ROGERS MEMORIAL LIBRARY

W9-ANI-383

Louise Thompson Patterson

LOUISE
THOMPSON
PATTERSON

*A Life of
Struggle for
Justice*

KEITH GILYARD

Duke University Press   Durham and London   2017

ROGERS MEMORIAL LIBRARY

© 2017 Duke University Press
All rights reserved

Printed in the United States of America on acid-free paper ∞
Designed by Heather Hensley
Typeset in Arno Pro by Westchester Publishing Services

Library of Congress Cataloging-in-Publication Data
Names: Gilyard, Keith, [date] author.
Title: Louise Thompson Patterson : a life of struggle for
    justice / Keith Gilyard.
Description: Durham : Duke University Press, 2017. | Includes
    bibliographical references and index. | Description based
    on print version record and CIP data provided by
    publisher; resource not viewed.
Identifiers: LCCN 2017015438 (print)
LCCN 2017018131 (ebook)
ISBN 9780822372318 (ebook)
ISBN 9780822369851 (hardcover : alk. paper)
ISBN 9780822369929 (pbk. : alk. paper)
Subjects: LCSH: Patterson, Louise Thompson, 1901–1999. |
    African American women political activists—Biography.
    | African American women social reformers—Biography. |
    African American communists—Biography.
Classification: LCC E185.6 (ebook) | LCC E185.6.G55 2017
    (print) | DDC 361.2092 [B]—dc23
LC record available at https://lccn.loc.gov/2017015438

Cover art: Louise Thompson Patterson in Europe, 1930s.
Louise Thompson Patterson Papers, Stuart A. Rose
Manuscript, Archives, and Rare Book Library, Emory
University, Atlanta, GA.

Frontispiece: Louise Thompson Patterson; her daughter,
MaryLouise Patterson; and young students in the Soviet
Union, early 1960s. Louise Thompson Patterson Papers,
Stuart A. Rose Manuscript, Archives, and Rare Book
Library, Emory University, Atlanta, GA.

For Ramón J. Jiménez (1948–2016)

CONTENTS

A gallery appears after p. 144.

ABBREVIATIONS

AIMS	American Institute for Marxist Studies
CAA	Council on African Affairs
CES	Congregational Education Society
CIO	Congress of Industrial Organizations
CPUSA	Communist Party USA
CRC	Civil Rights Congress
FBI	Federal Bureau of Investigation
HBCU	Historically Black College or University
ILD	International Labor Defense
IWO	International Workers Order
NAACP	National Association for the Advancement of Colored People
NAARPR	National Alliance against Racist and Political Repression
NNC	National Negro Congress
UPWA	United Packinghouse Workers of America
YMCA	Young Men's Christian Association
YWCA	Young Women's Christian Association

ACKNOWLEDGMENTS

Evelyn Crawford and MaryLouise Patterson receive my first thanks and heartfelt gratitude. They marvelously uphold the progressive tradition of the Crawford and Patterson families. Their interviews of Louise Thompson Patterson in the 1980s and 1990s formed much of the foundation on which a researcher could build. They also, in verbal and email exchanges with me, helped me to understand additional details of the life of their "aunt" and mother. MaryLouise not only supported the project from day one but literally created the day one. I had been thinking, somewhat ambivalently, about doing this research. A mutual friend, Lawrence Jackson, passed this information to MaryLouise. A phone call from her made me commit.

Margaret Wilkerson played a major role in pushing Louise to write a memoir, as did Linda Burnham. I thank them both for also pointing the way. I have benefited, additionally, from the insights of Alan Wald, Faith Berry, Judge Ted N. Berry, Dorothy Keller, and, of course, Lawrence Jackson, as well as an anonymous reviewer.

My researchers were a great and indispensable team with which to work: Karma deGruy, who filled my Dropbox space with photographed documents from Emory University; Monika Lehman, who performed similar work for me at Stanford University; and my Penn State research assistants, Mat Rude-Walker, Earl Brooks, and Mudiwa Pettus.

I thank Kathleen Shoemaker, Courtney Chartier, Heather Oswald, and the entire staff at the Stuart A. Rose Manuscript, Archives, and Rare Book Library at Emory University; and the staffs at the Bancroft Library, University of California, Berkeley; the Manuscripts Division of the Department of Special Collections, Stanford University Libraries; the Kheel Center for Labor-Management Documentation and Archives, Martin P. Catherwood

Library, Cornell University; the Moorland-Spingarn Research Center at Howard University; Special Collections and University Archives at Stony Brook University; the Tamiment Library and Robert F. Wagner Labor Archives, Elmer Holmes Bobst Library, New York University; and the Pattee and Paterno libraries at Penn State (particularly Shenetta Selden, Eric Novotny, and Sandra Stelts).

I thank all the staff members at Duke University Press, especially Gisela Fosado and Lydia Rose Rappoport-Hankins, for their enthusiasm and thoroughness.

Last, I thank my daughter, Kaamilah Gilyard, for her collaboration on several research trips. Despite health issues, we had fun and got the work done.

Introduction

On May 8, 1933, the diminutive and fair-skinned Louise Thompson, wearing a wraparound spring coat tied at the waist and looking determined, strode in a light but steady rain through the streets of Washington, DC. Having floated on the political left for several years, the confident thirty-one-year-old was now firmly grounded in a direct-action campaign as the principal organizer of a high-profile protest in support of the Scottsboro Nine. For a portion of the route from Florida and New York Avenues (in the northeastern section of the District of Columbia) to the White House, she had her left arm interlocked with the right arm of Ruby Bates, one of the two white women who had falsely accused the nine African American males of rape in Alabama two years earlier, a charge that had sparked an international firestorm. Plagued by a guilty conscience, Bates had changed course and had testified and demonstrated on behalf of the accused, who by that time had been convicted. Most had been sentenced to death. Bates's other arm was entwined with the right arm of Janie Patterson, the mother of Haywood Patterson, one of the defendants. Louise, Bates, and Patterson walked amid five thousand marchers, many of whom bore placards demanding justice not only for the Scottsboro Nine but also for death-row inmate Euel Lee, imprisoned labor leader Tom Mooney, and fledgling activist Angelo Herndon.[1]

Inside the White House, Louise mingled with a group of twenty-five demonstrators who demanded to see President Franklin Delano Roosevelt and refused to accept the word of Colonel Louis McHenry Howe, who received them politely, that the chief executive was busy in a conference. The hassled officer reached the president by phone, and FDR's words poured clearly from the receiver, audible to the entire group: "I will not see the committee."[2] After Louise, Bates, and Patterson, along with several others, spoke to Howe, they left a petition containing more than 200,000 signatures.[3]

After additional stops, the marchers eventually retreated to nearby Seaton Park. The demonstration—the first mass rally in Washington for racial justice—ended after a series of speakers held forth on the significance of the event and addressed an array of social issues. For her part, the jaunty Louise hailed the gathering as a watershed moment of interracial solidarity and noted the role of numerous women who "scoffed at hardship" to test the promise of mass protest. She argued that the day's actions were a harbinger of further political activism in the nation's capital and predicted that subsequent marches would number one million participants. It would not happen anytime soon. It would take Louis Farrakhan, who ironically was born the week of that Scottsboro march, to attain that number.[4]

But Louise's accomplishments over the course of a decades-long radical career of social activism are remarkable. She remained a pint-sized but potent hammer in a wave of counterattacks against Jim Crow. She was one of the early African American graduates of the University of California, Berkeley; a pioneering instructor at Pine Bluff Agricultural, Mechanical, and Normal School in Arkansas and at Hampton Institute in Virginia; and a valued cultural and political worker during the Harlem Renaissance. Her friends and acquaintances included W. E. B. Du Bois, Aaron Douglas, Augusta Savage, Arna Bontemps, Zora Neale Hurston, and Langston Hughes, and her first husband was the talented but tormented writer Wallace Thurman. She was central, along with Paul Robeson, to the labor fraternalism movement in the 1930s and 1940s. She steered proto-black-feminist activities in the 1950s with Charlotta Bass, Beah Richards, and others; was crucial to the efforts to free political prisoners, most notably Angela Davis, in the 1970s; and operated as a progressive intellectual and cultural resource in the 1980s and 1990s. In short, she embodied resistance to racial, economic, and gender exploitation, moving beyond theory to action. A socialist because she viewed such a political economy to be the key to eradicating poverty, racism, and sexism, she formed a long-term, vital political partnership with her second husband, the black Communist William L. Patterson, one of the most important American freedom fighters of the twentieth century and a victim of McCarthyism. Whether her political forecast was correct remains to be determined. Certainly, the problems that concerned her have not been eliminated under capitalism.

This book conveys the crucial events in the life of Louise Thompson Patterson, as she ultimately became known. Her portrait has remained blurry to date because, although numerous scholars have referred to her, no systematic and sustained attempt to represent clearly her actions and interiority has emerged; thus, smudges mar the literature. For example, Hampton Institute did not terminate her employment, as is widely reported. She resigned.[5] Neither did she ever divorce Thurman, which is another popular notion. In fact, she presented herself as the widow Mrs. Thurman when applying for her second marriage license.[6] But beyond getting some of the major facts straight and illustrating her formidable activism, this book is concerned with a psychological or at least interactive depiction of her.

What caused Louise to become politicized and act as she did? How did she construct the bountiful and elongated sample size—she was born in 1901 and died in 1999—that is a gift to current intellectuals and practitioners concerned with social change and progressive intervention? Relying on her unfinished memoir and other unpublished materials, her published articles and association writings, several hundred hours of audiotapes and videos produced as part of the Louise Thompson Patterson Memoirs Project sponsored by the Department of African American Studies at Berkeley, and the records of the Federal Bureau of Investigation (FBI), as well as interviews I conducted, I have provided a provisional answer in the following pages. In brief, a deeply felt color consciousness and sense of isolation and persecution as a child in the American West created a passionate yearning for justice, humanism, and community. In her view, this yearning was best consummated through the cultivation of a rebellious identity and participation in radical movements and projects. This story is largely one of a woman who rejected offers and opportunities to construct a sterling mainstream reputation and to pursue a materially comfortable professional life. Instead, despite the privilege of a college education and even her light complexion, she opted to traverse the harder path and committed herself to some of the most difficult struggles of her times for political transformation. All along she understood her predicament and the weight of her choice. As a young woman, she wrote to her best friend, "I know that my course won't be easy—I am saturated in bourgeois ideology and some of it is hard to get away from. I feel the necessity of maintaining a measure of economic security. But beside the march of world events my own seems very insignificant."[7]

Demonstrating her grasp of color politics in America, Louise noted in an interview in 1988 that the United States had been at odds with all other countries in its adoption of the one-drop rule for determining whether to characterize someone as black. Moreover, she understood that when those in power designated a person as black, they were classifying him or her as inferior. Specifically addressing the practice of such labeling during enslavement, she explained, "It was a question of private property."[8] Yet, unlike many postmodernists, particularly light-skinned African Americans, Louise was not preoccupied with drawing intraethnic distinctions, promoting talk of hybridity, or listening to claims about one-half or one-quarter ethnic membership. She knew that the only genetically pure thing we all are is human, but the narrative of the black freedom struggle in America totally captivated her. She embraced it as one who was fully Negro or black or Afro-American—all designations she used for herself at various times. In an essay titled "What Makes One an American Negro," she wrote of how the "greed for maintaining property rights and exploitation helped in the welding together of this new people—American Negroes—who with varying degrees of racial strains, forced into a new language, made to form a new culture from their now vague African background and the present life in America, emerged not as Africans or Europeans, but as a new people who have enriched not only the economy of America but given it its finest cultural contributions."[9] Rather than lingering on the ontological or biological nature of these new people, Louise concerned herself with how to position them for continued achievement. She settled on the view—and never wavered in it—that a leftist orientation offered the best way forward as an ethnic group.

Regarding her self-described status as a rebel, she considered it "just part of my makeup, I think." Of course, she was not suggesting that rebellion resided in her DNA. She meant that by the time she had come of age, she was determined to challenge the situations she thought unjust.[10] The roots of that resolve lay in a difficult childhood scarred by racism, and her public vocalizing of discontent began to manifest itself during her undergraduate days.

This volume contributes to the growing and much-needed scholarship on "black left feminism" or the "radical black female subject."[11] It joins recent biographies about several of Patterson's political allies and contemporaries, including Barbara Ransby's *Eslanda* on Eslanda Robeson, Gerald Horne's *Race Woman* on Shirley Graham Du Bois, Gregg Andrews's *Thyra J. Edwards*, and Carol Boyce Davies's *Left of Karl Marx* on Claudia Jones. This book also aligns with important themed analyses that consider Louise, such as Erik S. McDuffie's *Sojourning for Freedom* and Dayo Gore's *Radicalism at the Crossroads*.

Louise admirably and sometimes stunningly advanced a series of interconnected liberation efforts through such rhetorical efforts as writing, speaking, and demonstrating, as well as through handling a variety of movement logistics and serving as a key officer and organizer in several important organizations. To study her is to witness the courage, sacrifice, discipline, vision, and fortitude needed to organize and work over the course of a long lifetime for justice and liberation for all people.

CHAPTER 1

Louise Alone, 1901–1916

O n September 9, 1901, on the edge of the Black Belt of Chicago, a white-looking mother named Lulu Toles (née Brown) birthed a baby girl whose complexion hinted faintly of a brown world. Present in the apartment at Thirty-Fifth Street and Dearborn along with the delivering physician, Dr. Kelly, was the mother's best friend, Alone Townsend, who pronounced almost immediately that the infant's given name would be Louise Alone. The child would in the coming years consider the naming prophetic. She was never abandoned—her mother loved her fiercely and always hugged her firmly as they negotiated the complex poetry and politics of the assignment of racial identity and ethnic identification in America—but Louise experienced periods of intense alienation.

The twenty-four-year-old Lulu hailed from Bethel, Ohio, a village near Cincinnati.[1] Her mother, Emma Colwell Brown, a white woman, was the so-called illegitimate daughter of a young heiress in Kentucky and had been given to a black family to be raised. She eventually bore seven children to her fair-skinned African American husband, Moses Brown. Lulu was the eldest, born on July 10, 1877. She became the lead sibling within a pack of "half-white niggers," as she and her brothers and sisters were often derided by both whites and blacks; whites rejected them completely, whereas blacks regarded them with the traditional ambivalence.[2] Although light enough to pass for white in unfamiliar circles, as several of her siblings chose to do, Lulu apparently refused to consider that option seriously. She ultimately saw no reason during those vexing times to reject symbolically the biology of either of her parents. She focused instead on the dreams common to people of every hue—visions of excitement, good fortune, and romance. Her imagination drifted far beyond the confines of her work in her father's candy store.

Chicago proved to be irresistible to her; it had become the fifth-largest city in the world by the close of the nineteenth century.[3] The World's Columbian Exposition of 1893 had announced the city's preeminence and its role as a vital indicator of industrial progress. Problems were evident, to be sure, as a financial panic that same year clearly demonstrated. Moreover, labor relations would become particularly harsh, as indicated by the historic Pullman Strike in 1894, which paralyzed traffic on the nation's railways. Democracy also staggered under the weight of rapid urbanization and growing ethnic diversity. So the picture wasn't the rosiest for African Americans, even half-white ones. Blacks made up only 2 percent of Chicago's 1.7 million residents, numbering little more than thirty thousand.[4] They were disproportionately excluded from the city's industries and relegated to the domestic and service sectors. They mainly worked as porters, servants, waiters and waitresses, and janitors, though some did secure better service jobs, such as those generally available on the railroads.[5] In addition, blacks faced acute bias with regard to housing and schools. Such realities drew the attention of the National Afro-American Council, founded in 1898, and its secretary, Chicago resident Ida B. Wells, who had fled to the city from Tennessee after her militant, forthright journalism endangered her.[6] Another black activist, Bishop Reverdy Ransom, participated in uplift efforts by establishing the Institutional Church and Social Settlement in 1900.[7] Ransom's initiative resembled that of Jane Addams, whose work at Hull House more famously at that time highlighted struggles in the city at the turn of the century.[8]

Despite the possible hardships, Chicago seemed worth the gamble to Lulu. In 1899 she visited some female friends who had migrated to the city searching for opportunity in an attempt to escape or avoid segregation and faltering, smaller-scale Midwest economies. They had married men with some of the preferred service-sector jobs and thus enjoyed lifestyles that were relatively stable, though far from lavish (the black professional class in Chicago was miniscule). Lulu had little in the way of worldly possessions; when she decided to stay, she left nothing of material consequence behind in Ohio. Moreover, Lulu, like some of her friends, had the skin capital to realistically aspire to be more than a minor figure in an emerging black middle class (although she probably would not have stated this as her goal). She could join whatever skin color–based elites existed within black society—or at least gain access to them.

Chicago at the beginning of the twentieth century would prove difficult to negotiate, however. On April 23, 1900, within a year of her arrival, Lulu naively wed Will Toles, a twenty-six-year-old brown-skinned bartender who did fairly well moneywise.[9] He showered her with gifts and appeared to be a promising provider. But he proved to be a bit of a gallant and apparently developed a drinking problem as well. The couple divorced shortly after their daughter's birth. Toles subsequently extended little or no support, and the child would retain no lasting memory of him. Nor would she know his side of her family: although Toles had viewed the tall, attractive, high-toned, auburn-haired Lulu as a prize, her in-laws rejected her because of their own color chauvinism. It was no shock to her given the treatment she had experienced in Ohio. It merely represented another obstacle to overcome on the road to succeeding in Chicago. She never conceived of returning home as a viable choice. Always forward-looking, she viewed such a return as indicating failure.[10]

Lulu began using the name Louise, a less "country-sounding" signifier, and buckled down to work, mostly as a domestic and seamstress, to support herself and her light-complexioned, coarse-haired daughter.[11] Although she participated in the network of black Chicago, she remained open to other opportunities, which she would soon need rather desperately because her sewing business diminished, meaning she could no longer afford her apartment. Her social circle shrank; friends were not as welcoming to an unattached, striking, white-looking young woman with a small child. To crown matters, little Louise apparently contracted the measles and experienced complications that led to a weakening of her lower leg muscles, rendering it difficult to walk. Her doctor hoped that relocation to a temperate climate would enable the child to outgrow the crippling condition. If not, she might require orthopedic surgery, for which her mother had no funds.[12]

Naturally adventurous, Lulu was not afraid to take action, especially on her daughter's behalf. Besides, she felt a need to reignite her pride away from the scene of severe disappointment.[13] Exactly who paved the path from Chicago remains unclear, but her link to the black social network provided her with an introduction to one of the most prominent African American families in the nation. She wasn't middle class or upper class, but the middle and upper classes would help her and little Louise to get back on their feet, literally in the case of the latter. In 1906, at the age of twenty-eight, she took her hobbling four-year-old daughter and began a meandering train ride to Seattle, to people who were vigorously encouraging African Americans to give the West a try.

Their destination was the Cayton home. Susie Revels Cayton was the daughter of Hiram Revels, who in 1870, became the first African American elected to the U.S. Senate, representing Mississippi. A year later, he resigned his seat to become the first president of Alcorn Agricultural and Mechanical College (now Alcorn State University). He served several stints as the head of Alcorn, during which he also taught at the school. Susie, the fourth of six daughters, was particularly close to her father and became an educator as well. At the age of sixteen, she began teaching grade school in rural Mississippi. In 1889 she enrolled at Rust College in Holly Springs, finishing in 1893 after completing the nursing curriculum. She stayed on to teach at the college after graduation. A talented writer who had spun stories and verse by the time she was ten years old, she continued to practice her craft even as she engaged her other interests and duties.

She shortly had a notable publishing outlet. One of her father's former students at Alcorn, Horace Cayton, began publishing her stories and articles in his paper, the *Seattle Republican*, copies of which he sent to Hiram Revels, his mentor. Cayton had ventured west after completing his formal studies. Sharp-witted and sometimes brash, Cayton, who was born a slave on a Mississippi cotton plantation in 1859, knew that an outspoken, educated black man would be a high-priority target for white racists in the Jim Crow South. He left Mississippi for Kansas, living in such places as Nicodemus and Hill City. Kansas, though, had pitfalls as well. In the autumn of 1888, an attorney tricked Cayton into providing false testimony that Cayton thought would help the lawyer's clients, businessmen for whom Cayton was working. He subsequently was convicted of perjury and sentenced to a year in the Kansas State Penitentiary in Lansing. Fortunately, impassioned supporters in Nicodemus and Hill City prevailed on Governor Lyman Humphrey to pardon him, and Cayton was released from prison after serving a couple of months.[14]

After a stay in Hill City, Cayton set out for points farther west. His stops included Denver, Ogden, and Portland. In 1890 he set his sights on frontier Seattle, where he envisioned taking advantage of a true meritocracy and rising as a proverbial self-made man.[15] The Queen City, as Seattle was then known, doubled in population between 1890 and 1900, reaching eighty thousand inhabitants.[16] The lumber-industry boom and an expanding railroad network accounted for much of its growth. The next wave of growth—Seattle's population tripled over the next decade—would result primarily from the discovery of gold in the Yukon in 1896; the subsequent Klondike Gold Rush, which peaked in 1898; and the Nome Gold Rush in 1899, when gold was discovered at the other end of the Yukon River.[17] Only a few members of the stampede, less than 5 percent, ever found any gold, and even fewer cashed in significant ore deposits.[18] Suppliers made far more money than prospectors did, and Seattle garnered a large share of the gold-rush trade, even beating out San Francisco, its chief competitor, in that regard. Thus, the political economy that Cayton would attempt to negotiate involved free-flowing capital and a black population comprising less than 0.5 percent of the city's total.[19] He made several real estate investments and also gained a foothold in the publishing industry. In 1894 he established the highly successful *Seattle Republican*. When Susie sent him her stories, they also began an elaborate correspondence, and in 1896, with her father's blessing, Susie migrated to Seattle to marry Cayton.

She continued to write short fiction and columns for the newspaper and began serving as its associate editor in January 1900. In addition, she became a major cultural figure about town, often attending opera and symphony performances and eventually requiring her children to do so as well. She was active with her husband in the Sunday Forum, affairs at which local blacks convened several times a month to discuss the issues of the day. When Horace Cayton was present, the topics always included the recruitment of more blacks to live in the city.

By the time the Toleses arrived, the Caytons were living in an eight-room, two-story white house on Capitol Hill; they were the only African American family in one of the most exclusive residential areas in Seattle. The neighbors were not particularly friendly but respected the material attainments of the wealthiest black family in town. Their layout included a huge lawn and a horse stable, and they employed a Japanese servant named Nish. A giant portrait of Hiram Revels, who had died in 1901, hung in the front room, and the late senator remained a frequent topic of conversation among the family and the numerous guests who visited the Cayton residence. Exposed to such privilege, the three Cayton children were expected to measure up. As Horace Jr. would put it, "We were obligated by our family history to achievement in our fight for individual and racial equality."[20] The brood included seven-year-old Ruth, who seemed to possess a rebellious streak; five-year-old Madge, born the same year as the younger Louise; and three-year-old Horace Jr., who would grow up to become a prominent sociologist and coauthor, with St. Clair Drake, of the landmark *Black Metropolis*. The youngest Cayton scions, noted labor leader Revels Cayton and Lillie Cayton, would be born in 1907 and 1914, respectively.

In the stately, well-kept, olive-skinned Mrs. Cayton, Lulu glimpsed a future: financial success and refined motherhood, while still becoming a strong force in the home and in the community. She loved the parties and delighted in meeting all of the important visitors who came to the home, often recounting those events. She also grew fond of recalling how Susie, only seven years her senior, luxuriated in her bath while reading Shakespeare.[21]

But that was Susie's life of comfort and culture, in which Lulu at that point could only be a beneficiary of charity or seek employment outside of the home as a domestic while awkwardly being waited on by a servant in the Cayton household. For the sake of her self-esteem, she chose to depart after a few months. Her child had begun to walk well, so no medical reason existed to continue to rely on the Caytons. She preferred to slip into anonymity rather than face daily reminders of her own meager circumstances. In fact, she ceased communicating with friends and relatives back east for several years.[22]

Several Cayton associates and another gold rush directly influenced Lulu's choice of her next destination. Israel Walker, for example, a voracious reader and renowned raconteur, often entertained visitors to the Cayton household with tales of his eight years in the Yukon. He had not spent much time seeking gold. Instead, he established a lucrative barbershop after being grubstaked by Horace Cayton. When he returned to Seattle, he split the profits equally with Cayton and had enough remaining to buy a boardinghouse and start a mercantile business. Walker's tales and the example of his life epitomized the pioneer spirit, always celebrated in the Cayton home. While Lulu listened to Walker and others, news arrived that folks were crowding into Goldfield, Nevada, about halfway between Reno and Las Vegas. After three claims were filed in 1902, word spread among potential prospectors, particularly in Reno, San Francisco, Salt Lake City, Denver, and Seattle. The year 1906 brought high yields for the gold mines there, and about eight thousand people were creating the latest boomtown.[23] Ambitious building construction was under way, and the population would soon swell to more than twenty thousand, making Goldfield the largest city in Nevada.[24] Lulu had no appreciable life savings, nor would she become a prospector. Nonetheless, Goldfield drew her with its promise of an economic and psychic restart. In her estimation, she was risking nothing but escape from the judgments, real or imagined, of those who knew her.[25]

However, for a nonpassing African American to anticipate surviving in Nevada, he or she had to be unaware of or ignore much of the state's history. Blacks had enjoyed a relatively high legal and social status in the 1870s and early 1880s as they worked in service businesses supported by mining, most notably in Carson City and Virginia City. In fact, whites treated Indians and Chinese more poorly. However, blacks were in line for vitriolic treatment after a series of mining failures commenced in the mid-1880s.[26] Many whites fled Nevada, but those who remained typically grew hostile toward blacks as their own economic fortunes waned. They even forced blacks out of some communities, though a significant number of African Americans had already departed as work in service jobs catering to whites began to evaporate.[27] At any rate, no more than five hundred blacks were living in Nevada by the turn of the century, and the numbers had continued to decline as anti-immigrant and antiblack sentiments increased. Newspapers routinely included the epithet *nigger* in their stories.[28] Francis G. Newlands, who began serving as a Democratic senator from Nevada in 1903, supported the exclusion of the Chinese and Japanese on the grounds that the United States should be preserved for the white race. He argued that it was impossible to make "a homogenous people by the juxtaposition of races differing in color upon the same soil."[29] On Washington's Birthday in 1906, the Eagles of Tonopah, a silver-mining hub twenty-five miles north of Goldfield, staged a Coon Ball at which attendees were expected to darken their faces with burned cork.[30] In the nearby Fallon depot, a posted sign read, "No niggers or Japs allowed."[31] Notwithstanding, Goldfield represented a new opportunity for a handful of blacks, albeit in a dusty frontier town of tents and wooden shacks, with noisy construction, unpaved streets, rowdy behavior, and prevalent prostitution. It could hardly be more different from Capitol Hill, but Toles was determined to make the best of the situation.

As the fall of 1906 approached, she arrived in Goldfield with her daughter amid the buzz for a remarkable event that received more national press coverage than had the catastrophic earthquake in San Francisco five months earlier. This was the Fight of the Century, the boxing match between African American Joe Gans, the lightweight titleholder when that division was probably the most prestigious in the sport, and the challenger Oscar Mathaeus Nielsen, known more popularly as Battling Nelson and also as the Durable Dane. Gans, arguably the best pugilist who ever lived, first demonstrated his prodigious talent in degrading battle royals, the free-for-alls famously depicted by Ralph Ellison in the opening chapter of *Invisible Man*.[32] By the time of the Goldfield event, orchestrated by entrepreneur Tex Rickard, who would achieve fabled status as a promoter, Gans, a paragon of sportsmanship, had been the champion for four years and had generated the highest gates in boxing history up to that point.

If, as literary scholar Gerald Early suggests, boxer Jack Johnson is now correctly viewed as the prototypical New Negro whose excellence and assertiveness inflamed the youthful imaginations of Countee Cullen and his contemporaries (little Louise included), it is perhaps more correct to widen the scope to incorporate Gans, who served as Johnson's mentor.[33] A world-champion boxer before Johnson, he was the larger celebrity on the world stage and the bigger hero among African Americans during the first decade of the twentieth century. As was the case with Johnson's fights, the run-ups and responses to Gans's bouts revealed much about the American racial psyche. Many African Americans experienced his victories over white opponents as blows struck for dignity and freedom. Reverend Francis J. Grimke, a DC-based minister, while praising the uplift efforts of Booker T. Washington, avowed that Washington "never did one-tenth to place the black man in the front rank as a gentleman as has been done by Joe Gans."[34] In contrast, numerous whites viewed such triumphs as aberrations, mere glitches in a legitimate domain of white supremacy, which they often sought to reaffirm with violence outside of the ring. In fact, Gans was the first boxer whose wins led directly to serious attacks on blacks by whites.[35]

The racial tension in Goldfield was palpable, intensified by the challenger himself. Nielsen blithely remarked about the sadness that he imagined blacks would feel: "There will be crepe [mourning cloth] in Coontown on Labor Day while the Danish descendants are celebrating."[36] But he lost in the forty-second round on an egregious foul that he committed because he sensed imminent defeat.

Louise would not recall much about the racial dynamics surrounding the Fight of the Century because the bout took place six days before she turned five years old. She had a vague sense that Gans "was fighting for me, for us, for black people." Her most vivid memory, understandably, related to her own role. She was a recipient of the candy and pies that Gans's female companion dispensed to the town's children.[37]

Young Louise developed a more acute race consciousness amid the extracurricular activity of the first grade. The teacher did not explicitly denigrate blacks, but Louise was nonetheless aware of being regarded as lesser. *Nigger*, she said, was the word that "I went to school on and came home on."[38] Her mother encouraged her "poor baby," as she phrased it, to ignore racial taunts, though remaining oblivious to insults is not a stance many first graders can adopt.[39] In an episode reminiscent of *The Souls of Black Folk*, in which W. E. B. Du Bois tells how a white girl refused his offering when his grammar-school class exchanged visiting cards, Louise, the only black child in her class, was, in a reversal, the only student not invited to a classmate's birthday party.[40] Peer rejection tasted bitter enough, but the rejection was intensified because her teacher, an authority figure, communicated the message so callously. She piled the white envelopes on her desk and ceremoniously called the students' names in alphabetical order, working straight through the Ts with no mention of Toles. As the last few of her classmates collected their invitations, one by one, Louise felt both invisible and hypervisible, painfully and increasingly aware, as Du Bois had been before her, that she was considered a problem.[41]

Seeking relief from ridicule, she sometimes joined others in denigrating those who were seemingly more despised. With them she followed a Chinese man along a street, chanting, "Chink, Chink, Chinaman. Stole a load of wood. Chink, Chink, Chinaman. Ain't no good."[42] On another occasion, she remained silent when a group of children forced a dark-skinned boy called Rastus to dance on a box while they intoned, "Nigger, nigger, never die. Black face and shiny eye."[43]

At home, Louise received a harrowing lesson in racial animus. Her mother, who characteristically helped other women, sometimes at considerable danger to herself, temporarily housed a young Mexican woman who had borne a son to a black man from whom she was estranged. The woman lamented her son's genetic composition, sometimes expressing wistfully, "If I could only get this colored blood out of my baby."[44] Perhaps she did not perceive Lulu or herself as possessing colored blood, or maybe she thought the two had similar regrets. One wonders, though, how many noncolored women in Goldfield would have assisted or protected her as Lulu did, especially when the man appeared, gun in hand, to demand that his wife return home with their son. He threatened to murder everyone in the two-room shack, in a somewhat isolated location on the edge of town, if he did not get his way. However, Lulu, with her daughter clinging frantically to her lap, somehow persuaded the man to leave.

Indeed, little Louise was fearful much of the time in Goldfield and also grew increasingly in awe of Lulu's strength. Her mother nursed her through diphtheria in spite of not feeling well herself. Little Louise would clutch her mother's skirt whenever she heard a strange noise as they walked the dark streets after some work assignment or when they seemed on the verge of being accosted by some strange man. Her mother, in contrast, hardly ever seemed rattled. The only cracks in her emotional façade appeared when her daughter reported the racial insults that she suffered. Perhaps recalling her own abuse in Ohio, she wept on such occasions, which led her daughter to reveal less and less.[45]

Other struggles in Goldfield of which Louise became aware involved the running dispute between labor, mainly Local 220 of the Western Federation of Miners, and the Goldfield Consolidated Mining Company. Tensions peaked in the wake of the financial panic in the fall of 1907. Given the liquidity crisis, mine operators could no longer pay miners in cash, instead offering scrip that could be exchanged for cashier's checks at John S. Cook Bank, the only one of Goldfield's three banks to remain solvent. Multimillionaire George Wingfield and his business partner, Senator George S. Nixon, controlled both Goldfield Consolidated and the bank, and they gave no definite date for when the scrip could be redeemed for cash. The miners struck on November 27. Although Louise was too young to understand the politics of the strike, she witnessed the arrival, on December 7, of more than four hundred federal army troops sent to safeguard the lives and property of the bosses after Governor John Sparks, manipulated by Wingfield and Nixon, appealed to President Theodore Roosevelt. For three months, Goldfield's residents threaded their way through and among the soldiers.

The strike ended on April 3, 1908. By then, Rawhide, about 150 miles to the northwest, was experiencing a boom, drawing droves of prospectors and investors from Goldfield, including Rickard. Deserters often abandoned their burros to forage in the fields; the children who could catch them, like Louise, enjoyed riding them. As local industry declined, Lulu soon exhausted her employment options in Goldfield and nearby Tonopah. It was time for the fiercely proud, peripatetic mother with the bluesy, beleaguered daughter to consider her next move. They both guardedly hoped for better as they, now bearing the strains of having lived in the "Mississippi of the West," returned to the state of Washington, this time to Walla Walla, where they lived over the garage of a rich white family for whom Toles was working.[46]

Louise attended a convent school in Walla Walla because her mother preferred it to the area's public schools, not for religious reasons. Her mother never expressed much interest in religion. Atypically, she fit in well. She joked along with her schoolmates as they all clandestinely made faces while reciting the rosary on their knees. In more serious moments, Louise attended mass and genuinely enjoyed the elaborate ceremony of the Catholic Church.[47]

In the fall of 1909, she observed her first national African American leader in action when she was escorted by her mother to a downtown auditorium to see Booker T. Washington, who had traveled west to observe the Alaska-

Yukon-Pacific Exposition in Seattle, held to trumpet the city's rise as a commercial center. Washington spoke before a largely white audience and displayed, in the eyes of Louise and her embarrassed mother, a graceless embrace of darky stories. The eight-year-old, as one would expect, would not remember much of Washington's message about racial uplift and national progress. Fixed in her memory, though, was the image of Washington relaying a story in an overly stylized black dialect about Aunty, an old African American woman walking along a road.[48] Washington's affected manner provoked abundant laughter, but none from Louise's mother, who likely would not have appreciated any vernacular performance and definitely opposed humoring whites with black stereotypes. She much preferred the image of the Caytons—Victorian symbols of culture and money. Perhaps in a bit of wish fulfillment, both for herself and for her daughter, her favorite story about the time spent in Walla Walla involved a wealthy settler and his large family, whose complexions fueled rumors of black ancestry. But, bowing before wealth and status, no one dared to make the charge publicly. Race, Toles saw, could sometimes be trumped by enough mystery and money.[49]

The next stop was California. Louise's mother boarded her in West Oakland with a black family from Louisiana, the Davises, while she put in long hours as a waitress. Mrs. Davis had a terrible temper, likely related to her daily regimen of coffee laced with gin, and sometimes stretched her children across the dining room table to beat them with a razor strop. At times, she flogged with such frenzy that she had to be restrained by her husband and a couple of her sons. Louise was spared such punishment, however. Her mother, who never whipped her, left instructions to ensure that no one else would either. Nevertheless, the girl had to become tougher. As the only child of a doting parent, she was what many would have considered spoiled. But she would not be pampered in the Davis household. In return for the pleasure of having steady and close companions, she had to learn to steal and tussle. When she tagged along with the Davis children to the store, supposedly to purchase twenty-five cents' worth of some product for Mrs. Davis, they made her share in a plan to buy twenty cents' worth and spend the remaining nickel on candy or cookies, to be consumed before they reached home. The bonds were undermined, though, by her exemption from the risk of being beaten. For example, she and Beatrice Davis—the child closest to Louise in age— were sent to the dairy to buy a pitcher of milk, which they dropped and broke while playing carelessly. Beatrice alone received a whipping, which created animosity between the girls and eventually led to a brawl. Louise, with no experience at fighting, stood no chance against the battle-tested Beatrice and received a severe scratch on her cheek, which resulted in a scar.

In spite of the rough-and-tumble of life among the Davis family, as well as among the black children with whom she attended school, Louise felt that being centered in a community was worth it. In April 1910 she fit right in with dozens of black children praying that Halley's comet would not destroy Earth. She struggled, played, cried, laughed, and shared in mischief, and, most important to her, she was not particularly singled out for scorn. Obviously, she missed the daily contact with her mother. But her reliable caretaker never failed to visit on her days off and generally arrived loaded with treats for all of the kids. The Davis brood always beat Louise to the goodies, but she did not mind because she was proud that her mother could deliver such moments of joy.[50]

Louise's life would soon change again, however, when her mother, still an attractive woman with visions of a grander life, remarried. Her second husband, John Thompson, emerged somewhat mysteriously for the younger Louise. (He might have been in the background longer than she knew.) In any case, he seemed to her to be more shadow than substance. She asserted, "My stepfather played little or no importance in my life."[51] This surely represents a narrow recasting driven by her dislike. Thompson was an imposing presence, a large light-skinned man with "grey-green" eyes who rolled Bull Durham cigarettes.[52] He had two children by a previous marriage. Louise thought him mean and unsophisticated, definitely not good enough for her mother, or, perhaps, more precisely, not good enough to *come between* her and her mother.[53] Despite Louise's assessment, Thompson gave her a new surname and thus a new identity. The name she called him by, "Lovely," hardly indicates indifference or acrimony. More to the point, he was a major influence: his decisions strongly shaped her life over the next several years.

Thompson sought his fortune zealously throughout the West, convinced that it lay just over the horizon. A chef by trade, he never had trouble finding or holding jobs. However, he was always more interested in the prospects of striking a lucrative business deal, so whenever he had a stake he undertook some new enterprise, such as a lunch counter, sometimes venturing into a new town before his wife and stepdaughter joined him. He inevitably wound up broke and working once again for someone else, usually as a cook in a restaurant or on the railroads.

At one point, he became excited about farming, figuring that under the Homestead Act, a law under which up to 320 acres of federal land could be granted, he could obtain land for a nominal cost and build an economic empire.[54] He knew almost nothing about agriculture, or apparently about driving either, almost wrecking the car as he drove Louise and her mother to see a potential piece of property. His family was thankful that this idea never came to fruition. Later, with the advent of World War I, Thompson believed that he could make a mint trading in scrap iron. He bought a wagon and horse, gullibly buying an animal that had not been shod. He managed to trade the horse for another, a "pretty-looking, very high-spirited one," as his stepdaughter recalled.[55] When he hitched the horse to the wagon to take his family for a ride to impress them with his new endeavor, the horse rebelled at the first incline, backing away from, rather than climbing, the hill. Certainly no hauling of scrap iron would ensue. Thompson also tried bear trapping and bootlegging, and he even involved Louise and her mother in his scheme to prosper by selling hot tamales. They would prepare them, and he would travel about town trying to peddle them from a cart heated by a gas burner but finding little luck. To Louise, nothing symbolized his foibles more than when, presumably after getting a bargain on it, something he could never pass up, he presented her with an acoustic zither, a guitar-like instrument utilized most commonly in Europe and Asia.[56] She had no interest in learning how to play it. Her mother mostly indulged Thompson, a trait Louise perceived to be a weakness.[57]

During the summer of 1910, the family trekked back to Goldfield. Thompson left first; Louise and her mother followed on the train. Along the way they met another boxing legend, the heavyweight champion Johnson, who was en route from his training site in San Francisco to Reno for his famous Independence Day battle with "white hope" Jim Jeffries, a bout Johnson would win by knockout in the fifteenth round, sparking riots in more than fifty cities.[58] Mother and daughter were invited into the flamboyant champ's private car, where he entertained his entourage and guests with his bass viol. Louise never developed a liking for prizefighting. As an eight-year-old, she valued Johnson as a majestic and dignified symbol of black success, of triumph over adversity. She could always use the inspiration. As an adult, she did not take kindly to James Earl Jones's bumpkin-like portrayal of Johnson in the film *The Great White Hope*. The champ had been "no oaf," Louise declared; "he was an intelligent man."[59]

Once again ostracized by classmates in Goldfield—none would play with her during recess or walk homeward with her after school—she had to content herself with being a high-achieving student and with the resultant self-satisfaction. However, such attainment had limited effects on her immediate surroundings because academic excellence could not ward off the racist hostility of fellow students.

Her stepfather finally provided relief from the discrimination in Goldfield. Opportunity beckoned in Utah, and the Thompson trio soon landed in Ogden. From Louise's perspective, it seemed a better situation for her because she readily managed to form a friendship with a white girl named Thelma, though the latter may have been interested as much in food as in a new playmate. From a poor family, Thelma quickly figured out how generous Lulu could be. Louise's mother had grown fond of Alice Caldwell Hegan's novel *Mrs. Wiggs of the Cabbage Patch* (1901), which had been made into a successful play and later would be adapted several times for Hollywood, including a version produced in 1934 starring Pauline Lord and W. C. Fields.[60] Mrs. Wiggs was an old Irishwoman with lots of children who made ends meet and spun hardship into funny stories, abilities that Louise's mother tried to emulate. She also borrowed Mrs. Wiggs's announcement of her intent to accommodate additional guests for a meal: "We'll just put a little more water in the pot."[61] Thelma no doubt felt extremely thankful for the portions.

Thelma's motivation did not matter to Louise. After all of the ostracism, she appreciated having company her own age once again. Not surprisingly, though, racial pressures impinged on the friendship. After school one day, Thelma huddled among the other white students instead of falling in alongside Louise as had become her custom. She then approached Louise and declared, "My brother says I can't play with you anymore 'cause you're a nigger."[62] When the girl later drifted by the Thompson residence, probably because she was hungry, Louise shunned her, ending any association they would have outside of school.

Although that particular Thelma and Louise show closed early, the Thompsons lived in Ogden long enough for Louise to meet a few black playmates, the children of an African American community that was forming based on the railroad terminal in Ogden. Louise had fond memories of playing with black children in the snow after school and visiting some of their homes. One such occasion revealed the intensity of her craving for peer companionship. She became hungry while visiting a friend's house but opted against going home because she calculated that her mother would make her stay in for the rest of the day. The only thing the girl had to eat was tomatoes, a food Louise hated. But she stuffed herself with them rather than chance losing playtime.[63]

Ogden seemed to offer the opportunity for a stable family life. Steady work seemed in store for John Thompson. In addition, his wife had picked up the skills of a professional pastry cook. But Thompson soon became restless once again and decided to relocate to Boise, Idaho. Accordingly, Louise and her mother packed their few possessions—only a caged canary and a sewing machine were constants—and headed north.

Louise had a relatively pleasant, albeit brief, school experience in Idaho, impressing her teacher enough to skip a grade. There, she had less trouble with people than with her pets—a distempered cat and a rooster that pecked her in the thigh and drew blood. Her mother promptly rid them of the cat and beheaded the rooster to make soup, which Louise deemed delicious.[64]

She would not find social life so easy in Pendleton, Oregon, where they moved next. In school, racist taunting prevailed. Perhaps worse, her mother could not prevent racial insult in general. One day, for example, her mother took her and a white boy named Archie to the public swimming pool. The clerk on duty informed her mother, whom he assumed was white, that she could enter with Archie but that Louise would not be allowed. Lulu swallowed the hurt quietly. Her daughter recalled, "But how could she explain it to me? What did she and Archie feel? What did I feel? I will never know because we never talked about it."[65] On another occasion, a town official asked permission for Louise to participate in a parade. When her mother inquired about her specific role, she was told that her daughter would ride on a float in a grass skirt with wild hair, portraying an African savage. Of course, she refused.[66]

A third incident that Louise would never forget occurred on the Umatilla River. On a wintry day, while playing on the bank, Louise and another child spotted a dead bird on the ice and set out to inspect it. The ice broke under them, and they flailed in the water, yelling, until an adult passerby rescued them. During the harrowing escapade, Louise spotted a white man standing on a nearby overpass watching them. He never budged.[67]

Bend, Oregon, at the eastern edge of the Cascade Range, proved to be an even more hostile town than Pendleton. Louise imagined that the place served as a haven for defectors from the Confederate Army.[68] Students taunted her relentlessly. Worshippers at a local Protestant church barred her from attending Sunday school. She staged her first serious political protest, informing her mother that she refused to continue living in so racist a community. For the first time, her needs drove the decision to relocate.

Their last stop in central or northern Oregon was The Dalles, a small, hilly city on the Columbia River. They had friendly Italian neighbors who frequently gave them large pitchers of homemade red wine. Other students at school were friendly as well, or at least not unfriendly. The one indelible racist incident, in Louise's estimation, occurred when she, the proud owner of a new pair of roller skates, was racing down the steep hill on which she lived. Growing fearful because she had gathered considerable momentum, she grabbed hold of a white man who was approaching from the opposite direction. He cruelly pushed her away, causing her to topple to the pavement and bruise her forehead. He never glanced backward to see the damage he had inflicted.[69]

John Thompson soon left The Dalles for Marshfield, now known as Coos Bay.[70] Louise and her mother followed, first taking the train along the Columbia River to Portland, where they stayed at William D. Allen's six-year-old, five-story Golden West Hotel on Broadway. The hotel was the center of black life in Portland, and Louise encountered a substantial black community. She attended a black church and was "amazed and frightened" by the singing. She noticed the black businesses. Although the stay in Portland lasted only three days, the experience created, as Louise would recall, "an impression that would stay with me."[71]

The next legs of the trip were by ship along the Columbia River, first northwest to Astoria and then south along the coast to North Bend, the port for Marshfield. Eleven-year-old Louise proved hardy, but her mother became seasick during the rough final leg of the journey and thereafter would become nauseated whenever she saw a boat sail into the harbor. John Thompson met them at the dock to escort them to their new lodgings in town. They lived for a while at Second and Curtis Streets before moving out to the edge of town, in a wooded area that became known as Ferndale. Louise, racially isolated once again (there were fewer than twenty blacks in a town of five thousand), settled into a routine of going to school, then walking to the Chandler Hotel, where her parents held jobs, and finding a corner where she could do her homework and later eat dinner. Some of the staff encouraged her in her studies, particularly the politically conscious and unabashedly manipulative owner. On the day of the presidential election of 1912, he led his staff to the polls in an attempt to reelect the Republican candidate, William Howard Taft of Ohio. But Woodrow Wilson, a Virginian Democrat, captured the White House—and held a segregated inauguration parade.

Marshfield became the most stable environment of Louise's childhood. Her irrepressible stepfather soon quit his hotel job in his continuing bids to become a successful entrepreneur, and she was still mostly an outsider to whites as she progressed from the Marshfield School to Marshfield High. But she knew the pattern by then and handled it well enough to thrive. Immersing herself in books and magazines represented one coping technique. She frequently visited the library; a brand-new one opened in 1914. She worked through Martha Finley's popular Elsie Dinsmore series and the juvenile novels of Horatio Alger Jr. She pored over magazine ads because they suggested travel to her; she often imagined going to New York.[72] The only group-based cultural diversions for Louise were the annual visit to the Ringling Brothers' circus, the Circuit Chautauqua revue, and the revivalist meetings of Billy Sunday, the former professional baseball player who had become the country's most popular evangelist. Louise recalled her time under the tent: "He got up there preaching hell and damnation, you know, sad stories about you must be converted or you'll never get to see your dear old mother who'll be up there in heaven." Louise would sit wide-mouthed with awe: "Oh, did I want to be converted. Wash me whiter than snow." She vigorously debated the question with her mother, who never attended religious gatherings. But the elder Louise ruled that her daughter was too young. Her need to belong would have to find other avenues of expression.[73]

Although Louise had no friends in school, she did get to be a big sister of sorts when the Burdines moved from Oklahoma to Marshfield, followed by the Boles family. The two African American matriarchs were sisters, and their daughters, Dolores Burdine and Nattie Boles, were both seven years younger than Louise. By the time they were eight years old and able to walk about town unescorted, they were vying seriously for Louise's attention. The cousins visited the Thompson home regularly and tried to squeeze each other out for chances to spend the night. Louise would prepare lunch for them, make candy with them, or help them cut out paper dolls from Ladies' Home Journal.

Her mother remained ever supportive, even doing most of the cooking for the girls. Louise later stated, "As far as I was concerned, she gave me everything that she could. The only time that I would see her sad or crying was when she was unable to give me what I wanted or needed."[74] Although Lulu worked long hours, she tried to offset her daughter's essential loneliness by being her partner at cards or checkers, providing her with additional books (though dime novels were prohibited), and trying to keep her in good humor. In her late thirties, with the brightness of her own dreams beginning to dim, Lulu seemed to live more and more through her daughter, probably coddling her too much. She did not insist very forcefully, for example, that Louise dispatch her chores expediently. It would regularly take her daughter all day to wash the dishes. She would wash one dish and then read a book for an hour, letting the dishwater grow cold; she then had to reheat the water on the woodstove. Sometimes she opted for hiding the dirty pots and pans in the oven. A scolding would follow on discovery but was more perfunctory than fervent. Apparently, the only major offense would have been to neglect her formal studies. That never happened.

Although Louise later wrote reflections about her mother, her perspective remained child-centric; even factoring in her mother's characteristic reticence about personal matters, it isn't clear why Louise never tried, in print anyway, to explore the fuller contours of a life that had to have been more complicated than she described. Precisely how did her mother conjecture, evaluate, and love? Although, to her daughter's dismay, she showed the deference of a traditional wife, it may not have been the case that she was only being passive as she trailed her husband from town to town. She conceivably spurred him on given that she assisted him in several of his business ventures. Her habitual service as a waitress in his bound-for-failure eateries was doubtless limiting, but she was not overly docile by nature. After all, she was apparently resolute in divorcing Will Toles, dared to leave Chicago for Seattle, traded Seattle for Goldfield, and possessed nerve enough to remarry. It makes sense that she would have shared a good measure of John Thompson's dreams if she partnered with him on his journeys. But Louise remained reluctant to say, or genuinely failed to recall, much about the relationship between her mother and the man they called Lovely, a figure she regarded as somewhat farcical and somewhat tragic.[75]

Despite Louise's later omissions concerning John Thompson, it is clear that her mother's strongest emotional bond was indeed with her only child, whom she often referred to as "Babe." Louise remarked, "If I were unhappy, she was unhappy. Later on when I grew up and encountered difficulties of any sort, she would still reflect my unhappiness. I would spend my time consoling her rather than myself."[76] Although she came to believe that her mother's sort of selflessness was not mentally healthy for either of them, she relied on such a relationship in her youth.[77] How else would one make it through a world in which one perceives all kinds of differences but is mostly shackled to those of skin color and hair in territories where friends and allies are few?

Indeed, Louise developed a strong fear that her mother would die; she often tiptoed into her room in the middle of the night to check that she was still breathing.[78]

Louise did not grow up in the Jim Crow South, but she could not fathom that life in the South, though physically harsher and more dangerous, could have been any more psychologically brutal than her travails in the West.[79] By the time she left the picturesque, temperate coastal town of Marshfield at the age of fifteen, in her sophomore year, she had come to know what her mother knew about emotions: loneliness saddened, poverty gnawed, patriarchy constrained, and racial discrimination hurt profoundly. The omnipresent seagulls, a pretty sight, could not flap away those predicaments.

CHAPTER 2

California Community, 1917–1925

For once, John Thompson's and Louise's ideas aligned; she expressed absolutely no dissent when, in early 1917, riding a streak of good fortune and his usual optimism, he chose to relocate to Sacramento, which was becoming known as a growth town. Much of its commercial progress stemmed from the fact that it was a railway hub. Several popular lines served the city, and the original Sacramento station functioned as the western terminus of the Central Pacific Railroad. Thompson planned to work the trains until another opportunity for entrepreneurship surfaced. His aspirations were shared by a neighbor, George Dunlap, who was employed in dining cars on the Southern Pacific. Dunlap eventually operated the dining service on the Sacramento Northern Railway line and owned several restaurants, including the legendary Dunlap's Dining Room.[1]

Although Thompson possessed similar and sufficient ambition, he lacked, from Louise's perspective, the proper education and managerial skills.[2] In any event, the move represented a homecoming for him because of his family ties in the area. And he did get off to a good start overall. After staying for a brief period in an Oak Park boardinghouse run by John's sister, Frances, the Thompsons bought a cottage in the neighborhood. The presence of African Americans and Mexicans, though small in an area dominated by people of European descent, would have seemed very significant to Louise given her recent sojourns in Nevada, Utah, Idaho, and Oregon. Her parents splurged on new furnishings: a library table, rugs, leather chairs, and a dining room set. In July Lulu informed Margaret Burdine by mail that the house had begun to look like a home. She took special pride in the garden, which yielded onions, lettuce, wax beans, turnips, squash, and cucumbers. More important, she noted that she had never seen her husband prouder. Off on Mondays, he spent numerous hours tending to the soil and crops.[3]

Lulu, in fact, was faring better at the time than her old role model, Susie Revels Cayton. In imploring African Americans to move to the West, Horace Cayton had not reckoned adequately with the heightened racial antipathy among whites that an increased black presence would cause. The family had been driven from their home in Capitol Hill by business and political enemies. For the same reason, Cayton had ceased publishing the *Seattle Republican* in 1913, and his family had struggled economically since.[4] Just as the Thompsons seemed to be in ascent, the Caytons' fortunes had declined owing to racial politics.

Louise, as it turned out, was less than enthusiastic about life in Sacramento. She welcomed change but seemed to experience conflicted racial and class attitudes. She thought she wanted to be at the center of a black community, but she rejected the "colored Sunday school" because she judged the children's behavior to be too unruly.[5] Instead, she attended lessons at a Christian Science church. She did not favor Sacramento High, although she quickly established herself as a stellar student, finishing the academic year with high honors. She deemed the school environment too chaotic, an assessment perhaps related to the "colored" students of the working class.[6] Because she had been ostracized by whites and yearned nostalgically for connection with African Americans, such as she had experienced with the Davises in West Oakland, the teenage Louise possessed racial rumblings in the belly, but she did not embrace full black humanity in her heart and mind.

At the same time, she appreciated the entire Dunlap clan, from whom she learned about issues of concern to the African American community. She especially treasured the Dunlap women because they addressed a crucial matter that had been inadequately attended to: her hair. She and her mother were clueless regarding how to care for it fashionably. The elder Louise, lacking experience with the hair type, had always washed, greased, and braided it the best she could. Her best hardly sufficed now for her adolescent daughter, at least not in the Dunlaps' view, and they arranged for Louise to have her hair straightened. However, the decision had unintended emotional consequences. When Louise returned to school and met the stares and inquiries of the white girls, she realized that having her hair treated was much less embarrassing than having everyone call attention to the fact.[7]

While Louise dealt with the politics of hair and the wonders of cosmetology, her stepfather, true to form, set his sights on Oakland again, eighty miles to the southwest. The city was an even more prominent transportation hub. A huge railway yard sat on the west side, and a busy depot was located at Seventh Street and Broadway. The city was also undergoing rapid industrialization; its development had been accelerated by the earthquake and fire of 1906, which had destroyed much of San Francisco but left Oakland relatively unscathed. Thus, people had moved across the bay, as had businesses such as the important Moore Shipbuilding Company. In addition, the port city began to attract automobile manufacturers such as Chevrolet, Fageol, and Durant.

African Americans benefited from these changes in two ways. First, as the nation mobilized for World War I and a substantial number of white men entered military service, industrial jobs that would normally have been unavailable to blacks because of racial discrimination began to open up to them. Second, population increases meant more potential customers for black-owned businesses, which were primarily located along Seventh Street; this would have interested John Thompson the most. Although blacks made up little more than 2 percent of Oakland's 150,000 residents, they were concentrated in West Oakland, even more so than when Louise had lodged with the Davis family in 1910.[8] Prominent among this group were the Pullman porters, all of whom were black, according to company policy. Many of them settled in West Oakland because of the mild climate and the relative social freedom. Thompson would work an Oakland-to-Portland run until he launched his next business venture.

Louise, however, had to clear a major health obstacle to get to Oakland. In the fall of 1918, at the beginning of her senior year, the great influenza pandemic struck the West Coast. More than 115,000 Californians became infected, seventeen-year-old Louise among them.[9] She recalled that several fatalities occurred on surrounding blocks and that she was bedridden on Armistice Day, in contrast to the city's overall jubilance. In fact, the plague potentially altered her timetable for graduation given that city officials closed the schools. Therefore, after Louise had recovered and the family had moved to Oakland for the start of the spring term, it was impossible for her to carry a normal course load and still graduate in June. She found delaying her graduation to be unacceptable and committed instead to attending night sessions in trigonometry at Oakland Tech while taking classes as a day student at Oakland High School.

The Thompsons took up residence on Thirty-Sixth Street between Market and Grove (now Martin Luther King Jr. Way). Lulu, usually guarded, met a woman, Mrs. Allen, who became a lifelong friend. Mrs. Allen was "so proper."[10] For a woman raising an adolescent daughter in a bustling and unfamiliar city, that sense of propriety proved endearing. Mrs. Allen could reinforce teachings about the importance of style and a good reputation. As the diminutive yet maturing Louise traveled back and forth to school and encountered a much greater and more diverse volume of passersby and students than she had been accustomed to, her mother perhaps recalled her own arrival in Chicago, when she was too easily charmed. She could be somewhat of a social liberal at times, mainly because it was hard to begrudge her daughter fun, yet she remained naturally and maternally nervous about her daughter's welfare.

Louise's first steady boyfriend was a so-called pretty boy, a light-skinned man with "good hair."[11] Renner Cook had originally come west from Pittsburgh to visit friends Arthur Rickman and Bill Rickman. A couple of years older than Louise, he stayed for a while to attend school. A budding gentleman, he escorted Louise to her first formal dance, an affair held in a local hall by a social club known as the Ducks. She made her own dress for the occasion, a white crepe de chine number trimmed with beads. When Renner pinned on the corsage he brought, she must have felt as optimistic and as normal as she ever had. These feelings extended to her hormonal urgings; she was lively. But her Victorian side, carefully cultivated by her mother, kicked in. As she recalled the romances of her school years, she revealed that she and several of her friends were incurable teases. "We'd go to the door," she explained, "but that would be as far as we would go."[12]

Cook returned to Pennsylvania to enroll in dental school, but the couple corresponded diligently. When both were nearly finished with school, Cook broached the subject of marriage. Louise harbored no desire to be tied down to a life of "bungalows and babies."[13] But rather than reject the overture directly, she wrote to her beau about her plans to explore the world. She had cosmopolitan leanings born of both her deprivation and her wanderings. She explained her desire to visit Spain to master Spanish, of which she would complete three terms in high school.[14] Besides, the marriage she knew the most about was her mother's, an arrangement that seemed far from splendid.

Cook fatefully pressed his intentions. On a return trip west, he found Louise sitting with friends outside her current home on Thirty-Ninth and

Grove on a summery day. He approached her swiftly, took her in his arms, and kissed her passionately. He demonstrated possession, or at least that was how Louise disdainfully read the gesture. She remembered years later, "I was so embarrassed and so mad at him. You know, just like he owned me. He just, well, I guess that was his way. I didn't have a ring on. And that turned me against Renner."[15]

Louise graduated from Oakland High School on June 20, 1919, among a class of sixty-four seniors, including Becky London, the daughter of author Jack London, and future Academy Award–winning costume designer Walter Plunkett. Both classmates were headed to the University of California, Berkeley, the route Louise's mother wanted her to travel as well. The institution was open without examination to all graduates of an accredited California high school who had completed a college-prep curriculum, attended school for at least a year immediately before graduating, and were recommended by the principal. With the signature of Charles E. Keyes on Recommendation Form A, Louise could be on her way. Louise, however, preferred to begin working full-time so that she could become economically independent, which, she reasoned, would lead fairly soon to increased mobility.[16] She would agree to attend Berkeley only if her mother assured her that the family would not leave town after Louise matriculated at the university. They had made at least three moves in the Bay Area and were then living off of Forty-Seventh and San Pablo in Emeryville, a tiny municipality of two square miles adjacent to Oakland to the south and east, San Francisco Bay to the west, and Berkeley to the north. Nevertheless, they had remained in the area for three years, and Louise, knowing the proclivities of her stepfather, wanted to avoid a major disruption if she were going to attempt college.[17]

Her mother clinched the deal decisively. Not only did she agree to remain in the vicinity, but she moved even closer to the school shortly after Louise enrolled, coordinating the purchase of a house at 1125 Bancroft Way, near San Pablo, about a mile and a half west of campus. Because realtors steered blacks and Asians south of Dwight Way and west of Grove, Louise's mother probably passed as white—not actively but based on a racial don't-ask, don't-tell policy—to complete the transaction and move into a previously all-white section of Berkeley.[18] She passed for white at times in the labor market as well. Pragmatism superseded her youthful refusal to follow that strand of the Brown family's tradition.

The Cal that Louise entered was concluding a two-decade advance to prominence and distinction. Its first president, Daniel Coit Gilman, took the German research university as his model upon the school's founding in 1868.[19] However, because of political and financial problems, Cal remained an academic backwater in the landscape of higher education until the eve of the twentieth century, when its most important benefactor, Phoebe Apperson Hearst, an heiress and the first female regent, joined forces with the new president, Benjamin Ide Wheeler. By the time of Hearst's death in the spring of 1919, her collaboration with Wheeler had wrought the most radical transformation of the physical plant and the curriculum in Cal's history.[20] Indeed, the paradigm of the German research university had been put into operation. Louise would not attend under Wheeler's presidency, though. Although indisputably successful in many respects, Wheeler functioned autocratically, which led to his being forced from office. David Prescott Barrows presided over the university during Louise's studies.

She tackled the curriculum with aplomb. Enrolled in the College of Commerce, she amassed forty credits in her first year. In addition to required offerings in physical education, hygiene, and math, her coursework included Stenography and Typing, Fundamentals of Modern Geography, Introduction to Economic Geography, and Mathematical Theory of Investment. She also continued her study of Spanish and, because of her preparation in high school, was able to skip the most elementary course. During her sophomore year, with an eye to becoming a certified public accountant, she added nineteen more credits in economics, including Principles of Economics, Economic and Commercial History, and Principles of Accounting. She tackled a class in commercial law and pushed her Spanish studies with a yearlong sequence in conversation and composition. She finished the spring semester with significantly more credits than the sixty-four required for the junior certificate, which she received in May. She had also passed a foreign-language reading exam, tested out of the English composition requirement, and completed six units in history. Only nineteen years old, she had pulled within fifty credits of being eligible for graduation.

Louise's excellent academic progress unfolded despite her unease with the social environment on campus; Cal was not the most welcoming place for women or African Americans. She surely experienced at times, in the words of her schoolmate Ida Louise Jackson, the "cold spot," the reality of "sitting beside students who acted as if my seat were unoccupied, showing no sign of recognition, never giving a smile or nod."[21] During Louise's very first month at the university, the cover of the *California Pelican*, a student journal published monthly during the school year by the English Club, featured a mermaid ensnared in a fishing net. The caption proclaimed, "Fisherman's Luck."[22] Admittedly, the *Pelican* existed as a self-styled humor magazine. Nonetheless, it was a university-sponsored publication, and in issue after issue its bounty of jokes objectified women. One item announced that among the things a man hates to see on women are wool socks, spats, Bologne nose pinchers, bobbed hair, elongated bangs, and too much clothing.[23] The commentary about African Americans also proved to be tasteless. Black caricatures with bulging eyes and monstrously distorted white lips appeared in several editions. For example, in the installment for November 1919, the title "A Spirited Encounter or a Shot in the Dark" introduced a drawing of a fearful prohibition-era Negro (a "dark") sneaking a cup of liquor (a "spirit" or "shot") to a pleased white man.[24] The next issue featured a grotesque black figure snapping his fingers while tossing two bombs from a rooftop as though playing a game of craps. The text of "Force of Habit" explains the artwork: Negro Bolshevik— "Doan Fail Me, Dice."[25] In the issue dated December 1920, "Mammy's Little Coal Black Rose" is illustrated with a buffoonish figure (mammy's little coal black) dripping exaggerated beads of sweat who leapt (rose) six feet in the air after sitting on a pin.[26] In "Black and Blue," another minstrel-like figure is pummeled by a police officer for being in violation of a blue law.[27]

Occasionally, the *Pelican* contained more extended pieces about blacks, no less stereotypical, even if funny, such as:

FIRST COLORED GENT: "Whe' you all gwine?"
SECOND DITTO: "I'se gwine home to my wife an' chilluns."
FIRST C. G.: "Come on there, niggah; you all ain't got no wife an' chilluns."
SECOND DITTO: Yes ah has, too. Ah has a wife an' a bushel of chilluns."
FIRST C. G.: "Har, har! Who ebber heerd of a bushel of chilluns?"
SECOND DITTO: "Well, sah, ah married a widow named Peck with four chilluns, and four pecks make a bushel."[28]

And "He Got the Job" read:

The colonel of a colored regiment in France charged the adjutant with selecting a suitable soldier to serve as orderly at his billet. The adjutant combed the command for the proper man and finally found one who had been an elevator boy in a hotel—a smiling, gracious darky, neat and respectful. When the man reported the colonel impressed upon him the necessity for tact.

"Do you know what I mean by tact?"

"Yah, suh. W'en it comes to tac' I'se right on de spot. Why, cunel, es' las' week I went into the bathhouse near mah billet, an' foun' one of de madamselles there. I jest stepped back an' says 'Pardon, Monsieur!' Now ef dat warn't tac,' den I don't know what is."[29]

This second vignette about a darky soldier in France appeared two years after the 369th Infantry Regiment, the famous Harlem Hellfighters, achieved remarkable and crucial combat success in that country during World War I.[30] The unit was much celebrated by both the French and American governments—and might have had a good time at Cal.

Regardless, Louise had an outlet away from campus and enjoyed an active social life emanating from Bancroft Way. Mother Thompson, as the elder Louise became known among her daughter's closest friends, none of whom attended Cal, encouraged gatherings at her home. Along with perhaps compensating for her daughter's former isolation, this seemed to be a strategy to make home a preferred hangout, thereby lessening Louise's desire to be out in the streets. It was better to have her partying and entertaining inside the home than to fret about her external movements. Against the backdrop of the surrounding provincialism, she condoned card playing, dancing (which Louise loved), and even alcohol consumption on occasion. She could recognize the venturesome spirit in her daughter, which she had helped to instill, and she sought not to erase it but to add finesse.

Louise's closest friend during that period was Evelyn Phyllis Graves, known more informally as Nebby. How they met is unclear, but Nebby belonged to the Ducks. In any event, they liked each other immediately and soon regarded each other as sisters. Two years older than Louise, and with a complexion just as fair, Nebby moved in with the Thompsons on Bancroft Way. She and Louise shared a room on the upper floor. Nebby also brought her Victrola, a key implement for their merriment, and set it in the living room. A self-assured young woman, Nebby, a graduate of the High School of Commerce, had been working since she was sixteen years old and by that point had a job at Fort Mason. She and Louise were so supportive of each other that they focused less on organized social clubs and the attendant expectations. Both, for example, paid little attention to Lee Pernell, whom many other young women considered a prime bachelor. His mother, flabbergasted at such lack of deference to her son and to the dictates of black "high society," spread the rumor that they were lesbians.[31]

Dorothy (Dot) Fisher fit in perfectly with Louise and Nebby, both in temperament and in phenotype. In an allusion to Alexandre Dumas's famous novel *The Three Musketeers*, they were dubbed the Three Mosquitoes. Dot wasn't quite as light-skinned as the other two, but she had straight hair. Louise would later deny that they self-segregated based on traits such as skin color and hair, but Louise's closest female friends were all light-skinned.[32] Unless no dark-skinned young people, or even medium-brown ones, lived in the Bay Area, it appears that color chauvinism of the type infamously associated with some black sororities factored into the choosing of friends, subconsciously if not overtly. The group would eventually include Aleta Watkins, Irma Hopkins, and the Graves brothers, Wilbur and Milton, who were Nebby's cousins. Wilbur began dating Louise.

Driven by the quest for wholesome fun, the group arranged or attended a series of parties at the Bancroft Way residence, always under the watchful eye of Mother Thompson, employing her strategy of containment. She approved of the Sunday hikes in the area of Mt. Tamalpais, the 2,500-foot peak just north of San Francisco's Golden Gate strait that offered absorbing views of the bay, the ocean, and the neighboring cities and villages. She apparently wasn't worried that her daughter would get into trouble in that particular paradise. She was less sure about a weekend trip that her daughter and Nebby took, partly to give Nebby her first sight of snow. Using passes from John Thompson, then working as a cook on the Western Pacific, they rode the rails to Salt Lake City. They stayed overnight in a whites-only hotel, possible because of their ambiguous racial profile. Not fooled, however, were the black cooks and dishwashers, who were somewhat animated and amused by their presence. Before the pair departed from the city, they visited a black church, a livelier experience than the services of the Christian Science church they attended in Berkeley.

Mother Thompson fretted most about the temptations of West Oakland nightlife. Seventh Street had become a flourishing nexus of black cultural activity, particularly for jazz lovers; the widely traveled black railroad workers were cognizant of music innovations across the nation and eager to support visits by the likes of Jelly Roll Morton, Kid Ory, and King Oliver. But because it was a product of railroad culture, the neighborhood also featured gambling dens and houses of prostitution, especially after the shutdown in 1917 of San Francisco's infamous red light district, the Barbary Coast.

Louise, Wilbur Graves, and a few others went to Seventh Street to visit Sid Deering's Creole Café, where the sounds of New Orleans jazz radiated.

However, when Louise told Mother Thompson about the trip, the latter, knowing that the road to ruin often ran through speakeasies, broke down in tears.[33] Louise and her friends would hardly evolve into the most roaring of youngsters in the 1920s, but not because of the emotional blackmail that Mother Thompson attempted. The group was mainly searching for a satisfying middle ground between Victorian strictures and bohemian excess. For Louise, beginning to appreciate the various manifestations of black culture represented an essential aspect of the process.

Actually, for Mother Thompson, other family issues were more precarious than the immediate fate of her daughter. Tired of the railroads, John Thompson found a small restaurant between Oakland and San Jose that captured his fancy. As usual, he wanted to construct family life around his whims, in this case his fifth or sixth effort at being a restaurant owner, but Mother Thompson refused any major disassembling of her life. She calculated that her husband's absence would be the least of the possible disruptions. It is not known what verbal ultimatums, if any, were issued. Mother Thompson, predictably, visited her husband on occasion. The key outcome, however, was that John Thompson disappeared permanently from Bancroft Way.

By the time of her separation from her husband, Mother Thompson, long past the emotional devastation of Chicago and, strangely enough, having become an example of a successful Western pioneer, was back in contact with her family, several of whom would visit Berkeley. Her brother Charles stayed the longest and became, to Louise, a cautionary tale about the dangers of assimilation.

Charles Brown had run away from home and wound up in the army while still a teenager. For twenty years, he had lived the life of a white soldier in a (supposedly) segregated military, spending much of that time in the Philippines. He had virtually no knowledge of black people, remained aloof in their presence, and was moody and reclusive in general. "He knew nothing but army life," declared his niece. Yet he fell hopelessly and pathetically in love with Nebby, who viewed him just as Louise did: as the weird uncle who provoked aggravation along with tolerance and sympathy.[34]

He probably annoyed Louise more than he did Nebby: he snooped around for incriminating information, such as young men kissing her, to dish to Mother Thompson. Louise judged him to have an "inferiority complex of the worse type," her attempt to describe a lonely and despairing person with no motivation to pursue practical or serious matters.[35] Month after month, he, a grown man in his mid-thirties, lay about the house while Louise was on campus and Nebby and Mother Thompson were out working. His sister would not challenge him, but the girls began to pester him, initiating a war of wills. He was adamant that no one wanted to hire him. Finally, Nebby and Louise wrought a concession: he agreed to take the post office examination. He felt sure he would not pass owing to his limited education, and defeat would even strengthen his argument at home. But he passed—and was very upset. When he was called to work as a letter carrier, he sabotaged his own efforts. When he approached a building, rather than placing the mail in the appropriate boxes, he dumped it in one spot on the floor for the occupants to sort. He was promptly terminated and then boasted to Nebby and Louise, "I told you so."[36]

The girls kept firing back. Nebby secured him a position as a janitor in San Francisco and actually persuaded him to accept it. He then found a place in San Francisco and, apparently, even a girlfriend, though he remained a somewhat pitiable figure, often hanging around outside of Nebby's workplace to ask about the family. Although several factors were obviously at play, Louise attributed her uncle's downfall—and she clearly thought of it as such—to the failure to develop a healthy racial identity, something she herself was now trying to do. She bemoaned, "It was really tragic about him. . . . He wasn't black, he wasn't white, he wasn't anything."[37] She preferred to keep racial labeling simple and decisive at that juncture, reflecting her evolving racial consciousness and fear of psychological fracture. She felt one should just choose and stay the course.

This definitely described her approach during her somewhat-embattled time in the University of California social scene. Tarea Hall, who earned a master's in social welfare from the university in 1925 and would, as Tarea Hall Pittman, become a celebrated official in the National Association for the Advancement of Colored People (NAACP) and a civil rights activist, recalled matters this way: "Louise Thompson was a very fair girl, and she was always having some kind of problem because, you see, she looked like a white person. Well, you see, she'd be in a group and somebody would probably say, 'Well, I don't think these niggers ought to be here.' She'd overhear this, what with her being so light and with straight hair and looking so Caucasian. She'd be inclined to take up the cudgel and say something about it, 'What do you mean calling somebody nigger?'"[38] Such vigilance and flashes of a Hellfighter's moxie were surely valued by fellow black students, though Louise also felt irritated at times with the group she defended. As her fellow alumna remembered, "she had people that she felt were prejudiced against her because she was so fair."[39]

Despite such tensions, Louise collaborated on social and cultural projects with an outstanding, though small, group of young African American women (fewer than twenty black students attended Cal).[40] During 1921 and 1922, for example, she teamed up with Vivian Osborne, four years her senior, to help found the Kappa chapter of the Delta Sigma Theta Sorority (Osborne married Leon F. Marsh and became a government official). Intended to exemplify the double purpose of academic excellence and social service, in line with the original chapter, formed at Howard University in 1913, this was the first historically black sorority to exist west of the Mississippi River. It had the blessing of President Barrows and the full support of Lucy Stebbins, the dean of women, and it received official recognition, if not always respect, from other student organizations.[41] No black sorority members were included in the campus annual *Blue and Gold*.[42] Osborne, who earned bachelor's and master's degrees in anthropology, served as president of the chapter. The other charter officers were the vice president, Onilda Taylor; the treasurer, Elizabeth Gordon; and the secretary, Louise, who eventually became the chapter's leader.

Joining the Deltas on campus were Ida Louise Jackson and the charter members of the Rho chapter of Alpha Kappa Alpha. Jackson graduated with a bachelor's degree in education in 1922 and a master's degree in the same field in 1923. After battling discrimination for years, she became the first African American certified by the state to teach in a California public high school.[43]

The sorority sisters no doubt had a hand in welcoming the venerable W. E. B. Du Bois to campus on the afternoon of Monday, March 12, 1923. In room 11 of Wheeler Hall, under the auspices of the economics department, he delivered an address titled "The Economic Condition of the Negro in the United States."[44] Although the message was likely a modest reformulation of retrospective and prospective ideas about economics, race prejudice, education, uplift, and activism that he had presented in such forums as the *Publications of the American Economic Association* and the *Sociological Review*, Louise, a twenty-one-year-old senior, sat mesmerized listening to the masterful scholar and civil rights lion.[45] The medium proved paramount. Louise summarized the experience as follows: "He stood up. First of all, his presence was something, you know. He commands you just when he stands up. And then he spoke. He didn't look at a note. He didn't read it from a paper. He talked. And the hall, you could hear a pin drop. They listened. And I walked out feeling, well, it is something to be black."[46]

One needed such revelations or reminders at Cal. Neither the *Daily Californian*, which was the student newspaper, nor the *Berkeley Daily Gazette* covered Du Bois's talk. Yet the local media provided a detailed description of a Dixieland party held in Stephens Union four days before his appearance. Designed to promote friendship among women in the junior and senior classes, the Dixieland event included Professor C. W. Wells of the English department, touted as a "true Southerner," rendering Uncle Remus stories in a purportedly authentic "negro dialect."[47] The Thalian Players, with no African Americans among them, contributed entertainment "in the form of a negro sketch."[48]

But Cal wasn't totally backward on race that week, partly because an issue arose concerning sports, an activity that mitigated some, though certainly not all, of the prejudice against black males on campus. Stanford University officials threatened to cancel an intercollegiate boxing match because two "colored" boxers represented Cal, the host institution. Stanford athletic director W. H. Barrow argued, in obfuscating language, "Until the question of mixed bouts can be worked out on a basis that will be fair to all the participants, it seems best to discontinue boxing between the two universities."[49] However, Cal did not capitulate. I. A. Nichols, speaking on behalf of the Associated Students of the University of California, reasoned, "There is no other course open to the university. The men are good students, clean sportsmen, and have worked hard for their places on the team."[50] To modify Ida Louise Jackson's lingo, they had found a spot that was perhaps a bit warmer.

It is incontrovertible that Louise had learned much and felt flushed with black pride by the conclusion of Du Bois's lecture, given his brilliance, compelling oratorical style, and obvious self-esteem. Constantly the dreamer, she instantly conjured up visions of going to New York to work with him on the *Crisis*.[51] At the same time, the claim of ignorance about the worth of being black seems somewhat hyperbolic. Her own involvement with the Deltas belies any narrative that she was bereft of black pride. Moreover, she would have had to ignore several prominent developments in the racial politics of the Bay Area to not know that many committed people were making black perspectives count.

Both the NAACP and the Universal Negro Improvement Association were vibrantly active locally during Louise's time at Cal. In 1921 Marcus Garvey, who appealed enormously to the black proletariat, including the numerous railroad employees and dockworkers, spoke before an enthusiastic throng at the Oakland Civic Auditorium. Du Bois had toured the Bay Area in 1913 and stimulated enough interest to lead to the establishment in 1915 of the Northern California branch of the NAACP. More than a thousand members had joined the group, headquartered in Oakland, by 1917.[52] Louise was an area resident during most of the local controversy surrounding D. W. Griffith's *Birth of a Nation*, the pro–Ku Klux Klan movie that screened in San Francisco in 1915. Local NAACP members continued to agitate until the film was finally withdrawn six years later. Furthermore, while still in high school, she had attended an NAACP event at the Oakland Civic Auditorium presided over by William L. Patterson and featuring James Weldon Johnson.

However, if Louise exaggerated the depth of Du Bois's initial influence on her, it was understandable. After all, at the time of his lecture, she was taking an elective titled The History of Education, which made no mention of an important African American educationalist such as Du Bois.[53] She had also reached the midpoint of English 53B, Introduction to the Study of Poetry, which unambiguously meant, as stated in the college catalog, perusal and analysis of European verse.[54] Du Bois became for a while Louise's cultural, intellectual, political, and moral touchstone. To do right meant to make the decisions that Du Bois would.

Meanwhile, Louise negotiated the final leg toward graduation, finishing the last of her forty-two credits in economics and—never leaving behind her liberal-arts side, no matter how Eurocentric at that point—the last of four semesters studying Spanish literature with S. Griswold Morley, a future president of the Modern Language Association. With 135.5 units wrapped up, she had well beyond the total needed. Although technically an economics major, she accomplished what nowadays would be a double major, given her thirty-six credits in Spanish. Just as impressive, out of a total of 182 graduates, she was among the 16 students in the College of Commerce to be awarded the baccalaureate with honors.[55] Furthermore, Louise was among only a handful of African American students to have ever completed Cal, finishing only eighteen years after the university's first black graduate, Charles Edward Carpenter, and fourteen years after the first black female graduate, Vivian Logan Rodgers.[56] She received her degree in the university's Greek Theatre on May 16, 1923, as did her classmates from Oakland High School, London and Plunkett, as well as future novelist Irving Stone.

When Louise descended from the platform, she handed her diploma to Mother Thompson. Her mother grabbed it joyfully, then turned to her own mother, Emma Colwell Brown, on hand for the giddy occasion, and uttered emphatically, "Now I can die."[57] The words startled Louise, who thought the opposite declaration, "Now I can live," would be more to the point. Mother Thompson was only forty-five at the time. Louise learned an unintended lesson: "It taught me that selflessness in itself is not a virtue. It can be a handicap if you reserve nothing for yourself. It can handicap the other person as well as yourself. It made me resolve that I would never admit anyone else into my life who would only live through me."[58] She even understood that she might have been handicapped in ways she did not yet fully understand. In any case, she could never deeply fault her faithful guardian or even stop taking advantage of her mother's kindness and heroic dedication.

For all of the achievement it signaled, being among the early wave of African American graduates from the University of California also meant that one was living when blatant racial discrimination still prevailed in the state. In particular, the liberal political and social façade of the Bay Area never covered well the inexcusable racial exclusions in employment experienced by the area's fifteen thousand black residents.[59] Thus, the local options for Louise were limited. Viable teaching opportunities did not exist. The post office removed her from its list because she had worked during a holiday season. Furthermore, she was nowhere near marriage. Wilbur Graves had been secretly seeing another woman, named Ruth, whom he eventually wed. New prospects appeared limited; there were simply not enough black doctors, lawyers, and undertakers—or even working-class union members—to go around.[60] So with baccalaureate in hand and work as an elevator operator, stock clerk, or maid looming, Louise decided to pass ethnically. She never thought she looked white, despite the observations of schoolmates like Tarea Hall. After all, white people had ostracized her for much of her life. She judged that claiming to be Mexican was a better strategy, one she should be able to enact successfully with her passable Spanish if Mexicans were not evaluating her.[61]

She did office work for the General Equipment Company, a hardware jobber in San Francisco, earning about eighty dollars per month. However, her ruse strained her emotionally. She would not speak to some of her friends, who were complicit in her trickery, when she encountered them in San Francisco. On the Monday ferry ride across the bay, she and Nebby, who was also passing, often had to ignore the very guys they had been with all weekend. She kept quiet when she heard racial epithets in the workplace.[62] Sometimes her boss, a sportsman, would arrive unannounced on Bancroft Way to share the rewards of a day's fishing trip. These visits sent whatever friends happened to be on hand scrambling for the closets.[63]

Louise also recalled passing to obtain a temporary job one Christmas season at Capwell Department Store in downtown Oakland. She and her friends exchanged subtle greetings as she worked a booth in the middle of the floor. "It was a game that we played," she lamented, "an enormous deception, and all to work at a handkerchief counter!"[64]

By 1925 she could no longer persist in constructing her personal "mess of pottage."[65] She enthusiastically embraced the burgeoning car culture, combining funds with Nebby to purchase a Studebaker. Obviously, working had made that possible. In addition, she tried to amass funds for a move to New York, where the *Crisis* thrived and the New Negro flourished in Harlem. But she could no longer endure the environment in which she was maneuvering. Besides the racism and the subterfuge, it was too philistine an existence for someone longing more and more for the black intellectual and cultural communities that she knew existed elsewhere. Given her nomadic origins, she could easily conceive of leaving the Bay Area, unlike Nebby, who felt rooted in California. In general, her girlfriends talked more about a "good marriage and the trimmings" than about plans for travel.[66]

Although New York was Louise's preferred destination, Chicago became the practical choice. Some of Mother Thompson's siblings had migrated to the city, and the still very protective Mother Thompson would relocate along with her daughter. Nebby and Dot would accompany the two on the trusty Southern Pacific, but strictly as visitors.

Louise could not yet seize New York City, the brass ring that Du Bois had dangled before her in the University of California's Wheeler Hall on that auspicious occasion two years earlier. But she would perhaps enjoy a better angle of approach from the city of her birth.

CHAPTER 3

Shades of Control, 1925–1928

The Black Belt had grown considerably since 1906, when Louise and her mother had left Chicago. In 1925 there were six times as many black residents, and the black population would rise to 234,000 by the end of the decade.[1] The rapid population growth was accompanied by expanded opportunities for manufacturing jobs, segregationist residential policies, white violence, and evolving black institutional structures. This resulted in the oft-noted "black metropolis" or "city within a city."[2] The underclass, proletariat, middle class, and high society intermingled between Twenty-Second and Fifty-Fifth Streets, from Wentworth to Cottage Grove. Any initiatives for integrating Chicago had been repelled dramatically by the six-day race riots in the summer of 1919, during which thirty-eight people were killed and more than five hundred injured, followed in early 1920 by a wave of bombings designed to keep African Americans out of neighborhoods such as Hyde Park and Kenwood.[3] Naturally, civil rights activists would wage a battle for full housing rights, which were especially important given the general deterioration of the housing stock in the Black Belt. Nonetheless, the dominant agenda for black social, cultural, and political activity in Chicago was set. Amid the relative prosperity of the 1920s and the optimism of jazz spiriting forth from clubs on Thirty-First, Thirty-Fifth, and State Streets, many black Chicagoans believed that the ultimately fanciful idea of an *imperium in imperio* could work.[4]

Thus, upon settling in with her Aunt Irene at 3409 Giles Avenue, Louise received her most concentrated exposure to African American life up till then. Only Harlem could offer as much, albeit with what some would argue was a markedly different outlook. The sociologist E. Franklin Frazier remarked, "The feeling of rivalry between Harlem and Chicago has caused each to cast uncomplimentary epithets at the other. New York has charged Chicago Negroes with being a group of money getters, without any sense of the finer things in life; while Chicago has retorted that the 'homeless ones' of New York float in the clouds of spirit without any sound economic basis for their culture."[5] It is not known whether Louise ever weighed in on the controversy, but Chicago as portrayed by Frazier did not attract her. She was, despite her commerce degree, becoming more an aesthete than a money getter. Employed at the Chicago Mortgage and Credit Company, she turned down a chance to head the accounting department at Supreme Liberty Life Insurance, one of the nation's largest black-owned companies. She would remain too practical, though, for the life of an itinerant, and she needed more than a dream before she would move to Harlem. As a middle road, she gravitated toward the helping professions and began to consider a teaching career, perhaps one that would unfold in the Chicago public schools and later those in New York. She enrolled in education courses at the University of Chicago and in the autumn quarter of 1925 garnered As in Introductory Psychology and Elementary Italian, while earning a B in Methods of Teaching in High Schools. The following quarter, she received an A in Psychology of High School Subjects.

That summer, however, she fantasized again about living in New York, motivated by seeing W. E. B. Du Bois during the seventeenth annual convention of the NAACP, held in Chicago on June 23–29, 1926. The meeting was headquartered in the heart of the Black Belt, at Pilgrim Baptist Church on Indiana Avenue. Louise did not attend the convention proper but went to the social event sponsored by the Deltas, at which she danced with her idol. "I was in seventh heaven," she recalled.[6] The fifty-eight-year-old Du Bois seemed to Louise "not only a brilliant man, but a handsome, sophisticated man as well."[7] She followed up with a letter to Du Bois and included her résumé, which yielded a job offer.[8] She eventually explained to Du Bois, however, that she could not envision surviving in New York on the relatively meager salary available.[9]

With no viable plan to get to New York materializing as the summer wore on, she headed in another direction. In mid-August, she attended the Midwestern Tennis Championships, hosted by the Chicago Prairie Tennis Club, located at Thirty-Second Street and Vernon Avenue. Louise had become a tennis buff, but many of those who had not taken to the sport also placed the all-black tournament, one of the biggest social events in black Chicago, on their calendars. Louise rooted for Edgar Brown, the politically outspoken former American Tennis Association national champion. However, Wilber-force University star Ted Thompson defeated Brown in the finals. While at the tournament, Louise sat among a circle of acquaintances. She began inquiring about jobs and was informed that a school in Arkansas had advertised for a business teacher. Although Louise had never set foot in the South and experienced extreme trepidation about ever doing so, her bold streak enabled her to follow up with a telegram to the principal, Robert Emmick Malone. He responded promptly with a job offer.

When Louise first gazed on Pine Bluff Agricultural, Mechanical, and Normal School, it struck her as more a fifty-acre cow pasture than a junior-college campus. Dotting the uninspiring field were leftover army barracks, the primary infrastructure. An added touch was the mice-infested dormitory in which Louise spent a terrifying and sleepless first night. In all, the school remained decades away from living up to its current slogan, "flagship of the Delta."[10] Back then, the land-grant institution, created in 1873 as a branch of the Arkansas Industrial University (now the University of Arkansas), barely justified its junior-college billing, enrolling only 21 of 411 students in postsecondary courses.[11]

Despite the humble environs and the poor preparation of most students and teachers, Malone, a native of Louisville who had graduated from Tuskegee Institute and Cornell University, had made admirable strides in strengthening the curriculum since his tenure began in 1922, and he appeared committed to doing more. A corpulent forty-one-year-old prone to dozing off in meetings when attention shifted from him, he charged Louise with heading the grandiosely named Department of Commerce. In addition, as a gesture to the liberal arts and her other undergraduate concentration, he decided that Louise, whom he declared to be the most qualified member of the faculty overall (to the consternation of her peers), would teach Spanish classes. A coworker, Miss Wallace, who had attended Ohio State, was assigned to teach French, an attempt that quickly degenerated into farce. Louise recalled, "We used to listen outside Miss Wallace's class sometimes where we could overhear her saying 'Ow, ow, monsir,' for 'Oui, oui, monsieur.'"[12] Louise did not fare much better teaching Spanish—or English. Students typically pronounced her name, not Thompson, but Thomas, with a long vowel sound.

Her business classroom reflected the general quality of the school buildings—rough wooden floors, shabby furnishings, and a poor heating system. But Malone had procured shiny new Underwood typewriters and three glittering bookkeeping machines. When word of the technological largesse spread, students began to transfer from the trade school and home economics divisions. The work excited Louise, and she dived in exuberantly, impressed by the students' willingness and effort to learn. At the same time, she grew increasingly frustrated by the overall lack of investment in quality education on the part of the school's white overseers and by the derogatory way in which legislators and members of the board characteristically spoke, opining about "niggers."[13] She also became vexed because the demands of the cotton industry severely disrupted classes. The full complement of students would not be on hand until the crop had been harvested in November, and the ranks would thin again at the beginning of the planting season. The students as a whole were never going to transcend an elementary level of education.

The situation became crystallized for Louise when Malone appeared one day with visitors in tow to show off the commercial department, perhaps his greatest source of pride on campus. Louise had prepped the class for such visits; they were to act entirely business-like. Although she generally allowed students to wear coats in class because of the chill, she forbade them when observers came. The only student to resist the rule that day was a girl named Valentine. Louise demanded that she remove her coat, but the student protested before relenting just before the visitors arrived. Once she did, her teacher immediately understood her reluctance: under her coat Valentine wore a short-sleeved summer dress over long-sleeved white underwear. "There she was," Louise exclaimed, "this little black girl, sitting there in her white underwear! And she kept right on typing as I had instructed everyone to do! The absurdity of the entire situation suddenly hit me; the incongruity of an 'educational institution' capitalizing on the image, but rarely delivering the reality of education, despite the students' eagerness to learn, struck me suddenly. I was convulsed."[14] She remained composed, however, until the callers departed, at which point the entire class joined her in robust laughter, which was punctuated by Valentine's injured complaint, "Miss Thomas, I told you not to make me take off my coat."[15]

The disdain Louise began to feel about the educational process accompanied her contempt for school social customs. She became friends with Shields, the registrar, who hailed from Alabama. "To relieve our boredom," as she described it, they would take off in his Model T Ford, sometimes racing back to campus so that she could beat the ten o'clock dormitory curfew.[16] That she always made it did not impress Malone, who apparently had the matron-dean, Mrs. Stephens, inform Louise that her behavior seemed inappropriate. Louise refused to defend herself against suggestions of cavorting; instead, she told Stephens to tell Malone to mind his own business. She could be daring because she had no fear of the consequences. She would not quit— that would be defeat—but she did not mind the prospect of being fired. Unlike what faced most of the other teachers if they were dismissed, the worst that could happen to Louise was that she would go back to Chicago.[17]

She and Malone also clashed over Sunday behavior. Word quickly reached him that she had skipped church in favor of doing her laundry. No doubt he also heard about her forceful assertion to some of her peers, "I didn't sign a contract to go to church."[18] In response, Malone set up a Sunday school on campus and put Louise in charge.

Shields struggled with the codes of compliance as well and violated a protocol more serious than his relationship with Louise ever would have. A white board member called and asked to speak to "Malone." Shields, trying to engender respect for his African American boss, inquired, "You mean *Mr.* Malone?" The speaker replied, "I don't know about any *Mr.* I want Malone." Shields said he had the wrong number and hung up the phone, prompting the irate board member to make his way to the school to extract an apology from Malone for being insulted by a "nigger." Malone, in turn, fired Shields and banned him from campus.[19] Shields later left town, but while still living there, he would pull right up to the front gate of the school, just shy of technically being on campus and in full view of Malone, to pick up Louise.

Shields also remained around long enough to bring Louise face-to-face with the southern sharecropping system, that sprawling display of exploitation and dependency. On their rides through the countryside, she witnessed the subsistence farming that she eventually came to consider an extension of slavery. Landlords lent growers supplies at steep prices that ensured that only the landlords made money. The workers could not even stay out of debt. Louise knew that blacks were not much wanted out west—or even in Chicago outside of the Black Belt. She came to realize that they were welcome in the South—in some Arkansas Delta counties they made up 90 percent of the population—as long as they remained subservient. If black farmers organized to protest conditions, as they did in nearby Elaine in 1919, white mobs consisting mainly of men almost as poor as the blacks would enact violence against them on behalf of the economic elite. In what became known as the Elaine Massacre, more than a hundred blacks were killed. Dozens of black men were imprisoned, some on death row, in connection with the five white casualties, though they were all freed by 1925, largely through the efforts of Walter White and the NAACP. During the violence, rumors circulated in Pine Bluff, a hundred miles to the west, that weapons were being stashed on campus; the authorities reacted by confiscating the weapons of the ROTC program.

Not only did Louise become aware of this history, but she conversed with locals, who shared their memories and viewpoints. She would shortly have comparable memories of her own when the Mississippi River flooded in early 1927. One of the most powerful natural disasters of the twentieth century, that era's Hurricane Katrina, the flood resulted from unusually heavy rains and levee failures from southern Illinois to New Orleans. It affected an area of twenty-seven thousand square miles, and Arkansas was the state hit hardest. In all, 1.5 million people had to seek higher ground. Approximately 250 deaths were recorded. More than 130,000 homes were destroyed, and total property damage exceeded $1 billion.[20] Many plantation owners sought to prevent their workers from streaming to the various refugee camps that were established, one such site being Pine Bluff Agricultural, Mechanical, and Normal School. Counter to the mounting evidence, the bosses often contended that the flooding would be brief and that their lands would be secure. They capitulated when the American Red Cross, operating as an agent of the status quo, agreed to return the sharecroppers, sometimes using threats of violence, to their respective plantations when the waters subsided.[21] Louise likely had little knowledge of the regional pattern of policing the labor force, but she directly observed for weeks how the authorities tightly supervised the wagonloads of people who, with their few worldly belongings in croker sacks, were housed on campus. When refugees arrived, the white drivers would announce, as Louise spun it, "Niggers from Mr. So-and-So's plantation."[22]

Along with the other female faculty, Louise became a Red Cross aide and received instructions about how to handle "these people."[23] Only the men were allowed to leave campus—and then only to perform supervised flood-relief labor. The women were assigned a variety of tasks around the school. The children posed a particular challenge: "They had never seen white bath tubs and were frightened of them. It was a revealing and difficult experience. We had to hold the screaming children by force as they resisted our attempts to bathe them. However, our old-fashioned chain toilets were novel toys to them. We had to lock up the bathrooms because they loved to pull on the toilet chains."[24]

No joy or surprise accompanied the return to peonage. Overseers called for "Mr. So-and-So's niggers," who then piled into the respective wagons.[25] Louise reflected, "The flood of 1927 was a heart-rending experience that taught me more than I ever could have learned from books about the lives of sharecroppers."[26]

An even more haunting event was the lynching of John Carter in Little Rock, forty-five miles away, in May. On Saturday, April 30, 1927, after a three-week search, the body of a missing white girl, twelve-year-old Floella Mc-Donald, was found in the bell tower of First Presbyterian Church. Frank Dixon, a mulatto employed as the church janitor, became the prime suspect, along with his blue-eyed son, seventeen-year-old Lonnie Dixon. After a brief investigation—during which bloody clothing was found hidden in the church and an eight-year-old white girl supposedly told police that she had been accosted by Lonnie Dixon in the vicinity of the church a few weeks earlier—officials charged father and son with rape and murder. The Sunday papers—the *Arkansas Gazette* and the *Arkansas Democrat*—carried sensationalist stories about the case and ran photos of both Dixons.[27] Later that day, the police took a confession from Lonnie Dixon. For the next few days, white mobs in Little Rock demonstrated outside of the state prison and city hall, demanding that the Dixons be turned over to them. Two thousand demonstrators usurped Warden S. L. Todhunter's authority and stormed the penitentiary on Roosevelt Road in search of the Dixons. Mayor Charles Moyer and police chief Burl Rotenberry held off an even larger crowd at city hall, partially placating the lynch mob by allowing several of its leaders to search the facility. However, Rotenberry had secretly sent the prisoners to a jail in Texarkana. On Monday, May 2, the Association of Negro Ministers of All Denominations released a statement claiming Lonnie Dixon as a member of "our race," condemning his "dastardly crime," and praising the police work in the case.[28]

As the vigilantes simmered, word arrived on May 4 that six miles west of downtown Little Rock, John Carter, possibly in search of whiskey, had allegedly climbed into the horse-drawn wagon of Mrs. B. E. Stewart and her seventeen-year-old daughter, Glennie, and menaced them with an iron bar, causing Mrs. Stewart to fall from the wagon. Carter then supposedly dismounted, hurled rocks at the women, and grabbed a tree limb, striking Mrs. Stewart with it several times. The arrival of passersby scared Carter, who fled into the woods.

A posse hunted him down that same day, strung him from a telephone pole, and shot him more than two hundred times. The murderers then tied Carter's corpse to a car bumper and dragged it through the streets of Little Rock, past city hall, until they arrived at the intersection of Ninth Street and Broadway, the heart of Little Rock's African American community. For several hours, a mob that swelled to more than five thousand rioted throughout the neighborhood, while many locals cowered in their homes with the lights out. Goons soaked Carter's body with gasoline and kerosene and set it ablaze. They also raided local businesses for timber to set more fires, in some instances using pews from Bethel African Methodist Episcopal Church. One rioter directed traffic with a charred arm torn from Carter's body. If the city's police had the will to prevent the barbarism, they proved impotent. Only after Governor John Martineau, out of town at the time, received word of the events and deployed the National Guard did the crowd disperse, at around ten o'clock that night, three hours after it had begun rampaging through the black community.

Louise recalled her reaction: "I went about in a daze with a hatred of anything white—even a chicken. A fearful hush-hush pervaded our community. This was raw racism. It frightened me. I felt as helpless and lonely as when I was the sole black child in those little racist towns in Oregon or Nevada."[29] Martineau and other leaders condemned the lynching and riots. Even if their motives were pure, they also had reason to fear that the violence would damage the state's image and have a negative impact on flood-relief efforts and attempts to attract investments by "eastern capitalists."[30] Reverend J. O. Johnson of First Presbyterian had intimated as much the previous Sunday in reference to the Dixons, telling worshippers, "A lynching right now, when the attention of the nation is focused on Arkansas as a result of the flood situation, would cause irreparable harm to the reputation of the state. I beseech you to leave the matter to the courts."[31]

The courts were typical of segregated Arkansas. A trial jury convicted Lonnie Dixon on May 19 after seven minutes of deliberation. The state executed him in the electric chair on June 24, his eighteenth birthday. Meanwhile, a Pulaski County grand jury, convened by Judge Abner McGehee, met for several days concerning the Carter lynching but issued no indictments.

Terror would not drive Louise from Arkansas, however, nor would the indignities she suffered. Although she originally vowed not to accede to the mores of the South or accept Malone's constant advice not to rattle white folks, she reluctantly sat in "nigger heaven" at the movie house.[32] Nor would loneliness defeat her. Of course, she missed Nebby and Dot, but Mother Thompson, whom she sent for, filled a great void. In a victory over Malone, Louise wrangled permission to leave the dormitory and rented an upstairs apartment in the home of businesswoman Mrs. Swazy, at 1705 West Second Street, right across from campus. This drove a further wedge between her and the other women faculty, but their scorn mattered little compared to the chance to have Mother Thompson on hand.

In the final analysis, Louise departed Pine Bluff because she increasingly felt inadequate to address the needs of her students, concluding, "What I was doing was a sham."[33] She appreciated Malone's complete confidence in her abilities, despite how they bumped heads on occasion. But she perceived no sustainable model for change, feeling that a whole new system was required. Colleagues suggested that, given her qualifications, she should seek the more stimulating intellectual and cultural life they associated with Hampton Institute, which had the highest endowment of any school devoted strictly to the education of African Americans. She applied and was excited to be accepted by the Department of Business Administration, which caused an upset Malone to stop speaking to her for a while.

She remained in Pine Bluff to teach summer classes. The English teacher, Miss Wallace of the French classes, had not been retained, and Louise, needing the money, agreed to instruct teachers from the county schools, some of whom had taught the students who had been enrolled in Louise's business classes. She quickly learned more about shams. When she asked them as their first assignment to write autobiographical narratives, she discovered that they generally had no more than a fourth-grade education. Many had obtained their jobs by agreeing to kick back money to the local school board. At least the revelation resolved any anxiety that Louise had about the curriculum. She felt that, unlike with her other students, she was meeting this group at their point of need: "So all I had to do was haul out a grammar, a spelling book, a dictionary, and we had the beginning of a wonderful eight weeks."[34]

It was about much more than English. Her home became a social center, with Mother Thompson coordinating, of course. In the stifling heat of the Arkansas Delta, she kept the refreshments flowing. Students not only were keen about their formal lessons but pressed to learn what they could from Louise in all areas, while she, in turn, gained a greater sense of their lives. It was a reminder of the home on Bancroft Way, perhaps poignant because they no longer owned that residence. They had rented out the house when they left Berkeley, but the renters had failed to make payments and the real estate agent suspiciously did nothing about it. By the time Mrs. Allen's husband, J. T. Allen, investigated, Louise and her mother had lost the property. Louise later insisted that she received the news stoically because she had never planned to return to Berkeley to live.[35]

Despite Louise's appointment at Hampton, her ambition was still to reach New York, and she finally visited the city for the first time that summer when she accompanied Bella Taylor. Taylor, who would become a distinguished civil rights activist and director of the Cleveland branch of the NAACP, hailed from St. Paul. She had majored in sociology at the University of Minnesota, graduating, like Louise, in 1923. She and Louise met in Chicago when Taylor was working for the Young Women's Christian Association (YWCA) there. Taylor had recently been appointed the national secretary of the YWCA and was preparing to relocate to New York. She invited Louise to go to St. Paul with her; the two then returned to Chicago to start the sixteen-hour ride on the 20th Century Limited, "the most famous train in the world," from the LaSalle Street Station to Grand Central Terminal.[36]

From her first moments riding in a taxi through Central Park, the city did not disappoint Louise. Nor did Harlem, the emerging "Negro capital of the world."[37] A district of wide thoroughfares and remarkable architecture that had been populated almost exclusively by whites at the dawn of the twentieth century, the northern Manhattan province had become virtually all black by the time of Louise's visit. Racism and squalid living conditions in the middle West Side, the main black community in New York City at the turn of the century, had motivated multitudes of blacks to abandon the area for what seemed to be greener, if more expensive, pastures. They were also induced by opportunistic realtors and by land speculators who had created an oversupply of housing. These factors—along with the Great Migration, a significant influx of immigrants from the Caribbean and Africa, and other local developments like the construction of Penn Station, which drove additional residents out of the middle West Side—resulted in a radically altered Harlem in which tens of thousands of newly arrived blacks strove for better lives.[38] As in Chicago, the prospect of a black metropolis seemed plausible to many.

Louise experienced thrills at every turn. Even the theft of her handbag the first night in town—she had placed it on an empty seat next to her while watching a movie at the Paramount Theater in Times Square—did not dampen her spirits. She could replace the money, and after a nervous trip on a motorized cart through the luggage storage facility at Grand Central, she was able to overcome the loss of her claim check and retrieve her trunk.

As she ventured from the guesthouse on 132nd Street and strolled about Harlem, she did what all visitors from the Bay Area attempted: to visit attorney William Patterson in his office on the second floor, above Duncan Funeral Parlor, at 2303 Seventh Avenue, just north of 135th Street. This represented her first formal introduction to the San Francisco native and former University of California student. Patterson had just returned from Boston, where, on August 22, he had agitated outside of Charlestown Prison on behalf of the condemned Nicola Sacco and Bartolomeo Vanzetti.[39] In the novel *Boston*, Upton Sinclair immortalizes Patterson:

> The trooper speeds on; he has spied the black face, and wants that most of all. The Negro runs, and the rider rears the front feet of his steed, intending to strike him down with the iron-shod hoofs. But fortunately there is a tree and the Negro leaps behind it; a man can run round a tree faster than the best-trained police-mount—the dapper and genial William Patterson proves it by making five complete circuits before he runs into the arms of an ordinary cop, who grabs him by the collar and tears off his sign and tramples it in the dirt, and then starts to march him away.[40]

After being bailed out of jail, Patterson returned to the picket line. His efforts were ultimately futile, and Sacco and Vanzetti were executed shortly after midnight.

Transformed by his experiences in the prolonged protest, Patterson had already decided to leave the practice that he had established in 1923 with Thomas Benjamin Dyett and George Hall. Influenced by noted black Communists Richard B. Moore and Cyril Briggs—Briggs gave him his first copy of *The Communist Manifesto*—he had joined the Communist Party and was headed to Moscow to study at the University of the Toiling People of the Far East, known by its students as KUTVA, an acronym derived from the school's Russian name. He hoped to tackle racial discrimination in the context of a sharp class analysis. He later wrote, "Since I was beginning to identify my interests with those of the working class and to recognize that the interests of the great mass of Black people could not be otherwise identified, a study of the meaning of these two kinds of democracy was called for."[41]

By that time, Louise knew that thinkers attracted her. The brilliant Patterson, ten years her senior, certainly impressed her. A dance enthusiast, he also showed her a good time, escorting her on her first trip to the Savoy Ballroom. Their date was fairly light on flirtation, though, because Louise knew of Patterson's well-earned reputation as a ladies' man. While still married to Minnie Sumner, he had had a very public affair with musician and critic Nora Holt, which had been duly noted by a person ever inquisitive in those matters, Carl Van Vechten, author of *Nigger Heaven*.[42] So Louise and Patterson kept the conversation largely to the political, preventing a likely disaster. He inquired whether she had interest in going to the Soviet Union to study, a notion that intrigued her. Out of a sense of adventure, not commitment to Bolshevism, she agreed to have her name floated in connection with the Russian university. Overall, the delights of New York and the glimpses of possibility, particularly in Harlem, seemed all too brief. Louise reluctantly caught a steamship to Virginia, back to a Jim Crow world.

Although its well-funded, bucolic campus spread out along the scenic Chesapeake Bay, Louise quickly realized that Hampton Institute would not meet the lofty expectations she had formulated in Pine Bluff. The head of the school, James Edgar Gregg, had held the post since 1918 and firmly advocated the "Hampton Idea," that is, a focus on vocational training and moral doctrine. Louise became troubled by the paternalism inherent in the conception and in its instantiation. The administration was white, as were nearly all the heads of the various academic departments. The trade-school teachers were reputed to be members of the Ku Klux Klan. Blacks performed the menial labor and were kept almost totally apart from the white workers. Separate entrances and seating arrangements helped to accomplish that. Students were treated like servants; they cleaned dormitories and faculty houses, gardened, and helped staff the dining rooms while earning on average eight dollars per month.[43] Moreover, student behavior was tightly disciplined. Young women were forbidden to wear silk stockings, use cosmetics, or sport curls. They were sometimes stopped so that the length of their skirts could be measured, a ritual witnessed firsthand by Louise and Sue Bailey, a second-year faculty member and fast friend of Louise.

The male students wore uniforms, daily chapel services were compulsory, and no talking was permitted after curfew. Six faculty members sat on the student council. Students would be ejected from their dormitory to accommodate white visitors. As Hampton enhanced its college status, the average age of enrollment increased dramatically. Yet the school did not treat the more mature students accordingly. In a telling episode, a thirty-four-year old female student received probation for going shopping without permission.[44]

At orientation, Gregg prescribed the faculty roles, warning black and white teachers not to associate with each other in the segregated town of Hampton. Also, integrated groups were not supposed to walk along the campus waterfront because those grounds were visible to a trustee, the entrepreneur Frank W. Darling, who would disapprove. According to Louise, the first black faculty member in the Department of Business Administration, a number of the teachers had begun cross-ethnic friendships before the meeting, relationships that were seriously strained by Gregg's pronouncements.[45] In theory, Gregg was no segregationist, but the putatively liberal New Englander served as an agent of segregation because he never challenged that social formation. He tried, and ultimately failed, to steer a midcourse between positions—integration and segregation—that were irreconcilable. For example, he never fully stood up to Walter Scott Copeland, the powerful editor of the *Newport News Daily Press.* Copeland had been offended because his wife, upon arriving late for a show at Hampton's Ogden Hall in February 1925, had been seated near African Americans, much too near (in her hysterical estimation) given that the show featured scantily clad white women. As a result, Copeland, aiming to eliminate what he viewed as the threat of racial permissiveness, waged a strong segregationist campaign against Hampton and civil society in general. He expressed his bottom line clearly, explaining that, rather than accept integration, he "would prefer that every white child in the United States were sterilized and the Anglo-Saxon race left to perish in its purity."[46]

Copeland failed to affect life much at Hampton proper. Gregg resisted Copeland's extremism in that regard and received the backing of the board of trustees, led by former president William Howard Taft, at that time the chief justice of the Supreme Court. After all, Hampton Institute was private. At the same time, Gregg and Taft both remained on the political sidelines as Copeland's efforts resulted in the passage of the Public Assemblages Act of 1926, a measure "requiring the separation of white and colored persons at public halls, theaters, opera houses, motion picture shows and places of public entertainment and public assemblages."[47] This obviously affected life in the towns near campus. Neither Gregg nor Taft thought the state bill would pass, but their silence probably made it easier to accomplish.[48]

Gregg also behaved timidly when Robert Nathaniel Dett, an accomplished composer who in 1913 was appointed the first African American musical director at Hampton and who served from 1924 to 1926 as the president of the National Association of Negro Musicians, clashed with board member George Foster Peabody over the selections that student choral groups would perform.[49] Dett desired to blend black folk music with such forms as operas, concertos, and suites. In other words, Negro spirituals would be combined complexly with European romanticism. Peabody, for whom the famous broadcasting awards are named, opposed this adamantly. He had been a trustee at Hampton for more than forty years and had no use for Dett's musical innovation. He wanted straight, old-fashioned spirituals, and because Gregg would not back Dett, Peabody prevailed.

Lamentably, Gregg misjudged how these various decisions would be received by the student body, who saw them as triumphs of paternalism. Considerable tension already existed concerning the direction of the college. Would "New Negroes" have a real chance at education beyond manual training? Would they be treated with dignity and urged toward leadership? Because of similar issues, there had been student strikes the previous spring at Howard, Fisk, and Shaw. Before long, matters would come to a head at Hampton.

The school offered a featured movie on Saturday evening, October 8. Young men picked up their dates at Virginia Hall, where Louise served as a supervisor, for the walk to Ogden Hall. Chaperones were required. In fact, the right for men to escort women to the movies and other school functions had only recently been granted. Dissatisfied with the current level of supervision, however, the dean of women ordered that the lights be kept on in the auditorium during the film showing. Several students protested, feeling that the administration had sunk to a new low in terms of insulting African American women. Order was easily restored—the lights remained on—belying the degree of student anger. The Sunday vesper service would be the tipping point. Hampton hosted Sir Gordon Guggisberg, governor and commander-in-chief of the Gold Coast, who had recently established Prince of Wales College and School and was exploring education methods.[50] Guggisberg received an eyeful. To Gregg's chagrin, the students refused to sing at the event. Staffer Roy Lancaster sang the lead to "Ain't Gonna Study War No More," but no students joined him, instead filing quietly out of Ogden Hall. This action followed students' refusal earlier in the day to stand for ROTC inspection and sing grace at meals. The famous Hampton student strike or lockout of 1927 had begun.[51] Gregg formally dismissed the audience after intoning in prayer, "Father, forgive them, for they know not what they do."[52]

Louise sat in the mezzanine with other black faculty, supportive of the students in the drama unfolding below. Protesting the conditions at Hampton, tantamount to academic apartheid in her view, only appeared reasonable. As she left the auditorium, she wondered whether General Samuel Chapman Armstrong, Hampton's founder, was turning over in his grave.[53]

An exasperated Gregg suspended classes the following day and conducted meetings with students, who, realizing that Gregg had failed to address their concerns adequately, elected a twenty-member Student Protest Committee, which included several of the leading students among Hampton's nine hundred undergraduates.[54] The student body boycotted classes but agreed to return if Gregg discussed with them their demands for better academic standards and consistency in offering courses described in the catalog. Unlike at Pine Bluff, many students at Hampton were better educated than their teachers. In addition, students pushed for the relaxing of discipline and several other concessions. To Gregg's distress, the students refused to accept any punishment because, they reasoned, the protests had been peaceful. After several rounds of negotiation, Gregg instituted a lockout.

Louise and Bailey became unofficial advisers as female students flocked to them for counsel. In turn, the two women sought out mentors. Bailey knew Alain Locke and traveled to Washington to see him. Louise obtained an appointment with Du Bois and visited him in New York. Upon her return to campus, she wrote an expansive missive to Du Bois on October 17 explaining the "hypocrisy, racial prejudice, and backwardness" at Hampton and imploring him to support and publicize the students' cause.[55] She argued that the "wholesale slaughter that has come about of the school's best is too great for no good to come of it and the Negro world should be made to see the justice in the students' stand."[56] It was an easy sell, as she knew from her recent meeting. Moreover, Du Bois had been critical of the Hampton Idea for decades and had never been invited back to the school after delivering an address at a campus conference in 1906.[57]

Louise considered resigning because she did not want her silence to be construed as loyalty to the administration. Bailey and others dissuaded her because they thought the outside world would not understand the battle as one against racism but would see the matter as strictly a student issue not worthy of faculty involvement.[58] On that point they were largely correct. Parents as a whole did not back the students, nor did alumni. Perhaps most damaging, most of the black media weighed in against them.[59] So Louise concluded, along with her colleagues, that to leave would be to abandon the struggle, one in which the students possessed little leverage.

By the time Gregg officially reopened Hampton on October 25, sixty-nine students had been expelled or suspended, and hundreds more had been placed on probation.[60] The moves significantly drained the school's talent pool. Some of those students fortunate enough to gain admission to other institutions prospered as undergraduate and graduate students at places such as Columbia, Cornell, and the University of Pennsylvania. As one scholar noted, "with unerring accuracy the college singled out the backbone of its student leadership: young people whose subsequent careers in higher education, government service, business and public school teaching and administration would mark them as probably one of the most talented groups ever to leave a college or university campus."[61]

Cecil Lloyd Spellman, a member of the protest committee and a casualty of the purge, received a letter during the lockout alleging that he had "brought a great amount of damage, not only to the school but to many innocent individuals."[62] Spellman, who fortunately gained admission to Negro Agricultural and Technical College of North Carolina (now North Carolina Agricultural and Technical State University) and eventually became a prominent educator, countered the assertion in his published memoir, *Rough Steps on My Stairway*:

> I firmly believe that if ever an institution owed a debt of gratitude to a group of students, Hampton owed one to that student committee. As a committee we insisted that the vital functions of the college be maintained. Students having duties in connection with care of livestock, sanitation of premises, preparation and service of meals, care of the sick, and so forth were requested to perform their services well during the time. Obedience to law and conservation of property were stressed. To the best of my knowledge not a single dollar's worth of institutional property was damaged during the time, although I know there were irresponsible students among us. So complete was our control over the students that it is my opinion that they would have literally torn buildings down brick by brick if the word had been given. But we visualized ours as a job of helping toward a greater school, not that of destroying one. We would not condone one mite of destruction.[63]

Apparently, Spellman had lined up on the right side of history. Twenty years after having been dismissed from Hampton, after having earned two graduate degrees, he received a letter from university president Ralph P.

Bridgman informing him, almost pointlessly, that he had been "reinstated in good standing in so far as your standing may have been affected by the October 1927 student strike."[64]

As for Louise, the nerve-wracking experience proved transformative: "The strike had begun to frame my experiences as a teacher in the South and I began to see everything else that year through an emerging political prism."[65] Part of that process involved comprehending a theory of labor and racial exploitation, as developed by Karl Marx in *Das Kapital*. Patterson had recommended the work to her, one of numerous suggestions that he forwarded in a series of letters. She found the volume in the stacks of the Hampton library. She hardly grasped Marx, whom she had not heard of at the University of California. As she recalled, "I started too high up, not with the A B C's."[66] Notwithstanding, she comprehended enough to link the racial discrimination she had experienced and witnessed to the idea that exploiters manipulate broad systems to ensure that they collect a disproportionate share of the surpluses created by workers. This partly explained both the raw working-class racism of Arkansas and the paternalism sponsored by aristocrats in Virginia. Educational efforts devoid of a critical dimension helped to entrench inequities.[67]

Louise remained mindful of this as she continued to deal with fallout from the strike. Du Bois ran excerpts from her letter in the December issue of the *Crisis*, which she became aware of only when chemistry professor Collis Davis handed her a copy on campus.[68] Although Du Bois did not identify her by name, Gregg strongly suspected her of being the author. He summoned Louise, not to his office, but to his residence. After small talk, mostly about his Scottish terrier, Louise shifted to the business of why she had been called. Gregg, clearly uncomfortable, expressed his opinion that Louise did not sufficiently grasp the current principles of Hampton or the ideas of General Armstrong. He divulged that he had heard that she supported the strike. She neither confirmed nor denied the allegation, and she invited Gregg to produce the person who had heard her utter any statement to that effect. Gregg gave up on the intervention.[69] As Armstrong would have put it, "the darky is an ugly thing to manage."[70]

Gregg then suspected that Bailey had authored the letter. Two years younger than Louise and a graduate of Spelman Seminary and Oberlin College, Bailey, who later married the esteemed theologian Howard Thurman, had joined the music department the previous academic year. Gregg made no headway with her either. In any case, he knew that student sympathizers like Louise and Bailey existed among the faculty; though he elicited no confessions, he conveyed clearly that they were not wanted at the Hampton over which he presided.[71]

Around the same time, Louise made her first deliberate decision about the organized Left. Prompted by Patterson, Richard B. Moore sent her an application for study in the Soviet Union. Still curious about traveling abroad, she nevertheless balked at the required pledge of total commitment to the cause, one she barely understood, and did not submit the paperwork. Rather, she concentrated on life at Hampton after the strike. As at Pine Bluff, she proved an extremely capable instructor, possessing faith in her students and challenging them accordingly. She rode especially hard on some of the male students, who took her youthful appearance and friendly demeanor as license to propose dates or be lax in their preparation for class. Demerits, which were enforced through the ROTC program, remedied the problem. Louise would remind her students, "If you're not on business here, you have no business here."[72] In turn, some of her charges noted in admiration, "Miss Thompson's tough, but she's a good teacher; she'll make you work."[73]

Tennis and travel were Louise's primary leisure activities. It was common to see her lugging her racquet to class along with her course materials. She played with some of the girls at noon and after school. Bailey was her travel partner. They would borrow nurse Rogers's car, an old Dodge, and visit surrounding towns. They also ventured to Richmond, Greensboro, or Washington, DC. On her first trip to Washington, Bailey introduced Louise to Locke. Louise also visited with Deltas at Howard and spent an afternoon conversing with the distinguished scientist Ernest Everett Just, head of the university's zoology department, whom she had been introduced to by his sister. Professor Just tried to recruit her to the natural sciences but expressed support for her work and interests.

Through either Just or Locke, Louise found out about a fellowship program established by National Urban League secretary Eugene Kinckle Jones, who believed that a core of black social workers would be needed to address the problems of the black multitudes who migrated north after World War I.[74] E. Franklin Frazier and Inabel Lindsey (later the first dean of the Howard University School of Social Work) had already benefited from Jones's vision. Successful applicants would attend a one-year advanced degree program at the New York School of Social Work.[75] Louise had no firm desire to become a social worker, though the possibility seemed fathomable to her. Moreover, she had to reflect on her status at Hampton. Even if she wanted to stay, she had no guarantee that she would be retained—and had ample reason to suspect that she would not. Given this uncertainty, it made sense to explore other options, especially ones located in the city of her dreams. Thus, she applied for the fellowship, listing as her recommenders Just, Du Bois, and Hampton Institute's chaplain, Laurence Fenninger. Final adjudication of her bid would not occur until after classes ended at Hampton. This did not prevent Louise from heading to New York anyway and trusting her chances.

Bailey also planned to move. She agreed to join the staff of the YWCA as the national secretary for colleges in the South. In the meantime, she tried to finish the academic year in style, which prompted her to invite to campus Langston Hughes; two years earlier, in 1926, she had arranged his visit to Oberlin. Five months after protesting students had exited Ogden Hall, the ebullient author of *The Weary Blues* received a warm welcome as he read his poetry in that venue on March 11, 1928. Louise appreciated the poet Hughes much as she had valued the teacher Du Bois in Berkeley. But Du Bois was ultimately for idolizing; Hughes, several months younger than Louise, could be befriended. Introduced by Bailey, she reacted to Hughes as most people fortunate enough to meet him did; she liked him immediately. He seconded her decision to try New York.

For the record, Gregg in fact tendered an offer to Louise for the following year, a gesture known as an "Ask Back." Louise and some of her colleagues called it an "Ass Back."[76] Gregg actually offered her a raise yet continued to insinuate, as did her department head, that she would be happier elsewhere.[77] The principal overplayed his hand. The balance of power at Hampton had shifted, and although Louise and Bailey left, that could not be interpreted as much of a victory for Gregg. Their presence as black professors with activist tendencies signaled a change in the culture of white paternalism. Gregg would, in fact, barely outlast them. The following year, amid renewed student pressure, the board of trustees finally acknowledged the shortcomings of Gregg's leadership style and dismissed him. By the time his ship sank, Louise, as did the stoker Shine in some versions of the glorious toast about the *Titanic*, was striding confidently about Harlem.

CHAPTER 4

Harlem Kaleidoscope, 1928–1932

arly in the summer of 1928, Bella Taylor positioned Louise Thompson squarely within the Niggerati, a band of writers, artists, and intellectuals flourishing in Harlem, by introducing her to a couple, Aaron and Alta Douglas, who were at its core.[1] The Douglases, a visual artist and an educator, embraced her right away, and she became a regular at the parties and gab sessions they hosted. At the Douglases she became familiar with bathtub gin and orange blossoms (gin and orange juice). Through them she met other cultural figures such as Gwendolyn Bennett, Dorothy West, Helene Johnson, Arna Bontemps, and Bruce Nugent. She joined Aaron Douglas, known by his friends as Doug, as a member of the newly formed Negro Experimental Theatre, also known as the Harlem Experimental Theatre. A spinoff of the defunct Krigwa Players that had been established by W. E. B. Du Bois and dramatist and future librarian legend Regina Anderson, the group met at the 135th Street branch of the New York Public Library, where Anderson worked. It emphasized community roots and educational programs along with dramatic productions.[2]

Quickly becoming a regular on the Harlem society scene, Louise soon met other writers such as Countee Cullen, Jessie Redmon Fauset, and Rudolph Fisher. She became happily reacquainted with Langston Hughes, whose manifesto "The Negro Artist and the Racial Mountain" (1926), championing art by African Americans that broke free of bourgeois norms and the white gaze, struck a chord with Louise and expressed the sentiments of the group with whom, to various degrees, she bonded.[3] She saw this "Hughes bunch," the Douglases, Nugent, and West among them, as possessing a different temperament than Nella Larsen, Fauset, and even Anderson. She stated, "They were what we would call the 'dicty' ones, you know. The proper. They didn't get down in the groove."[4] Louise also met the civil rights activists Elmer Carter, Walter White, and Roy Wilkins. Just as important, she mixed with political radicals, including Cyril Briggs, Otto Huiswood, and Harry Haywood, in addition to Richard B. Moore.[5]

While Hughes expressed the fundamental ethos of the more artistically adventurous members of the Niggerati, the well-read Wallace Thurman set the intellectual pace. Another habitué of the Douglases' apartment who previously had been anchored at 267 West 136th Street, the official Niggerati Manor, Thurman by then was living in a rooming house on 128th Street between Lenox and Fifth. A year younger than Louise, he was youthful and attractive. West portrayed him as possessing "the most agreeable smile in Harlem and a rich infectious laugh. His was without accent, deep and resonant; it was the most memorable thing about him welling out of his frail body and wasting its richness in unprintable recountings."[6]

Thurman, like Louise, had grown up in the West. Born in Salt Lake City, he excelled in school and attended the University of Utah as a premed major. He transferred to the University of Southern California to study journalism but did not complete his degree. While working at the post office in Los Angeles, he met Arna Bontemps, a friendship partly responsible for leading him to New York in 1925, where he served for a spell as the managing editor of Chandler Owen and A. Philip Randolph's *The Messenger*. By the following year, he had collaborated with Hughes, Bennett, Nugent, Douglas, Zora Neale Hurston, and John P. Davis to create perhaps the most discussed one-issue literary journal in American history: *Fire!! A Quarterly Devoted to the Younger Negro Artists*. Not only did the group lack the funding to sustain the vehicle, but they couldn't pay the printer for the inaugural issue. Thurman got stuck with the tab, which he had to satisfy through garnishment of his wages. Ironically, a blaze consumed the building where copies of *Fire!!* were stockpiled, destroying a considerable portion of the print run.

Because of his fertile mind, accomplishments, and literary promise, as well as, perhaps, his dark skin and nonthreatening slightness of build, Thurman could hardly have avoided intriguing Louise. The only question was what avenues the affinity between them would take. Framed another way, would Louise allow the train of her desire to jump the teasing, petting, quasi-platonic rails on which she had always managed to keep it?

Louise and Thurman (mostly known as Wally) would traverse Harlem looking for small restaurants and clubs that white initiates had yet to discover or make popular. At other times, they would hang out on 135th Street and comment on the passing crowd, his laugh a steady feature of the sound track. She alienated people like Nugent, who considered her too possessive of Thurman. In Thurman's room, she eagerly typed his manuscript of *The Blacker the Berry*, which explored intraracial colorism. Like many others, she could see that Thurman was very much the dark, traumatized Emma Lou Morgan, a victim of intraracial discrimination. And now he was the dark man spending more and more time with one of the fairest black women in Harlem. Was he slaying the god of complexion or succumbing to it? Was she?

An answer would come soon enough. In the meantime, she took an emotional detour to welcome to New York her mother, Nebby, and Mrs. Allen. Also, she needed to press for an answer regarding the National Urban League fellowship and perhaps scout for employment. Nebby arrived first at the apartment on 142nd Street that Louise was sharing for the summer with Taylor, Sue Bailey, and Marion Cuthbert. She and Nebby hit the night scene hard, sometimes with Thurman. Then her mother showed up, in good spirits. On the taxi ride through Central Park, Louise prepared her mother for the liberated, flapper-style attitudes of young women of the 1920s: "You know, Mama, the girls, they smoke." Louise herself was practically a chain smoker by then. "Oh, that's all right," her liberated-sounding mother smoothly replied. "I may smoke myself."[7]

Mother Thompson went on a few outings with her daughter and Nebby. She had her own partner when Mrs. Allen visited. The two scared Louise and Nebby on one occasion when it was well past midnight and they had failed to come in. As the younger women were about to call the police, Mother Thompson and Mrs. Allen arrived, full of laughter, and did not divulge where they had been. "We've been worried about you," the younger women offered. The elders replied, "Well, we're just paying you back for you all going out and staying all the time."[8] It turned out that the night out had been a nod out. The two had taken the Seventh Avenue bus downtown and sat in the upper deck enjoying the summer breeze. On the ride back uptown from Washington Square Park, they fell asleep before the bus reached 142nd Street. When they awakened, they were by Columbia Presbyterian Hospital and had to wait for a bus to head back south. Once on that bus, the merrymakers fell asleep again. They rode well past 142nd Street, perhaps all the way back to Washington Square Park, before boarding a return bus.

Louise and Thurman wed at city hall on August 22, 1928, two months after they met. It was a case of blunders. Louise, not mature in romance, equated love with admiration and fun, and she thought marriage and sexual pleasure would make the latter qualities permanent.[9] But no carnal enjoyment was forthcoming that summer because vaginal penetration proved impossible to achieve. Not until several months after the marriage would Louise undergo the needed surgery.

Thurman's error was even clearer, and the marriage sent shock waves through the Niggerati and beyond because no one in that crowd viewed him as a prospective husband. His general ambivalence and contrariness were fabled. As Hughes described it, Thurman was a person who "liked to drink gin, but *didn't* like to drink gin; who liked being a Negro, but felt it a great handicap; who adored bohemianism, but thought it wrong to be a bohemian. He liked to waste a lot of time, but he always felt guilty wasting time. He loathed crowds, yet he hated being alone. He almost always felt bad, yet he didn't write poetry."[10] Hughes probably knew enough to continue and thereby cover the critical point regarding Thurman's relationship to marriage. Sexually, he liked women, and he didn't like women. He liked men, and he didn't like men. Louise, slow all of her life, picked the wrong time to speed.

It is jejune to label the marriage one of convenience. All marriages are to some extent, so meaningfully accurate descriptions are complicated. Evident is that the marriage never worked—Thurman considered it over in three months—and that the implosion hurt Louise deeply.[11] Thurman stayed drunk a good deal of the time. He grew volatile, though never violent, and generally made life miserable in apartment 56, their fifth-floor walk-up at 90 Edgecombe Avenue, just below the majestic neo-Gothic buildings of City College. In October he informed Claude McKay by letter, "I still do not believe in marriage for an artist of any type." Realizing, however, that it made sense to explain why he had wed, he continued unromantically, "My only point of extenuation is that I have married a very intelligent woman who has her own career and who also does not believe in marriage and who is as anxious as I am to avoid the conventional pitfalls into which most marriages throw one."[12] Thurman never elucidated why two so-called nonbelievers took wedding vows.

In addition to getting off to a rocky beginning, the marriage jeopardized Louise's Urban League fellowship, the career to which Thurman alluded. That meant the potential loss of $1,800, the equivalent of Louise's annual salary at Hampton. News of the wedding reached Eugene Kinckle Jones, and he responded furiously, accusing Louise of deception because she had not listed on the application that she was married. Of course, her application involved no ruse because she had not been married or even engaged back in the spring. Charles S. Johnson, who was serving as the industrial secretary of the Urban League before leaving to start the sociology department at Fisk, had confirmed the fellowship for Louise, albeit reluctantly because he fancied that she might join him at Fisk as his secretary. Jones wanted to cancel the grant but backed down after a shouting match with Louise in his cubicle at the Urban League offices on Twenty-Third Street and Madison Avenue. She could be assertive and effective with everyone but Thurman.

Although seriously distracted, Louise began classes that fall at the New York School of Social Work, housed at the Russell Sage Foundation at Twenty-Second Street and Lexington Avenue. Early on, she discovered that casework held little interest for her; she much preferred research. The training included reading cases and providing diagnoses and prognoses. She invariably proposed to give people jobs. In one instance, a woman was suspected of living with a boyfriend but claimed he was her uncle. Louise wondered whether they would give the young woman a job if they proved the man was not her uncle. She declined to investigate. The school referred her to a counselor, who told her, "I think you're the sanest thing I've seen come out of social work."[13]

If only one could say the same about her and matrimony. In that area, frustrations only mounted. Thurman rode a high tide artistically; he submitted *The Blacker the Berry* for publication; launched another journal, *Harlem: A Forum of Negro Life*; and placed the finishing touches, in collaboration with William Jourdan Rapp, on a play, *Harlem: A Melodrama of Negro Life in Harlem*, which was slated for Broadway. Yet, plagued by self-doubt, a permanent condition with him, and unfulfilled with domestic life, he became unhinged and concocted a scheme to get away. He had a friend send him telegrams from Salt Lake City announcing that his mother had fallen ill and that he should come to Utah as soon as possible. He departed at the end of November and didn't return until January, shortly before the release of his book. He and Louise, keeping up appearances, hosted a party on January 19.

During that month, they were also trying sex. Louise had had the needed surgery while Thurman was out of town. It didn't ignite their relationship, though. Neither would claim that any passion existed in their lovemaking. As the emotional environment in the home grew more toxic, Louise's mother, who had been a fixture, fled, taking a room at a midtown YWCA. In mid-February, Louise joined her, choosing, ironically, an auspicious occasion, the opening night of Thurman and Rapp's play at the Apollo Theater on Forty-Second Street. West later criticized her, arguing that in abandoning Thurman at that moment Louise failed as a writer's wife.[14]

The snub failed to rattle Thurman. While Louise moped away from Harlem, he swaggered about town and boasted that his wife had abandoned their home and left him with everything. His behavior went unchecked until Louise, after putting in a rather pathetic phone call to Alta Douglas, was summoned to the Douglases for a constructive scolding that stiffened her spine. She then felt bold and energized enough to stride the twenty minutes downhill from where the Douglases now lived, at 155th and Edgecombe, to her and Thurman's apartment at 139th Street. She roused her husband from his sleep and threw him out, an action he did not contest.

Her next major move was to enlist Morris Ernst of the American Civil Liberties Union to be her divorce lawyer. She and her mother tracked him down at a bowling alley to discuss the case, which appeared to him to be a weak one under the fairly strict New York law. Certainly any claim to alimony would be tenuous because Louise had been married fewer than six months, was only twenty-seven, and had no children. On the simple matter of divorce, Ernst thought it best to seek it in the more liberal Nevada. A three-month residency would entitle her to file, and Ernst could set her up with an attorney in Reno. On the question of financial compensation—Louise had definitely become vengeful—Ernst advised negotiating directly with Thurman rather than through the courts. Subsequently, Louise summoned her husband to 90 Edgecombe Avenue and presented her proposal for fifty dollars per week—significantly more than she had ever earned at a job—plus the expenses for attaining the divorce, which she planned to pursue after her classes ended. He eventually agreed to support her at that rate for a year and to handle the divorce expenses. He was motivated to strike a quick accord in part by a desire to protect his future income, but, though he could be prickly, he seemed to genuinely care about Louise's welfare. Thus, he ignored advice to withhold payments until a signed agreement had been executed.[15] He was to pay her fare to Reno and $300 for the Nevada attorney. Even after Thurman left New York on April 6, 1929, to pursue writing projects on the West Coast, he arranged for the weekly payments to be made.

Back at school, Louise plotted out her master's thesis. Concerned that African American high school girls were typically pushed toward domestic or nursing tracks, she wanted to study the social choices they made. She began to conduct evening interviews with students and parents throughout Harlem, not just in tony Sugar Hill. This prospect alarmed Aaron Douglas, who felt that she should be accompanied on her rounds. Douglas mentioned the situation to a friend, Lyle Carter, who in turn introduced Louise to Ruben

Young, a successful Jamaican doctor who had trained at McGill University. He proved quite eager to escort the attractive ethnographer in his car. Young became an ardent suitor, maybe even a welcome dalliance for Louise after her marriage's blow to her self-esteem.

Perhaps time spent with Young compromised her ability to finish the paper, not that she tried too hard. Never more than lukewarm about being a social worker, she dismissed the idea altogether when her perception strengthened that paternalism defined traditional social work in both conception and administration, not unlike the situation at Hampton Institute. Jones, having become a solid friend of Louise's after their initial contretemps, tried to convince her otherwise. He thought she might become an Urban League official, but the remedies she envisioned were posed tantalizingly by the Left. Perhaps she could make headway in that regard after resolving her issues with Thurman, which had turned particularly contentious; he had begun to experience diminishing income from his writing and complain about the negotiations.

She had acquired more ammunition, having become aware of Thurman's arrest four years earlier for accepting money when propositioned by a man in a subway bathroom. She now threatened to make homosexuality an issue in the divorce suit. Thurman, updating Rapp from Santa Monica in May, acknowledged the scandal in 1925 while denying that it proved homosexuality. He implied that because he was broke at the time, he was merely hustling, not making a definitive statement about his sexual preferences. Defiantly, he blamed any sexual incompatibility in the marriage on Louise. He mentioned the penetration problem and her operation. Furthermore, he claimed that even though the marriage was eventually consummated, by the time the procedure had been performed he had lost his sexual desire for her. Seemingly dejected about being, in his view, blackmailed, he confided to Rapp, "And such is my tale of woe. Doesn't it read like a novel? You can understand now what a mental state I was in during those last few weeks in New York, and why I had to get away. And you can also imagine with what relish a certain group of Negroes in Harlem received and relayed the news that I was a homo. No evidence is needed of course beyond the initial rumor. Such is life."[16]

Thurman added touches of spice to the tale. Not an aggressive person, he wrote to Rapp a little later, "I would like to have a nice poke at the honorable Louise's jaw."[17] In a subsequent message, he opined that Louise knew the charge of homosexuality had no merit because he had, in fact, had sex with her on April 6, the same day he left New York.[18] He seemed to be pushing a double, quintessentially Thurmanesque premise: Louise wanted to reconcile with him and at the same time wreck him in a divorce case. He gave no explanation for his own involvement in the alleged April tryst, which would have occurred at least six weeks after their formal separation.

Meanwhile, Louise headed to Reno. The reliable Young sublet her apartment, and she left New York by train with the Douglases, who were off to visit their native Topeka, and Bontemps, who was headed to St. Louis. In Topeka, Louise encountered her weakness, another intellect. She became infatuated with Loren Miller, a brilliant young Kansan two years her junior, who was destined to make notable contributions in both journalism and law. After meeting, they talked all night. She did not, however, immediately follow her passion with respect to Miller.

The strangest aspect of Louise's journey is that she made a point of spending a couple of days with Thurman's relatives in Salt Lake City. She met his mother, Beaulah Jackson, with whom he had always had a strained relationship, and his grandmother, Emma Jackson, or "Ma Jack," who was his bedrock. Louise reported that the family received her warmly, with no hint of blame.[19] Thurman suggested a different outcome. It so happened that he missed Louise in Salt Lake City by only a few days; the fresh tale that he supposedly heard involved a sobbing, polarizing Louise blaming outsiders for the breakup and impolitely mentioning inflated assessments of how much alimony he could pay.[20]

It is likely that Thurman cared little about the objective truth. He enjoyed all of the narratives. If he grumbled to Rapp about his domestic life turning into a bad dream, he nonetheless seemed to thoroughly enjoy his nightmares. It is telling how sympathetically he portrays Louise in the five or six brief appearances she makes in his classic roman à clef *Infants of the Spring*, which he was composing at the time. No character is treated better. He writes of Raymond (himself) and Lucille (Louise), "Raymond had been attracted to her, because she personified what he was wont to call an intelligent woman."[21] This is the same description he used for Louise in his letter to McKay. He also casts Lucille as appropriately revolting against the "stodgy" and "prim," just as Louise had been doing for years.[22] In a wishful scene:

> " 'Cile, we ought to get married."
> "Do you want another drink?"
> "No, really, I'm serious."

"My dear Ray. Don't you realize that should we marry you'd probably cut my throat after the first week or else I'd bash you over the head with your typewriter?"

"But I love you."

"I don't doubt that. And I love you, too."[23]

They agree to have an affair instead of getting married—a case of art not imitating, but being wiser than, life.

Six weeks in Reno awaited Louise, a stay reminiscent of her time in Goldfield as a little girl. Nebby came to see her, and Louise, in turn, snuck out to the Bay Area. However, she missed the wedding of Nebby and Matt Crawford on September 1—and fell far short of establishing residency in Nevada—because her mother had entered Bellevue Hospital and was diagnosed with stomach cancer. Distraught, Louise wired ahead to inform Thurman's family that she would be passing through Ogden, about thirty-five miles from Salt Lake City. Inadvertently, she provided fodder for another absorbing vignette. Thurman suggested to Rapp that he had no choice but to meet her in Ogden, at which point a supposedly tearful Louise asked that he ride the train with her a while at her expense. Thurman consented but claimed that he held his emotions in check along the way by thinking of the money he had forked over and the fact that he was "in exile." In his yarn, he rejected Louise's request for a loan and rebuffed her attempt at reconciliation, which he perceived to be "angled for most subtly." Expressing disgust, Thurman dubiously declared, "If I had the money I would put in for the divorce right here in Salt Lake and have no trouble getting it at all. And god knows I wish it could be over."[24] But it remains hard to imagine Thurman voluntarily dispensing with chaos or contradiction.

He rode as far as Green River, Wyoming, and faced a five-hour wait for a return train. He gleefully described to Rapp the interim spent in a hedonist paradise. He marveled at "whores of all races, white, black, mulatto, Mexican, and what have you. A bar almost a half block long. A dance hall. A hotel (?). Poker, dice and blackjack, roulette, and fan-tan." He confided to Rapp, perhaps unwittingly and ironically providing insight into his suitability as a mate, "I spent a glorious five hours exploring and almost missed my train. I arrived back in Salt Lake full of pep and ready to work."[25]

Although they would remain apart, Louise and Thurman never divorced. She was certainly willing, growing far more tired of him than he was of her. When both were back in New York, he exasperated her to no end by sometimes showing up at a restaurant where she was dining with a date. In a possessive move, Thurman would scoop her glass from the table and drink from it.[26] On other occasions, he would come to her home at five o'clock in the morning and threaten to kill himself, a dramatic gesture he had employed at many parties around Harlem. Louise learned to retort calmly, "Go ahead. You're not going to do it."[27] She became much more animated when she pressed him to explain in rational terms all of his behavior toward her. However, he would only reply, in a manner that countered the tone of his letters to Rapp and reflected *Infants of the Spring*, "Well, Louise, I love you."[28] Unlike the character Lucille, his wife did not affirm the same.

As Louise began to focus on caring for her mother, she received enormous assistance from Bailey, Young, and Alain Locke. The first mission involved abandoning the fifth-floor walk-up, which her mother would not be able to negotiate. They moved to 132nd Street but were driven out by the combination of a sanctified church below, a buffet flat above, and a bedbug infestation. Fortunately, Bailey welcomed the two after purchasing a spacious co-op at 435 Convent Avenue. Young, predictably, discerned no need for such an arrangement because he aimed to capture Louise through marriage, virtually the last proposition she would entertain. But the amorous physician attended assiduously to Mother Thompson, which didn't hurt his chances.

Locke led Louise to the job she needed by introducing her in September to noted patron of the arts Charlotte Osgood Mason. The kindly seventy-five-year-old aristocrat, who primarily lived at 339 Park Avenue, hired Louise at a salary of $150 per month to help Hughes, who had graduated from Lincoln University the previous month, produce the third and final draft of his novel *Not without Laughter*. Mason sponsored his set-up, including a new typewriter and desk for Louise, in a rooming house in Westfield, New Jersey. Louise also performed other tasks for Mason, such as organizing numerous newspaper clippings and covering events. For example, Mason assigned her to cover the appearance of South African statesman Jan Christiaan Smuts at New York City's Town Hall on January 9, 1930. Louise could work at home much of the time, allowing her more time to keep an eye on her mother than would have been afforded by most employment options. As a bonus, the charitable Mason sometimes gave Louise an extra twenty-five or thirty dollars to spend on Mother Thompson.

The Hughes project proceeded smoothly. Louise kept the typewriter keys jumping in tune with the author's voluminous revisions, surely appreciating his merging of an autobiographical perspective with a vision of common black personhood. For his part, Hughes recognized the allure and intellect of someone who was no ordinary typist. Their friendship deepened, grounded in similarity. Like him, she was a fair-skinned, radically inclined native mid-westerner who had experienced a nomadic, alienated upbringing and had come late, and zealously, to both black pride and Harlem. No romance ensued. Hughes in his own peculiar way generally hovered beyond avail-ability.[29] Louise might have entertained the notion at some point but never had to consider the matter seriously. Instead, she regarded him as a brother, which meant he became an adopted son for the ailing Mother Thompson. He was always welcome on Convent Avenue, as fine a visitor as any that had been attracted to the Cayton residence twenty-five years earlier.

The situation failed to amuse Young. He simmered when Louise, because Hughes asked her first, attended the Hampton-Lincoln football game with Hughes at the Polo Grounds on November 2, 1929, at which "brilliant, fight-ing" Lincoln beat "snarling, slashing, never-say-die" Hampton 18–6.[30] Aware of Young's controlling nature, Louise vowed to herself, regardless of his help with her mother, "Nobody is going to chain me."[31] Young erupted after Eddie Perry reported in the *Inter-State Tattler* that Louise and Hughes had been seen holding hands while walking along Seventh Avenue.[32] He accused Louise of making a fool out of him in front of his Jamaican friends and even charged that she was anti–West Indian. Louise's ultimate refusal to embrace him on his terms contributed to his decision to leave New York.[33]

Hughes delivered the final draft of his book manuscript to Knopf in the middle of February, which pleased Mason. That eased his demanding patron's pressure for him to produce, but her expectations of production in Westfield increased with the arrival of Zora Neale Hurston in the spring of 1930. As part of her duties, Louise was assigned to help Hurston ready for publication the folklore materials she had collected during her travels over the previous two years. She worked twelve-hour days at Hurston's place, a few doors from Hughes, working so much that her arm grew sore from returning the manual typewriter carriage. It mattered little, though; she enjoyed the work and ad-mired immensely the flamboyant, irrepressible Hurston, ten years her senior. Hurston, too, was feted at the Thompson home.

Unfortunately, this harmony failed to last long, and Louise found herself at the center of the well-known dispute between Hughes and Hurston that dissolved their friendship. At issue was the ownership of *Mule Bone*, a fair-to-middling drama that was ultimately not worth fighting over as it did noth-ing for either writer's pockets and little for their legacies. Their collaboration was urgent in 1930, however, because it seemed to them the best way forward creatively. Hughes had stalled somewhat as a poet, and Hurston felt overwhelmed trying to rush her anthropology manuscript. As a result, the two returned to an idea they had once discussed: collaborating on a folk opera. The aim shifted to creating a folk comedy, an initiative in which Hurston would take the lead. She fascinated Louise with her ability to play each character in an uproarious fashion. Hughes would lend his technical sense to tighten up the structure.

Hughes and Hurston, as well as Louise, knew that they were all treading in dangerous waters as far as Mason was concerned. She never intended to fund this work and found the activity in Westfield unacceptable. In a paroxysm of recriminations, Mason began to withdraw her emotional and financial support. Most likely, she was egged on by Locke, who obviously could be generous but tended to be petty when he felt it time to settle old scores—he had long desired Hughes—or protect the perks he enjoyed from his patron. Mason's maneuvers unnerved the writers, especially given the onset of the Great Depression. In a further complication, Hughes and Hurston had not yet figured out how to compensate Louise for her time. Hughes proposed to cut her in on any future profits, a show of disrespect in Hurston's view. With the play unfinished, she began to distance herself from the other two; she soon left Westfield altogether and would later claim sole authorship.

Hurston's umbrage at Hughes's ill-conceived attempt to reward Louise was certainly legitimate. But her decision to leave apparently involved more. For one, she seemed envious of the closeness between Hughes and Louise. Louise surmised, speaking of Hurston's emotional needs, "Maybe she wanted to be the only pebble on the beach."[34] In fact, a perceptive Bailey had warned Louise, who had little or no experience with overly competitive girlfriends, to be wary of Hurston.[35]

Another explanation for Hurston's actions is that she perceived a need to sacrifice Hughes and Louise to have any chance of placating Mason and preserving an arrangement that paid $200 per month. Her rhetorical approach to effecting appeasement required distancing herself from the "error" of Westfield.

Months followed with Louise in limbo. She heard nothing from Mason about additional work. She didn't fantasize about philanthropic assistance or about advances and royalties as did Hughes and Hurston; she focused on remaining employed. Through contacts in the YMCA and the National Council of Churches, she met Hubert C. Herring, secretary of the Department of

Social Relations of the Congregational Education Society (CES). The department dealt with labor and race issues. Several years later, Herring, who had graduated from Union Theological Seminary in 1913, flashed his progressive streak with his highly publicized criticism of Union president Henry Sloane Coffin, who attempted to suppress student radicals.[36] In August 1930 Herring offered Louise a job; because she hadn't heard from Mason about plans beyond the one-year contract that was about to expire, she accepted.

In September Mason finally summoned Louise to the Barclay Hotel, where she sometimes quartered, and formally terminated their relationship. Dressed in purple velvet, which caused Louise to conjure up images of Queen Victoria, Mason berated her, accusing her, among other things, of betrayal of trust and of not even being an authentic Negro.[37] Louise was stunned by the attack but left with her dignity intact. She recounted, "I walked around that corner, around that block, I didn't know where I was. But when I got over it, contrary to the way Langston took it, I got angry. I hadn't done anything to her."[38] Louise could be more philosophical about being dumped than could Hughes because she had never been connected viscerally to Mason as he had. Therefore, she never wallowed in deference. Sensitive to condescension, as she had been at Pine Bluff, Hampton, and the New York School of Social Work, she never called the patron "Godmother" as Hughes and other sponsored artists did at Mason's insistence, nor did she sweat over the precise wording of the expected thank-you notes.

One of Louise's first ventures with CES was the American Interracial Seminar, a series of events over a two-week period during the fall of 1930 intended to promote interracial understanding. Herring assumed the post of executive director; Louise served as assistant to the director. The approximately twenty-five-member touring group included Mary McLeod Bethune, one of Louise's three favorite educators, the other two being Nannie Helen Burroughs and Charlotte Hawkins Brown. From November 11 to November 21, the interracial group undertook a whirlwind tour of black college campuses, including Howard, Virginia Union, Hampton, Bennett, Morehouse, Clark, Spelman, Talladega, Tuskegee, Alabama State, and Fisk. In the South, they all went through the "colored" entrances and exits, and they were advised to pull the shades inside their Pullman car. On November 16, while the group was en route to Talladega, local terrorists threatened to dynamite their car. A couple of days later, while in Montgomery, they were warned not to visit Birmingham, where they were scheduled to tour industrial sites and hold a session at a Masonic temple. After a contentious discussion within the group, they caved in. Promoting interracial understanding could go but so far southward on that occasion. Instead, the group headed for Nashville to spend a couple of days at Fisk.

Later that fall, Louise, representing the American Interracial Seminar, accepted the invitation of labor leader A. J. Muste to attend the Conference for Progressive Labor Action, which he chaired. The event, focused on the problems of Negro workers in the labor movement, took place at the Brookwood Labor College in Katonah, New York, on December 27. Also participating were Hughes, Du Bois, Carter, White, and Howard University faculty members Abram Harris and Emmett Dorsey. Proposals were sought for eliminating discrimination against blacks in labor unions, making unions more progressive overall, and developing worker education programs.[39]

In January Louise visited Cleveland, where Hughes was living after his banishment by Mason, and once again found herself in the middle of the *Mule Bone* controversy. The Gilpin Players, headed by Rowena and Russell Jelliffe, planned to stage the play, which, unbeknown to Hurston, the group had received from the Samuel French literary agency. Hughes's name was not affixed to the script or to the copyright document. While in Cleveland, Louise confirmed to the Jelliffes that Hughes and Hurston had collaborated on the play. Her testimony, rather than aiding in negotiations to have the play produced, torpedoed the project because Hurston became enraged when she arrived in Cleveland a few weeks later and became aware of Louise's presence and comments. Hurston's erratic behavior caused the Gilpin Players to cancel plans to perform the drama.

Back in New York, Hurston told numerous acquaintances that she was going to thrash Louise, whom she had once referred to as a "vile wretch," the next time she ran into her.[40] The opportunity occurred at the Savoy. Louise spotted Hurston standing along a wall. She informed her dance partner that there might be some action, but she kept dancing. A bit later, Hurston managed to approach from the rear. She threw her arms affectionately around Louise and kissed her fondly. It was the last time Louise ever saw Hurston.

Louise continued her work with the CES, but she was decidedly a "fellow traveler" by 1931 and seeking other outlets for her activist impulses. Although she had resisted formal recruitment by Communist Party stalwart Richard B. Moore when she was at Hampton, he had remained a significant influence, and in Harlem she drew closer to him ideologically. More broadly, the party was making inroads among blacks as material conditions worsened in the nation's largest black community. Blacks in Harlem never embraced

Marxism-Leninism in overwhelming numbers; even at its peak, party membership among African Americans in Harlem never reached more than one thousand. But against a backdrop of bank failures, drastically reduced wages, rampant unemployment, exorbitant rents, mundane evictions, and pervasive police brutality, the party's visibility in somewhat-successful campaigns to address immediate needs in ways that liberal reformers and Garveyites did not made it an increasingly viable player in the Harlem market of ideas and models for political engagement.[41] Louise did not organize at the grassroots level, but because of her contacts with artists and civil rights officials, she became a conduit to the Left for the Harlem intelligentsia. Whether in Marxist study circles at the Douglas home, sessions at 435 Convent Avenue, or classes downtown at the Workers School, she developed and communicated an understanding of the link between class oppression and racial oppression, seeing the second as a highly exploitative instance of the first. Of course, she was passionately interested in the "Negro Question," but she thought more and more in terms of the Negro worker and the potential fate of that worker in a Soviet-style social order.

In March 1931 William L. Patterson, having been assigned to the Harlem section of the Communist Party as an organizer, returned from the Soviet Union. In Louise's estimation, he was "redder than a rose."[42] He was also the father of a daughter, Lola, a product of his marriage to Vera Gorohovskaya. According to Patterson, Gorohovskaya thought it unwise to accompany him to the United States because of the racial climate.[43] Louise, as always, was impressed by Patterson's intellect, which would get him close to her heart. But his situation still seemed too complicated for a serious romantic claim. In any event, she worked closely with Patterson in "campaigns," as he would put it, before he was reassigned to teach at a school in Pittsburgh.[44] She met a number of people through him and featured him at several of her gatherings.

Louise's actions on behalf of the organized Left intensified with the Scottsboro case, which broke into the national headlines in the spring of 1931. Indeed, the legal battle to save the lives of nine innocent Alabama youths charged, convicted, and sentenced to death for the rape of two white women proved to be the best chance to date for the Communist Party to garner the support of African Americans nationwide. The party was not motivated solely by political opportunism, as popular cynicism suggested; it was not uncommon to hear that the Communist Party wanted the young men to die and therefore was pursuing a confrontational politics that some felt would doom any defense. Yet the Scottsboro case represented an explicit examination of whether the party could be more effective on a major legal issue than the NAACP, an organization that specialized in legal solutions to racial discrimination. History confirms that the confrontational, mass-movement strategy of the Communist-backed International Labor Defense (ILD), executed in large part by Patterson after he was later recalled from Pittsburgh to take over from J. Louis Engdahl as the national secretary, was correct. After much mass pressure and several years of appeals and reversals of death sentences, the lives of the Scottsboro Boys were saved.

From the beginning, Louise made Scottsboro central to her political discussions, presentations, and organizing efforts. She tried to push the CES to become directly involved, but that would have been too bright a spotlight for Herring. He was not hostile to Louise's thinking. He knew, for example, that she attended the Workers School and would support her political development. But he remained invested in his own vision of the CES, a liberal approach that would not satisfy Louise in the long term. In the meantime, she planned a foray to Mexico in July that was essentially a vacation but officially a study trip for approximately a hundred members of the organization to expand their knowledge about social issues. Louise handled the railway logistics; she greeted the passengers who joined the group at different stops along the way, distributed information, and saw them to their berths. Sue Bailey boarded in Laredo, joining her good friend as only the second black person on the junket. From Texas, the group proceeded to Guadalajara, Mexico City, Cuernavaca, and Taxco. Louise became sick with a stomach virus along the way but recovered in time for the grand celebration in the famous Chapultepec Park.

By the end of the year, Louise had become firmly aligned with the League of Struggle for Negro Rights, the Communist Party's national civil rights initiative. She attended its ball, intended to become an annual affair, on December 19 at the New Harlem Casino on 116th Street.[45] On hand were Cyril Briggs, Harry Haywood, and Patterson, visiting from Pittsburgh. She and Patterson, recalling their first trip to the Savoy, danced to the music of the popular Casa Loma Orchestra, also known as the O.K. Rhythm Kings.

Not only were leftist politics becoming more important to Louise, but she was increasingly becoming important to radicalism in Harlem. In consultation with party officials, she formed a chapter of the Soviet Friendship Society.[46] Fifty people attended the founding meeting at her apartment, at which films were shown about Soviet industrial progress.[47] Russia loomed even larger in Louise's imagination when James Ford returned in early 1932 from two years of study abroad. He conveyed news of a proposal by the Mezhrabpomfilm company, a Russian-German studio, to make a film titled *Black and White* about the struggles of African American workers in the United States. The interracial theme had become popular in Russian cultural and political circles, particularly with respect to deepening a critique of the United States, after the celebrated poet Vladimir Mayakovsky wrote a poem "Black and White," apparently based on observations in Cuba en route to the United States in 1925. Mayakovsky provoked a stirring response in several American cities when he read the poem, which included a reflection about an oppressed black worker named Willie: "How was he to know / that his question / should be directed / to the Comintern / in Moscow?"[48] The proposed film cast for *Black and White* would not meet Mayakovsky, however. He died under mysterious circumstances in the spring of 1930 at the age of thirty-six.[49]

On March 9, 1932, Louise joined Ford to meet with Charles Rumford Walker and John Henry Hammond Jr., a heir and former NAACP supporter, to sketch out plans for the film. They envisioned recruiting a cast of fifteen for a trip of five or six months that would commence May 1. Louise thus became the corresponding secretary for what became known as the Co-operating Committee for Production of a Soviet Film on Negro Life, which meant she did most of the work. Ford assumed the post of executive secretary, and radical pamphleteer W. A. Domingo served as the chairman. They were joined as officers by publicity director Deene Young, representing the Workers' Laboratory Theatre, and *Amsterdam News* reporter Henry Lee Moon, who served as the vice chairman. Moon was like a brother to Louise, in her eyes anyway.[50] He lived right around the corner from her, and she saw him almost every day. She had also visited him several times when he was a student at the Brookwood Labor College. Sponsors of the committee included Waldo Frank, Rose McClendon, and Hughes, whose names, it was imagined, would attract donations.

Trying to generate money and enthusiasm for the project, Ford keynoted a meeting of the international branch of the Soviet Friendship Society, with Louise presiding, on March 27.[51] The strategy proved unsuccessful, at least in the short run. It was hard to entice established actors to make commitments without contracts redeemable in U.S. currency. The rubles that Meschrabpom promised, even if forthcoming, meant economic survival only in Russia. By mid-April no actors had been found, nor had any contributions been generated, and the envisioned start date was no longer possible. At this point, Ford shifted the focus to people who could pay their own way.[52] Louise was not able to do so herself, but she expended enormous energy trying to make the trip happen for others.

She also remained drawn to the Scottsboro case and worked with another of the endlessly overlapping progressive organizations, the National Committee for the Defense of Political Prisoners, to stage a benefit at the Rockland Palace, on the northern boundary of Harlem, on May 15. She considered the occasion to be her debut as a "revolutionary speaker" and confided in Hughes by mail that she felt somewhat intimidated.[53] However, she succeeded in speaking before more than a thousand people, before performances by Cab Calloway's band and McClendon, "without any knee trembling," in her own words.[54] It helped, of course, that her concluding statement was a telegram of support sent by Hughes. She noted that Countee Cullen, Harold Jackman, Alta Douglas, and a variety of other folks she called "the people" were in attendance.[55]

Louise's good fortune ballooned the following day. After listening to her talk about the trip and her desire to go, Herring, feeling somewhat comradely, advanced her several months' salary so that she could both make the journey and leave money with her cousin Mary Savage and Sue Bailey, who would care for Mother Thompson. She wrote ecstatically to Hughes, who had recently committed to taking the journey.[56]

By late May, Ford had quit working on the Meschrabpom project because he had to attend to other party duties, including touring as the party's candidate for vice president in the upcoming election. He wisely put Louise in charge; her work ethic and organizational skills would ensure that the voyage occurred. Using all of her contacts, she continued to recruit tirelessly and eventually secured commitments from what she deemed a worthy assemblage, including Loren Miller, whom she admitted to being in love with at the time of the trip, and Matt Crawford.[57] Moon brought in Dorothy West, whom he was dating, and probably helped to make the expedition salable to a fellow reporter at the *Amsterdam News*, Ted Poston. Communist Party member Allan McKenzie was naturally interested (or appointed) for obvious political reasons. Wayland Rudd, Sylvia Garner, Thurston McNairy Lewis, and Juanita Lewis were perhaps the most sensible recruits, along with Hughes and West, because they had stage or singing backgrounds. Katherine Jenkins (who had roomed with Louise), George Sample (Jenkins's fiancé), former Hampton student Lloyd Patterson, Howard student Frank Montero, Minneapolis journalist and postal worker Homer Smith, social workers Leonard Hill and Constance White, Jamaican agricultural worker Laurence Alberga, art student Mildred Jones, and Teachers College student Mollie Lewis rounded out the group of fourteen men and eight women who would board a German liner, the SS *Europa*.

Nebby, to Louise's disappointment, couldn't make it. She tried to avoid a second setback by keeping Hughes, then reading and lecturing in California, interested; the departure was now scheduled for June 15. Hughes proved more than willing and made plans to travel cross-country by car with Miller and Crawford. He telegrammed Louise on June 6: "YOU HOLD THAT BOAT, CAUSE ITS AN ARK TO ME."[58]

Unbeknown to Louise, Alain Locke tried to sabotage her mission. On his way to Europe once again courtesy of Mason, he happened to book passage on the same ship as the *Black and White* group. He expressed considerable angst about this turn of events to Mason, though it's hard to imagine he was sincere.[59] He was serious, though, about further discrediting Louise. He told Mason that he had dissuaded a "fine youngster" from Howard University from joining the travelers. Concerning the student, Locke claimed in a Hurston-inspired bit of reasoning that the lad "might have been harmed—as he is very good looking and I do not trust Louise in matters like this. Why should I, after what happened with L.!"[60]

In contrast to Locke's spiteful actions and comments, the bon-voyage celebrations were large and lively. Many responded positively to Domingo's letter of invitation, which proclaimed:

> The American Negro has never been portrayed on screen or stage in his true character, and this film, *Black and White*, to be produced by the Meschrabpom Film Company of Moscow, will be the first departure from the traditional pattern. It will trace the development of the Negro people in America, their work, their play, their progress, their difficulties—devoid of sentimentality as well as of buffoonery. Meanwhile, Hollywood producers continue to manufacture sentimental and banal pictures, and particularly cling to traditional types in portraying the Negro. We therefore believe that *Black and White*, produced under the best technical and artistic experience of Russia, will be welcomed by discriminating patrons of the cinema and those people sincerely interested in the Negro.[61]

Domingo and the sponsoring committee threw a cabaret party at the Green and Gold Studio on Friday, June 3, that attracted two hundred guests to the 135th Street location. The following Friday, the League of Struggle for Negro Rights held a similar affair at the Bronze Studio on Lenox Avenue.

Four nights later, a hearty crowd gathered at the pier for the final send-off. An exhausted Louise was relieved when the traveler with the most star power, Hughes, made it, just barely in time. Shortly after midnight, the improbable cast of twenty-two, all connected in some way to the varied social aspects and political circumstances of Harlem, set off for Moscow in search of fun, perhaps acclaim, and possibly an up-close and in-depth examination of other ways to configure the world.

CHAPTER 5

Madam Moscow, 1932

Blissfully unburdened with logistical details, Louise relaxed for much of the trip across the Atlantic. She experienced no motion sickness, which she had feared she might.[1] After a refreshing seawater bath at seven o'clock each morning, she spent the days reading, writing letters, partaking in feasts, playing cards in the salon until closing time, and talking on the deck late into the night. She wrote to her mother, "We don't seem to sleep on this here boat."[2] She easily befriended many of the white passengers, who were curious about the Negroes in their midst but for the most part did not gawk or intrude. However, not all was idyllic. Among the travelers connected to the proposed Meschrabpom film, political and personality differences surfaced and presaged rather sharp divisions. Early in the trip, for example, they could not agree to send a group cable of support to Ada Wright, the mother of two of the Scottsboro defendants. The largest faction formed what Louise considered to be a relatively apolitical middle. They were curious about the Soviet Union and tended toward progressive positions but were motivated primarily by acting dreams and the desire for a great, nearly all-expenses-paid vacation. Louise pushed from the left, along with Matt Crawford, Langston Hughes, Loren Miller, and, at times, Allan Mc-Kenzie, though Louise considered him basically a "fool and of no use to any-one."[3] The married McKenzie startled the group by bringing along his mistress.

Amsterdam News reporters Henry Lee Moon and Ted Poston, along with former party member Thurston McNairy Lewis, made up the oppositional clique. They were leftists but suspicious of the Soviet example. Louise felt that Moon, one of her closest associates, might have been driven, at least in part, by jealousy because she spent most of her time with Crawford, Hughes, and Miller.[4] Poston, the last person to sign up for the venture, was an impetuous twenty-five-year-old who was undoubtedly Louise's main nemesis on the trip. She judged him to be the "evilest Negro I ever met."[5]

A caviling Alain Locke remained mostly a backstage adversary during the voyage across the sea. Although he traveled first class while the cast members resided down in steerage, he found them often enough to fuel a series of messages to his patron that disparaged Louise, Hughes, and the entire *Black and White* initiative.[6] In one, he cattishly described Louise as "bloated with drink."[7] In person, Locke proved civil to Louise and Hughes; he introduced them to his traveling companion, Ralph Bunche, then the head of the political science department at Howard University. At the same time, Locke was quite friendly with former Howard students Moon and Leonard Hill, as well as current Howard student Frank Montero. They (especially Montero) provided grist for his spy mill.[8] For their part, Louise and Hughes were happy to keep conversation with Locke, and Bunche as well, to a minimum. She wrote to her mother, "Lang and I gave old Locke the cold shoulder and he didn't bother around us at all. And Bunche is so stuffy now since he has been gaining the status of professor at Howard and is now bound for French East Africa for a study that he is a frightful bore. Both Lang and I remarked on how he has changed."[9]

The *Europa* docked at Bremerhaven, Germany, on June 22. After meeting with a representative from Meschrabpom, the group caught a train for a day-long trip to Berlin, where the Russian consul had not been informed of their impending arrival. After a distressing snag that Louise as the group organizer had to resolve, they received their visas. While in the German capital, Louise walked the streets with Hughes. Both were struck by the poverty in the city and the prostitutes desperate enough to try to entice a man right off of a woman's arm. Hughes was propositioned repeatedly while in her company.

A train ride to Stettin followed; then came the most pleasurable segment of the voyage for Louise, the sail across the Baltic Sea to Helsinki on the *Ariadne*. The waters were calm, the breeze warm, and the culinary fare magnificent. As an added bonus, because they were traveling in Scandinavia around the time of the June solstice, she had the opportunity to experience the so-called white nights, when the sun stays above the horizon for more than twenty hours—and never sets at all in some locales. On the deck of the *Ariadne*, Louise could read by natural light until past midnight and witness sunrise less than two hours later.

After reaching Helsinki on June 24, the travelers toured the city briefly before boarding a train for the Soviet Union. As the train reached the Russian border, no passenger could have been more exuberant than Louise. Hughes, though, possessed the most dramatic flair. He leaped from the train to be the first to scoop up a handful of Russian soil. In Leningrad the "Negro comrades" were greeted by a brass band and feted at the October Hotel. Among the welcoming delegation was Lovett Fort-Whiteman, the first native African American—he was born in Texas—to join the Communist Party. He had collaborated on the *Black and White* script with Russian screenwriter Georgi Grebner and German director Karl Junghans. A flamboyant iconoclast, a trait that would lead to his death in Stalin's purges of the late 1930s, Fort-Whiteman, to Louise's dismay, seemed to become a hero to Poston and Thurston McNairy Lewis.

The travelers reached Moscow on the morning of June 26 and were transferred by automobile to the Grand Hotel, one block from the majestic Kremlin. Louise roomed with Mollie Lewis, whom she knew from New York social circles. Louise had, in fact, been a dinner guest of Lewis and Dorothy West the previous Christmas. She described the twenty-four-year-old Lewis as a sort of butterfly, "glamorous and flighty."[10] Lewis would remain glamorous but acquired more substance (though of a reformist variety) than Louise seems to have predicted. She would marry Moon in 1938 and became in 1942 the founding chair of the National Urban League Guild, a crucial fundraising venture. Also, like Louise, she would live in fiction, serving as the model for the character Mamie Mason in *Pinktoes*, a satiric novel by Moon's cousin Chester Himes.

Louise had few solitary moments in Moscow. The list of commitments appeared endless: meetings, rallies, media inquiries, and parties. Not that Louise was complaining. Early in the trip, she closed a letter to her mother by drawing a smiley face, captioning it, "Me in the USSR."[11]

Sergei Eisenstein, acknowledged as the finest Soviet filmmaker of his era based on films like *Battleship Potemkin* and *October*, welcomed the Americans to his home. In addition, the group received celebrity treatment among Muscovites whenever they appeared in public. Crowds parted for them as they went to ride the trolleys. Passersby flooded their interpreters with questions about things American, including the much-publicized Scottsboro case. Somewhat amusingly, when Louise and Hughes wandered away from the group, the locals did not recognize them as Negro comrades. They were probably mistaken for Uzbeks and were sometimes asked for street directions, the requester not understanding that Louise and Hughes probably could not even direct them around the nearest corner. Indeed, Muscovites, as well as Meschrabpom officials, gazed quizzically on this light-skinned crew that Louise had assembled. *Shouldn't they have been much darker?* Louise spent considerable time explaining the multihued saga of the descendants of Africa in the United States.

Meschrabpom officials had additional reservations. For a film about steel-workers and domestics, the cast seemed not only fair of complexion but also physically soft. According to Homer Smith, a staff member muttered, "We needed genuine Negroes and they send us a bunch of *metisi* [mixed bloods]."[12] Another staffer seemed puzzled after shaking the callous-free hands of several of Louise's recruits.[13] The revelation that hardly any of the cast members could carry a tune only added to the distress of Junghans and the film company. At the same time, Meschrabpom itself was far from executing a perfect game plan. Apparently, no one in the organization thought it curious to deliver a script in Russian.

Translation would take several weeks. In the meantime, the cast worked on what were euphemistically called rehearsals. They chanted slogans and sang what were supposedly Negro work songs. Male actors swung sledgehammers but "not very convincingly."[14] The cast, comprising mostly students, artists, and office workers, fittingly laughed at their own performances. They were not industrial workers, domestics, southerners, or trained actors; they had no chance of capturing the ethos of southern black industrial workers and domestics. If Meschrabpom officials thought that genuine workers would be arriving, as seems to have been the case, then they were extremely naive. What workers could take four months off from their jobs? As scholar Joy Gleason Carew noted, "workers' priorities would be to stay in the United States and to hold on to whatever jobs they had."[15]

No one, however, questioned whether the film cast was black or plebian enough in spirit. Hughes warded off any queries in that vein with his Victrola and abundant collection of jazz, blues, and gospel records. Although the celebrated poet was easily the most recognizable and popular member of the entourage, his function as disc jockey may have most pleased their hosts, who habitually reminded the group not to forget the musical equipment.

As July unfolded, the American visitors settled into a routine. They had to be somewhat austere because a stipend of four hundred rubles per month wouldn't stretch far if one bought thirty-ruble dinners at the high-end Metropole Hotel, a preferred gathering place. The Meschrabpom support was not boundless but proved reliable. The firm even delivered food generally unavailable to the public. This saved the Americans from a diet consisting predominantly of borsch, potatoes, cabbage, and black bread. While the Great Depression deepened in the United States and a famine gripped much of the Soviet Union, the contingent at the Grand Hotel could hardly have imagined a better period of leisure.

With nothing meaningful happening with *Black and White*, plenty of time remained available to explore Moscow and pursue a variety of capers ranging from the discreet to the madcap to the bizarre. Given Russian men's fascination with the female visitors, none of the women had trouble securing dates if they desired them. Most of this activity was tame, except that the extremely attractive Mildred Jones became an object of obsession for Constantine Oumansky, head of the Soviet People's Commissariat of Foreign Affairs. He subsequently had to endure a term of banishment to Siberia. The bisexual Jones was known to explain her interest in women by stating to her male suitors, "Sorry, I want what you want."[16]

Smith relayed a whimsical account of his own romantic exploits. He supposedly arranged an evening outing to the Aquarium Summer Garden for himself, a Russian woman he was dating, Hughes, and a woman his girlfriend brought along to accompany Hughes. Apparently, the women wanted to swap dates, but the men wanted to adhere to the original arrangement. In Smith's account, this led to a hair-pulling brawl between the women that "would have done justice to 125th Street and 7th Avenue."[17] Hughes purportedly remarked, "Man, I've seen us fighting over white women, but this is the first time I've seen white women fighting over us."[18] Hughes's account of the incident is perhaps more plausible: he claimed that Smith got the days mixed up and inadvertently invited two women who did not know each other to his room at the same time, thus sparking the fight. Hughes recalled that news of the incident spread all over Moscow.[19] Surely another gossip item was the possible suicide attempt—it was at least a suicidal gesture—made by a cast member. A despondent Sylvia Garner, after being spurned by Constance White for a Russian woman, began to drink formaldehyde, which burned her digestive tract and prompted a fit of screaming heard by many of the guests in the hotel. Fortunately, she recovered swiftly after hospital treatment.[20]

Such incidents led Louise to convene solemn meetings about the need to avoid disgracing their race. The worst violators in her view were Poston and Thurston McNairy Lewis, who wantonly pursued Russian women. In Louise's view, they acted in accord with the worst racial stereotypes. Seemingly lacking all restraint, they became particularly fond of the nude beaches in the Park of Culture and Rest and subsequently chose to go naked even on beaches not designated for nude bathing. They were impervious to any moralizing effects of the group meetings, remaining, in Louise's words, "thoroughly irresponsible."[21] Poston, who earned the moniker "Daddy Long Legs" for his footwork on the dance floor in the Metropole Hotel, apparently thought that a steady supply of Russian women was his payment for a hoped-for conversion to Communism.[22] Lewis, though, seemed the worse of the two to Louise. She considered him "really incorrigible."[23]

Louise figured that the social problems could be reduced if work could begin on *Black and White*. The film's story culminated in the triumph of steel-workers and domestics in Birmingham, Alabama, after they unite across race and class lines to defeat their exploiters. But no viable script existed. When the translated screenplay arrived, its ineptitude rivaled the cast's. Hughes could only laugh when he read it. Scene after scene depicted implausible events in stilted language—not a surprising result from writers who were largely unfamiliar with African American history and culture and who con-sidered fidelity to that history and culture less important than an overarch-ing black-and-white-unite-and-fight message. Fort-Whiteman presumably was supposed to ensure authenticity, but the result was nonetheless a failure. In an ideologically pristine packaging of the Civil War, a white officer ad-dresses his troops, "You black workers in our factories in the North; you are free men. Arise, help us to battle against the cruel and godless planters of the South, who keep your black brothers in bondage in order to undermine the glorious rise of our industrial North!"[24] In another scene, wealthy African Americans in Birmingham, under attack during a riot, scramble to the radio stations they own and broadcast for help from the North. In response, hordes of white workers pile into cars and buses to ride to the rescue. In yet another scene, it is suggested that the Red Army would be deployed to counter lynch-ing. Hughes showed the script to Louise, who agreed that "it really was im-possible."[25] In a meeting with Meschrabpom officials, Hughes marked all of the problems in the script with a red pencil, then asked, "Now what is left from which to make a picture?"[26]

Junghans and Meschrabpom tried to recover from this, but the project encountered other difficulties. Colonel Hugh Lincoln Cooper, an influential civil engineer who had supervised the construction of the Dnieprostroi Dam, a massive hydroelectric power station, and figured prominently in Sta-lin's plans for building the infrastructure for heavy industry, disapproved of the proposed film. He conveyed his views to McKenzie and United Press correspondent Eugene Lyons at the Metropole Hotel bar. But he also scuttled the project by appealing to Vyacheslav Molotov, chairman of the Council of People's Commissars of the Soviet Union. In essence, Soviet officials saw the wisdom of mollifying Cooper in hopes of achieving diplomatic recognition from the United States, which would open the gates for investment capital to flow into the USSR. Of course, the Soviets understood the potential value of Black and White for their goal of global hegemony; for this, the film was possibly as important as Communist involvement in the Scottsboro case. By illustrating in film the oppression of African Americans, they hoped to draw more blacks in America into the Communist ranks and eventually make a strong appeal to nonwhite populations (with Africans perhaps the biggest prize). The reasoning was sound and prophetic. Decades later, the United States clearly realized that its tolerance of racism weakened its attempts to gain influence over independent African nations, a realization not unrelated to subsequent domestic civil rights concessions. In 1932, however, the Soviets shelved their strategy of embarrassing the United States on race relations with a proselytizing film about Negro-and-white proletarian unity, instead prioritizing diplomatic recognition and the unfettered investments needed to foster economic progress.[27]

Cooper knew almost immediately that his visit to Molotov had been successful. He made no secret of it, which emboldened Lyons and others to circulate stories of the movie's cancellation. When and how Meschrabpom officials received word of this is unknown. In any event, on August 3 they sent the cast by train to the resort city of Odessa. The stated goal was to garner location shots beginning on August 15; with the snow-capped Caucasus Mountains in the background, Louise couldn't fathom which part of Alabama Odessa resembled.[28] In the meantime, waiting on artistic direction from Meschrabpom, they cruised the Black Sea, visiting the ports of Sebastopol, Yalta, Gagra and Sukhumi. As they neared a landing, Lewis and Poston, true to form, despite Louise's pleading, would strip naked and swim to shore. She urged them to at least be on time for departures, but they were generally late, adding to Louise's frustration by showing up with "women on one arm and souvenirs in the other."[29] Lewis further irritated her by disparaging their political guide and their interpreter.[30]

When the group returned to Odessa and their lodgings at the luxurious Londres Hotel, they were greeted by Moon, who, having been ill, had taken a later train to Odessa. He brandished a copy of the international edition of the Herald-Tribune for August 12, which announced, "Soviet Calls Off Film on U.S. Negroes; Fear of American Reaction Cause." The story carried no by-line but was Lyons's handiwork. The same day, the *New York Herald-Tribune* ran a story submitted by correspondent Ralph Barnes: "Negroes Adrift in Uncle Tom's Russian Cabin." This second story linked the decision to cancel the film to the Soviet Union's desire to strengthen its position in the Far East given the imperialist aims of Japan, a longtime enemy, which had invaded Manchuria eleven months earlier. In this endeavor, it needed the support of the United States, which, in fact, became its military ally against Japan during World War II.

Clutching his copy of the international edition, Moon intoned, "Comrades, we've been screwed!"[31] Turmoil promptly ensued. Although doubts must have plagued the proposed cast members, they still thought they were making a movie and were committed to the process. Boris Babitsky, a manager from Meschrabpom, arrived to reassure them that the film had merely been postponed, not canceled. Because the Russian winter would soon begin, work on the film would be discontinued in any case until the following year. Babitsky informed the cast that their current contracts would be honored and that shooting would begin in the spring. Furthermore, Babitsky suggested that the group might want to return to the United States directly from Odessa.

Skeptics abounded. Moon, Poston, and Thurston McNairy Lewis denounced Meschrabpom for capitulating to a Kremlin–Wall Street alliance. Moon charged that Otto Katz, the director of Meschrabpom, had admitted to him that the film had been scuttled. Louise, along with Hughes, took Babitsky at his word and defended the company. They agreed about Meschrabpom's incompetence but refused to ascribe deep political motives to the decision. There was accord, however, on rejecting the invitation to depart for the United States directly from Odessa. All returned to Moscow to seek further clarification and take their case to whatever authorities would hear it. They also had to communicate to worried friends and family that they were okay and not at all in the dire straits erroneously indicated by Barnes. Louise wrote at length to her mother, winding up:

> You can see from what I have said that all has not been pleasant. Ted and Thurston have been more venomous than I imagined any two people could be. I haven't minded this as much as their actions which reflect on the group. . . . On the whole, the group has acted very well and I am sure they would have a much better understanding of everything if Meschrab-

pom had given us a bit more leadership. We were given very excellent living accommodations, food and hotel but their neglect came in not providing sufficient guidance. Whiteman has turned out to be an awful person and such a person that one can only have contempt for.[32]

A sign of their dropping stature awaited them upon their arrival on August 20. They had been booted from the Grand Hotel and moved to the sparser and less commodious Mininskya Hotel, though they were still in a prime location on Red Square, directly across from the Kremlin. Had they been making a documentary about themselves, it would have been the perfect setting, given the political infighting that followed. They debated fiercely for three days how to comment publicly. These deliberations became known as the son-of-a-bitch sessions because of how frequently the appellation was used to refer to a debate opponent.[33] Poston, particularly caustic, accused Hughes of currying favor with the Soviets because his literary reputation in the United States had sagged.[34] He bitterly dubbed Louise "Madam Moscow."[35] Poston and Moon weren't going to be bound by a group decision; they were intent on writing scathing stories for the *Amsterdam News* and possibly other outlets. Thurston McNairy Lewis and Laurence Alberga matched their contempt for Meschrabpom and joined them in signing what became the minority statement, which was published in the international edition of the *Herald-Tribune* on August 24. "Rejecting as unsound, insufficient, and insulting to our intelligence the reasons offered by Meschrabpom-Film Corporation for the cancellation of the 'Black and White' film project," the quartet of dissenters argued that the cancellation represented a "compromise with the racial prejudice of American Capitalism and World Imperialism, sacrificing the furtherance of the permanent revolution among the 12,000,000 Negroes of America and all the darker exploited colonial peoples of the world."

Miller and Crawford helped Louise and Hughes win over the middle. The majority statement, signed by the remaining members of the group, with the exception of Hill, Katherine Jenkins, and George Sample, stressed how well the cast had been treated in the USSR and maintained that the charges made by Moon, Poston, Alberga, and Thurston McNairy Lewis had no basis in fact. "These fake allegations," it continued, "are ridiculous and have already been repudiated by the majority of this group. Such statements are readily utilized in consistent attempts to arouse distrust on the part of white and black workers in the success of socialist construction in the Soviet Union, where exploitation and the oppression of racial minorities have been eliminated."[36]

To Louise's embarrassment, Poston and Moon wanted to press their case before the Comintern and managed to secure a hearing, at which Hughes and Miller also spoke. Nothing said before that body had any bearing on Meschrabpom's decision.

Next, Louise and Hughes tried to win the media battle unfolding in the United States, but they lacked access to mainstream outlets like the *Herald-Tribune*. For example, Hughes had to be content with papers such as the *Daily Worker*.[37] In contrast, Moon and Poston were on a highly public roll. They filed a story from Berlin, "*Amsterdam News* Reporters Tell Why Soviet Russia Dropped Film," which appeared during the first week of October.[38] The *New York Times* published an item based on their work: "Say Race Bias Here Halted Soviet Film."[39] Moon and Poston reiterated their perspective in the *Amsterdam News* after they arrived back in the United States on October 12.[40] The newspaper also ran an article on the views of Thurston McNairy Lewis, attributing to him the idea that "Russia cares nothing for the interests of the Negro beyond the point where they can serve their purposes."[41] Moon's, Poston's, and Lewis's words set Harlem astir. Louise worried about the impact on W. A. Domingo and James Ford. She didn't want either man embarrassed by the failure of a project they had sanctioned. Moreover, perhaps blooming fully into Madam Moscow after all, she wanted to ward off or counteract any damage to party recruiting. Ford, for instance, was not a serious contender for vice president in established circles, but his candidacy was an opportunity to gauge the party's appeal to African American voters. In line with this thinking, Domingo expressed to Louise his belief that the film "MUST BE MADE."[42]

Louise could not guarantee that outcome, but she did manage to get the majority opinion in the *Amsterdam News* by the end of October.[43] In the meantime, the League of Struggle for Negro Rights organized a demonstration against the newspaper to protest its one-sided coverage of the *Black and White* situation. Similarly, Louise called on her old mentor, W. E. B. Du Bois, to publish her perspective in the *Crisis*, though the piece wouldn't appear until the February issue. Responding to the accusation that no satisfactory explanation for the postponement of the film had been given, Louise wrote vigorously, "It is quite true that such statements have not been given such publicity in the white capitalist press of America as have the false allegations of complete abandonment of the picture for political reasons. The reason must be obvious to you, knowing as you do the attitude of this press to the Negro, as well as to the Soviet Union. Many statements have been issued collectively and individually by the majority of our group and have been steadily ignored by the representatives of the press through whom adverse statements were released."[44] She specifically blamed Lyons for not making United Press services available to her faction, as he was eager to do for the other side.

Reserving her most vituperative comments about Moon and Poston for private correspondence, she told her mother:

> Here we come from a country where everything is denied us—work, protection of life and property, freedom to go where we will and to live where we will—where we are despised and humiliated at every turn. And here we are, accorded every courtesy—free to go where we will and are eagerly welcomed—given every opportunity to enjoy ourselves and to travel—free to pursue any work that we choose. And these *boys* play right into the hands of American newspaper men who of course do everything they can to turn Negroes against the only land that gives them perfect equality. [emphasis added][45]

Her hopes blinded her. Moon and Poston were actually correct, and it should have been evident that the film would never be completed.

To mollify the disappointed and disgruntled *Black and White* cast, Meschrabpom offered them three options. They could return to the United States as soon as possible, a choice that appealed to several, including Moon, Poston, and Thurston McNairy Lewis. They left the Soviet Union on September 17, prompting the rest of the group to hold a jubilant party in Louise's room. Cast members were also invited to stay in the USSR indefinitely, pursuing whatever employment or career options interested them. Smith, Garner, West, Hughes, Wayland Rudd, and Lloyd Patterson found that offer appealing. Hughes, however, would also avail himself of the third alternative: a tour of Central Asia as guests of Theatrical Trade Unions. Of course, the propagandistic aim of the trip was to acquaint the travelers with postrevolutionary developments, especially with respect to racial progress, and to equip them with rhetorical material with which to recruit blacks in the United States to the Communist cause. In other words, Louise and the others would receive a positive spin on the much-discussed "national question."[46]

This was precisely what Louise desired. Just as earlier generations had reshaped the story of Exodus into an American tale of black deliverance into the promised lands, Louise wanted to contribute to the construction of a strong narrative about the feasible application of Soviet principles as a solution to U.S.-style racism. If Central Asia, where ethnic minorities had been ruthlessly exploited under czarist rule, had indeed been transformed for the better, then she would certainly spread the news. To her, this constituted a better justification for traveling abroad than the proposed filming of *Black and White*. Indeed, Louise wanted to study in the Soviet Union until the end of November to gather material for articles and lectures. Her deal with the CES called for her to return to work at the beginning of January; thus, aside from her educational interests, it was more beneficial economically to remain in the Soviet Union in the meantime. She planned to leave around the first of December and take a few weeks to work her way home through Leningrad, Berlin, and Paris.

However, two health matters had to be considered and clarified. If Mother Thompson's cancer were immediately life-threatening, Louise would head home rather than go on the junket through Central Asia. But her mother, happy to see Louise pursuing her dreams, encouraged her to continue. The second issue was Louise's decision to terminate her pregnancy. The only precisely stated points in her recollection decades later were that she had the procedure; that Sylvia, their guide, handled the arrangements; that Miller knew about it; and that she spent a couple of days quite ill before the trip to Central Asia.[47] She did not link Miller more explicitly to the situation and didn't exactly identify who the father was, though she implied that it was Miller and indicated that their romance ended at that point. Concerning her ultimate fortune with him, she remarked, "Well I guess he didn't want to marry me. I would certainly have married him, but I would never beg him to marry me. . . . I wasn't going to beg anybody to marry me."[48] Her tone was matter-of-fact, with no hint of conflict around the decision. It appears that Louise had always been on the short end in the emotional economy between her and Miller. In letters to his fiancée, Juanita Ellsworth, he portrayed Louise as overbearing and spoiled.[49]

Certain is that on September 20, 1932, an under-the-weather Louise set out on the Central Asia trip with Miller (with whom she managed to maintain a friendship), Hughes (and his always-in-tow Victrola), Crawford, McKenzie, White, Juanita Lewis, Mollie Lewis, Jones, Jenkins, and Sample. Otto Huiswood, then living in Moscow, accompanied them. The first major stop was Tashkent, the capital of Uzbekistan. Louise was keenly aware of being among non-Europeans. She remarked, "In my photographs of Langston in Central Asia, he looks as though he is among his own people."[50] Indeed, many Central Asians were darker than Hughes and Louise.

After arriving in Tashkent on September 26, the tourists had a long meeting with President Akhun Babayev, who spoke with them about Russians' historical contempt for the Uzbek people and the brutal czarist repression. Not surprisingly, he compared this to the plight of blacks under Jim Crow. As she listened to Babayez, a former sharecropper, speak of former restrictions, including the paucity of opportunities for education, Louise conjured up images of Pine Bluff, Arkansas.[51] She could not imagine that any of the farmers she had met could become governor of Arkansas anytime soon—or that African Americans in Arkansas would be provided decent schools. She wrote later, "It was astounding to me to listen to Babayev, a man who before the Revolution had been too poor to visit the capital, though he lived only twenty-five miles away, and who now served as president of the Republic."[52]

She also met Vice President Jahan Obidava, who at the age of eleven had been sold by her parents to a man for 150 rubles and became his fourth wife. In 1923 she became one of the first women in Uzbekistan to discard the veil. She vowed to never again live under her husband's authority; instead, she attended school and became literate. She was elected to office in 1929. Louise may have been even more impressed by Obidava than by Babayev because the former symbolized a new status for women. Louise had not trumpeted gender concerns as she had racial and economic ones. Nevertheless, as a woman who had long flouted social norms, she obviously viewed the condition of women as a vital concern. She noted women's contributions to industrial advances in Uzbekistan; they appeared to have the expansive role in production that woman in the United States had experienced only during wartime (as Rosie-the-Riveter types).

In an especially welcome development, Louise's contingent met other African Americans in Tashkent. Oliver Golden, Bernard Powers, George Tynes, and a dozen or so other men trained in agriculture had gone to Moscow near the end of 1931 and arrived in Uzbekistan shortly thereafter to help the locals modernize cotton farming and build improved farm machinery. The group had been split up and assigned to various locations, but several, including Golden and Powers, were in Tashkent. Louise wrote, "Though we had never met these men before, the time spent with them was like a reunion. We brought them news and gossip from the States and they regaled us with stories of adjusting to life in Uzbekistan."[53]

From Tashkent, Louise and company traveled to Samarkand and Bukhara. In each city, the itinerary included visits to farm collectives, factories, schools, hospitals, and trade union headquarters. Signs proclaiming "Welcome to

Our Negro Comrades" often awaited. Thinking of future lectures and articles, Louise furiously scribbled notes about cotton cultivation, labor and machinery problems, the cost of camels and donkeys in Bukhara, and declining illiteracy and infant mortality rates.[54] Louise marveled at the "spectacular craftsmanship" of the mosques and palaces, the splendid designs of tiles and mirrors.[55] Cultural festivities were plentiful, a series of multicultural displays of poetry, drama, music, and dance performed by Uzbeks, Jews, and Tajiks.

But not all was convivial. In Samarkand Louise witnessed the trial of Basmachi rebels, Muslim opponents of Soviet rule in Central Asia. Such opposition had declined over the previous decade as the Soviet central government made placating gestures, but counterrevolutionary flare-ups still occurred. "Madam Moscow," who admittedly could not follow the proceedings closely, dismissed the defendants as "terrorists."[56] Although a student of the "national question," she voiced no understanding of Basmachi resistance as anti-imperialist.

From Bukhara the group headed to Ashgabat. Before leaving Bukhara, they composed a message to the workers and peasants of Uzbekistan:

> We have been able to see the practical application of the Leninist national policy successfully converting Middle Asia from a czarist colony of oppressed peoples and an undeveloped country to an industrialized country under working class rule. The emancipation of women, the complete elimination of national antagonisms, the stimulation of national proletarian culture, the proletarization and collectivization of workers and poor peasants we have found realized in Uzbekistan since the Revolution. . . . We shall carry the warm proletarian greetings of the various workers and peasants of Uzbekistan to the black and white workers and peasants of the United States.[57]

"The past ten days," Louise confided to her mother, "have been the greatest of my whole life."[58] Ironically, it was the exact same period of time that John Reed claimed "shook the world."[59]

In Turkmenistan the group, over Hughes's objection, decided to forgo a tour of Ashgabat. The capital city was his last stop with the group; he had landed an assignment with *Izvestia*, a Russian newspaper, which would require him to spend an extended period in Central Asia. Yet he felt unceremoniously abandoned. Louise recalled, "Lang looked rather forlorn at that desert station, and I hated to lose such a fine traveling companion. But we were, as usual, behind schedule, so our good-byes were brief."[60]

On October 9, after an eighteen-hour sail across the Caspian Sea, the travelers reached Baku, the capital of Azerbaijan and the most industrialized city they had visited in Central Asia. The republic's vast oil fields, once controlled by the Rothschild and Rockefeller conglomerates, had been socialized. Louise, however, was more interested in the Baku Women's Club, which was dedicated to eliminating illiteracy among women. The literacy rate among Azerbaijani women stood at 2 percent at the time of the revolution; women had been beaten and in some cases killed by their husbands for trying to read. Although wrathful husbands still tried to block female education, they were beginning to be prosecuted and imprisoned for violence against women. The Baku Women's Club sent tutors to the homes of women who could participate in lessons but not study outside of the home. The organization also ran a dormitory. Louise, who took copious notes on economic development, observed, "In the fourteen years since the Revolution, opportunities had been opened up for women that had been closed to them for centuries. This meant far more to me than the introduction of new drilling machinery to the Baku oil fields."[61]

During the final week of the journey, they drove through Georgia and went to Ukraine to see, ironically, the Dnieprostroi Dam, the facility built by Cooper. They met the head of an all-woman concrete brigade that held some sort of production record. As the weary passengers proceeded by train to Moscow, a satisfied Louise wrote to her mother, "In a few days we shall be back in Moscow with a month's experience that cannot be duplicated. We will have traveled over 6,000 kilometers and visited six republics. Each place held different interests and at the same time fitted into the general plan of the Soviet Union, which is uniting one-sixth of the globe and almost 200 nationalities into one whole. We have learned more in this time than in all the time prior in our stay in Russia. We have been able to see put into practice the policies and plan we have read about."[62]

Unfortunately, a dispiriting telegram awaited Louise in Moscow. Her mother's condition had deteriorated. After an exchange of messages, Louise calculated somewhat guiltily that she could remain in Moscow for a few more weeks to participate in one more event that tugged at her, the annual parade on November 7 to celebrate the Bolshevik victory in 1917.

She did not possess the ticket required to enter Red Square as a viewer. In a fortuitous turn, however, some Russians who had befriended her invited her to join their contingent. As was the case with *Black and White*, failure opened onto a better opportunity. Her sponsors escorted her about Moscow on the night of November 6, steering her through the crowds of revelers until morning. Then she stood with her adoptive group for hours until their turn came to march through the square, proceeding past Stalin and other luminaries on the reviewing stand.

A day later she was en route home. While traveling, she thought about the setbacks and triumphs of the five-month sojourn in the Soviet Union. Obviously, the film fiasco and resultant fallout were negatives. She had lost her close friendship with Moon; they would merely be civil in the years to come. Thurston McNairy Lewis and Poston, the future "Dean of Black Journalists," would remain "implacable enemies."[63] And there was repair work to do to bolster the Soviet image in Harlem. However, her attachments to Hughes and Crawford had strengthened through working and playing in close proximity, exploring ideological common ground, and enduring political battles together. There was, for better or worse, clarity about her relationship to Miller. Moreover, her course in terms of activism had also become clear. She later expounded, "What I had witnessed, especially in Central Asia, convinced me that only a new social order could remedy the American racial injustices I knew so well. I went to the Soviet Union with leftist leanings; I returned home a committed revolutionary."[64]

However, political thoughts did not remain uppermost in her mind as she steamed across the ocean. She grew increasingly anxious about her mother. Exactly how much had she declined? What awaited Louise when, after the longest separation yet between the two, they finally reunited?

CHAPTER 6

The Struggle Has Nine Lives, 1932–1934

L ulu Thompson, when lucid, listened intently to her daughter's tales of adventure. But she declined rapidly through the holiday season and spent much of the new year under sedation. She died very early on the morning of February 23, 1933, at the age of fifty-five. Gone was Mother Thompson, who had worn out her flesh prematurely against a hard world. Gone was the valiant protector from whom Louise had acquired or learned so much curiosity, fearlessness, strength, and determination. In a sense, Mother Thompson's spirit had long passed to her daughter and held her in good stead. Louise charged toward horizons and knew how to fight for her dreams. She was prepared to do justice to Mother Thompson's sacrifice. Three days after Mother Thompson's death, Louise wrote to Langston Hughes, "I shall go ahead living as I know Mother would wish it—missing her very much—but indulging in no morbidity. The Scottsboro boys and Angelo Herndon must be saved and one must sublimate his personal problems to the great struggle."[1]

Indeed, Louise remained a political whirlwind. After returning from the Soviet Union, she participated in a series of decompressing events. During her first week home, she gave an interview to the *Amsterdam News* in her apartment. Drawing mostly on her experiences in Central Asia, she declared frankly, "Russia today is the only country in the world that's really fit to live in. I'd live there any time in preference to America." Given the still-fresh thrill of her trip, one understands the overstatement. In reality, Louise would never have chosen residence in Russia over life in the United States. If the main obstacle to relocating, as she articulated during the interview, had been concern about her mother's well-being, that lingered as an issue for only three months. Yet she never made serious gestures to return to the Soviet Union and reside there. Even Madam Moscow had to know that she had essentially received a guided tour designed to cast Stalin's Five Year Plan in the most favorable light. Although she maintained, "Russia was the only place where I was able to forget entirely that I was a Negro," it is unfathomable that she was ever unaware of having been a special Negro visitor asked to rehearse for *Black and White*, speak about the Scottsboro case, and view progress on the national question. Beyond the psychological bombast, the most salient points that Louise made during the interview were that international contacts and a transnational view of the black freedom struggle should be maintained, that the "industrially emancipated" Soviet example could be instructive to a Depression-era United States seeking to provide jobs and relief and to reduce mass insecurity and dispossession, that Soviet women on the whole enjoyed more economic progress and civic emancipation—she mentioned the legality of abortion—than their American counterparts, and that Soviet progress on the question of national minorities should inform efforts to dismantle American racism. When the reporter skeptically suggested that a reversal in the Russian attitude might occur if ten million Negroes lived there, Louise indignantly replied, "The real cause of oppression here is economic exploitation not biological aversions. With neither of those causes existing in Russia, why would there be any change of attitude toward Negroes, regardless of numbers?"[2]

For the next couple of months, Louise continued to explain her view of the Soviet Union's significance for African Americans, making presentations to enthusiastic audiences, for example, at the Harlem Interracial Forum in the Urban League building on 136th Street and at the Savage Studio of Arts and Crafts on 143rd Street.[3] She became particularly close to the latter's proprietor, Augusta Savage, a renowned sculptor and teacher who had been a Julius Rosenwald fellow and student in Paris. Louise described the native Floridian as a fairly quiet woman, sometimes melancholic. But she also saw that Savage was a deeply caring artist genuinely interested in finding solutions to social problems. When Louise aided Savage in sponsoring political forums, their joint effort became known as the Vanguard Club. "Parties on Saturday, forums on Sunday, and we talked about everything under the sun," Louise recalled.[4] At larger venues around Harlem, they presented events such as a debate between William L. Patterson and Kelly Miller, the elder statesman and somewhat conservative former dean of the College of Arts and Sciences at Howard University. They also hosted a lecture by Mary Abby Van Kleeck, a reformer widely known for her advocacy on behalf of women workers; like Louise, Van Kleeck spent a significant amount of time in the Soviet Union during 1932 studying economic policies and conditions there.

Louise decided against returning to the CES because she felt hamstrung by the organization's moderation. Whereas she wanted to speak as a CES representative to workers about labor issues, CES preferred to consult with employers. Rather than continuing with CES, she chose to work with the ILD and accepted the position of assistant secretary with its affiliate, the National Committee for the Defense of Political Prisoners. The latter body, composed of intellectuals, had originated two years earlier and was led by Theodore Dreiser, Lincoln Steffens, Elliot Cohen, Adelaide Walker, and Diana Trilling.[5] Most important to Louise, it championed the causes of the Scottsboro defendants and Angelo Herndon, a nineteen-year-old Communist organizer who had been charged the previous July with attempting to incite an insurrection in Atlanta. He was convicted and given a sentence of eighteen to twenty years.

As Louise sought to maintain and even increase her activism in the wake of her mother's death, startling developments in the Scottsboro case attracted her attention and energy. Nineteen-year-old Ruby Bates, one of the alleged victims, had written a letter in January to a boyfriend, Earl Streetman, that absolved the defendants. Through a court order, the ILD obtained a copy of the letter, and attorney Joseph Brodsky prepared to reveal its existence to the general public. Louise, in her role with the National Committee for the Defense of Political Prisoners, organized a meeting featuring Brodsky at Abyssian Baptist Church on February 8; more than a thousand cheering supporters attended. Louise spoke briefly at the event, as did Countee Cullen.[6] The letter itself was made public on Monday, February 13.[7]

Bates had gone into hiding and was working at a camp in a New York City suburb. With heavy coverage of the Scottsboro case pricking her conscience, she sought out Harry Emerson Fosdick, the pastor at New York's Riverside Church and probably the most famous preacher in America, given that his radio sermons were broadcast to millions every week. She affirmed to Fosdick that the contents of her letter were accurate, and he convinced her to testify to that effect in court.

Once back in the public eye, Bates became a celebrity witness and later a spokesperson for the ILD. On several occasions, she stayed with Louise on Edgecombe Avenue, and Louise came to know her fairly well. She saw no hardened racist, only a teenager who had been bullied and exploited by bigots to maintain white supremacy. At the time of the alleged crimes, Bates was a seventeen-year-old wandering mill worker and prostitute who, along with Victoria Price, the other purported victim, had reason to fear charges under the vagrancy laws and the Mann Act. Dressed in overalls, they were not immediately recognized as women by police responding to reports of a racial fracas. Only after they were separated from the men did they make the charge of rape.[8] A shaky and vague testifier who mainly followed Price's lead, Bates had never been credible in the courtroom, though trustworthiness was beside the point for juries hell-bent on issuing convictions and dealing death sentences like cards at a southern gentlemen's club. A wave of pro-segregation critics charged that the ILD had paid Bates to recant, but Louise, closer to Bates than any of those critics, put the matter differently: "Some whites got to her to convince her to tell the truth. And there was enough decency in her heart that she had to be honest. She was a decent person who wasn't ready to kill nine black boys who didn't rape her."[9] In contrast, Louise had no sympathy for Price, whom she termed a "hussy."[10]

Bates confirmed Louise's faith in her with her performance on April 7, 1933, at the retrial of Haywood Patterson in Decatur, Alabama. Her exchange with defense attorney Sam Leibowitz got directly to the point:

Q: You told the story you had seen six negroes rape Victoria Price and six negroes raped you; you told a story like that?

A: I told it before, but I was excited.

Q: You testified at Scottsboro that six negroes raped you and six negroes raped her, and one had a knife on your throat; what happened to her was exactly the same thing that happened to you. Who coached you to say that?

A: She told it and I told it just like she told it.

Q: Who told you to tell that story?

A: I told it like she told it.

Q: Who told you to do that, who coached you to do that?

A: She did.

Q: Did she tell you what would happen to you if you didn't follow her story?

A: She said we might have to lay out a sentence in jail.[11]

In addition, Bates acknowledged that semen discovered during the physical examination of her and Price had been deposited during sexual relations with their boyfriends the night before.[12]

Although noble, Bates could not sway the jury. Neither could the firebrand Leibowitz, an enormously successful trial lawyer second only in prominence to Clarence Darrow among his generation.[13] No radical, Leibowitz was a mainstream Democrat with political ambitions. Known primarily for mob trials, including a murder defense for Al Capone, he understood that working on the Scottsboro case, which he did gratis, could enhance his image in New York.[14] The Communist Party leadership viewed Leibowitz with skepticism, and members of the National Committee for the Defense of Political Prisoners split over his appointment.[15] Cohen and Trilling objected to the attorney's use of racist stereotypes as he defended his "ignorant" and "inferior" clients.[16] But William L. Patterson, appreciative of the attorney's skill and tenacity, had insisted that Leibowitz join the defense team.[17]

On April 9, Palm Sunday, an Alabama jury again convicted Haywood Patterson (no relation to William), prompting a bitter Leibowitz to call the verdict the "act of bigots spitting on the tomb of Abraham Lincoln."[18] For Louise, in line with the ILD's mass-based strategy, the outcome meant taking the struggle back into the streets. She became instrumental in many of the numerous rallies in the New York area and in plans to conduct a march on Washington. The publisher of the *Amsterdam News*, William H. Davis, called for the action immediately after Patterson's conviction but later advocated for petitions to be presented to government officials by a "delegate of representative citizens."[19] The Left, though, seized on his original idea and stepped up their organizing accordingly.[20] From a storefront office on 135th Street near the YMCA, with a staff of three or four young women, Louise successfully coordinated fund-raising, outreach, and logistics. To focus her efforts and maximize their effect, she helped to form the allied Scottsboro Action Committee and served as its national secretary. Harlemites were not her only target; she sought, with a "united front" perspective, to mobilize the entire Eastern Seaboard and beyond.[21]

Harlem certainly responded. On the morning of May 6, 135th Street, cordoned off between Lenox and Seventh Avenues, resembled a black national mall. Louise recalled the scene outside of her office: "The streets, the whole block was just like a huge mass gathering itself. And people of every category were there: old people, young people, mothers with babies in their arms, children. It was something else. I think it actually frightened me when I saw what was happening."[22] Louise scrambled to order additional charter buses to accommodate the surging crowd. Although a morning departure had been envisioned, the caravan didn't leave for Philadelphia until one o'clock in the afternoon. Louise traveled by car because she wanted more flexibility in her route.[23]

The group of marchers snowballed in Philadelphia and Baltimore. In the latter city, Bates addressed a crowd of several thousand. On the evening of May 7, she addressed another throng at Mount Carmel Baptist Church in Washington, DC. Regarding the Scottsboro Boys, she stated unequivocally that they had been framed *"not only by the boys and girls on the freight train, of which I was one, but by the bosses of the southern counties."*[24] The next day, the marchers reached the White House, where President Franklin Delano Roosevelt, two months into his first term, refused to see them, though an official did accept a petition. The wave of people moved on to the Capitol. Inside, William Patterson and a small group of supporters managed to secure a brief meeting with Vice President John Garner and Speaker of the House Henry Rainey.

In the June edition of *Working Woman*, Louise summarized her perspective, arguing that the march represented a watershed moment of interracial solidarity, symbolized by the joint appearance of Bates and Janie Patterson, Haywood Patterson's mother.[25] That same month, Judge Horton, not convinced by the prosecution's case, set aside Patterson's conviction and ordered a new trial, which Louise took as proof that mass-pressure tactics worked. But Horton did considerably less than he could have. Because voiding the conviction and releasing Patterson was an option, Horton's decision not to do so delayed but did not resolve matters.[26] Yet he provided hope that eventually the defense would prevail.

During this time, Louise welcomed Ada Wright and Janie Patterson to her home on several occasions. She described Wright as very alert and likened her to Frederick Douglass given her travels in Europe to elicit support for antiracist endeavors back home.[27] Patterson proved much quieter, staring out of the window for hours; she chewed snuff and used a tin can as an improvised spittoon. "I don't know that I ever knew what she was thinking about," Louise recalled.[28] However, she stressed that Patterson, along with Wright, was always engaged when it was time to face the crowds.[29]

In the lull between dramatic legal developments, funding for the work of the ILD and the National Committee for the Defense of Political Prisoners, always precarious, became even more problematic. Louise had been making only twenty-five dollars per week, but there was no guarantee that even that arrangement would last. She started inquiring about a more stable position, and through her connection to James Ford and, through him, Communist Party USA (CPUSA) general secretary Earl Browder, she found employment with the International Workers Order (IWO), the fraternal insurance society operated by the Communist Party; its Harlem headquarters were located over Frank's Restaurant, a popular eatery on 125th Street off of St. Nicholas Avenue. "They had a business to run," she explained, "so you got paid."[30] She would still receive only twenty-five dollars per week as a clerical worker, but she could count on it. The IWO, founded in 1930, had sprung from the left wing of the Workmen's Circle, a Jewish mutual benefit society. A rapidly growing federation of nearly forty thousand members, the IWO, besides offering insurance, provided a cultural and familial grounding for large numbers of immigrant workers. It incorporated a large Jewish division as well as English, Hungarian, Italian, Polish, Romanian, Russian, Slovak, and Ukrainian sections. The job suited Louise's political temperament. As she assessed, "it wasn't the Congregationalists or Mrs. Mason or the social workers or the staff at Hampton doing things for somebody else. It was people working together to do something for themselves."[31]

While working with the IWO, Louise joined the Communist Party. However, she minimized the momentous decision: "When they found out that I was not a member of the Party, somebody came and just put a card in my hand, and I signed it just like that."[32] In a way, Louise's almost-parenthetical remarks about joining the party were appropriate. She mainly performed political and cultural work among artists and intellectuals. That would not change. In addition, she would still be involved with the ILD. She didn't work in the party apparatus, and given that the party embraced a united-front strategy in the spring of 1933, no pressure existed for her to be more of a hard-liner than she already was. She dismissed the inquiry of Mike Gold, a left-wing Jewish writer, when he greeted her, "Hi, Louise, you still working for that damned petit bourgeois insurance organization?"[33] For her, joining the party fulfilled a desire to voice and develop her political convictions freely and confidently while being anchored in and supported by a powerful organization seeking fundamental change.[34]

If Louise later downplayed her decision to join the Communist Party, several concerned friends and mentors immediately perceived the danger in her enrollment. Mary McCleod Bethune tried to dissuade her. Elmer Carter, the editor of *Opportunity*, argued that a person with her qualifications could enjoy a big future in the Democratic Party. Her mentor W. E. B. Du Bois also expressed concern; emotionally, it was probably hardest for Louise to disagree with him.[35] He was not a strong ideological opponent of Communism; in fact, he had recently published an anticapitalist essay, "Marxism and the Negro Problem," in the *Crisis*. He acknowledged the merits of Marxism, despite some logical flaws, with respect to its analysis of Europe in the nineteenth century. But he saw the need for modifications in the theory for application to the U.S. context, especially the situation of African American workers, who were being exploited not by a black capitalist class but by white capitalists *and* a white proletariat. Du Bois therefore concluded that "internal organization" to ward off both white usurpation and black capitalist tendencies was required.[36] Obviously, Du Bois had reservations about whether Communist plans best addressed the needs of the African American proletariat. However, Louise saw a future in Communism that worked. She conveyed her final decision to Du Bois firmly but respectfully: "Well, it has been your way for all of this time and look where we are. Some of us younger people have the right to move further."[37]

Louise also tried to expand her activities within the IWO. As she sat in the office writing low-cost coverage that would yield several thousand dollars per customer, she began to think that African Americans could benefit from joining the IWO because the available term policies were better than what most of them had access to, especially in the South. She knew that insurance salesmen worked their "debt routes" and collected dimes and quarters every week for virtually worthless financial instruments.[38] They hawked the notorious industrial insurance, policies that were more expensive and had lower face values than ordinary life insurance. Because of the resultant ratio of premiums to face values, policyholders would often have been better off if they had remained uninsured. Over a thirty-year period, for example, one would typically pay almost 90 percent of the face value of a burial policy of only $150–$200. The same money saved, plus interest, would have yielded almost as much—or could have purchased much more insurance at competitive rates. However, companies like Metropolitan Life provided incentives to salesmen to saddle African Americans with industrial insurance.[39]

Ultimately, Louise construed the discriminatory practices as an issue of workers' rights as well, and she took to the pages of the *Negro Liberator* to explain the relationship between "proletarian fraternalism" and "Negro liberation." She saw the IWO, with its egalitarian approach, as a model and mechanism for uniting workers across ethnicities in a fight for broader social protections such as unemployment benefits. She urged support for the Workers Unemployment Insurance Bill, introduced in the House of Representatives by Minnesota congressman Ernest Lundeen. At the same time, she hurled acid remarks at conservatives within the leadership of the American Federation of Labor, whom she felt had betrayed workers by collaborating with government authorities to quell labor demonstrations. Speaking directly to African Americans among her readership, she ripped the idea of unconditional race loyalty, arguing that black bourgeois leaders who scrambled for crumbs in Washington and tried to sabotage a working-class agenda did not deserve African American allegiance. Nor did they, in her view, fool Negro workers.[40]

By the time she wrote this for the *Negro Liberator*, Louise had maneuvered her way from clerical worker to field organizer in the IWO. Relying on trade unions and churches as primary contact points, she traveled widely to organize chapters of the IWO. The effort took her back to the South on many occasions, to states like Virginia, Georgia, Louisiana, and Alabama. The southern campaign tripped, not surprisingly, over Jim Crow. States resisted issuing insurance licenses to interracial groups. The IWO eventually deemphasized the region but not before Louise had added some intense and sometimes harrowing episodes to her activist résumé.

In the spring of 1934, she was in Birmingham, the meanest city she ever visited.[41] The city stirred with many causes in which the organized Left could become involved.[42] The center of the heaviest industry in the South because of the abundant supply of iron ore and coal, Birmingham was also an arena of rampant unemployment and pitched battles between bosses and workers. Strikes were commonplace and involved thousands of launderers, textile hands, and packinghouse employees, as well as miners.[43] By the beginning of May, the city was abuzz with the impending strike by the International Union of Mine, Mill and Smelter Workers against the area's iron, steel, and coal companies. The integrated union, known locally by some as the "nigger union," demanded shorter hours, better wages, and improved work conditions overall.[44] Tensions reached a climax at the May Day rally in Capitol Park. Five thousand people attended even though the city had revoked the parade permit. The police, using their own force and the violence of the White Legionnaires, shut down the proposed program. As a follow-up tactic, police chief E. I. Hollums ordered raids by the Red Squad, a unit headed by detective J. T. Moser. The net ensnared Louise.

In her quest to learn all she could about local struggles so that she could convey that information to progressive allies, she had sought out Elizabeth Lawson, who wrote for and edited the *Southern Worker*. Louise entered

Lawson's apartment building, located in a white community, and knocked on the door of the apartment to which she had been directed. A policeman opened the door while Lawson announced in the background, "We don't have any sewing for you today."[45] Not fooled, the officer brusquely ordered Louise into the apartment and arrested her along with several others. She was jailed and "held for investigation," without being allowed to contact friends or an attorney.[46] "Upon the head of Louise Thompson," the ILD would later argue, "the rulers of Birmingham hope to pour their vengeance for the strike wave, for the startlingly powerful May Day demonstration."[47]

After a night in a holding pen with fourteen other black women, and after being served what could only liberally be called breakfast, Louise was photographed, fingerprinted, and hauled before a judge at the Jefferson County courthouse, where, ironically, three of the Scottsboro defendants were being held. During hostile questioning, her jailers made suggestive remarks about her possible intimacy with the white men with whom she had been arrested. When she refused to answer certain questions before consulting with an attorney, the authorities threatened to beat her with a rubber hose or turn her over to the Ku Klux Klan. Although she still did not know the formal charges against her, she knew that she had committed at least one more "crime" by violating the rules of courtroom decorum. An officer wagged his finger and admonished, "See here, gal, you're arrested now, see. And you say 'yes sir' and 'no sir.' "[48] Actually, one of her cell mates, an accused pickpocket named Pinky, had offered the same advice, albeit in a friendly manner: "When you go down there, don't you be no goddam fool. When that white man asks you a question, you say, 'yes, sir, no sir.' That won't cost you nothing, Honey, but it'll save you plenty of hard knocks."[49] Louise became too enraged to heed Pinky's words. She recalled, "I was ready to die before 'Sir' would cross my lips."[50]

Later that day, friends managed to establish contact with Louise and secure Brodsky as her attorney; he filed a writ of habeas corpus so that Louise had to be either charged or released. Thus, she was returned to the courthouse, where Moser escorted her into the courtroom. The detective, who boasted of eleven notches on his gun representing Negroes he had shot, told Louise, "We ought to handle you reds like Mussolini does 'em in Italy—take you out and shoot you against a wall. And I sure would like to have the pleasure of doing it."[51] He settled for producing a warrant for arrest for vagrancy. Louise paid the bail of $300 and had to appear for trial ten days later.

As Louise sat in the Negro section of the courthouse waiting for her case to be called by Judge Abernathy, she noted that police officers and White Legion members interceded in cases, suggesting to Abernathy or the prosecutors how to interrogate African Americans. A standard retort to a defendant who disputed incriminating testimony was "Nigger, do you dare to dispute the word of a white man?" Louise wrote afterward, "Here was 'southern justice' undisturbed by any militant interference!"[52]

Louise easily won her own case given her documented employment. During the proceedings, she upbraided Judge Abernathy for his, the prosecutor's, and the witnesses' use of the epithet *nigger*.[53] Abernathy, however, seemed more interested in the threat that her phenotype posed to segregation in Birmingham. As she recounted, "Wonder where this gal is from? Looks like she came from Mississippi—that's the way they mix up down there. Course it's got nothing to do with the case, but I'm going to ask her where she was born as I'm mighty interested in how these mixtures turn out."[54]

At the conclusion of the trial, another warrant was issued charging Louise with concealing her identity, which she had done until the trial to protect the family with whom she had lodged. The police promptly rearrested her, but the warrant was shortly vacated. In Louise's estimation, the Birmingham power structure, having become aware that significant numbers were prepared to mobilize on her behalf, didn't feel that her case was important enough to justify engaging in such controversy on top of all the protests already under way.[55] She was spared those hard knocks about which Pinky had warned her. However, the details of the matter were slightly more legally involved and dramatic than Louise revealed in her memoir.

After arriving in Atlanta, the next stop on her campaign, Louise wrote to C. B. Powell, the Birmingham attorney who had assisted Brodsky with her case. She expressed thoughts about her second arrest: "I have been thinking of this quite a bit since Friday and I cannot see how in the world giving another name under such circumstances can be construed as a crime, that is legally. Suppose that is a name under which I do writing? Or what about people who use other names professionally? Or just suppose, as was my case, that I did not care to have known my real identity in the frame-up perpetrated? I shall appreciate your legal opinion on the case."[56]

That same day, after reading the current issue of the *Negro Liberator*, she wrote even more spirited letters to Brodsky and IWO official Sadie Doroshkin. The paper had incorrectly reported that Louise had been organizing among the striking mill workers and miners, including picketing, and that those activities had led her to run afoul of the "ruling class and Birmingham police."[57] She asked Doroshkin to consult with Brodsky and IWO head Max

Bedacht to address the question of proper publicity. "As it is," she wrote, "I scarcely think it is going to be possible for me to work in Birmingham for I suspect the White Legion will have this article posted on their front window and I will be watched constantly every minute I am in town."[58] More urgently, she worried that the article would expose her to further liability in court. Reasoning along with Atlanta-based Communist lawyer Ben Davis, who would move to New York the following year and would, in fact, edit the *Negro Liberator*, she felt that Birmingham authorities might press more charges given that "now the LIBERATOR comes out and pretty damn near makes me the leader of the strike."[59] "It isn't necessary in order to make a story," she continued, "for the fact that I was picked up with absolutely no grounds for arrest and that they are trying to hold me with no basis for it whatsoever is damaging enough."[60] Imagining that Brodsky would deal with the matter appropriately, she concluded, "I hope you give them hell!"[61]

It turned out that Powell provided the speediest relief. A few days after Louise's letter, he secured the solicitor's recommendation to nol-pros the case before Abernathy, providing a payment of $8.25, which Powell had made from the bail money. He stated that there was "little question" Louise would have been acquitted, but the expenses involved would have exceeded the amount paid.[62] Fortunately, the rougher scenario envisioned by Louise and Davis never materialized. Louise was perhaps correct to credit activists in Birmingham for that. She also felt gratitude toward the Deltas. Jeannette Triplett Jones, the national president of the Deltas, wrote, "This message comes from hundreds of sorors who want to stretch out their hands to you across the distance and silence that separates to say that your welfare, your comfort and your safety is our heartfelt concern. Thoughts of love and cheer and consolation go out from us to you for are you not one with us through the bond of devotion?"[63]

In the *Crisis*, a tried-and-true vehicle for Louise, Du Bois agreed to publish a written account of her experiences in Birmingham. She titled the article "Southern Terror," and Du Bois ran it in the November issue; he described Louise as the "leading colored woman in the Communist movement in this country."[64] If nothing else, she wrote like it. Beyond recounting the legal aspects, she blasted the White Legion as an "openly fascist," anticommunist organization, and she excoriated the local press in Birmingham for its biased and inflammatory reportage regarding "red violence," "red plots," and "social equality." She aimed barbs at African American organizations that opposed militant mass protest by blacks; she considered them pawns of the ruling class. Such groups, in her view, "accept the present system of capitalism and are willing to be satisfied with what hollow reforms may come without any fundamental change." Louise argued that a true program for Negro rights had to be revolutionary because it had to seek the destruction of American capitalism, the system through which millionaire financiers and a managerial stratum exploited black and white labor and perpetuated white supremacy. She concluded, "Any organizations among the Negro people which do not point out these class alignments must therefore become the voice of reaction in the midst of a people struggling for freedom. So it is that the leadership among the Negro people must pass into new hands—into the hands of working class leaders, the Angelo Herndons, who will not be stopped by jail, by a desire to cling on to jobs, by death itself in leading the Negro people through the final conflict to complete emancipation."[65]

Louise was also in the South in October when she received word that the relationship between Leibowitz and the ILD, always fragile, had almost irretrievably disintegrated. After two ILD attorneys, Samuel Schriftman and Sol Kone, were arrested in Nashville for allegedly trying to bribe Victoria Price (a case that was never prosecuted), the opportunistic Leibowitz, who always asserted that he was more concerned with the "rights of man" and racial fairness than any "controversial theory of economy or government," seized the chance to wrest control from the ILD and distance himself from the Communist Party.[66] He hurriedly met with several influential Harlem clergymen and with publisher William H. Davis to get the unqualified backing of the *Amsterdam News*. He began to publicly allege that the Communist Party and the ILD were benefiting from the Scottsboro "cash cow" while jeopardizing the lives of the nine Scottsboro defendants for political purposes and using the case to foment racial discord in the South.[67] In the meantime, even as he threatened to remove himself as counsel, he dispatched an assistant to Kilby Prison in Montgomery, while his secretary (John Terry) and several political allies traveled to Chattanooga to meet with Ada Wright and the parents of Haywood Patterson. As a result, Patterson and Clarence Norris signed on with Leibowitz, while Ada Wright announced in writing that she wished no further involvement by the ILD in the defense of her sons.[68]

Leibowitz had proved to be a more formidable opponent of the ILD than the NAACP because of his personal relationships with his clients. William L. Patterson and the ILD responded by further playing to what had been their strengths, that is, their connections with several of the parents. Knowing that those bonds could again be the trump card, Patterson sent word to Louise in

Atlanta, where she was traveling for the IWO, to see if she would go to Chattanooga to counter the blitz by Leibowitz. Because the IWO had provided her with a car, she could proceed with haste. At the same time, attorney Ben Davis headed to Montgomery to reason with Clarence Norris, his mother (Ida Norris), and Haywood Patterson.

Louise visited Ada Wright the following day. She picked her up from her job in an affluent section of town where she worked as a domestic. Her boss happened to be leaving at the same time as Wright, and Louise offered him a ride as well. During the trip he remarked, "You know, I don't mind if Ada teams up with you, you folks. I've no objection about it. But the thing is you gotta tell her not to be sassy. Don't talk back and stay in her place." Louise was somewhat enlightened: "Now, that was a liberal!"[69]

She persuaded Wright, who agreed to ride with her to Montgomery for a demonstration. She changed Janie Patterson's mind also, but the second woman wouldn't agree to leave for Alabama because she said she had to care for her granddaughter. In the meantime, Terry had Janie's husband, Claude Patterson, in tow and was headed to Montgomery by train. Louise rushed to the depot to contest for Patterson, literally tugging at him when he boarded the train. But she lost the encounter. Heartbroken, she turned back to Janie Patterson and begged as hard as she knew how. When Louise pulled out of Chattanooga, she had Janie Patterson in the passenger seat. They beat Claude Patterson and Terry to Montgomery—a shock to both—because the men had to wait on the train from Birmingham. The women linked up with Davis, who had managed to keep Ida Norris under the ILD banner but not (for the moment) Clarence Norris and Haywood Patterson. (The defendants would jump back and forth between the ILD and Leibowitz at least half a dozen times.)

By October 23 Leibowitz had temporarily gained control of all nine cases. Moreover, several defendants had written to the governor of Alabama, Benjamin Miller, asking that he bar Communists and their representatives from further participation on their behalf. On October 24 Janie Patterson arrived in New York by train, ostensibly to support Leibowitz. He was among the group that greeted her at Pennsylvania Station, as were Terry and entertainer Bill "Bojangles" Robinson, who had become visible and active in raising funds for the newly formed American Scottsboro Committee, which rivaled the older committees concerned with the defense of the Scottsboro Boys. Not to be outdone, Ben Davis, accompanied by Ida Norris and Ada Wright, reached New York on October 25. They would appear with Scottsboro mothers Josephine Powell and Viola Montgomery at the Rockland Palace on Friday evening, October 29. All of the ILD mainstays in Harlem, with the exception of William L. Patterson (who had left for Russia suffering from exhaustion and possibly tuberculosis), mounted an offensive against Leibowitz. However, they faced an especially difficult rhetorical challenge. Many among the subdued audience of three hundred had copies of the latest issue of the *Amsterdam News*, in which Leibowitz and his associate George Chamlee had charged that by failing to request an appeal and file a bill of exception within the required time period, the ILD had flubbed the appeal process in the case of Haywood Patterson, who had been convicted and sentenced a third time, and thus had perhaps doomed him to the electric chair.[70] In fact, Janie Patterson reportedly threatened lawsuits against Brodsky and ILD appeal attorney Osmond Fraenkel if their errors prevented her son's case from being argued before the U.S. Supreme Court. Therefore, Ben Davis had no takers when, after attacking Leibowitz, William H. Davis, and others for more than an hour, he thundered, "Who'll give $10 to support the International Labor Defense and run Sam Leibowitz out of the Scottsboro case?" Flustered, he tried soliciting five-dollar and then two-dollar contributions while the speakers on the platform shifted anxiously. Ada Wright eyed her copy of the *Amsterdam News* and then handed it to Ida Norris. Only when Davis lowered the asking price to one dollar did he provoke a positive, though scattered, response.[71]

Whatever support, courtesy, and patience the audience extended were undoubtedly due to the presence of the four Scottsboro mothers. Josephine Powell, Viola Montgomery, and Ida Norris unequivocally endorsed the ILD, but Ada Wright spoke with mixed feelings. She recounted the visit to Chattanooga by Reverend Lorenzo H. King and Reverend Richard M. Bolden, which had led her to sign an affidavit ousting the ILD. Then she spoke of Louise's subsequent visit, during which Louise convinced her to back the ILD once again. However, she reminded the audience that she had not been able to persuade her sons to remain with the ILD, and, to Davis's chagrin, she aired Roy Wright's criticism of the organization. Growing increasingly bitter, young Wright, echoing Leibowitz, had questioned how the funds raised for the Scottsboro defendants were being disbursed and had wondered whether the ILD had been focused enough. "I don't want to know what they're doing for somebody in Germany," he had told his mother. "I want to know what they're doing for Roy Wright in Alabama."[72] Actually, ILD lawyers would perform further work for all of the defendants and eventually renewed a degree of cooperation with Leibowitz.

As machinations involving the Scottsboro Nine resonated in Harlem and beyond, Louise received a poignant reminder of how far she had traveled both emotionally and politically over the past six years when Wallace Thurman died from tuberculosis in City Hospital on Welfare Island on December 22, 1934. He was thirty-two years old. A newspaper account indicated that Louise had chosen the class struggle while Thurman remained a bohemian.[73] Of course, their breakup refused so neat an explanation. Deep feelings and much confusion had been in play and perhaps still were. Louise once remarked that she was glad that Thurman died, a statement that was not cruelly meant but reflected her exasperation; she had felt she would never be fully free of him in life.[74] But she acted humanely toward him during his final days, tending to him at the hospital after he had summoned her through Hughes.[75] And she respectfully attended his funeral on Christmas Eve, held at Levy and Delany Funeral Home on 134th Street, virtually around the corner from where he and Louise, in the early days of their friendship, had watched the crowds go by. On hand were Louise's good friend Alta Douglas, through whom she had met Thurman, and a significant portion of Thurman's Harlem Renaissance cohort, including Iolanthe Sidney, Countee Cullen, Harold Jackman, Bruce Nugent, Rose McClendon, and Dorothy West.

Now that she was officially no longer married, what were Louise's prospects? She never revealed very much or seemed particularly stressed about it. She remained cryptic about the fact that she once dated the handsome James Ford, her impressive comrade and former Fisk footballer.[76] She implied that she had rejected the advances of Harry Haywood.[77] Loren Miller had married Juanita Ellsworth and sometimes, according to Louise, expressed regret about it.[78] But she had closed that door to her heart. She later summed up, "Don't waste any sleepless nights over love affairs that didn't last or didn't exist."[79] William L. Patterson always held her attention when he was around, even as she remained wary of him. It didn't matter at that point, however, because Patterson was back in the Soviet Union with his wife. So, viewed from the outside, it seemed that Louise's firmest romantic attachments were to her crusades for justice. Perhaps she surmised that ideology was less fickle than people.

CHAPTER 7

Popular Fronts, 1935–1937

ino Rivera sparked the next phase of Louise Thompson's political development by shoplifting a penknife in the E. H. Kress Five and Ten Store at 256 West 125th Street on the afternoon of Tuesday, March 19, 1935. When two employees, Steve Urban and Charles Hurley, nabbed Rivera and threatened to take him downstairs for punishment, the teenager frantically grabbed hold of a pillar and bit the hands of his captors. Despite the boy's resistance, the two men managed to deliver him, not to the basement, but to the front entrance. There they turned him over to a mounted policeman, Officer Raymond Donahue. Donahue took Rivera to the rear of the store and asked the manager, Jackson Smith, if he wanted Rivera arrested. By that time, another officer, based with the Crime Prevention Bureau, had arrived. Smith decided that the boy should be released, and Donahue, nervous about the forming crowd of curious and agitated onlookers, took the shoplifter to the basement and let him out the rear exit, which opened onto 124th Street. But an excited witness, who was subsequently arrested, screamed that the cops had hauled Rivera to the basement to beat him.[1] Given the history of police brutality in Harlem, the assertion seemed plausible to the African American spectators, and their anxiety escalated when an ambulance arrived at Kress. The medics treated the employees' bite wounds and departed. However, the ambulance's departure without a patient inside signaled to some that Rivera had been killed. This supposition gained traction when a hearse pulled up to the back entrance. The driver was visiting his brother-in-law; however, most thought he came to transport a lifeless body. Thus converged a petty theft, an improbable sequence of events, and a history of adversarial relations between disenchanted Harlem residents and discriminatory merchants like the owners of Kress, who despite protests had refused to hire black clerks. One woman punctuated the proceedings by exclaiming, "Just like down South where they lynch us."[2]

Whether Louise happened on the scene or had been directed to it remains a matter of dispute. She claimed it was a coincidence.[3] Her office at the IWO was only one block away, and by five o'clock she had joined the observers inside Kress trying to ascertain what had transpired. The lower level of the store was fairly quiet. No clerks manned the various counters, but staff could be spotted on the mezzanine peeking out of their offices. As frustrations mounted, a woman next to Louise waved an umbrella and knocked an arrangement of drinking glasses to the floor. More people surged in from the street and began trashing merchandise and toppling displays. Rather than attempting to defuse the situation, the police began to chase people from the store and answered queries by stating that the Rivera affair was none of their business.[4] Louise later said she had asked a cop, "Officer, why don't you tell people what happened to the boy?" She had added, "That's all they want to know. They don't want to make any trouble." Whatever her efforts, the cop yelled at her, "Get the hell out of here," and shoved her. "Then I realized how you create a riot," recalled Louise. "Because at that time, anger flushed in me. You know, you are trying to help. Although he didn't hit me, his words provoked me as much as a blow would have."[5]

The people around her also realized how to create a riot. Although Kress had closed by 5:30, a furious crowd remained outside the store; the numbers swelled into the thousands as the Young Liberators, the youth wing of the League of Struggle for Negro Rights, set up for a demonstration. But people were not in the mood for speeches. Shortly into the flow of words, someone threw a rock through the front window of Kress, a rock symbolizing all of the community's rage about unemployment, job discrimination, high prices, bad meat, high rents, evictions, ineffective bureaucracies, police violence, and their general subjugation. The sound and sight of shattering glass set off frenzied destruction and looting all along the block. As the police battled to restore order, Louise saw black women pull African American officers off of their horses. The women declared, "Shame, shame, going against your kind."[6] She admired them, commenting, "They had lost all sense of danger. They were ready to do anything. They were so outraged."[7]

By seven o'clock, the worst outburst of Harlem's first major riot had ended. All plate glass windows between Seventh and Eighth Avenues had been smashed. The police arrested dozens of protestors and dispersed the main group, but the violence flared out, reaching from St. Nicholas Avenue in the west to Fifth Avenue in the east, and from 120th Street in the south to 138th Street in the north. Rioters targeted white-owned businesses but not exclusively. Posted signs announcing "COLORED STORE" or "COLORED HELP EMPLOYED HERE" likely saved a business or two. Louise saw a sign in a Chinese laundry, "ME COLORED TOO," anticipating by fifty-four years the Korean merchant's "ME BLACK, ME BLACK, ME NO WHITE" overture in Spike Lee's *Do the Right Thing*.[8] Therefore, the riot was not strictly racial. It was widely known that the police had assaulted white protesters during the riot, and the black community evinced sympathy for those victims. But when a group that Louise was walking among approached a white couple on Seventh Avenue, a woman in the group smacked the white woman in the face without breaking stride.

Louise observed looters throwing groceries up to people in second-floor apartments. She saw folks in dry cleaning establishments trying on clothes and absconding with the articles they chose. She undoubtedly saw the leaflets distributed by the Young Liberators and the Young Communist League claiming that Rivera had been brutally beaten. Police in riot gear patrolled the streets. Gunfire and sirens echoed through the darkness. Perhaps the most tragic incident occurred when patrolman John Heineray fatally wounded Lloyd Hobbs, a high school student who was returning home from the movies. Amid a crowd on Seventh Avenue near 128th Street that scattered when Heineray approached, brandishing his weapon, Hobbs was shot as he ran away. He survived the night but died several days later.

In a belated attempt to halt the disturbance, authorities fetched Rivera from his home and photographed him with an African American police lieutenant, Samuel Battle. This led only to charges that Rivera was not the real victim but had been cast as such to deceive the public. Also ineffective were the posters urging peace that were circulated by the order of Mayor Fiorello La Guardia. By the time the turmoil ceased, looters had struck hundreds of business establishments, and the police had arrested dozens of rioters. Louise roamed the streets until two o'clock in the morning talking with numerous people and hearing firsthand of their combustive resentment.

In the aftermath of the riot, critics reserved their harshest judgments for the Communists. William Dodge, the Manhattan district attorney, ordered raids on the party offices with the aim of gathering material for indictments on charges of anarchy. One of Randolph Hearst's newspapers, the *New York American*, featured an editorial questioning the wisdom of granting Communists freedom of speech.[9] La Guardia, however, did not condemn the

Communists or the rioters. Instead, he formed the biracial Mayor's Commission on Conditions in Harlem, headed by Dr. Charles Roberts, to which he appointed Eunice Hunton Carter, Countee Cullen, Hubert Delany, Morris Ernst, Colonel John Grimley, Arthur Garfield Hays, Father William Mc-Cann, A. Philip Randolph, William Jay Schieffelin, Judge Charles Toney, and Oswald Garrison Villard. The committee conducted twenty-five hearings over the next two months, intended to frame accurately the problems in the district. In addition, La Guardia charged the committee to propose solutions.

Supremely organized and prepared, Louise and her comrades turned the hearings into forums in which they could articulate at length many of their ideas and platforms to a broad cross section of Harlem residents. Led in theorizing and strategizing by the chief Communist Party organizer in Harlem, James Ford, who had begun pushing the notion of the "popular front," the party's top leaders in Harlem who were of the professional class spoke at the hearings.[10] Coming off as clear-eyed and articulate, these spokespersons, along with Abner Berry and Merrill Work, seemed every bit as respectable as other positive civic leaders. The hearings provided them crucial leverage in Harlem and enabled them to build important alliances, including with Adam Clayton Powell Jr., who was destined to become Harlem's most popular political advocate, and labor leader Randolph, a former party nemesis. Locally, Louise and her colleagues also rose in stature relative to the NAACP, which had remained curiously passive in the months following the riot and did not participate formally in the commission's activities.

The first session, held on March 30 at the Seventh District Municipal Building on 151st Street with six hundred people in attendance, addressed the immediate causes of the uprising.[11] Louise, Ford, Berry, radical journalist Robert Minor, and attorneys Edward Kuntz and Joseph Tauber represented the Communist Party. Asked by Hays, the general counsel of the American Civil Liberties Union, about what immediately precipitated the mass violence, Louise blamed the police while defending the actions of the Young Liberators.[12]

After listening to her testimony, Delany declared Louise to be the "best liar that he ever heard."[13] She later commented, "He seemed to go for the Communist-agitators story."[14] Plenty of others were skeptical as well, but additional witnesses supported her testimony, and in the end the commission determined that Louise's claims were tenable. In fact, members of the police department admitted under cross-examination that the riot could have been avoided had the officers on the scene been more responsive to the concerned black citizens who surrounded them.[15] As for the role of the Young Liberators and the Young Communist League in fomenting unrest, the panel ascertained that the leaflets distributed by those groups, while irresponsible, appeared *after* the worst of the rioting and therefore had not instigated it.[16] It wrote, "At no time does it seem that these crowds were under the direction of any single individual or that they acted as a part of a conspiracy against law and order."[17] Further, the commission concluded that Communist organizations deserved "more credit than any other element in Harlem for preventing a physical conflict between whites and blacks."[18] Most notably, the final report reflected the dominant interpretation in the community: "The explosion on March 19 would never have been set off by the trifling incident described above had not existing economic and social forces created a state of emotional tension which sought release upon the slightest provocation. As long as the economic and social forces which were responsible for that condition continue to operate, a state of tension will exist in Harlem and recurrent outbursts may occur."[19]

With an enhanced image in Harlem political and social circles, Louise and fellow members of the Communist Party were well positioned to help forge the prescribed Popular Front, officially confirmed at the Comintern's Seventh World Congress in August. In street and town hall meetings across Harlem, they participated in various movements, from transethnic labor union efforts to nationalist protests against Benito Mussolini's militarism toward Ethiopia to electoral bargaining. From the party's perspective, strengthening the panoply of organizations fighting racial discrimination and economic exploitation served the party's emphasis on class struggle and anti-Fascism. Simultaneously, party advocates stressed that their analyses of race, class, and Fascism should be central to how other progressive groups envisioned their own work.

This reasoning found expression at the national level with the formation of the National Negro Congress, in part an outgrowth of the Joint Committee on National Recovery established by John P. Davis and Robert Weaver in 1933. By the spring of 1935, Weaver had accepted a position in the Roosevelt administration, and Davis had become disgruntled with the attempts at control made by the NAACP, the most prominent member of the lobbying consortium. By that time, party leaders in Harlem, most prominently Ford, who was in conversation with Davis, were contemplating the creation of a federation of black organizations. Ultimately, Ford and the party relied on Davis to take the initiative, which led the latter to convene a conference in

May at Howard University under the title "The Position of the Negro in Our National Economic Crisis." The conference attracted 150 workers, political operatives, administrators, and academics from around the country. At its conclusion, Davis and Ralph Bunche gathered a select assemblage at Bunche's apartment to concretize plans for the new organization. The members of the resultant National Sponsoring Committee included Ford, Randolph, Elmer Carter, Alain Locke, and Charles Houston.[20] When Davis and Bunche's cadre announced that the founding convention would take place in mid-February in Chicago, a New York sponsoring committee was organized during a meeting at the Harlem YWCA. Louise, Ford, and Ben Davis joined the likes of Powell, Houston, and Roy Wilkins as members of that body. Even though august NAACP officers Wilkins and Houston participated, Walter White and the NAACP board, fearing Communist dominance, refused to align formally with the incipient congress or support it financially. Notwithstanding, tremendous support existed for the idea of the National Negro Congress, a council that would rival the NAACP in influence.

Although the founding convention proved successful, it did not run entirely according to plan. Inside the Eighth Regiment Armory, just one block from her former residence on Giles Avenue, Louise mixed with 816 other delegates for three days, on February 14–16, 1936. All told, they represented almost six hundred organizations nationwide.[21] Plenary sessions drew several thousand visitors, largely from the South Side community. Crowds even listened outside the armory, where loudspeakers kept them informed. Also on hand, however, was Chicago's Red Squad, reminding conventioneers of the censorship threat that hung over the gathering, a foreshadowing that became real when Colonel William Warfield, hinting at orders from "higher up," barred Earl Browder, the chairman and general secretary of the National Committee of the CPUSA, from speaking at the closing session. Socialist Party leader Norman Thomas said that he was humiliated that the ban did not also include him.[22] Certainly, Communists participated freely in the meetings, among them Louise, Ford, Berry, Work, Manning Johnson, Ben Davis, Richard B. Moore, and Angelo Herndon (out on bail). But the authorities drew the line at Browder. They provoked a brief uproar—and Thomas's comment—but the organizers and attendees remained disciplined in conveying a Popular-Front disposition. John P. Davis articulated, "The Congress was not formed and does not exist to duplicate the work of any existing organization. Rather it exists to add strength and to give support to every progressive and meaningful program in aid of the Negro people in their just demand for equal opportunity and complete social and economic rights."[23]

Louise and her Harlem colleagues applauded John P. Davis's election to the post of national secretary. Randolph was elected president in absentia. The convention selected Louise's former apartment mate Marion Cuthbert to be treasurer; Ford, Berry, and Ben Davis landed on the executive committee. The sessions themselves covered anticipated topics: sharecroppers' rights, union organizing, arts initiatives, economic efforts, lynching, Jim Crow, and the Second Italo-Ethiopian War—Mussolini's forces were close to claiming victory. Also addressed was the issue of how black women fit into the labor movement, a matter of particular interest to Louise. In the preamble to a resolution, conventioneers acknowledged that black women were subjected to "three-fold exploitation as women, as workers and as Negroes and . . . forced through discrimination into the most menial labor under the worst conditions without organizational protection."[24] The National Negro Congress unanimously adopted the resolution, presented by Nellie Hazell of the Negro Democratic League of Philadelphia, to unionize domestic workers, promote housewives' leagues, and organize women's groups into a united front to improve the conditions of all working-class families.[25] Louise saw the passage of the measure as the beginning of a practical program.[26] Equally important, she optimistically read the attendees' actions as first steps toward the broad coalition of women needed to address effectively the relevant concerns: "Women club leaders from California greeted women trade unionists from New York. Women schoolteachers made friends with women domestic workers. Women from the relief agencies talked over relief problems with women relief clients. Women from mothers' clubs and housewives' leagues exchanged experiences in fighting against the high cost of living. Negro women welcomed the white women delegates who came to the Congress as an evidence of the growing sense of unity between them."[27]

Louise included her reflections on the conference in an article titled "Toward a Brighter Dawn," published in the April issue of *Woman Today*. She coupled them with an analysis of the "triple exploitation" discussed in Chicago.[28] Although she had alluded to black female subjectivity in writings and musings about the Russian experiment, the Scottsboro mothers, her own arrest in Birmingham, and the outrage of Harlem rioters, she had not made an expansive theoretical statement explicitly linking such a subject position to oppression. To do so, she paralleled the plight of black southern domestic workers and field hands with the situation of the black women who assembled daily in Bronx Park to be chosen for day labor at ten or fifteen cents per hour. This latter practice, known as the "Bronx Slave Market," had been the subject of an exposé in the *Crisis* five months earlier, written by activist Ella Baker and the muckraker Marvel Cooke.[29] Louise explained how black women, in her view the most exploited members of the American working class, faced almost-insurmountable odds as they tried to hold their families together while enduring racism and coping with a prolonged economic crisis. Then, turning to her memories of the National Negro Congress convention, she mentioned a number of the dynamic participants, including Tarea Hall Pittman, formerly a fellow student at Berkeley and now the president of the Federation of Women's Clubs of California. She forecast that they would have tales of significant progress to share at the next convention.[30]

As the National Negro Congress and allied women's groups struggled to gain momentum, Louise continued her ascent through the ranks of the IWO and kept her hand in cultural and political developments in Harlem. At the end of February, Max Bedacht, IWO's general executive secretary, announced her promotion to national secretary of the English section, which consisted of ten thousand members.[31] She soon left for a two-week tour of Virginia on behalf of the IWO, then returned home in time to cosponsor a forum at the Delano Hotel on the minimum wage, an urgent issue given the recent abrogation of the minimum-wage law for women in New York City. Speakers included Congressman Vito Marcantonio, Mrs. E. M. Herrick of the National Labor Relations Board, Francis Gorman of the United Textile Workers of America, and Jessie Taft of the Laundry Workers' Union. Taking advantage of a relative respite at home, she caught the opening night of *Macbeth* at the Lafayette Theatre.[32]

During this period, Louise spent time with Langston Hughes, who alternated between Cleveland and New York while checking on literary matters, and she was a crucial component of Ralph Ellison's welcome—and indeed his radicalization—when he arrived in July from Tuskegee Institute. She likely did not recruit the aspiring artist in any official sense. During the Popular Front, building the Communist Party ranks proved far less important than increasing the number of those orbiting around or intersecting with the party. Louise drew young Ellison close enough; he spent many days reading literature and theory in her apartment at 530 Manhattan Avenue, off of 122nd Street, and at the end of the year he moved into an apartment in the same building. Moreover, through Louise's and Hughes's contacts, Ellison gained access to some of the most prominent figures, both leftist and moderate, in Harlem.[33]

Ellison surely heard her pronouncements on the Spanish Civil War, the latest crisis on the left and the one with the most romantic appeal. Economic progress under the New Deal was unfolding in a slow, circuitous, and sometimes Sisyphean manner. Angelo Herndon claimed an unqualified victory before the U.S. Supreme Court. Sam Leibowitz accepted a compromise that freed four of the Scottsboro defendants—Olen Montgomery, Willie Roberson, Eugene Williams, and Roy Wright—and took the death penalty off the table for the rest.[34] And the conquest of Ethiopia had the ring of finality to some. But when General Franco led a revolt against the newly elected republican government of Spain (known as the Frente Popular) on July 17, 1936, many activists mobilized energetically in protest. Harry Haywood, who became involved in the war, commented, "Spain was the next logical step" as he later reflected on that nation's significance in the worldwide imperative to defeat Fascism and prevent a second world war.[35] Or, as fellow volunteer Oscar Hunter, a coworker from Chicago, phrased the matter succinctly, "It ain't Ethiopia, but it'll do."[36]

Louise delivered a round of anti-Fascist speeches. On August 25 she joined James Baker, chairman of the New York chapter of the National Negro Congress, to address a teeming crowd on Seventeenth Street after a parade organized by the American League against War and Fascism. Billed as the spokesperson for the women of the congress, she enumerated the "crushing effects of Fascism." If oppressed minorities in the United States were "most liable" regarding Fascist incursions, as Baker argued, Louise stressed the potential hardship for women in those groups.[37] By the following spring, as Guernica became a "burned skeleton," the threat in Spain had become a staple in Louise's public and private conversations, including, of course, those involving Hughes and Ellison.[38]

The conflict beckoned the three friends. The first opportunity fell to Hughes, who embarked for Paris on June 30, 1937, to attend the Second International Writers' Conference. He would continue to Spain to cover the war for several black newspapers. Louise bid him farewell as he boarded the *Aquitania* at the Fiftieth Street pier; he somewhat jokingly said, "I might not come back."[39] Hughes was to track the activities of African Americans in the International Brigades. Ellison was also on hand at Hughes's departure and was inclined to follow him as soon as possible, but he could not obtain a passport or apparently figure out an alternative.[40] Louise's chance came courtesy of the IWO, which funded her to join a delegation of church officials, educators, and businesspeople to gain authentic knowledge and establish priorities for relief. On August 11 the deputized representatives composing the North American Committee to Aid Spanish Democracy set sail for Paris on the *Queen Mary*. Louise, as an IWO representative, was also slated to attend the World Assembly against Racism and Anti-Semitism scheduled for September 10–12 in Paris. Much of the enthusiasm in the United States for the conference had been spurred by Samuel Untermyer, the president of the Non-sectarian Anti-Nazi League, the American affiliate of the conference sponsor, the International Federation of Leagues against Racism and Anti-Semitism.

Once in Europe, Louise realized that the fighting spirit of the Republican forces was their only advantage. Given the support from Adolf Hitler, Mussolini, and Antonio Salazar (Portugal's dictator), Franco's manpower, resources, and tactical advantages would almost inevitably lead to military triumph. The Germans and Italians, clearly muscling up for further conquest, conducted bombing raids and controlled crucial supply routes. To have any hope of winning, the Republicans needed strong allies, but Great Britain, which had massive investments in the Franco-controlled northern provinces and feared a massive European armed conflict, pursued a noninterventionist policy, and the United States was a partner in appeasement. France sympathized with the Republican cause but feared a war with Germany. The material aid the Soviet Union provided arrived intermittently, and technical support from Mexico amounted to little.[41] The biggest boost proved to be the Comintern-sponsored International Brigades, which attracted thirty-five thousand volunteers from around the world over the course of the war, although no more than seventy-five hundred were in battle at any one time. The five brigades were organized mostly according to nationality and language: the Eleventh comprised German exiles and refugees; the Twelfth, Italian anti-Fascists; the Thirteenth, the Poles; the Fourteenth, the French and Belgians; and the Fifteenth, also known popularly as the Abraham Lincoln Brigade, the Americans, Canadians, and British.[42]

Crossing from France, Louise became enchanted with the beauty of the Mediterranean Sea and the Spanish countryside, which to her seemed manicured, "just a gorgeous sight."[43] Closing in on Barcelona, however, she began to see the devastation caused by bombing. Part of their hotel's façade had been blown off. In Barcelona she witnessed her first air attack: "You'd hear the signals. It evidently was not near where we were, but I remember going to windows, looking out and seeing fire against the sky. You could see, and you could hear. But you began to lose your fear because you didn't find the people panicking."[44]

She would see evidence of a similar resolve in Madrid after she endured a hot, dusty, seeming interminable bus ride. When the group stopped at an inn to dine, she ate her first dish of paella—and thought it delicious although she didn't look at it because of the wormy creatures in it. She whimsically imagined the fare to contain "everything that lives in the sea."[45] On the bus, as the hills rolled by, she noticed signs of poverty dotting the idyllic landscape. She saw people living in caves and grew more cognizant of the harsh conditions that the Spanish masses had faced even before the civil war.

In Madrid she saw more ravages of war. When Franco failed to seize the capital city quickly, he decided to bomb it, sparing only Salamanca, a neighborhood in which he expected support. Yet the locals had held, often yelling their famous slogan, "No Pasarán!" (They Shall Not Pass!). Subsequently, the Madrid front had become the scene of some of the most intense skirmishes in Spain. In her memoir, Louise remarked, "Although it was the first time I'd ever been in a war zone, it was exciting." As she drew strength from the Madrileños, their visitors, and the people in the surrounding villages, she wasn't unduly afraid for her safety: "Everywhere you could feel the unity of the people fighting against Franco. The little kids held up their hands in every village we went through."[46] A variety of posters were on display throughout Madrid. Some were tributes to General José Miaja, head of the Madrid Defense Committee and deemed by many to be the city's hero.[47] Other posters featured a globe and faces of different ethnicities along with the wording, "TODOS LOS PUEBLOS DEL MUNDO ESTÁN EN LAS BRIGADAS INTERNACIONALES AL LADO DEL PUEBLO ESPAÑOL."[48]

Louise observed that even in the midst of violence and food shortages, the people of Madrid seemed to find humor in spite of the war experience. Their gaiety functioned alongside their sober determination that Madrid would be the tomb of Fascism. Indeed, the city remained lively up until curfew, with theaters, concert halls, and cabarets doing brisk business.

In Madrid she caught up with Hughes, who was residing on the top floor of a club for artists and writers, the Alianza de Intelectuales Antifascistas. She met a writer important to Hughes, the Afro-Cuban poet Nicolás Guillén. She was taken with the graciousness of Ludwig Renn, the German novelist who had been imprisoned by the Nazis for so-called literary treason. On the street, she stumbled onto the eccentric screenwriter Dorothy Parker, who thirty years later would controversially leave her literary estate to Martin Luther King Jr.[49] Of course, Ernest Hemingway, sympathetic to the Republican cause, was on hand as a war correspondent. The Republicans weren't winning the war, but they were easily ahead on the scorecards of Western artists and intellectuals.

Walter Garland and Harry Haywood, Communist comrades and colleagues from the National Negro Congress, had also landed in Madrid. Garland, a New Yorker who had been a private in the U.S. Army, commanded troops in Spain. The previous February, he had been wounded on the southeastern Madrid front in the Battle of Jarama, in which Republican forces foiled Franco's offensive, an attempt to gain control of the strategically critical Madrid-Valencia highway. Garland recovered to lead a machine-gun company in the Washington Battalion and later commanded the Mackenzie-Papineau Battalion before returning to America to engage in fund-raising and lobbying. Born in 1913, the same year as Ellison, he had undoubtedly served the Republicans with distinction.[50] Haywood, fifteen years older and a veteran of World War I, had a wound-free tour but in some ways a more trying time. A deputy brigade commissar—a political officer whose main tasks were to inspire discipline, inform troops about progress and objectives, and coordinate logistics—he clashed with military officers and was eventually accused of leaving the front without permission, allegations that haunted him back in the United States and hurt his status in the party.[51]

Haywood seemed carefree in Madrid, however. Always interested in Louise, he trailed behind her as much as he could. On August 27, to his delight, they would work together. On August 26, 1937, the city of Santander fell to the Fascists, and soldiers jubilantly paraded huge signs of Mussolini through the streets; the following night, Louise and Haywood joined Garland, Hughes, and others, likely including Captain Basilio Cueria and Lieutenant Valentín González González (known as "El Campesino"), to broadcast three-minute appeals via shortwave radio back to the United States, urging support for the Republican cause and the lifting of the embargo.[52] The Republicans were as committed as ever to fighting; they just needed a fighting chance. Haywood claimed to need assistance with his text, so Louise and a few others, defying curfew, walked through the pitch-black streets over to his hotel, only to find him stretched out drunk in unforgettably loud wide-striped pajamas. At any rate, they wrote his speech and left, whereupon they were stopped by a soldier who spoke neither English nor Spanish. Fortunately, he let them go, though he would have had the right to detain or even shoot them.[53]

At midnight they were escorted to the communications building by car; radio station E.A.R. was located in the basement. Haywood showed up in surprisingly fine form, and they sent their pleas across the airwaves, though Louise was never sure whether they were heard in the United States. Garland, who obviously had the most front-line experience among the Americans, spoke most movingly. He ventured that in some respects the black soldier in Spain found himself in a better situation than many African Americans because he could strike back physically at oppressors. Emphasizing that the battle against injustice needed to unfold everywhere and that all people of good will had a responsibility to join or support it, he noted that, despite the United States' noninterventionist pose, the Fascists were firing American-made bullets at him and his fellow soldiers. He highlighted the bravery of the black soldiers with whom he had served, including the now-hospitalized Doug Roach, barely five feet tall but with enough energy to drag a machine gun more than nine miles and make Fascists dance to his fire, and Oliver Law, the commander of the Abraham Lincoln Brigade who had been killed in July at the Battle of Brunete on the western Madrid front.[54] Law was the first military commander from the United States to lead a racially integrated unit.[55] No matter the setbacks, Garland maintained that battlefield victories had been achieved and that more would follow because the Republican troops possessed unbreakable unity. The other speakers, with Louise and Haywood in synch, sculpted the generic anti-Fascist vision and connected it to African American concerns. Defeating Franco, the reasoning went, would weaken Mussolini's forces and lead to the liberation of Ethiopia, thus impeding the spread of Fascism worldwide. "If you can imagine the Klan in control of America," Haywood intoned, "you know why Negroes have to fight fascism everywhere in the world."[56] Louise contributed:

> Reactions tumble over one another—they come so thick and fast. In these minutes I can only tell you a few. I feel at home here, though one is in the midst of the strain of a war-ridden country. Though my Spanish is miserably inadequate, I talk to the people. We have a common language. They are fighting oppression, and I come from a people whose oppression is centuries old. I am part of their feeling against the Italian fascism which has participated in the devastation of their country, because we in America felt keenly the devastation by the same forces of Ethiopia. I sense

their determination to maintain democracy in Spain, because in America we Negroes have been striving for democratic rights since the days of slavery.[57]

Seeking out the trenches in the Casa de Campo section, on the western flank of Madrid, Louise accompanied Hughes in his role as an embedded correspondent. Bullets whizzing by overhead failed to diminish, and perhaps even enhanced, what she termed a "very great experience."[58] She was struck by how illiterate peasants from the countryside were devoted to learning to read and write during their rest periods.[59] They were encouraged by the broadsides promoting literacy that circulated throughout the Republican zone. "Illiteracy blinds the spirit" (*el analfabetismo ciega el espíritu*), they were told. The soldiers were pushed to study, *soldado instruyete* (soldier, instruct yourself!), and encouraged to read periodicals such as the socialist morning paper *Adelante* and the Republican version of *ABC*.[60] Eagerly, the men showed Louise their notebooks before picking up their weapons to resume combat.[61] "No Pasarán!"

During her three weeks in Spain, Louise visited several prisons and encountered Moors who had fought for Franco. Although she understood that they had been ruthlessly exploited, often being paid in worthless German marks, she found it bitterly ironic that they had done the bidding of a man whose most powerful supporter preached Aryan superiority. She found fascinating the juxtaposition of Moors and African Americans. She would tell Richard Wright, then writing for the *Daily Worker*, "I wanted to see with my own eyes the differences between the two dark-skinned people fighting on opposite sides of the struggle."[62] Moreover, she understood the further irony that the Moors were helping to obliterate the contributions of their own culture. She seconded Hughes's summation: "The Moors are assisting in the destruction of a country stamped indelibly with the mark of Moorish culture, a country whose wine grapes were watered by Moorish aqueducts, whose Moorish castles cast geometrical shadows on peasants singing Moorish songs. They are shelling universities founded by Moors a thousand years ago. They are killing men, women, and children whose ancestors gained their olive skin and black hair from a common bloodstream."[63]

Two women shone brightly for Louise. Twenty-three-year-old Salaria Kee, the only African American nurse working in Spain, ran the operating room at the base hospital of Villa Paz, near Madrid. After training at Harlem Hospital, she had been funded by the medical bureau of the North American

Committee to Aid Spanish Democracy to travel to Spain the previous March. "American Negro women should feel very proud of Salaria Kee," declared Louise, noting Kee's courage, commitment, and joy.[64]

Likewise, they should celebrate Dolores Ibarruri, the famous La Passionaria (Passion Flower), the Spanish Communist who was one of two preeminent female politicians in Republican Spain, the other being Margarita Nelken.[65] In fact, the forty-one-year-old Ibarruri perhaps contributed directly to the outbreak of the war when she admonished (or, some say, threatened) the right-wing finance minister, José Calvo Sotelo, during a session of the Spanish Parliament on July 11, 1936. She declared that his tirade against the Republican government was his last speech. Although Ibarruri denied involvement, Sotelo was slain by leftists two days later, which precipitated the mass advance of Franco's military.[66] Ibarruri, whom Louise saw in Valencia, the Republicans' provisional capital, "embodied the whole sentiment," as an adoring Haywood put it.[67] Louise agreed about her role in the resistance to tyranny. Ibarruri thrillingly epitomized to Louise the indispensable leadership of women in global progressive campaigns.[68]

Before Louise left Spain, she visited Albacete, the headquarters and training camp of the International Brigades. She met Oliver Frankson, a master mechanic from Jamaica who was working in the auto park and proved instrumental in keeping the supply lines open. She consulted with Carlos Contreras, who was headed for the Aragon front in the northeast to funnel propaganda to enemy troops in the trenches. Contreras discussed with her the critical and worsening refugee problem—thousands displaced from Málaga, Almería, Bilbao, Santander, and other places—and reminded her to pursue relief work when she returned home.[69]

In Paris Louise encountered another dimension of difficulty related to anti-Fascist movements. The conference was predictable but needed. Several hundred delegates from more than twenty countries, including Bedacht and William Weiner, the president of the IWO, heard greetings from Maurice Violette, the minister of state of the ruling coalition Front Populaire. Violette stressed that the French government sympathized with oppressed people around the globe and wished the conventioneers success. Supportive messages from Untermyer and the writers Thomas Mann and Emil Ludwig were read to the audience, and radical French journalist Bernard Lecache, president of the International League against Anti-Semitism, delivered a stirring opening keynote. Tributes were offered to victims of racial persecution. The delegates approved a manifesto calling for everyone to "reject the bloody lie of racialism, that of the theoreticians as well as the dictators."[70] Throughout the conference, attendees strategized about how to optimize the pressure of public opinion, coordinate propaganda internationally, promote intercultural contact and communication, utilize boycotts judiciously, and advocate for the right of political asylum for those persecuted because of their race or religion.[71] One could become giddy with solidarity. But, for Louise, the most dramatic moment in Paris occurred on a park bench near the small hotel where she was staying. There, she was distressed to discern how the French petit bourgeoisie were embracing the Nazi appeal. The son of the hotel owners expressed resolute support for Hitler and blamed the Communists for disrupting France and undermining the values he held as a French patriot and future entrepreneur. He blamed not business owners but workers and their confederates. Thus, for him, Hitler-style order as a prescription for a nobler France made perfect sense. Louise, like many observers, thought that defeat of the Republicans in Spain would mean a second world war. She grew firmer in such thinking as she conversed, not with defenders of democracy, but with a youthful, innocent-looking member of the European right wing.[72]

There were also positive occasions, however. Louise talked with conferee Thyra Edwards, who had been funded by aid organizations to do work in Europe. A transplanted Texan living in Chicago, the forty-year-old Edwards left for Spain after the conference to assess the conditions, particularly for women and children, in Puigcerdà, Barcelona, and Valencia.[73] And the most fun aspect of her time in Paris had to be becoming reacquainted with William L. Patterson. Recovered from his illness—and also the father of a second daughter—he was at the conference and on the verge of returning to the United States for the first time in three years. As Louise celebrated her thirty-sixth birthday, one imagines that Patterson, her old Savoy Ballroom escort, proved to be at least an enthusiastic dance partner for a still-attractive woman in the City of Light.

CHAPTER 8

Ba Ba Ba Bop, 1937–1940

Back on U.S. soil, Louise pursued an array of follow-up commitments. For one, she brought Carlos Contreras's message about the refugees of the Spanish Civil War to every available constituency. She pleaded for donations at a memorial banquet that the IWO threw at the Commodore Hotel on October 6, 1937, to honor members who had lost their lives in the conflict. Speaking in front of IWO president William Weiner and general secretary Max Bedacht, as well as guest Ludwig Renn, she stressed the extreme financial sacrifices already made by Spanish freedom fighters.[1] She made similar appeals at the Harlem YMCA and additional venues. At virtually every stop, she delineated her perspective on the Republican cause and lauded the optimism and courage of the defenders of the Second Spanish Republic. Extending her myriad organizational involvements, she became an officer in the Harlem Committee to Aid Spanish Democracy, which counted among its members Adam Clayton Powell Jr., William Lloyd Imes, Countee Cullen, and Richard Wright, a growing cultural force on the Harlem scene. The group welcomed the newly wed Salaria Kee to New York after her fourteen-month stint abroad.[2] Kee, along with Thyra Edwards, who stayed at Louise's apartment for a week after returning to the United States on November 8, spearheaded a drive to send a fully supplied ambulance to the war zone.[3] The vehicle was to be adorned with the words, "From the Negro People of America to the Heroic People of Spain."[4] Edwards also envisioned building a home in Spain for child refugees, and Louise played an important role in fund-raising for both efforts, spreading the word while touring for the IWO.[5] Sometimes, in her weariness, she had to laugh at herself to keep going. She wrote wryly to Hughes, "Pittsburgh, Chicago, St. Louis, Detroit, Cleveland, and way points. Philadelphia and New York. Come, all ye Negroes, hear the tale of Spain. See the blight of the fascist touch, hear the roar of the bombas and obuses. Be inspired by the morale of the Spanish people. Learn the lessons of unity and 'one command.' Keep fascism out of America by keeping it out of Spain. Aid yourselves by aiding Spain. Ole! Salud!"[6]

Louise also attended to "Hughesiana," as Hughes put it.[7] About a year earlier, she had convinced her artistic doppelgänger to assemble a booklet of poems to be published by her employer. She often enhanced her lectures with his poetry and sought a broader audience for it. Somewhat bossy with Hughes, as usual, she chose the title *A New Song*, based on a poem Hughes had published in *Opportunity* and *Crisis*: "I have this word to bring / This thing to say / This song to sing." The poet rails against past injustices and promotes resistance—even black and white workers' revolt in the revised version included in the collection.[8]

Given his trouble with mainstream publishers at the time, Hughes enthusiastically embraced the chance at a print run of fifteen thousand copies, the largest of his career to that point. He completed the book in the spring of 1937. However, when Louise returned from Europe, she found to her disappointment that publication had not been expedited. After she applied pressure, the IWO finally printed ten thousand copies, selling at fifteen cents each, in the spring of 1938. The publisher officially explained its rationale for the collection in a foreword. It wished to put literature within the reach of wage earners, and "it chose the poetry of Langston Hughes because as a fraternal society the IWO considers it as one of its missions to create a better understanding and closer solidarity between nationalities. It believes that in the brotherhood of people is the path to that security and well being, which, as a fraternal society, the IWO tries to provide through mutual aid."[9] One of the most popular figures on the American literary left, Mike Gold, provided an introduction for the collection.

Hughes contemplated a second project for the IWO, a collection of articles to be titled *Negroes in Spain*. A week after Louise returned to New York, he sent her six dispatches to be forwarded to the *Baltimore Afro-American*; others for the Associated Negro Press would follow. He advised Louise that she should keep copies of all the articles and that he would soon send her a book outline. With a full agenda for Louise, Hughes also pressed for news about the upcoming second convention of the National Negro Congress, to be held in Philadelphia on October 15–17, 1937, and he sent messages for her to relay to Ralph Ellison. To try to balance the scale, he sent something for her: photographs he had taken of her along with the note, "You sure come out lovely."[10]

The convention's content seemed fairly commonplace to Louise and probably would have to Hughes as well. At the Metropolitan Opera House on October 15, during the sesquicentennial of the U.S. Constitution, she along with 1,148 other delegates heard John P. Davis and other leaders describe a general plan for united mass action. Battle lines were drawn around such domestic issues as proposed federal antilynching legislation, Franklin Delano Roosevelt's intent to revamp the judiciary, increased organizing by trade unions (most black workers, especially domestics and farmers, remained outside of them), and the question of release for the five Scottsboro men still incarcerated. Two of the freed men, Olen Montgomery and Eugene Williams, attended the convention with Ada Wright. Casting an eye on international matters, National Negro Congress officers championed the cause of the Republicans in Spain; condemned the militarism of Italy, Germany, and Japan; and affirmed both the Kellogg-Briand Pact, which repudiated war in favor of conciliation among nations, and the Nine-Power Treaty, which recognized the sovereignty of China.[11] Several references were made to similar points by President Roosevelt in his famous "Quarantine Speech" on foreign policy, given the previous week in Chicago.[12] Likewise, A. Philip Randolph sounded the key theme of the Popular Front: "It is well nigh accepted quite generally by the thoughtful peoples everywhere that if the dykes of democracy break in the land of the little Iberian peninsula, a world flood of fascism may not be far behind, and imperil peoples everywhere."[13]

Given his eagerness for news about the convention, Hughes certainly would have enjoyed, and at points been amused by, the cultural session. In remarks titled "The Problems of the Negro Writer," Sterling A. Brown recapitulated some of the analysis in his seminal essay on racial stereotyping, "Negro Characters as Seen by White Authors" (1933). In Philadelphia he implored African American writers to produce social realism—not a move he makes in the essay—as a way to negotiate literarily between the extremes of, on one hand, the "contented slave, clown, and brute" (types promoted by American novelists from James Fenimore Cooper to Margaret Mitchell) and, on the other hand, the equally stereotypical character who is "faultless, unbelievably intelligent, and upper-class with a vengeance."[14] On the same panel, Alain Locke, admittedly weaned on aesthetic individualism and notions of art for art's sake, seconded, though cautiously, Brown's call for social realism. Offering an insightful take on the failure of Harlem Renaissance writers to make their work speak more directly to the black masses, Locke saluted Brown and Hughes as exemplars in the movement from "cultural racialism" to "class proletarian art."[15]

As one would expect, Louise found Davis, Randolph, Brown, and Locke convincing, and also one of her idols, Charlotte Hawkins Brown, who gave a speech titled "What Negro Youth Have a Right to Expect from the Constitution of These United States."[16] However, Louise had to imagine that the National Negro Congress could have done a stronger job of promoting women. The percentage of women attendees was somewhat higher than in 1935, and several sessions were devoted to women's concerns, but the four honorees chosen for the convention were all male: Abraham Lincoln, John Brown, Richard Allen, and Frederick Douglass.[17] Giant banners of the four, like a Mount Rushmore of civil rights leaders, hung suspended from the rafters over the auditorium stage.

Louise remained a popular speaker at political rallies. Typical was her participation in a torchlight parade and mass meeting to protest the firing of Alma Vessells, a nurse and union organizer at Harlem Hospital. Louise credited Vessells with improving work conditions for staff and called on the commissioner of hospitals, Dr. Sigismund Schulz Goldwater, to reinstate her. Urging the crowd at the Congress Casino on Seventh Avenue to keep pressing systematically for gains, she remonstrated, "Don't get down on your knees and say 'Please, Mr. Boss Man, give me an eight-hour day,' but get it by organizing into trade unions."[18]

Such exhortation lay at the core of her recruiting for the IWO as she crisscrossed the country to spread the gospel of proletarian fraternalism with a threefold approach. Insurance policies were the opening gambit because acquiring one made sense in any event. Louise was always eager to explain benefits to the uninsured as well as to those who held what she considered inferior contracts. She took particular delight in pointing out the limitations and, in her view, the bad faith of Metropolitan Life, which she considered an archenemy of the working class, especially the African American segment. Whenever she passed the offices of Metropolitan Life in New York, she was reminded that the company had been built largely on the exploitation of black people.[19] While she pitched coverage, she kept in mind Bedacht's directive to solicit not just subscribers but active pro-labor and anti-Fascist supporters. Thus, the growth of the IWO was linked to explicit political initiatives, especially the incipient Congress of Industrial Organizations (CIO) headed by John L. Lewis. Considered more progressive than the dominant American Federation of Labor, from which it was expelled in 1935, the CIO was crucial to labor organizing in the heavily industrialized Midwest, the region that became the strongest base for the IWO. A CIO organizer told Louise, "If you help us win this strike by winning our women for the strike, we will promise to put the IWO over the mountain when we get back to work."[20]

That was certainly Louise's intent, but she and other IWO officials understood that business and political success would come only through social and cultural conduits, the very fraternalism at the heart of the original IWO mission. The construction of a national network of lodges would undergird business and political recruiting. Through social and cultural activities, current lodge members would attract new ones; existing lodges would help to found others. Naturally, the lodges did not produce the full political yield envisioned by higher-ups in the IWO, or by the sponsoring Communist Party for that matter. Sometimes socializing is just socializing, and the business and political results were uneven across lodges. Nationalists did not always convert to class-based reasoning. Nonetheless, as components of the largest and fastest-growing Communist-led mass organization, the lodges on the whole were indispensable as a base of support.[21]

As the national secretary of the English section, Louise focused on managing and establishing lodges in that division, with an emphasis on building the African American ranks, though she also met with members of the immigrant units and enlisted their help. She would use an interpreter as she tried to become more familiar with various immigrant groups. Curious about ethnic dynamics, she learned early on that she could not read the facial expressions of Poles. She paid particular attention to the demeanor of various women and judged Italian women to be perhaps the least aggressive.

Louise spent a lot of time in saloons and poolrooms because they were the only meeting places available in many of the areas where no lodge existed yet. In these cities and towns of the Midwest and adjacent states, her focal region during this period, no one within the sphere of the IWO balked significantly at accepting leadership from an African American woman. In fact, she stayed in numerous white homes, with the families feeling it an honor to host her. In this context she began to make significant progress in conveying the IWO's political platform and getting both black and white audiences to understand the interconnectedness of the fights for labor and for African American rights. A key IWO gesture in her eyes was the organization's insistence that its convention at the Fort Pitt Hotel in Pittsburgh in 1938 be completely integrated, reportedly the first time that blacks and whites mingled freely in all of the hotel's facilities.[22] This contrasted with the racial and ethnic geography she discerned in various mining camps. Although all workers had similar housing, the accommodations of native-born white Americans were often found along paved and lighted streets while those of immigrants were located along dimly lighted wooden boardwalks, and those of blacks along unlighted dirt roads.[23] In West Virginia, a place Louise thought "very raw," she went with a group of workers to a restaurant where a sign in the window indicated that no "colored" were served.[24] Passing as white, she ate with her colleagues, who were aware of the deception. She remembered, though, "I had the hardest time swallowing that food down. I couldn't help looking at that sign."[25]

Although an odious experience, such racial discrimination by small proprietors proved to be less of an obstacle to Louise's organizing efforts than the power and intimidation of plant and mine owners. At every stop, she explained that IWO members, being workers in the mines and mills, should be interested in the CIO.[26] On several occasions she was requested not to mention the union during her presentation.[27] Nonetheless, some Czech, Polish, Hungarian, and Russian organizers, at considerable risk of injury and retribution, courageously helped her to make her point. Louise considered them to be the unsung heroes of the CIO.[28]

Gains would be hard won, and even advances were subject to erosion. In Homestead, Pennsylvania, the site of famous steelworker lockouts and strikes, and the town where Mary Harris "Mother" Jones had been arrested, Louise ascertained that membership in the Amalgamated Association of Iron and Steel Workers had sunk to only a fraction of what it had been in earlier decades. In general, she thought that steelworkers lagged behind miners in unionizing.[29] She knew of the setbacks suffered by the Steel Workers Organizing Committee after the strike against "Little Steel" in 1937.[30] Lorain, Ohio, where Louise spent considerable time, was a "Big Steel" city, dominated by the giant U.S. Steel Corporation. The company-town politics were apparently less fractious, but the workers, in Louise's estimation, were being bullied and exploited nonetheless. Hoeing the union row, then, was one of the roughest but most gratifying tasks Louise had ever undertaken. She saw workers living hard but also, when sober and focused, organizing hard. Some of the mining camps were particularly trying in personal terms; she had to spend a week without bathing during one stretch in West Virginia.[31] Yet she made admirable strides in her primary mission to expand the English section of the IWO and give it a darker hue. She also made progress in fostering inter-changes between African Americans and members of other sections, such as the Jewish and Ukrainian groups.

Of the various aspects of her work, Louise enjoyed the cultural dimension as much as any, the choirs, dance groups, and almost ubiquitous drum and bugle corps that sprang up along with the lodges. She fondly recalled how the IWO "took over" the Golden Gate International Exposition, or World's Fair, in 1939.[32] She helped to develop cultural centers in Chicago, Norfolk, and the Watts section of Los Angeles. Her own local base, from which she had been elected to the IWO executive committee, was Lodge 691 at 317 West 125th Street in New York City. Like other such units around the country, this one reflected its surrounding community, in this case a bustling ideological hodgepodge of black striving, with enclaves of bright optimism even amid the tailspin of an economic depression. The lodge, of which Louise was a cofounder, drew from trade unions, churches, and other civic and political organizations, including the Communist Party. It was not highly political in a formal sense compared to other lodges, though the message of proletarian fraternalism circulated freely, of course.

The Harlem lodge featured a vibrant series of cultural events that appealed to Harlemites of all classes and pulled in aficionados from downtown. Rich-ard Wright was presented at the IWO hall upon his appointment to the edito-rial board of *New Masses*. Louise joined Alta Douglas, Ben Davis, and Eugene Gordon to pay tribute to Wright, Harlem's latest literary star, who was riding the success of *Uncle Tom's Children*.[33] The career of Lead Belly, a friend of Wright's, was on the downswing, but he found a receptive audience at Lodge 691.[34] The hottest ticket was for a celebration of W. C. Handy's sixty-fifth birthday. Many of Harlem's leading socialites, to their surprise and dismay, were denied entry because there simply was no room. Hughes-Thompson insiders Alta Douglas, Marion Cuthbert, Ralph Ellison, Richmond Barthe, Waring Cuney, Gwendolyn Bennett, Dorothy Peterson, Arthur Spingarn, and Mollie Lewis—by then Mollie Moon—squeezed in. Although the actual birthday party took place at the Cotton Club, the patrons at Lodge 691 en-joyed a stellar program on the blues in the arts, highlighted by Hughes's demonstration of "blues in poetry." A longtime Hughes friend, Zell Ingram, took on a similar theme regarding painting. Composer and arranger Robert Kingsley accompanied Felicia Sorel, the only established dancer in America who performed interpretations of the blues. Toy Harper, Hughes's adoptive "aunt," both sang and helped to illustrate the blues in drama.[35]

By far the most significant cultural legacy of the IWO Lodge 691 is that it served as the initial site for the Harlem Suitcase Theater. Hughes had the idea for such an enterprise as early as 1931.[36] However, he began to concretize his desire only when he returned home from Spain at the beginning of 1938. Sitting with Ellison in Louise's apartment on Manhattan Avenue, he remarked simply, in the casual manner in which he usually addressed her, "Lou, I want a theater."[37] She had heard the spiel before, but on this occasion, inspired by the poems in *A New Song*, she suggested specifically that Hughes link some of his poetry within a narrative frame for production. The author loved the idea immediately and within a day had drafted *Don't You Want to Be Free?*[38] With music, songs, dance numbers, and speeches to be incorporated—reflective of traditional African drama, later exemplified by Wole Soyinka and Femi Osofisan—Hughes's protest pageant traced, with tragicomic breadth, the trajectory of African American struggle from enslavement to current participation in interracial, working-class resistance.[39] At the end of the play, a group of actors would come forward and talk about black and white workers uniting. The troupe normally featured only one white actor, lodge member Ernest Goldstein, so they would draw from the audience to display black-white solidarity. Louise sometimes served as one of the background singers who chimed, "Who wants to join hands with me? Who wants to ba ba ba bop?"[40]

It appears that Hughes wrote a script that fulfilled the vision held by Meschrabpom six years earlier. Moreover, this concept, unlike the ill-fated *Black and White*, would come to fruition once Louise secured the IWO hall, outlined an organizational structure, and coordinated the fund-raising. Eventually, the theater operated under an elaborate constitution, a set of by-laws, and a system of rules and regulations. Membership, numbering fifty or so, was divided into voting and studio categories, with voting privileges each season earned by accumulating merits for acting, production work, and volunteer services and avoiding demerits for absences, lateness, and otherwise-uncooperative behavior. Much of the membership was drawn from the IWO youth groups, and thus the organizers felt a need for tight supervision. All participants received the frequent reminder, "You are part of a workers' cooperative theater!"[41] The membership rolls included Cuney, Bennett, Barthe, Ellison, and Romare Bearden.[42] Louise chaired the nine-member executive committee but remained clear about the essence of the theater: "It was amusing, it was innovative, and it was Langston."[43]

It was also, in Louise's opinion, part Vsevolod Meyerhold. She recalled that Hughes met the legendary Russian dramatist during the Soviet Union trip in 1932 and that he had been excited about Meyerhold's experimentation and the Moscow theaters in general.[44] Ironically, just as the Harlem Suitcase Theater came into being, the sixty-four-year-old Meyerhold's avant-garde theater was shut down by Stalinist authorities for violating precepts of social realism. He was later declared an enemy of the state and executed in 1940.

Hughes's folk theater would be in the round with minimalist sets. As its name implied, it was intended to be portable enough to transport easily to clubs, schools, churches, and community centers. Given his fame, Louise's contacts, and the lure of the stage, assembling a cast posed little problem. Many came from the lodge's children, youth, and adult sections. In choosing his principal actor, Hughes pulled a Meyerhold-like move, selecting twenty-eight-year-old Robert Earl Jones because of his physique.[45] A Mississippi-born former professional boxer who had sparred with Joe Louis, the strapping Jones had a beautiful voice and smile, attributes shared with his son James Earl. His presence screamed "leading man" if the project were folk drama. The only drawback was that Jones impressed neither Hughes nor Louise as much of an actor.[46] Not only was he obviously inexperienced, but he had trouble remembering his lines, which distressed other players waiting on their cues. Largely because of Jones, no two performances of Don't You Want to Be Free? unfolded quite the same. Louise did acknowledge that Jones, whom she and others called "Brown Rice" because of his affinity for the dish, improved a great deal, especially during his later years, when he appeared in Hollywood movies such as The Sting.[47] In Harlem in 1938, however, he had to rely heavily on the coaching of Harper, one of the senior cast members, to get through his first major role. Strangely enough, half a century later, Jones acted in the Hughes–Hurston vehicle Mule Bone.[48]

Because Hughes traveled too much to oversee rehearsals closely, he tapped Hilary Phillips to be the production director. Louise judged him to be a polarizing figure, an excitable and shrill gossip who liked to play one person against another. She refereed a lot of disputes, although, to be fair, not all were instigated by Phillips. A young, volatile, unruly, prone-to-attrition assortment of unpaid performers would prove difficult for anyone to discipline and professionalize. It seems that rule 13 encountered a lot of infractions: "Refrain from entering the theatre intoxicated or with liquor on your breath. Not only is it a bad reflection on your theatre, but annoying to the person playing opposite you."[49] Phillips therefore had no easy path to travel to get to opening night.

Despite all, the precariously constituted troupe blended well enough. The Harlem Suitcase Theater premiered *Don't You Want to Be Free?* in front of a wildly cheering audience on April 24. Marvel Cooke, writing in the *Amsterdam News*, called the play "brilliant" and a "significant proletarian drama," one that was "startling in its stark realism." She judged the magnetic though flawed Jones to be "majestic," proof that "an actor is born and not made," and she lauded Harper, Edith Jones (Robert Earl Jones's wife), Clifford Brown, and musical director Carroll Tate. She saw a need for tightening the script, as she felt it dragged in spots, but saw the show as a compelling addition to the cultural tapestry of Harlem.[50] Indeed, attendance proved robust until the close of the season in July.

Wary of saturation, Hughes added skits for the fall performances, which began at the end of October. Leaning on his strength as a humorist, he created to good effect satires such as *Limitations of Life*, *Colonel Tom's Cabin*, and *The Em-Fuehrer Jones*. The first parodies *Imitation of Life*, John Stahl's Hollywood melodrama starring Claudette Colbert, produced in 1934 and based on Fanny Hurst's novel of the same title. Hughes deploys puns and racial reversals—the maid, Audette Aubert, is white, for example—as he "undermines the Aunt Jemima stereotype."[51] Louise considered the sketch "a riot!"[52] *Colonel Tom's Cabin*, also known as *Little Eva's End*, plays on Harriet Beecher Stowe's classic abolitionist but also sentimental and stereotypical *Uncle Tom's Cabin* and *Dimples*, the spinoff film directed by William Seiter and released in 1936, in which Shirley Temple plays Little Eva. Hughes inverts the traditional relationship between the so-called benevolent Eva and the submissive Uncle Tom and presents an empowered Uncle Tom by the close of the vignette. *The Em-Fuehrer Jones* invokes Eugene O'Neill's *The Emperor Jones* in a humorous meditation on German Fascism.

Unfortunately, an artistically vibrant second season could not resolve brewing tensions. Hughes commanded absolute respect, but during his frequent absences differences among members of the theater came to the fore. Some, of course, were personality conflicts. Harper, always protective of her "nephew," would "fight in a minute" if she felt his interests were being undermined.[53] Louise, a hyperfocused taskmaster, knew of her own impatience; tact was never her strongest suit. She tried to mediate several stormy sessions, some of which occurred in her apartment, three blocks from the IWO hall. The results were mixed, and given that she was also on the road a great deal, any diplomatic gains she managed to achieve while home were vulnerable to erasure. In the end, the fundamental divide involved clashing artistic visions. Not all remained committed to the idea of a people's theater despite the obvious value of *Don't You Want to Be Free?* According to Louise, much of the cast did not want to wear overalls all the time. Influenced by commercialism, they wanted to imitate Broadway productions and perform more comedy. Key board members such as technical director Dorothy Peterson, a close associate of Jessie Fauset, shared and reinforced that perspective. Louise maintained, "I didn't see any point to doing Noel Coward or that kind of material. As a novice group, we weren't likely to do it well. So what was the point?"[54]

By the beginning of the summer season in 1939, the Harlem Suitcase Theater had begun suffering seriously from attrition; in July Hughes resigned from the post of executive director. He remained committed to the suitcase-theater concept. In fact, the show had already been widely transported. He had brought it, for example, to a Los Angeles stage in March under the auspices of the New Negro Theater. But he also felt overcommitted and overwhelmed, and perhaps realized that his peripatetic ways and his need to focus on making a living made him unfit to supervise the theater.

Because of building-code issues, the Harlem Suitcase Theater relocated to the basement auditorium of the 135th Street library. Tommy Richardson became the guest executive director for the summer offerings and would also assume control for the season of 1939–1940. He knew that weaknesses needed to be addressed, and he attempted to shore up business, production, and repertory operations. However, Richardson turned out to be more polarizing, in Louise's view, than any other figure associated with the troupe. Conflicts related to his style and personality led to the ultimate breakup of a group whose primary production, ironically, stressed the theme of unity.

Although it fell short of its ambitions, the theater was no failure. It did not, as planned, stage charter member Powell Lindsay's *Young Man of Harlem*; Hughes's adaptation, in collaboration with Peterson, of Lope de Vega's *Fuenteovejuna*, a play Louise knew from her studies in Spanish literature at Berkeley; or Hughes's *Front Porch* and *De Organizer*.[55] In addition, Hughes had wanted to put on dramatizations of Wright's "Fire and Cloud" and "Bright and Morning Star."[56] That failed to happen. Nevertheless, *Don't You Want to Be Free?* ran for almost 150 appearances in New York all told and inspired folk dramatists in several other cities.[57] Thus, the Harlem Suitcase Theater served as a watershed of cultural work in the 1930s.

On the broader political scene, serious schisms took place inside the Popular Front after the signing of the Nazi-Soviet nonaggression pact in August 1939. Spain had fallen to Franco, and Austria and Czechoslovakia to Adolf Hitler. Viewing Poland as the next jewel in the empire but concerned that the Soviet Union would attempt to repel a German invasion of Poland, Hitler eventually agreed to share the country with the Russians, then launched the fateful offensive against Poland on September 1. The Soviet Union soon invaded its agreed-upon section of Poland, and by the end of the month Hitler and Joseph Stalin had signed a friendship agreement. Backers of Soviet policy mainly ignored Russia's imperialist aims and perceived the nonaggression pact and friendship agreement as necessary defensive measures. Many leftists in the United States adopted that position and thought its wisdom revealed when Hitler invaded the Soviet Union less than two years later. In contrast, an equal or perhaps larger faction construed the maneuver to be at best futile appeasement, the sort that led inevitably to World War II and actions like, ironically, Hitler's invasion of the Soviet Union. At worst, the pact could be seen to cement the collaboration between totalitarian, imperialist regimes. Louise sided with the first argument and was correct insofar as she was concerned with the immediate defense of the Soviet Union, although, as a transformed "radical democrat," one probably suspicious of Stalin's show trials, she had toned down her pro-Soviet rhetoric from earlier in the decade.[58] But she did not escape self-contradiction: as a staunch supporter of war against Fascism in Spain, she logically should have been an early advocate of war against Fascist Germany.

At any rate, defending the Soviet policy would become increasingly difficult, especially in the black community, once the word came from Moscow to abandon the Popular Front. The new strategic goals were to deemphasize anti-Fascist activism; oppose social democracy and the New Deal; keep the United States from entering the war on the side of England and France; play up England's role as a colonial, imperialist power; and stress the class struggle once again. This mandate required some creative but largely ineffectual flip-flopping by African American Communists, including the Harlem cadre, in which Louise remained central, and it left the CPUSA, extracted from a popular front, mostly out of step with the expressed aspirations of the black masses.[59] African Americans by and large understood the powerful argument that linked Fascism to Jim Crow, Hitler to Senator Theodore Bilbo. Many of them would not comprehend a line that promoted an alliance with Hitler, the greatest symbol of Fascism, and seemed rather far removed from their own fight to achieve a nonracist democracy. Close colleagues of Louise such as Ben Davis and James Ford tried to push the new Communist Party positions among Harlem residents, but the public meetings they sponsored drew fewer than a hundred curiosity seekers.[60] Overall, the black coalitions involving the party in Harlem crumbled; even party membership losses were sizable, and its recruitment stunted.[61] By no means, however, was the talented and resilient Harlem cadre finished as an influence in the community. Although deprived of a credible political voice among the masses, it still held sway in local intellectual and cultural circles, in which Louise had long been a tremendous asset; she was, in fact, still active with the Harlem Suitcase Theater. To remain relevant and seek potential political triumphs, the Harlem Communists had to accentuate the cultural front and consolidate their victories in union organizing, particularly within the CIO, into a practical message.

Fallout from the Nazi-Soviet Pact permeated the atmosphere at the third convention of the National Negro Congress, held on April 26–28, 1940, at the U.S. Labor Department Auditorium in Washington, DC.[62] Fewer than half as many delegates attended the Washington event as had been present in Philadelphia, and few signs of a broad alliance existed. Because of dwindling streams of financial support, John P. Davis made concessions to the Communist Party and the CIO, effectively putting the convention in their hands.[63] Randolph responded furiously. In his address "The World Crisis and the Negro People Today," he condemned the Soviet Union and criticized the CPUSA, especially its white members, as Moscow lackeys too unstable to be partners in the black struggle for democratic rights. Most of the audience had left the hall by the conclusion of his speech. Subsequently, citing domination by Communists, Randolph, who had pronounced forcefully three years earlier that the National Negro Congress "shun[ned] the Scylla and Charybdis of the extreme left and the extreme right," stepped down from his post and quit the congress altogether.[64] Randolph had issued the minority view of the National Negro Congress's state at that time, but he found a receptive audience among African Americans in general and would always, for better or worse, enjoy an increased stature in the African American community relative to the Communist Party. Max Yergan, who had headed the congress's International Committee on African Affairs and had been an associate to the national secretary, succeeded Randolph. Not coincidentally, Yergan approved of the Nazi-Soviet Pact. No doubt the politics of the National Negro Congress were a prominent discussion topic when Louise attended a party for a select group of conventioneers thrown on April 27 by Henry Lee Moon and Mollie Moon, who at that time occupied an apartment in the home of Robert Weaver.

Meanwhile, the IWO's annual convention at Carnegie Hall unfolded more smoothly. Already a member of the executive board, and therefore the highest-ranking African American or woman in the society, Louise was elected a vice president in recognition of her work on behalf of proletarian fraternalism, a concept Bedacht, still thinking of the Popular Front, had relabeled "labor fraternalism."[65] The membership of the IWO stood at more than 155,000, roughly quadruple what it had been when Louise came aboard seven years earlier.[66]

The Committee to Defend America by Keeping Out of War became another hopeful formation for Louise. Promoting nonintervention, the position of the Communists but also of numerous others of various political persuasions, the committee convened an Emergency Peace Mobilization conference in Chicago from August 31 to September 2. More than twenty thousand people turned out, including six thousand delegates.[67] The conference resulted in the formation of the Washington-based American Peace Mobilization under the chairmanship of Reverend John B. Thompson. Louise would be named to the American Peace Mobilization's national council, which also included Hughes and Richard Wright.

For those who knew Louise, the most surprising aspect of the trip was that she married William L. Patterson. The divorced Patterson had moved to Chicago two years earlier to work as an editor for the *Daily Record*, a newspaper designed, as he described it, to "present the Midwest public with an organ reflecting a working-class point of view."[68] Neither Louise nor Pat (as Patterson was generally known) had talked publicly about having a serious personal relationship. In his memoirs Pat devoted less than a page to their romantic affairs, writing without embellishment, "After I came to Chicago to work on the paper, Louise came on vacation and we were married over the Labor Day weekend."[69]

Obviously, things were a bit more involved. Louise had spent time in Chicago during the summer, mostly staying on Prairie Avenue at the home of a friend, Helen Glover, a schoolteacher, and her physician husband, Nelson. She was perhaps taking an emotional break because she had recently ended a relationship with Joseph North, the Ukrainian-born Communist journalist who wrote for the *Daily Worker* and served as the editor of *New Masses*. He had been married to the former Helen Oken since 1931 but seemed to want

Louise to be the third corner of a triangle. She acknowledged being "very much in love with him." North, she elaborated, "was good for me. He made me write. He was very helpful in that respect. If I was doing articles, he'd stand over me and make me do it. . . . I always liked to be around men who made me think. . . . He was always a good, stimulating companion." Louise required more, though, to keep moving forward with North. She insisted on a "clear break with his wife," who apparently knew of his affair.[70] North and his wife did not divorce until 1957.

During her time at the Glovers, Louise started seeing Pat and even spent time with him at a country resort in Michigan. After their various political and intellectual collaborations, she felt that Pat was finally getting serious about her. By midsummer they had decided to wed but had not committed to a date. They then tried to marry in relative secrecy while the peace conference was under way, taking into their confidence John P. Davis, who accompanied them to city hall. However, after they encountered delays, the news broke about their intentions, which caused Helen Glover to dismiss vehemently the idea of a plain ceremony downtown and insist that the nuptials take place in her home. She and Horace Cayton Jr., Louise's playmate from toddler days, with whom Louise had become reacquainted in movement circles, arranged the event, a fairly easy task given that so many of Pat's and Louise's friends were already in Chicago.[71] Louise asked Yergan, whom she assumed was ordained, to perform the ceremony. But once Yergan indicated that he wasn't, the job fell to Archibald Carey, the "boy orator," then a young pastor at Woodlawn African Methodist Episcopal Church. On the evening of September 3, 1940, he joined Pat and Louise in matrimony. One of Louise's aunts, Mrs. Mabel Mitchell, stood with her. Lawrence Brown, known widely as Paul Robeson's accompanist, stood by Pat.[72] Robeson himself, on his first major singing tour since his return to the United States in the fall of 1939, was present at some point during the ceremony. He and Pat had been good friends since their time in Harlem in the early 1920s. After the wedding, the entire gathering proceeded to a Chicago landmark, Morris Perfect Eat Shop, for a rousing supper.

No honeymoon followed immediately. Louise recalled spending almost as much time at Cayton's apartment, consoling him about a bad turn in his marriage, as attending to hers. In any case, Louise shortly landed back at 409 Edgecombe Avenue, planning her relocation. She would go to Chicago as the head of the iwo's Midwest district. While in New York, she opened up a little about the marriage, giving an interview to the *Daily Worker*.[73] One tidbit she dropped was that she and Pat thought it important to stay inside the race, a point neither had previously prioritized. It bothered them now that the Communist Party, a group with a disproportionate share of interracial marriages, which provoked criticism even from some on the left, was certainly short on African American power couples.

Friends in New York rushed to fete Louise Thompson Patterson, no one more enthusiastically or elegantly than the dependable social butterfly Mollie Moon, who on Saturday evening, October 5, hosted an exquisite dinner featuring her renowned shrimp creole. Those on hand included Alta Douglas, Frank Horne, and Eddie "Mr. Tattler" Perry, who had not had time to gossip.[74]

Louise, circa 1909. LOUISE
THOMPSON PATTERSON PAPERS,
STUART A. ROSE MANUSCRIPT,
ARCHIVES, AND RARE BOOK LIBRARY,
EMORY UNIVERSITY, ATLANTA.

Louise and her mother, Lulu
Thompson, circa 1920s. LOUISE
THOMPSON PATTERSON PAPERS,
STUART A. ROSE MANUSCRIPT,
ARCHIVES, AND RARE BOOK LIBRARY,
EMORY UNIVERSITY, ATLANTA.

W. E. B. Du Bois, who lectured in Wheeler Hall at the University of California in 1923, with Louise in attendance. He became her first political mentor.

Langston Hughes in 1928, the year Louise met him. She followed his advice to move to New York City; the two became lifelong friends.

Wallace Thurman, who was married to Louise from 1928 until his death in 1934, although they were separated for all but a few months of that time.

Zora Neale Hurston, for whom Louise worked as a secretary in 1930.

Louise at the podium, late 1920s or early 1930s. LOUISE THOMPSON
PATTERSON PAPERS, STUART A. ROSE MANUSCRIPT, ARCHIVES, AND RARE BOOK
LIBRARY, EMORY UNIVERSITY, ATLANTA.

The Scottsboro defendants, pictured with attorney Samuel Leibowitz. Louise led the first national rally on their behalf and sometimes clashed with Leibowitz over their defense. Haywood Patterson is seated next to Leibowitz. *Standing, front row, left to right:* Olen Montgomery, Clarence Norris, and Willie Roberson. *Back row, left to right:* Andrew Wright, Ozie Powell, Eugene Williams, Charley Weems, and Roy Wright.

Louise and most of the cast of the proposed film *Black and White* aboard ship en route to the Soviet Union in 1932. Louise is seated on the deck to the left; Dorothy West is to the right. *Next row, left to right:* Mildred Jones, Constance White, Katherine Jenkins, Sylvia Garner, and Mollie Lewis. *First row standing:* Wayland Rudd, Frank Montero, Matt Crawford, George Sample, Laurence Alberga, Langston Hughes, Juanita Lewis, and Allan McKenzie. *Last row:* Ted Poston, Henry Lee Moon, Thurston McNairy Lewis, Lloyd Patterson, and Loren Miller. Leonard Hill and Homer Smith are not pictured.

Louise and Harry Haywood (to her right) in Spain in 1937. LOUISE THOMPSON PATTERSON PAPERS, STUART A. ROSE MANUSCRIPT, ARCHIVES, AND RARE BOOK LIBRARY, EMORY UNIVERSITY, ATLANTA.

Louise in Madrid during the Spanish Civil War. *To her right (r–l):* Lieutenant Valentín González González (El Campesino), Langston Hughes, and Captain Basilio Cueria. LOUISE THOMPSON PATTERSON PAPERS, STUART A. ROSE MANUSCRIPT, ARCHIVES, AND RARE BOOK LIBRARY, EMORY UNIVERSITY, ATLANTA.

Paul Robeson. Performance for troops in the Spanish Civil War, 1936. CHARLES L. BLOCKSON
COLLECTION ON PAUL ROBESON, 1894–2005, RBM 9411. EBERLY FAMILY SPECIAL COLLECTIONS LIBRARY,
PENNSYLVANIA STATE UNIVERSITY LIBRARIES, UNIVERSITY PARK.

Traveling in Europe, 1930s. LOUISE THOMPSON PATTERSON PAPERS, STUART A. ROSE MANUSCRIPT,
ARCHIVES, AND RARE BOOK LIBRARY, EMORY UNIVERSITY, ATLANTA.

Louise performed in the chorus of this Harlem Suitcase Theater performance, which ran in Harlem in 1938 and 1939.

Louise and William Patterson, her second husband, circa 1940s.

Louise, William Patterson, and their daughter, MaryLouise Patterson, mid-1940s.

A Fraternal
Organization
Sentenced to Death!

The Strange Case
of
the International Workers Order
Now Before the U. S. Supreme Court

The International Workers Order, a fraternal insurance society of some 160,000 Americans, has been sentenced to *death by liquidation* by the courts of New York State.

In the appeal of the International Workers Order from this unprecedented act of injustice, the United States Supreme Court is now faced with a decision which will be momentous to the maintenance or destruction of American liberty and the right of free association.

What are the facts in the strange case of the IWO? How does this case affect the lives, not only of the organization's members, but of all Americans in every walk of life?

The logo that appeared on Louise's IWO membership certificate. She joined the IWO in 1933.

Excerpt from an IWO pamphlet regarding the government case against the organization. Louise testified on behalf of the IWO during the trial in 1951.

Louise; her daughter, MaryLouise; and young students in the Soviet Union, early 1960s. LOUISE THOMPSON PATTERSON PAPERS, STUART A. ROSE MANUSCRIPT, ARCHIVES, AND RARE BOOK LIBRARY, EMORY UNIVERSITY, ATLANTA.

Louise (front center) with Evelyn (Nebby) Crawford (behind Louise), Margaret Burnham (to Louise's left), and others at a demonstration in New York City in 1965. LOUISE THOMPSON PATTERSON PAPERS, STUART A. ROSE MANUSCRIPT, ARCHIVES, AND RARE BOOK LIBRARY, EMORY UNIVERSITY, ATLANTA.

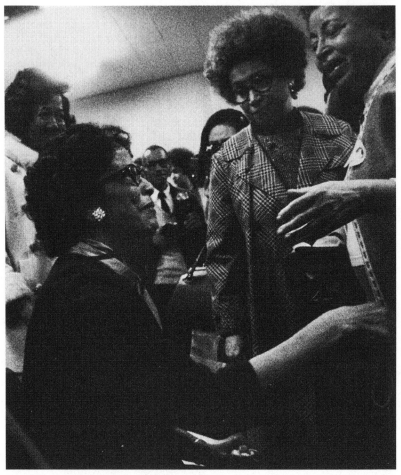

Louise (far right) with Alice Childress and Sallye Davis (seated) in New York, 1970s.

Angela Davis, 1970s. Louise was central to Davis's defense efforts and was particularly interested in the critical reception accorded to Davis's autobiography. LOUISE THOMPSON PATTERSON PAPERS, STUART A. ROSE MANUSCRIPT, ARCHIVES, AND RARE BOOK LIBRARY, EMORY UNIVERSITY, ATLANTA.

Louise (third from left) in May 1991 at the Seventeenth Annual Black Graduation Ceremony at the University of California, Berkeley. She received the Fannie Lou Hamer Award at the event. LOUISE THOMPSON PATTERSON PAPERS, STUART A. ROSE MANUSCRIPT, ARCHIVES, AND RARE BOOK LIBRARY, EMORY UNIVERSITY, ATLANTA.

Louise on the occasion of her ninety-third birthday. She is accompanied by her daughter, MaryLouise; her granddaughter Joanna; and her great-grandson, Roberto. LOUISE THOMPSON PATTERSON PAPERS, STUART A. ROSE MANUSCRIPT, ARCHIVES, AND RARE BOOK LIBRARY, EMORY UNIVERSITY, ATLANTA.

CHAPTER 9

Bronzeville Brigades, 1941–1949

H aving stretched south to Sixty-Third Street and grown rapidly, with its population now exceeding a quarter million, the Black Belt of Chicago, known more popularly among residents as Bronzeville, represented the most logical territory for Louise to work, even without considering her marriage.[1] With its steel and meatpacking industries, Chicago possessed the heavy industrial base that New York City lacked, making it fertile if dangerously contentious ground for union organizers and proponents of the labor fraternalism sponsored by the IWO. The mature voice that Louise had developed in New York, a strong, Communist-inflected advocacy for labor, radical culture, and black freedom, would not sound at all unfamiliar in a citadel of left-wing activity. Richard Wright, partly a Chicago product, opined that the city had produced the "most incisive and radical Negro thought."[2] Wright chose not to provide evidence for that proposition but surely had in mind that the City of Big Shoulders was the original home of the American Communist Party and the site of the launching of the National Negro Congress. Indeed, reflective of this dual development, half of the nation's thousand or so black Communists were located in Bronzeville, and the community had spawned at least three Louise knew well: Wright himself, James Ford, and Harry Haywood.[3] Although suspicious of the party's motives at times, African Americans in Chicago on the whole were not instinctively or deeply hostile toward Communists, black or white, given the history of Communist endeavors on the legal, housing, relief, labor, and cultural fronts. Communists, including Pat, encountered fairly receptive crowds in Washington Park, the open-air market of ideas where political black nationalists also held court, along with Garveyites and Muslims. Even public critics of Communists sometimes remarked in private, "If the Reds can feed the people, let 'em."[4]

Louise tried concretely to help feed the people by growing and strengthening the IWO-CIO alliance. Local labor unionists certainly needed her support as they took on the bosses, who assiduously fomented conflict among native white Chicagoans, Eastern European immigrants, and African Americans and only grudgingly conceded improvements in workers' rights, workplace conditions, and compensation. Under her maiden name, Louise Thompson (her usual choice, as Pat approved), she set up shop in the Loop to continue recruiting members and establishing lodges.[5] She was the president of the Midwest district, which already, largely owing to her personal energy, included more than two hundred lodges; her responsibilities included not only Bronzeville, where she cofounded the Du Sable Lodge, but all of Illinois, Indiana, Wisconsin, Iowa, and Michigan. Yet Bronzeville would be an obvious focus given how big a prize it could be. Only a small percentage of the IWO's members were African American at the onset of the 1940s, and no city had more potential for black membership growth than Chicago. Louise's main contacts on the general executive board for the membership drive were national organizer Sam Patterson (no relation to her husband) and director of organizing Sam Milgrom. Two of her strongest boosters were her husband and Paul Robeson. Robeson, in fact, made a guest appearance at the IWO general executive board meeting at the Riverside Plaza in New York on Saturday, February 22, 1941. Rockwell Kent, a noted painter, author, and longtime political progressive who served as an IWO vice president, introduced the renowned entertainer and strong supporter of both the CIO and the IWO. Also on hand as a guest was composer and IWO member Earl Robinson.

Although the appearance of Robeson and Robinson was the highlight of the meeting, the board members buzzed aplenty about several other developments. For one, the meeting began less than a week following the U.S. Supreme Court's unanimous decision to uphold the conviction of CPUSA general secretary and IWO member Earl Browder on charges of passport fraud. Less sensational in terms of the media coverage was the conviction on similar charges of CPUSA treasurer and IWO president William Weiner. During the Sunday morning session, presided over by Louise, IWO general secretary Max Bedacht, a founding member and former head of the CPUSA, thundered his indignation: "Bros Weiner and Browder are to be clapped into jail and in our hearts we know that the real 'crime' of which they have been convicted is that they never ceased to combat fascism and war; that they have ever been militant in the fight for peace; that they have been ever more effective in the struggle for the emancipation of the underprivileged, the persecuted and the oppressed."[6] The board subsequently passed a resolution to channel its outrage into intensified efforts to keep the United States out of the war in Europe; Louise voted for it.[7] This affirmed the position she had taken with the American Peace Mobilization, that is, that the war extended a fight among imperialists over capitalist markets and colonial holdings. Or, as Bedacht put the matter somewhat poetically, with regard to the motives of England and France, "when [they] realized that the fox Hitler considered the eastern grapes too sour, they began rattling their sabers to spoil his appetite for sweeter-looking western fruit."[8]

Louise—or Sister Thompson, as she was called at IWO gatherings—also had the gavel for the closing session on Monday, at which Sam Patterson called for a thorough discussion throughout the organization about African American issues. A committee consisting of Pat, Louise, Bedacht, Dave Greene, and Peter Chaunt was charged with bringing recommendations to the board.

In Chicago, Louise and Pat settled in at the Vincennes Hotel on East Thirty-Sixth Street. Because of the housing shortage in Chicago, they could not find an apartment yet had to move out of Pat's cluttered room at the Grand Hotel on South State Street. Their solution was to book adjoining rooms in the Vincennes and use one of the bathrooms as a kitchen—an odd improvisation but useful enough for a couple who constantly moved in various circles outside of the home. As in New York, Louise gravitated toward the arts scene and engaged artists in conversation about culture and politics. Almost forty, she could not be the young and central presence she had been on Convent Avenue. The twenty-three-year-old printmaker and writer Margaret Taylor Goss (later Margaret Burroughs) played a role similar to what Louise's had been in Harlem; she, along with her husband, the painter Bernard Goss, hosted numerous artists and activists in their apartment, dubbed "Little Bohemia," on Michigan Avenue. At the Goss residence one could regularly encounter other fledgling local artists such as Charles White, Gordon Parks, Gwendolyn Brooks, and Margaret Walker, who wrote for the *Daily Record*. Participating in their second renaissance, the ever-curious Louise, the ever-animated Pat (who never shied away from a get-together), and the ever-inspirational Robeson, a frequent visitor to Chicago, constituted a core of elders.

Louise's link to the black art world of Chicago became solidified after the opening of the South Side Community Art Center, located at 3831 South

Michigan Avenue. Dedicated by Eleanor Roosevelt on May 7, 1941, the facility constituted an extension of the Works Progress Administration. A home to innovative African American artists, the center became a model of how to infuse "cultural and political radicalism into black public space."[9] Margaret Taylor Goss served on the board of directors, as did a rising star on the left, Ishmael Flory, with whom Louise would work closely. Like Louise, Flory had graduated from Berkeley. In 1934, while a graduate student in sociology at Fisk University, he was expelled for organizing protests against racist violence and Jim Crow policies. In Chicago Flory, a Communist, had become a trade unionist and the president of the Chicago chapter of the National Negro Congress. It was a simple move, therefore, to connect the work of the IWO to the South Side Community Art Center, a point illustrated by the reception for the IWO held at the center in August.

Langston Hughes also contributed to the arts in Chicago. While a guest of Noel Sullivan on the West Coast, he wrote to tell Louise that he would arrive in Chicago during the second half of November. She wanted him to stay at the Vincennes, but he had accepted Horace and Irma Cayton's invitation to stay in one of the residential halls at the Good Shepherd Community Center, the social project that Horace Cayton directed, known after 1942 as Parkway Community House. Hughes had accepted a Julius Rosenwald fellowship and would be in town periodically through April working on a play, *The Sun Do Move*, to be performed by his Skyloft Players, and collaborating on a separate project with Arna Bontemps, who had been in Chicago for six years. The official debut of his latest collection of poems, *Shakespeare in Harlem*, which he dedicated to Louise, took place at Good Shepherd on February 15.

While Louise was surveying the arts scene, a crucial shift occurred within the leftist discourse on the war. After Germany invaded the Soviet Union on June 22, 1941, Louise agreed with the CPUSA's abandonment of Yanks-are-not-coming reasoning in favor of the argument that everyone should support the war and the Soviet cause as proper responses to the spread of Fascism; her husband and Robeson, the most high-profile figure among black radicals, concurred. The Soviet Union was the enemy of Germany and thus, ipso facto, a friend of England, France, and the United States. When the British and Soviets pledged to assist each other three weeks after the invasion, interventionism gained momentum across the entire spectrum of American public opinion, especially on the left. At the September meeting of the general executive board, the IWO, with Louise in step, called for the "complete military destruction of Hitlerism and Nazi Germany."[10] Mindful of resistance to the war in many quarters of the African American community, the organization tethered its hawkishness to the domestic struggle against racist discrimination, calling for racial equality in the armed forces and the abolition of poll taxes. Of course, the attack on Pearl Harbor in December and the ensuing declaration of war by Germany made for an easier sell in the United States, including among blacks, though some veered sharply toward ethnocentrism and preferred to see Japan as the champion of the so-called darker races. The National Negro Congress countered this tendency with a hastily published pamphlet, *The Negro People Will Defend America*, in which it stressed how the war against Fascism was tied to the possibilities for racial advancement. It urged African Americans to enlist "by tens of thousands" while making sure to agitate simultaneously for equal opportunities in labor markets, particularly in war industries. Addressing nationalist sympathies, the congress pointed to the Japanese occupation of China. In the eyes of the congress, feelings of solidarity with the Japanese should have been directed toward the rank-and-file citizens, themselves victims of the Japanese war machine.[11]

Similarly, Louise and Sam Patterson slanted the IWO's pitch to African Americans toward intervention by publishing *The IWO and the Negro People: A Message and an Appeal*. Arguing that democratic and patriotic aims undergirded the civic, cultural, and benefit activities of the organization, the authors explained that those aims now coincided with the stated objectives of the United States and its allies: "to destroy Fascism, to preserve Freedom and Democracy and to enlarge them throughout the world."[12] Then, with a twofold argument, they connected the international fight against Fascism to the domestic struggle for racial equality. They insisted that no victory over Fascism could be complete without the total defeat of Jim Crow and, conversely, that the immediate removal of Jim Crow barriers, especially with regard to employment in the war industries, was the only way to ensure the full and indispensable participation of African Americans in the war effort. With regard to the IWO's ethos, the authors pointed to their high positions in the IWO as proof of the group's sincere attempts to construct a racially inclusive, radically democratic culture.[13]

The IWO brass tried to normalize interventionist discourse by conflating it with patriotism throughout 1942. Before rapping the gavel to commence the June 27 meeting of the general executive board, Louise led the assembly in reciting the Pledge of Allegiance and singing the national anthem. Throughout the session, leaders expressed support for President Franklin Delano Roosevelt, who had tossed a bone to the international Left in May by commuting Browder's sentence to time served, and they were planning to back mainstream political candidates who supported Roosevelt's military policies.[14] The board acknowledged, however, that the general membership was on the whole less enthusiastic about a pro-war posture. An easier sell did not mean an *easy* sell. The arguments of pacifists, including the IWO, had been persuasive, and members were reluctant to embrace war on the warrant that Hitlerism represented the greatest threat to them.[15] The IWO prolocutors faced, then, the task of continuing to drum up support for a pro-war, "national unity" program while, ironically, fending off assaults from recalcitrant right-wing forces such as the House Un-American Activities Committee, led by Texas representative Martin Dies; the committee had been requesting the IWO's membership lists as part of a campaign to harass and destabilize progressive organizations. The IWO followed the CIO in denouncing the committee and calling for its abolition.[16]

In the summer of 1942, Louise had a concern shared by no other IWO leader in the wartime political vortex, however. She was unmistakably pregnant. If her and Pat's marriage had been a surprise, they now seemed to have ventured into the miraculous given that Louise, over the age of forty, was probably perimenopausal and unlikely to conceive. Oddly enough, her good friend Nebby had faced a similar situation, delivering a daughter, Evelyn Louise (Nebby Lou) Crawford, on July 28, 1938, three weeks before her own thirty-ninth birthday.[17]

Louise scaled back her schedule, missing the November session of the IWO general executive board in New York. But her political fervor did not dim, nor did her desire to see such zest matched on the cultural front. Reflecting on some of Hughes's recent poetry, for example, she informed him that it needed to include "that grim, stern note of hate which we must feel toward Hitler and Hitlerism abroad and at home." Sounding a note of urgency, she avowed, "We must destroy or be destroyed!"[18] As the baby neared full term, health complications arose. Louise had fibroid tumors, which raised the specter of a miscarriage or difficult delivery; she would also need surgery immediately after the birth. She became extremely fretful and cautious, choosing to mainly stay inside because she feared slipping on a snowy sidewalk.

Mary Louise Patterson arrived on March 15, 1943, at 9:15 p.m. Her parents called her their income-tax baby because she was born on the day of the filing deadline then in effect. Delivered by cesarean section at American Hospital, she weighed about seven and a half pounds and had black hair, brown eyes, and pretty much her father's thoroughly brown complexion. She received her political and curricular instructions almost immediately. On National Negro Congress stationery, Edward Strong, Thelma Dale, and Hermina Dumont wrote, "The National Negro Congress greets you [Louise and Pat] upon the birth of a new anti-fascist freedom fighter, Mary Louise. With best wishes for her immediate initiation to the American Youth Movement as a valiant and courageous inheritor of a fighting tradition."[19] Hughes furnished a collection of radical poems he had written for the occasion and ordered Mary Louise to take her cod liver oil and grow strong so that she would be able to read them and, presumably, enact their themes. He hoped that by the time she was a big girl the red star would be shining everywhere.[20]

Well-wishers sent dozens of messages over the course of several weeks. Bedacht, Peter Shipka, John Middleton, and Sylvia Schatzkammer sent greetings from the IWO.[21] Rubin Saltzman, the national secretary of the Jewish-American division, sent two letters, one from himself and one on behalf of the executive committee.[22] Chicago educator Roma Jones, a good friend to Louise, and her husband, labor attorney and future Cook County circuit court judge Sidney Jones Jr., called the baby the "heiress of a New Day."[23] A local member of the Communist Party, Claude Lightfoot, and his wife, Geraldyne, sent a note of congratulations.[24] James Ford wrote on behalf of the "comrades on the ninth floor."[25] Thyra Edwards also wrote from New York and expressed a desire to meet Mary Louise.[26]

Of course, Louise's dearest friend, Nebby Crawford, responded anxiously from California. Pat had wired the Crawfords to convey that the baby was fine and that Louise had come through the delivery and fibroid removal okay; she felt sick mostly because of the prolonged anesthesia. Louise had followed with a memo. But Nebby, knowing her friend's tenacity, worried that she would not take the proper recovery time. She recommended a minimum hospital stay of two weeks. Nebby hoped that Mary Louise (she loved the name, taken from the baby's grandmothers) developed a healthy appetite and "raised the devil for food."[27] A precocious Nebby Lou, now four years old, was demanding to see the baby and threatening to travel alone to Chicago to see her "sister."[28]

Perhaps most poignantly, Louise received lengthy letters from her two "othermothers," Susie Revels Cayton and Mrs. Allen.[29] Cayton, at her children's insistence, had moved to Chicago shortly after her husband died in 1940. In her mid-seventies and suffering from diabetes, she had not seen Louise recently and learned of the birth only when Robeson paid her a visit. Tugging on Louise's heartstrings, she wrote, "It does not seem so very long ago since I walked the streets of Seattle holding your little hand in mine and now to think you have a daughter of your own—these would be happy days for your mother. . . . I feel very close to your baby although I have not seen her because I love you and also loved your mother."[30] Unfortunately, limited by her illness, Cayton did not get to bond with Mary Louise. She died a few months later at the age of seventy-four. Mrs. Allen, excitedly referring to herself as a "grandma," also evoked memories of Louise's mother by speculating about how proud she would have been. More future oriented, practical, and humorous than Cayton, she advised, "Mr. A says more power to you and Pat; now bring him a boy next time."[31]

Louise's own mission had more to do with getting back to work. Bored with staying home and washing diapers, she hired a babysitter and resumed IWO tasks when Mary Louise was six weeks old. Indeed, for several years afterward, Louise would spend a large share of her salary on babysitters, but she felt the investment worthwhile because it made her, in her estimation, a better mother. In the evenings, she was eager to entertain her daughter. That time along with the time she spent with Mary Louise in the mornings before she went to the office—Pat typically rose first and brought the baby to Louise in bed—represented a satisfying balance with work.[32] The inevitable transition from the Vincennes Hotel was spurred by Roma Jones, who directed Louise to a second-floor apartment at 5341 South Maryland Avenue. The Jones family, including three playmates for Mary Louise, occupied the first floor.

By February 1944 Louise was back in full swing concerning IWO matters, though technically she no longer belonged to its sponsoring organization, the CPUSA. Browder had been theorizing the rapprochement of socialism and capitalism at least as far back as his release from prison, as was evident in his monograph *Victory and After*, and he had recently convinced the National Committee to dissolve the party in favor of becoming the Communist Political Association. In his book Browder argued, with regard to the mutual future of the Soviet Union and the United States, "The truth is that a socialist country, led by Communists and the working class, must coexist and collaborate with a capitalist country, led by lawyers, business men, industrialists, and financiers, on the basis of mutual respect and toleration of their differing systems, finding thereby a common road to the post-war reconstruction of the world."[33]

Louise did not necessarily agree with Browder's reasoning, nor did she necessarily disagree. She likely flip-flopped, as did her husband, seeing "class collaboration" as a poor long-term strategy but viewing the significant wartime increase in new party members, a third of whom were African American, as a positive result of more flexible thinking.[34] But the point was moot in IWO circles because cooperation with New Dealers was already the practical order of the day. Presiding over the first business session of the sixth convention of the IWO, held in early July at Manhattan Center, a week after the Republicans had nominated Thomas Dewey, Louise told the audience, to tumultuous applause:

> With the knowledge of that convention of the Republican Party before us, we of the IWO who are of all political affiliations, religions, as well as nationalities, will hammer out in this convention that kind of unifying, non-partisan program that we can then take to the people of our various communities and various national groups, and bring home to them how we must work, how we must guarantee that when the elections are held this fall, we shall have not only a glorious victory, but an overwhelming victory—the answer of the American people to that convention that took place in Chicago—by putting Franklin D. Roosevelt back in the White House as President.[35]

On July 5, in a meeting of the conference of general lodges, a few dozen participants, energized by talk of the election, revisited the question of increasing IWO membership among a key bloc of voters: African Americans. It had become apparent to Sam Patterson that any drive to increase black enrollment would stall if not propelled by an offer of greater autonomy than was currently afforded to African Americans within the general section.[36] The progressive impulse among blacks was largely nationalist, as it was among the nationality groups. Thus, the IWO faced an organizing dilemma. On one hand, Bedacht had always felt that a fraternal order should serve as the conscience of a community. A vibrant, egalitarian, integrated general section could be the paradigmatic example of this function.[37] On the other hand, the general section and the IWO lacked vibrancy to the extent that it failed to draw blacks in sufficient numbers with its integrationist appeal. With no ideal solution forthcoming, Patterson sensed that pitching a broader tent was the best option, and he helped to establish the momentum that led to the creation of the Douglass Lincoln section. On the afternoon of July 5, he worked with Louise and Sam Milgrom in particular to fashion a "resolution on Negro work," which was adopted the following day by the general convention.[38] Naturally, Louise and Patterson had created much more work for themselves because they were specifically tasked with bringing masses of blacks into the IWO. Louise would serve as the chair of a new national organizing committee and would concentrate on the Midwest in addition to her overall district duties, while Patterson, as the executive secretary of the organizing committee, would handle the rest of the country.

The chief members of Louise's Chicago unit included Dr. Luther Peck, a prominent civic torchbearer and the president of the Du Sable Lodge, along with Eurah Gerrard, Anna Mae Mohn, and Harriette Gray, a trade union leader at Douglas Aircraft Company, who was still in her twenties.[39] They concentrated on unions in industries such as mining, steel, machinery production, meatpacking, and transport. They also established connections with the strategically vital Canaan Baptist Church.

Organizing did not go as well in Detroit, where local lodges had perceived the previous IWO leadership as heavy-handed and now resented outsiders. Louise began taking a monthly train trip to Detroit and also began to rely on local leaders such as Reverend Charles A. Hill, pastor of Hartford Avenue Baptist Church, who had expressed strong support for the IWO at the convention, and Eleanor Broady, who had experience as an IWO operative. Louise felt confident enough to write, "We can begin to hammer out leadership and a program."[40]

By the time the general council met in November, two weeks after Roosevelt's reelection, black membership in the IWO stood at thirty-five hundred, a significant increase but not enough to satisfy Bedacht and other leaders, including Louise and Sam Patterson. On the afternoon of November 25, Louise presided over yet another discussion about recruiting. This time, she had assembled a rather large group of black activists to introduce to the IWO leadership, among them the Communist Party stalwarts James Ford, Maude White, and Ben Davis, now a New York City councilman. Also on hand were Ada Jackson (a city council candidate from Brooklyn) and Urban League official Frank Montero, who had sometimes been Louise's adversary on the trip to Russia in 1932. All pledged support for the recruiting initiative, which became crystallized as a campaign to enroll six thousand new black members, two thousand of them in the Windy City, during the first six months of 1945.

The Chicago crew, most notably Peck, Gerrard, Mohn, Benjamin Browning, James Tate, Theodore Green, Gladys Durham, Maude Clements, Fred

Jackson, and La Ursa Hedrick, gladly accepted the challenge. After a slow start because of the holidays, business picked up dramatically in February, bolstered by a Negro history program at Canaan Baptist. Robeson helped to keep the momentum rolling through May with an appearance at Canaan that, according to Louise, "worked wonders."[41] More than a thousand new applications were in hand by the end of May. Louise, operating out of an office on East Thirty-Fifth Street, reported to Milgrom, "It's a madhouse." Of course, she was not complaining. In fact, she conveyed to Milgrom concerning the campaign, "I personally feel better about it than ever before, for I see that we have something that can take on proportions of a real mass movement."[42]

On June 17, 1945, fifteen hundred new members were inducted into the Du Sable Lodge. Louise organized a celebratory program at the Du Sable High School auditorium. In a bit of rhetorical wisdom, the event doubled as a tribute to President Roosevelt, who had died in April. Robeson once again made an inspiring appearance, which played no small part in convincing five hundred additional people to sign up by July 1. Headquarters gushed about the campaign's success for weeks afterward, with Milgrom scrambling to place congratulatory ads in the black press. Louise seized on the success of the membership drive to expand the influence of the Du Sable Lodge. Working with Peck, other lodge leaders, and an array of community activists and trade unionists, she helped to establish the Du Sable Community Center to provide broader cultural programming for children and adults.

However, claiming victory with an IWO membership drive and cultural initiatives did not ensure workers' success with regard to labor issues. In the immediate postwar period, they met stiff resistance as they tried to parlay their acquiescence to wartime austerity measures into material advances. As a result, more than six thousand strikes, involving more than seven million employees, were called during the first eighteen months following the surrender of the Axis powers.[43] Black veterans returning from the war fueled much of the militant action. As one soldier explained, "I couldn't see myself being discriminated against. . . . We died, our blood had been shed for this country, and I felt . . . that we should get a better deal out of it. Instead of crumbs we wanted a slice of the pie."[44] The new mood saturated the United Packinghouse Workers of America (UPWA), which was largely African American by 1946. Going head to head with three giants of the meatpacking industry—Armour, Swift, and Wilson—the union, perhaps the most militant in Chicago, refused to settle for an easy peace with postwar liberal democracy.[45] Moreover, given that the massive Union Stockyards sat little more than a mile from the Black Belt and drew many of its forty thousand workers from that community, the union agenda and broader civil rights platform developed literally alongside one another.

Louise could hardly avoid that phase of the struggle, and she readily backed the efforts of unionists such as Herbert March and Sam Parks. March, a Brooklyn native and former member of the Young Communist League, had moved to Chicago in 1933, when he was twenty years old, and had begun working at Armour. Committed to building a Communist presence in the stockyards, he eventually became the district director of the UPWA.[46] Parks, one of the most eloquent Washington Park orators, studied law in night school after arriving in Chicago from Memphis in 1940. His goal was to become a sharp, unscrupulous lawyer who could "fuck over, freak up, rob Negroes" and grow rich.[47] In the meantime, he began work as a freezer man for Wilson in 1941 and, shifting to nobler aims, became a dynamic leader in UPWA Local 25. He won the union presidency in 1944. Understanding the strength of focused interracial alliances, Parks reasoned in retrospect, "The thing that made the Packinghouse Workers a progressive union was the combination of the blacks and the white Left. The Communists and the blacks, that's what made it. And there were the whites in the union that weren't Communist, but they were progressive. I think that the Left whites and the Communist whites helped to make a hell of a difference in that union: standing out as an example, cooperating and working with blacks, and then talking to a lot of white workers in the plant."[48] Charles Hayes, an officer in UPWA Local 25 along with Parks, felt similarly: "Black folks didn't get caught up in the syndrome of looking under the rug in every room for a red. It just didn't ring a bell with them. We wanted to get free. I don't care who helps us, help us, you know, that was the general attitude."[49]

By January 1946 the UPWA had demanded a 25 percent pay hike nationally. When negotiations stalled, the union called a strike on January 16. Louise gathered with Parks, March, and other Southside leaders at Morris Perfect Eat Shop, in the heart of Bronzeville, to discuss strategy and organize a citizens' committee to support the union. The members included Flory, Oscar C. Brown, and radical poet and journalist Frank Marshall Davis. The *Chicago Defender* photographed a smiling trio—Louise, Parks, and March—examining a document related to the deliberations.[50]

Once the strike went into effect and the industry, with the exception of a few independents, ceased production nationwide, President Harry S. Truman, feeling pressured because the auto workers and steelworkers had already struck, countered decisively by seizing the packinghouses on January 24. The Amalgamated Meat Cutters, an allied union, capitulated.[51] However, the UPWA held out and secured a heady victory. Wage increases didn't reach 25 percent, but it was a better deal than the Amalgamated Meat Cutters obtained.[52]

Louise also teamed with Parks on civic efforts, including the demand that Mayor Edward J. Kelly overhaul the ineffective Commission on Human Relations, which had been established in 1943 to combat racism but had functioned in a decidedly "weak-kneed" manner, according to critics.[53] Local cleric James Horace of Monumental Baptist Church charged the commission, headed by Thomas Wright, with "shadow boxing with occasional issues instead of constantly hammering at the city's vicious race discrimination."[54] Wright had, in fact, opposed involving the agency in the fight against restrictive housing covenants. Advocating for substantive action, Louise, Parks, and several others delivered a letter to Kelly outlining their concerns at the beginning of April.

Perhaps no political issue lay closer to the heart for Louise and Pat than the fate of the Abraham Lincoln School, born of his experiences teaching at a workers' school in Pittsburgh in the 1930s and recently at the one on South Dearborn Street. Pat had conceived of the school as a nonselective, nonpartisan institution for workers, writers, and sympathizers that would foster deeply analytic study of race and class, primarily to build a bridge of understanding between migrant African Americans and European immigrants, two groups new to the "American urban industrial complex."[55] He explained:

> I had in mind a school in which we would teach how society had developed its class structure, how it functioned and was held together, what social forces dominated it and how those who were exploited and oppressed could escape. Above all, I believed that the many and varied contributions of Black Americans to the economic, political, artistic and social life of our country had to be uncovered. In a word, the acquisition of knowledge that would make it easier for those who fought together for better conditions on the job to see the dire need that they also fight together on the political front.[56]

After eliciting encouragement from Robeson, Henry Winston, and a then-tolerable Browder, he approached "merchant prince" Marshall Field III at the suggestion of Clara Taylor, who assisted Pat with the project.[57] Field was becoming increasingly known for his progressive leanings and served on the board of Saul Alinsky's Industrial Areas Foundation. He provided funds that enabled Pat to open the school in 1944 on the top floor of a building on West Washington Street. Historian A. D. Winspear assumed the post of director, and civil liberties lawyer Pearl Hart chaired the board. Faculty members included Pat, Flory, and Frank Marshall Davis, who taught pioneering courses on the history of jazz.[58]

In Pat's estimation, the Abraham Lincoln School "gave impetus to the cultural and educational life of Chicago."[59] Louise devoted substantial time and energy to keeping the school in operation. Although hobbled by a leg injury in the fall of 1946 and still saddled with numerous obligations to the Du Sable Lodge and IWO, she managed to coordinate several fund-raising efforts to support the school and the Du Sable Community Center, with the aid of Robeson and the latest celebrity she could depend on, Lena Horne. The flower of the films *Stormy Weather* and *Cabin in the Sky* had blossomed into a social activist and embraced Louise's work. On April 27, 1947, during a tremendously successful month-long engagement in Chicago, Horne participated in "Chicago Salutes Paul Robeson," an affair held at the Civic Opera House.[60] In conjunction with the event, she presented Louise with a check for $1,000.[61]

Although Louise and the Left-labor coalition could certainly point to tangible achievements—IWO membership would swell to 188,000 by the end of 1947, making it by far the largest and most viable left-wing organization of its era—it was clear that the legacy of her years in Chicago would be decidedly mixed.[62] American-Soviet détente and widespread sympathy for Communism had already become the casualties of history after talk of the Marshall Plan, Iron Curtain, and Cold War, as well as a Soviet-controlled coup in Czechoslovakia; the Right sought to further stagger a disoriented Left with a legislative and law-enforcement blitz. In particular, the union-busting Taft-Hartley Act became law on June 23, 1947, over Truman's veto, and the FBI engaged in heightened surveillance and harassment, jousting with Red windmills while wreaking far more havoc than the average Quixote.[63] The FBI's intimidation tactics contributed to people shying away from the Abraham Lincoln School and led to its closing despite its obvious value.[64] On the labor front, the UPWA, Louise's most important union connection, suffered an unequivocal setback in a second strike. To punctuate the defeat, Red Squads led by police captain George Barnes attacked strikers and detained so-called Communist agitators.[65] Moreover, the CIO overall began to succumb to pressure to purge its ranks of its most radical advocates. Emboldened authorities raided the CPUSA's offices and indicted twelve of its leaders under the Smith Act.

Nonetheless, Henry A. Wallace's candidacy for president inspired hope. The former vice president and standard-bearer of the newly formed Progressive Party had been persuaded by W. E. B. Du Bois to seek the presidency as a third-party candidate. Following Du Bois's lead, Louise, Pat, Robeson, and much of the black Left poured tremendous energy into the campaign. They did not expect electoral triumph, of course. Rather, they sought to keep progressive arguments a respectable part of American political discourse. Two months before the election of 1948, a Wallace rally at Yankee Stadium sponsored by the American Labor Party drew a crowd of almost fifty thousand.[66]

Louise also felt guardedly optimistic about the CPUSA-affiliated Civil Rights Congress, formed in 1946 at a conference in Detroit, initially as a consolidation of the ILD and the National Federation for Constitutional Liberties. The group merged with what was left of the National Negro Congress in December 1947. As in the Scottsboro days, Pat continued slugging it out within the legal system and the court of public opinion on behalf of wronged defendants in high-profile cases. Willie McGee, a married father of four, had been wrongly convicted of raping a white woman in Mississippi. Rosa Lee Ingram and her teenage sons, Wallace and Sammie Lee, were found guilty of murdering a white neighbor in Georgia, despite a lack of legitimate evidence and the denial of adequate legal representation. Murder judgments and death penalties were hung on the Trenton Six—Ralph Cooper, Collis English, McKinley Forrest, John McKenzie, James Thorpe, and Horace Wilson—though all had plausible alibis. With a demanding job and a five-year-old daughter, Louise could not be the organizing buzz saw of 1933 but attended her share of rallies and made speeches before the final split decision: the state executed McGee; the Ingrams' lives were spared, but lengthy stretches in prison awaited them; four of the Trenton Six won reversals, and none served more than six years.

As the legal battles unfolded, Pat, in many ways the heart and soul of the Civil Rights Congress, assumed the top post, an assignment that required relocation to New York near the end of 1948. Louise's resultant decision was simple, at least in retrospect: "We, the family, followed the father."[67] She meant geographically, not in terms of specific organizational work. Concluding a fifteen-year run with the IWO, she would become the director of organizing for the Council on African Affairs (CAA). Established in 1937, the CAA, also affiliated with the CPUSA, was the primary American entity bringing attention to the problems and struggles of Africans. In addition to providing speakers, films, and reports—the kind of work Louise had done during her Soviet-friendship phase in Harlem—the CAA organized some direct aid to the continent. Moreover, the council promoted an understanding of the link between African and African American struggles. The current executive director, Alphaeus Hunton, taught, "Racial oppression and exploitation have a universal pattern, and whether they occur in South Africa, Mississippi or New Jersey, they must be exposed and fought as part of a worldwide system of oppression, the fountain-head of which is today among the reactionary and fascist-minded ruling circles of white America."[68] In this analysis, masses of Africans and African Americans were natural allies in a battle against capitalism, imperialism, and Jim Crow.

The urbane Hunton, a former English professor, had become an officer of the CAA in 1943 while on leave from Howard University. The following year, he resigned from Howard and moved to New York to manage the council's daily operations. During 1948, like many agencies on the left, the CAA endured internal power struggles, particularly between Robeson, Du Bois, and Hunton on one side and executive director Max Yergan, whom Louise had regarded highly, on the other. A founder of the CAA and the former head of the National Negro Congress, Yergan had begun a process of self-reinvention in the face of anti-Communist hysteria. He charged that Communists were running the organization, fired Hunton, and tried to seize control from Robeson, the council's chair. After a series of moves and countermoves, the apostate Yergan, who had committed several fiscal improprieties and later ranged so far right that he became an apologist for apartheid South Africa and Moïse Tshombe's warped ambitions in the Congo, was expelled in September 1948.[69]

The infighting cost the CAA some of its mainstream membership, including Mary McLeod Bethune, Adam Clayton Powell Jr., and Judge Hubert Delany (who had called Louise a liar extraordinaire during the Harlem-riot hearings in 1935). All insults could have been forgiven, though, had Delany kept up his fight in the council for African empowerment. Ben Davis remained integral, as did Doxey Wilkerson and Henry Winston, both of whom had become prominent in New York after Louise's departure in 1940. Her first mentor, Du Bois (now eighty years old), moved his headquarters to the CAA after being forced out of the NAACP by Walter White, largely because of disagreements about Truman's foreign policy.[70] But a wobbly CAA needed an outreach campaign, a task Louise was perfectly suited to undertake in the aftermath of a rift she had observed from afar. After she conferred with Hunton about recruiting, the executive committee announced the appointment, in April 1949, of the organization's new political dynamo.

CHAPTER 10

Sojourns and Sojourners, 1949–1959

L ouise Thompson Patterson landed simultaneously in New York City and at ground zero of the Red Scare. In the midst of the frenzy created by loyalty oaths, union busting, waves of faculty firings, deportation cases, and espionage prosecutions, the first of the Smith Act trials was under way. On March 7, 1949, eleven Communist Party leaders, including Ben Davis, Louise's former collaborator in the Harlem section and on the Scottsboro case, appeared before Judge Harold Medina in the federal courthouse on Foley Square in Lower Manhattan.[1] On this overall McCarthyite political terrain, Louise searched for the organizing magic to jumpstart the CAA. No one reasonably expected her to match her phenomenal accomplishments at the IWO. The council was still experiencing the fallout from Max Yergan's failed bid for control, and its rolls listed only a few dozen members.[2] Its most solid fiscal resource, personal financing by its chairman, Paul Robeson, would not enable a significant expansion of activities. But the always-accommodating Robeson retained drawing power. Thus, it made perfect sense to send him on a national fund-raising tour benefiting several causes in the fall of 1949 and to incorporate a membership drive for the CAA. Louise would serve as the advance person for a man she regarded as a tower of strength, fearlessness, and commitment.[3] They targeted six cities: Philadelphia, Washington, Cleveland, Detroit, Chicago, and Los Angeles. Louise envisioned establishing numerous CAA chapters and sustaining a national presence.[4] However, she had to dial down such optimism in the wake of increasing intolerance, especially toward Robeson, in the latter half of 1949.

The first damper resulted from Robeson's remarks at the Paris Peace Conference in April. He declared, "Our will for peace is strong. We shall not make war on anyone. We shall not make war on the Soviet Union."[5] This represented normative discourse at the convention; several other featured participants provided similar antiwar fare. To the dismay of many, however, a wire service somewhat inaccurately reported that Robeson also commented, "It is unthinkable that American Negroes would go to war on behalf of those who have oppressed us for generations against a country which in one generation has raised our people to the full dignity of mankind."[6] Robeson's opponents branded him a traitor and mobilized against him, forcing the cancellation of speaking engagements and concert performances.

Anti-Robeson hysteria had reached its apex by late summer, yet the activist performer was poised to make a breakthrough as he prepared for a concert on behalf of the Harlem chapter of the Civil Rights Congress at a venue familiar to him, the Lakeland Acres Picnic Area just outside of Peekskill, New York. Regrettably, organizers of the event did not seem to be fully aware of the danger in the air. Some locals, particularly upset because Lakeland Acres lay directly across Hillside Avenue from the Hillside and Assumption Cemeteries, where some veterans of foreign wars were buried, became indignant that Robeson and his supporters were coming to town. "Let us leave no doubt in their minds that they are unwelcome around here either now or in the future," wrote Vincent Boyle in a letter to the *Peekskill Evening Star* published on August 18.[7] Four days later, an editorial titled "The Discordant Note" ran in the paper advising Robeson that the proper use of his talent would have earned him a place as a truly great Negro American alongside Booker T. Washington and George Washington Carver. That opportunity, in the observer's mind, had been irreversibly lost.[8]

In contrast to the angry mood, Louise celebrated her husband's fifty-eighth birthday, which fell on August 27, the day of the planned concert. Feeling fatigued after a series of fund-raising events in the Catskills, she decided to forgo the show and stay home with Mary Lou. However, she invited all of her and Pat's friends who were attending the concert to stop by the cottage where the Pattersons were vacationing, located on Mount Airy Road in the nearby Croton-on-Hudson, to enjoy refreshments en route.[9] Collective merriment soon turned to horror, though, when rioting right-wing whites, in league with the police, forced postponement of the show. Robeson avoided bodily harm, as did Pat. But in a stunning display of the ultra-authoritarian white nationalism and faux patriotism that characterized Fascist impulses in the United States, rioters assaulted numerous members of the audience and also smashed the stage and set fire to chairs. Pat and Robeson retreated to

Harlem for an emergency meeting, and Pat did not arrive home to a worried Louise until nearly midnight.

With a much-enhanced pro-Robeson security presence, the rescheduled concert took place on September 4 at the former Hollow Brook Country Club, about half a mile north of the first site. Twenty thousand people attended, and the singer performed without interruption. Yet proto-Fascist forces, perhaps even more frenzied after the Soviet Union tested an atomic bomb on August 29, lined the sides of Route 9 to attack those attempting to leave town.[10] Louise saw rioters overturn a car and shatter its windows.[11] Later, after she had escaped via back roads and had enough distance from the event to allow humor, she reflected whimsically about how she characteristically seemed to get caught up in such chaos, as she had in Harlem in 1935.[12]

Possessing as good a phone book as anyone on the left, Louise proved to be an ideal agent for Robeson as they pushed forward in the aftermath of reactionary and racist violence. She secured major performance venues and meeting halls, and used her contacts to help create a considerable buzz despite a veritable blackout by the white press.[13] Typically, she would arrive in town three days before Robeson and check his accommodations, beat the drums of local publicity, and meet with local authorities about security, which usually included police motorcades.[14] Her efforts paid off as enthusiastic audiences awaited Robeson at places such as the Paradise Auditorium in the heart of Cleveland's Cedar-Central neighborhood and Bakers Hall on the North Side of Chicago, as well as Tabernacle Baptist Church on the South Side. Along with displaying his marvelous baritone in song, Robeson usually wove in criticism of Harry S. Truman's foreign policy and expressed his own ideas about peaceful coexistence with world Communism. He condemned the war preparations in Korea and favored instead sending troops to Mississippi and Alabama to ensure the freedom of African Americans.[15] Louise noticed that many African American police officers—Robeson preferred an all-black detail—were eager to get the embattled star's signature even if they could not or would not express their support publicly.[16]

The tour unfolded without major disturbances, though shrewd opponents in Detroit accused Louise and her colleagues of trying to foment violence. George Schermer, head of the Detroit Interracial Committee, explained to members that Robeson was a valuable Communist Party asset and that a standard party ploy was to orchestrate violence to get attention. Schermer acknowledged that Robeson's attempts to raise funds and champion the downtrodden were laudable, but he warned the committee members not to be provoked to displays of brutality or even spirited demonstrations, and to encourage others to avoid this as well. The best strategy, in Schermer's estimation, was the opposite of that deployed in Peekskill. In other words, they should ignore Robeson and refuse to fan the flames of controversy.[17] Schermer also distributed his memorandum to newspapers, veterans' organizations, and other groups. Eugene Van Antwerp, the mayor of Detroit, endorsed his efforts, as did the Michigan Committee on Civil Rights.[18] Nevertheless, thousands came to hear Robeson at Sunny Wilson's Forest Club, where an overflow crowd stretched for six blocks outside.[19] As part of his show, he offered observations about the changing political climate: "When I came here many times for concerts, I got the finest reviews from the press. When Joe Louis and Marian Anderson and I came here to speak and sing at bond rallies during the war we were given a civic reception, greeted by the mayor and governor. What has happened? I am still the same man. I still speak and fight for justice, against fascism, for peace, like I did in those days. Just what has happened is that I am fighting for it now; that's why the atmosphere is changed."[20] Afterward, he walked the relatively short distance to Shiloh Baptist Church and performed again. He followed up the next day with an appearance at Hartford Avenue Baptist Church. "There," his son wrote, "he recalled the tribulations of his father, who escaped from slavery as a teenager, and reemphasized his two main themes: racism, not communism, loomed as humankind's greatest enemy, and communists, who were both antiracist and anticolonialist, could not possibly be the enemies of black people."[21]

In Los Angeles Louise connected with the estimable Charlotta Bass, a woman she likened to Ida B. Wells because of her moral courage and journalistic vision.[22] Almost three decades older than Louise, Bass, a native of South Carolina, published the *California Eagle*, the largest African American newspaper on the West Coast. She had been a leader in the local chapters of both the NAACP and Marcus Garvey's Universal Negro Improvement Association. For more than twenty years, she had used her weekly column, "On the Sidewalk," to make a multipronged argument for political and social change. Aware of Bass's reach as a power player in black Los Angeles, actress Beah Richards, who assisted Bass during the 1940s, quipped fondly, "You had to go through Mrs. Bass if you wanted to go to the toilet."[23] Louise worked with Bass, whose newspaper benefited financially from Robeson's appearance, to stage a concert at Wrigley Field. During the hectic preparations, Louise admired Bass's calmness and serenity: "I remember everybody was running around and going out of their minds, and Mrs. Bass was just sitting in that room as cool as a cucumber."[24]

Bass had little reason to fret on that occasion. Even though the city council took the unprecedented step of passing a resolution urging citizens to boycott the event, an enthusiastic audience of seventeen thousand people welcomed Robeson. Standing in the area near second base, he dedicated his first number, "Go Down, Moses," to Bass. Later in the show, he articulated his primary political message for the day: "Black people throughout the world are calling for their freedom. War cannot gain that freedom for them. They want peace. War cannot gain us the right to vote, civil rights and the right not to be lynched. War will be in the interest of a few people, not in the interest of the great masses."[25]

The buoyant reception that Robeson received across the country convinced Louise once again of people's capacity and readiness to mobilize. "We were walking on air when we got back," she noted.[26] Unfortunately, long-lasting tangible gains were few. Numerical strength displayed in a stadium did not equate to growth for the CAA or stabilize it against harassment and persecution. At any rate, as concrete support for black radicalism diminished, an elaborate infrastructure for the CAA remained little more than wishful thinking. Moreover, its leadership was subjected to increased attacks—though more for being pro-Soviet than pro-Africa at that point—after the conviction in October of the defendants in the Smith Act trial. The Justice Department pressed for disclosure of the names of those who had contributed to the Civil Rights Bail Fund, which had enabled the convicted defendants to remain free pending appeal. Initiated by the Civil Rights Congress to support leftists facing legal problems because of their political beliefs, the fund, which contained more than $700,000, was administered by writer Dashiell Hammett; progressive scion Frederick Vanderbilt Field; Abner Green, who served as the executive secretary of the American Committee for Protection of Foreign Born; and CAA director Alphaeus Hunton.[27] The four trustees refused the government's demand that they furnish the contributors' names and were subsequently charged with criminal contempt. Meanwhile, the government zeroed in on Robeson and infamously canceled his passport in July 1950. Louise arranged the meeting at which he was to surrender his passport to Internal Security agents.[28] Robeson decided not to surrender the document, however, at which point the government voided it.[29]

The following month, inquisitors struck even closer to home for Louise when Congress, the House Lobbying Committee in particular, subpoenaed

Pat to question him about the Civil Rights Congress's membership list. Louise, along with many on the left in New York, including Eslanda Robeson and Claudia Jones, traveled to Washington several times to show support. The most dramatic point of the proceedings, during which Pat never revealed the names of any Civil Rights Congress backers, occurred when he agitated committee member Henderson Lanham, a representative from Georgia. Patterson asked Lanham, "How many Negroes have you lynched?" Lanham notoriously responded by calling Patterson a "god-damned black son-of-a-bitch!" and charging the witness, who prepared to defend himself before the guards interceded. After a quick adjournment, the congressman reportedly declared, "We've got to keep those black apes down!"[30] In a strikingly perverse turn of jurisprudence, Lanham, the physically aggressive hurler of invective, filed contempt charges against Pat, who then had more to worry about than just concealing the congress's membership.

Before standing trial, Pat, with Louise as his primary respondent, worked intensely on the document that would be published the following year as *We Charge Genocide: The Crime of Government against the Negro People*. Known popularly as the "genocide petition," the treatise spoke directly to the Genocide Convention adopted on December 9, 1948, by the UN General Assembly and signed by the United States. It was scheduled to take effect on January 12, 1951. Thus, Pat had a stronger legal claim than advocates such as the National Negro Congress and W. E. B. Du Bois, who had submitted earlier pleas to the United Nations regarding redress for African Americans.[31] In a rhetorical high-wire act, he argued that America's tolerance for and perpetuation of lynching, police brutality, voting disfranchisement, and health disparities fit the convention's definition of genocide as the "intent to destroy, in whole or part, a national, ethnical, racial or religious group."[32] With regard to racist crimes committed between January 1945 and June 1951, Pat included synopses of more than 150 cases of murder or state executions and more than 350 instances of beating, maiming, rape, or threats.[33] He contended that his evidence, though voluminous, did not capture the vast majority of such crimes, which remained unreported and unpublicized.[34] Moreover, he argued that given their poor living conditions and health care, 32,000 African Americans were killed each year, for a total of 200,000 since the United States' signing of the UN charter in 1945.[35]

Louise certainly thought this proper conversation for the dinner table. Indeed, political understanding and alignment fueled the Patterson marriage as much as anything else. Friends for nearly a quarter century and activist allies well before they were married, neither Louise nor Pat expected or desired that domestic life would curtail their activist commitments. Moreover, their home life was never insular, with the Patterson residence being a jovial hub for visitors, as had been the case every place Louise had lived in New York. More card player than dancer by then, Pat loved company, as did Louise. Although firm in their political commitments, they entertained friends of various persuasions. "The only people not welcome," she recalled, "would be traitors."[36] Some guests were semipermanent, part of Louise's plan to ensure that Mary Lou was taken care of during her parents' extended absences. Louise mostly felt secure that she had found the ideal strategy for nurturing her daughter. But, perhaps expressing regret, she once asked an adult Mary Lou whether she had been happy with the arrangements, a question her daughter sidestepped.[37]

But there was no other way at that time for the Pattersons. Late that summer, a couple of days before Louise's forty-ninth birthday, Pat traveled to Europe for several months to push the preliminary genocide petition in England, France, Hungary, Czechoslovakia, Germany, Switzerland, and Austria. Domestically, Louise and the CAA had to accept that, never able to recover fully from the Yergan fiasco, it would be more a local community group than a national force. Consequently, there was no practical need for a director of organizing. Undeterred, however, Louise followed a familiar path—a harrowing trail of Jim Crow insults and atrocities, as well as the shared outrage of friends—to her next broad-based venture, her most significant one in the 1950s.

On February 2 and February 5, 1951, the Martinsville Seven were executed in Virginia. Arrested two years earlier for allegedly raping Ruby Floyd, a white woman, the men—Frank Hairston Jr., Booker Millner, Howard Lee Hairston, James Luther Hairston, John Claybon Taylor, Francis DeSales Grayson, and Joe Hampton—had been convicted by all-white, all-male juries. With less verbally vulgar racism than the Alabama authorities in the Scottsboro case, Virginia officials overrode the public outcry, took advantage of the U.S. Supreme Court's silence in the matter, and carried out the largest mass execution for rape in the nation's history.

A far less grisly affair, but one no less telling of intolerance, involved the arrest of Du Bois a few days later. Having served as the chairman of the Peace Information Center, a short-lived organization created in April 1950 to publicize the Stockholm Peace Appeal, Du Bois was indicted on February 9, 1951—well after the organization had disbanded—for failing to register as an agent of a foreign principal within the United States. The charges were eventually dismissed, but not before many liberals deserted Du Bois. So many people canceled their scheduled appearance at his birthday celebration that the event was moved from the Essex House in midtown Manhattan to the friendly confines of Small's Paradise in Harlem.

The Pattersons backed Du Bois even in the midst of their own legal battles. Pat scored a partial victory in the spring of 1951 when a racially integrated jury failed to convict him in the contempt trial. But he faced a retrial, still feeling the legal heat along with fellow black radicals and friends Ben Davis and Henry Winston. At the time of her husband's trial in Washington, Louise suddenly faced a courtroom date in New York in connection to her work with the IWO, which had become a priority target for right-wing forces after then United States attorney general Tom Clark included the group on his list of subversive organizations in 1947. Although the IWO's fiscal practices had on several occasions been proven to be sound, Governor Thomas Dewey and the State of New York Insurance Department moved to liquidate the organization, to which one million people had belonged at one time or another.[38] Essentially, they hounded the IWO for being Communist and sought to root out Communist leadership. If witnesses lied about their political affiliations, they could face perjury charges. The trial typified the tight one-two combination employed by red-baiting officials: the Smith Act for the openly Communist, and provocation to perjury or contempt of court for suspected Communists.

As Red Scare trials went, this one involved relatively low stakes. No one faced jail time, for example, related to the primary charges. In this civil case, the prosecution sought to prove that the IWO's leadership was Communist, which it knew would persuade the judge to liquidate the organization. If witnesses invoked the Fifth Amendment when asked about direct involvement in the Communist Party, that would constitute proof enough, the prosecution figured, in those proceedings. So the point was not to convict Louise of anything but to get her to take the Fifth. Besides, less active in higher party circles, she was not as attractive a prize for the Right as the current leading black woman in the CPUSA, the perpetually hounded Claudia Jones.[39] If Louise exposed herself to further legal jeopardy, that would have been a bonus for prosecutors. But this was not their main goal on April 6, 1951, when she took the stand, stylish and stately at the age of forty-nine, before a packed house in room 300 of the Supreme Court of the County of New York.

Defense attorney Raphael Weissman handled the first part of her testimony. Likely retained by the IWO in an effort to appear mainstream during the deliberations, the "basically conservative" Weissman led Louise through a lengthy retelling of the major contours of her life journey.[40] He aimed to depict Louise, and through her the IWO, as primarily concerned with racial and ethnic equality.[41] The questioning and testimony dragged into a second day as assistant prosecutor James B. Henry focused during cross-examination on establishing that Louise had been a prominent Communist throughout her years as an IWO officer. He pointed to New York City voting records for 1936, which indicated that Louise had registered as a Communist to participate in an election primary.[42] When asked directly about party membership, Louise followed her counsel's advice not to answer. It mattered little. They were not after her, and no testimony she could provide, nor the amicus brief filed by Du Bois, Robeson, and some two hundred supporters, in which they decried the "menace to the democratic structure of American life," would save the IWO.[43] Prosecutors and judges remained on a roll. In June, the same month in which the U.S. Supreme Court upheld the first-wave Smith Act convictions, Judge Henry Clay Greenberg issued his opinion against the IWO.

A few weeks later, racist violence erupted in the Chicago suburb of Cicero, Illinois, as a mob of several thousand whites attacked the apartment building into which Harvey Clark, a black World War II veteran, had moved with his family over the objections of locals, including the police. Rioters proceeded in their destruction virtually unchecked until Governor Adlai Stevenson dispatched the National Guard, which had to fend off attacks. Although the violence lasted several days, the Cook County grand jury indicted no rioters, bringing charges instead against Clark's lawyer, the landlord, and the landlord's representatives for inciting a riot and conspiring to damage property.

While the lengthening list of absurdities primed Louise for organizing beyond the confines of the CAA, or her husband's Civil Rights Congress for that matter, it took the spark of Beah Richards, also known by her birth name, Beulah Richardson, to establish the action agenda for carrying forward cutting-edge political work. An elegant dancer, poet, playwright, and essayist as well as actress, Richards—perhaps best remembered these days for playing Baby Suggs in the film *Beloved* (released in 1998)—was also intellectually impressive and, about twenty years younger than Louise, very energetic. The two met at the home of actress Frances Williams in Los Angeles. After hearing Richards read, Louise encouraged her to move to New York, as several people had encouraged Louise to do in her youth. Following a stay with the writer Alice Childress on Riverside Drive, Richards ended up on Edgecombe Avenue with Louise, whom she considered her mentor.[44] The two were central to the formation of the initiating committee for what became the militant, black-feminist Sojourners for Truth and Justice. The committee consisted of fourteen formidable women, including Bass, Childress, Shirley Graham, Dorothy Hunton, Rosalie McGee, and Eslanda Robeson.

In the spirit of her signature and now-classic poem, "A Black Woman Speaks of White Womanhood, of White Supremacy, of Peace," Richards began to craft with Louise on behalf of the committee a response to the recent wave of repression.[45] With Louise pacing the floor for hours and Richards fixing sentences onto the page, the dynamic duo produced "A Call to Negro Women," which was made public in September above the signature of the acting secretary, "Beah Richardson." The manifesto implored "dear Negro sisters everywhere in the United States" to assemble in Washington, DC, from Saturday, September 29, through Monday, October 1, for a "sojourn for truth and justice." Linking feminist, domestic civil rights, and internationalist human rights visions, the conveners argued, "Our action will carry forward the tradition of Harriet Tubman and Sojourner Truth and will give inspiration and courage to women the world over, especially the colored women of Africa and Asia who expect us to make this challenge."[46] And challenge they did, as they planned a blitz of the power corridors of Washington, starting at the top. They sent a letter to the White House requesting a meeting with President Truman. Citing several problems, including the legal judgments in Cicero and the spilling of black blood in Korea, they were curious to see whether Truman would "heed the voice of Negro women who come to Washington in a Sojourn for Truth and Justice for unconditional redress of our long insulted, long impoverished, legally and illegally lynched people." They reminded the president of his speech on September 17 at the Constitution Day ceremonies at the Library of Congress, during which he told the nation that the Declaration of Independence and the Constitution were "more than historical relics."[47] It seemed logical to them, therefore, that the president would grant an audience to "hear from us with your own ears—from us, the most oppressed in this great land of ours, that the Constitution—nor the unenforced Amendments—does not protect us from the evils of tyranny or against the illegal use of power."[48]

They also sought to meet with the secretary of the army, Frank Pace Jr., because they wanted him to explain to "the Negro women of these United States" how the army can "take peace and freedom to the people of any nation while at home our government has never and does not now protect the lives and liberties of fifteen million of its own citizens." The committee cited abuses such as the shooting death of John Derrick by police officers in Harlem and the conviction of Lieutenant Leon Gilbert, which, in its view, had caused Kay Gilbert to deliver a stillborn baby.[49] The soon-to-be Sojourners—they used no official title yet—pressed Secretary of State Dean Acheson to spell out "with what honesty representatives of our government can protest through the Voice of America and the United Nations forced labor or lack of basic freedom in other parts of the world, yet utter no word of protest about peonage and chain gangs in our poll tax states, the lynching and flogging of Negroes by the Ku Klux Klan as they seek to exercise their right to vote, the bombing and burning of homes of Negroes seeking decent places in which to live."[50]

Of Attorney General J. Howard McGrath they demanded an explanation for, among other things, the failure of his department to identify and convict mob members who committed violence against blacks, as in Peekskill and Cicero. Reminding or lecturing McGrath, they spelled out that "the implementation of the 13th, 14th and 15th Amendments to the U.S. Constitution, the execution of the Bill of Rights demands a Department of Justice that will vigilantly and energetically prosecute their flagrant subversion." The group also conveyed their intention to file indemnity claims on behalf of African American women who had been deprived of their husbands, homes, or land because of racist violence and who, with children to rear, had been rendered destitute.[51]

The organizers' sweep of Washington included the Democratic National Committee. The sojourners urged the "ruling majority political party" to outline its intended response to the events in Cicero and to account for its failure to curb or censure racist acts by members (such as Lanham's insult of Pat).[52] In similar fashion, they criticized William L. Dawson, an African American congressman from Chicago, for allowing Lanham to use him as a character reference in an attempt to prove impartiality regarding race. More important, they sought to push Dawson to be more active concerning the Cicero indictments and wanted to know whether Dawson would support them as they pressed claims for indemnity on behalf of African American women. Referencing Truman's Constitution Day speech, the initiating committee communicated to Dawson its wish to "tell you and other representatives of our government how we feel these documents can be implemented to realize full justice and dignity for 15,000,000 Negro Americans."[53] For good measure, the committee submitted a petition to the Justice Department demanding the dismissal of the indictment against Du Bois and the restoration of Robeson's passport privileges.

Of course, Louise, Richards, and their collaborators knew that they would not get all of that action in Washington. Nevertheless, enthusiasm ran high among the 117 women from coast to coast who answered the call. The largest delegation, with seventy-one members, arrived on the noon train from New York.[54] Claudia Jones, who had been indicted under the Smith Act and placed under house arrest, was denied permission to travel by Judge Gregory Noonan of the District Court for the Southern District of New York. She lent her support through a telegram, declaring, "Though I cannot be with you in person, I am with you in mind, heart, and spirit. You may count on me to continue our mutual fight for peace and freedom."[55]

After eagerly reporting to the headquarters of the Cafeteria Workers Union, a reliably left-leaning outfit operating from 1015 M Street, NW, the sojourners worked out the logistics of housing and subcommittees. Emma Robinson of the Washington group welcomed everyone; Pauline Taylor of Youngstown, Ohio, presided over the afternoon's plenary session. After the group sang the Negro national anthem, Richards read the "Call to Negro Women" and led a new song she had composed, "We Are Sojourners for Our Rights, till We Wake Up the Conscience of the Land." Eighty-eight-year-old Mary Church Terrell, regarded by many in attendance as the "dean of Negro women," congratulated the conveners on the inspiring call and on their determination to hold the nation to its ideals.[56]

Several women testified as to why they were attending the gathering. Emma Westray, for example, spoke of the murder of her only son by a New York City policeman. "I am ready to fight on," she offered bravely. "Just tell me where to fight." Josephine Grayson, a mother of five and the wife of Francis DeSales Grayson, one of the victims in the Martinsville executions, also vowed to keep battling. Dorothy Hunton spoke of the imprisonment of Alphaeus Hunton, who had been serving time in the federal penitentiary in Petersburg, Virginia, after his contempt conviction. Eslanda Robeson addressed her husband's passport case.[57] At 5:30 the delegation headed to the Frederick Douglass home in Anacostia, in the District of Columbia, for a tour guided by the Federation of Colored Women. From the front steps, Lorraine Hansberry, twenty-one years old, read the clarion call setting forth the aims expressed by the initiating committee:

> We claim that this government cannot honestly, convincingly and sincerely spend billions, send troops and draft treaties for the peace and freedom of other nations while it never has and does not now protect the

lives and liberties of 15,000,000 of its own Negro citizens. Only when our government abolishes the lynch justice of Mississippi, when it publicly declares there shall be no more Ciceros or Peekskills, only when it moves to enforce with its might the 13th and 15th Amendments to the United States Constitution, then and only then can it speak as a free nation for a free world. And to this end, we, the Negro Women of this our land, must and now dedicate our every effort.[58]

On Sunday the group held a "camp meeting" at Salem Baptist Church, featuring Amy Ballard, the widow of Robert Mallard, who had been murdered by white supremacists in Georgia for voting. The charismatic Richards read a new poem, "Harriet Tubman." Angie Dickerson, second in command at the New York chapter of the Civil Rights Congress, detailed the following day's schedule. Only two of the requested appointments had been granted. However, this failed to thwart their efforts significantly. After being called to order on Monday morning by Bass, the chair of the initiating committee, the sojourners set out in two brigades. Dickerson led a contingent to the War Department, where six members were received not by Pace but by Major General Shaw. He made no commitments. When asked by visitor Mary Luke whether he believed that discrimination was happening in the military, Shaw replied that he did not know what he believed. He said he only took orders.[59]

Bass led the second crew, including Louise, to the Justice Department for a meeting in the office of Maceo Hubbard, an assistant to the director of the civil rights section. They presented demands for the release of Rosa Lee Ingram, indemnities for the widows and children of lynch victims, federal intervention in Cicero, a cessation to the prosecution of Du Bois and Pat, the release of Alphaeus Hunton, and the return of Robeson's passport. Like Shaw, the polite Hubbard offered precious little, though he did indicate that a federal grand jury would investigate the events in Cicero. The delegation did not harass Hubbard, the son-in-law of former Tuskegee Institute president Robert Moton, but the women left a message for Attorney General McGrath that they would remain unsatisfied until he heard their grievances directly.[60] Several sojourners dropped by Congressman Dawson's office and were received by his secretary, who informed them that Dawson was away for the week, whereupon they left written demands for the legislator to take a stand on Cicero and publicly distance himself from Lanham.[61] Completing the foray into the polite-on-the-surface but deeply hostile circles of Washington politics, the entire group of sojourners staged a silent vigil outside of the White House to protest being denied an audience with President Truman.[62]

Back in New York, Louise slipped into organizing overdrive trying to expand the influence of the group that became formally known as the Sojourners for Truth and Justice. Serving as its executive secretary, she was central to the debriefing and planning meetings held on October 19 and 20 at the Harriet Tubman Center on Lenox Avenue. She crisscrossed the New York metropolitan area, often with the much-requested Richards in tow, to meet with small groups of women she hoped would merge into strong chapters. At the same time, she and Bass were traveling extensively in an attempt to orchestrate a national membership drive, and Louise became the point person to establish alliances between the Sojourners and groups such as the Emma Lazarus Federation of Jewish Women's Clubs as well as various trade unions. She and the Sojourners thought grandly, imagining a much larger subsequent demonstration in Washington and greater participation in the following year's national political conventions.

However, they expected too much too soon. They certainly made strides. Alphaeus Hunton was released from prison in mid-December, and the Sojourners held a fund-raising event at Small's Paradise at which they honored him and Dorothy Hunton. The celebration, held on December 27, was, however, sabotaged in a sense by white supremacists in Florida, who threw dynamite through a bedroom window on Christmas day, killing NAACP leader Harry Moore and his wife, Harriet. Reflecting on yet another heinous crime for which the white culprits would go unpunished, the Sojourners, in a statement titled "Our Cup Runneth Over," declared the Moore murders to be the "climactic drop to the bitter cup of grief and outrage poured for the Negro people of this nation in the year 1951." They vowed, "[Our] indignation, courage and determination to fight transcends our grief and mourning." They drew inspiration from "that other brave Harriet, who, in the long hours of bondage, fought for the freedom of our people till the chains of slavery gave way to emancipation."[63]

The Sojourners also welcomed Pat, who returned home in January after his latest trip abroad. During his trip he had presented the full genocide petition, of which the Sojourners were signers, to the UN General Assembly in France on December 17, while Robeson had delivered a copy to the UN headquarters in New York. The Sojourners sponsored a rally at the Rockland Palace that drew twenty-five hundred people, many more than Louise saw at the political gatherings she had attended in Harlem during the collapse of the Popular Front. She hoped the momentum would translate into memberships.

On March 23, 1952, the Sojourners sponsored a two-part political event at the Harlem YMCA. At noon a unity luncheon was held with representatives of the Emma Lazarus Federation. Tributes were paid to Emma Lazarus, Ernestine Rose, Harriet Tubman, and Sojourner Truth, and the Emma Lazarus Federation pledged moral and financial support for the Sojourners. In addition, the two groups signed an alliance, expressing that it represented an "important link in that bond of unity, which must embrace all American women." They elaborated, "We hold that none of us can feel secure in the rights upon which these United States were founded—Life, Liberty, and the Pursuit of Happiness—until the country is cleansed of white supremacy and all the evils that flow therefrom."[64]

After the luncheon, 105 delegates assembled in the YMCA's Little Theater for the Sojourners' Eastern Seaboard Conference.[65] As Louise delivered a speech on the triple oppression of black women, she no doubt felt that she was addressing a group still on the rise. And she redoubled her efforts to ensure its growth. But later that spring, a sobering letter arrived from Evelyn Burrell in Baltimore. Burrell reported that it was becoming "increasingly difficult" to recruit people for activities, especially "those who have anything at all at stake," meaning those whom the establishment could intimidate. Burrell had, in fact, been fired from her job after her loyalty was questioned. She said she would fight on, and apparently did for a while, but her letter suggested the organization's ultimate fate.[66] Indeed, it became, despite its promising and not-inconsequential outcry, a casualty of conservative politics and the evaporation of the most prominent left-liberal coalitions.[67] Although embraced by the Emma Lazarus group and several others, the Sojourners received a telling blow in April 1952 when Walter White rejected Bass's request for a formal aligning of the NAACP with the Sojourners.[68] The power centrists had deemed the group untouchable, and no rescue in terms of resources was forthcoming from the beleaguered and sometimes imploding hard Left.[69]

Louise became less active, and to some extent less exuberant, in the years immediately following her work with the CAA and the Sojourners for Truth and Justice. She worked a series of pedestrian clerical jobs and mostly watched from the sidelines as a new generation of activists began to transform the landscape of civil rights activism in places such as Montgomery, Little Rock, and even New York City. She obviously took satisfaction in a series of legal victories in which she had no small hand. The charges against

Du Bois were dropped, and fines were levied in the Cicero case. The Supreme Court outlawed segregation in *Brown v. Board of Education*, stilled the prosecutorial frenzy under the Smith Act in *Yates v. United States*, and restored Robeson's passport via *Kent v. Dulles*.[70] Perhaps most heartwarming, prison authorities in Georgia paroled Rosa Lee Ingram and her sons in the summer of 1959.

But plenty of Old-Left dues still had to be paid along the way, and Louise suffered from the strain. For example, Pat's luck ran out with regard to the justice system. Although he had been acquitted in the contempt retrial in 1952, in 1954 he was given a series of rolling sentences, of ninety days each, for refusing to provide a list of Civil Rights Congress donors to the Internal Revenue Service. By the summer, the sixty-two-year-old Pat was locked away, conceivably for life, in the federal penitentiary in Danbury, Connecticut. He would have enjoyed speaking at length with two former Danbury political prisoners, poet Robert Lowell and screenwriter Ring Lardner Jr.[71] At the same time, the current prison environment, replicating as it did the most extreme anti-Communist sentiment of the outside world, was, as Pat knew, a dangerous place in which to speak at all.[72]

Pat spent much of his time writing to Louise, mostly about political matters, organizing to be done, and his adjustment to prison, where he reread Victor Hugo's *Les Misérables*, which he praised profusely, and perused John Gunther's *Inside U.S.A.*, which he did not.[73] He expressed delight that Louise remained in some demand and had speaking engagements upcoming.[74] He even joked that he had missed a meeting with Robeson but figured Robeson would understand.[75] To eleven-year-old Mary Lou, away at summer camp, he explained, "There are people who truly fight for better things. Those people gave money to the organization daddy leads, and the men who run the courts wanted to know the names of those who support this fight. Daddy did not give them the names for they would have had those good people kicked out of their jobs and maybe jailed. Besides, I did not have the names. But they—the bad men—said that I did and that if I did not give the names up they would put me in prison. So dear here I am." He encouraged his daughter to be a "brave little girl and a fighter."[76] Louise's inclination was to spare her daughter the sight of her father behind prison walls. Mary Lou, however, with a spirit her father appreciated, insisted on making the trip through the hills of Fairfield County. Louise had little choice but to concede.

Naturally, Louise folded her husband's situation into her organizing efforts. On July 20 she sent a letter to numerous friends to inquire if they would be interested in initiating the National Committee to Defend the Rights of William L. Patterson, which she imagined would be led by Du Bois. But a prompt reply from her former mentor provided a hard reality check: "I am convinced that my name at the head of any committee would not help its objects today. On the other hand, if you think that using my name as a member of a committee to defend your husband would help, I should be very glad to let you use it."[77] At the end of the month, after a visit to Danbury, she wrote a second letter to solicit support, along with a fact sheet, without broaching the idea of a national committee. Instead, she made three alternative suggestions. The first was that supporters write to United States attorney general Herbert Brownell to demand bail and to protest the "injustice and hypocrisy of persecuting one whose 'contempt' is for the lynchers and violators of the rights of the Negro people." She felt that Justice Department resources would be better expended solving cases like the bombing of the Moores. Second, she urged friends to send greeting cards to Pat. Last, she appealed for funds, which she did receive from some quarters, to cover legal fees and to disseminate materials with the purpose of influencing public opinion. She solemnly informed her friends, "Mary Lou and I, while terribly distressed by Pat's jailing, are more proud of him than ever, as a father and husband who, in these hysterical times, is no 'summer patriot.' And while neither we nor Pat desire martyrdom for him, we know that if our people are to be free and our nation kept from becoming a police state, some Americans must stand firm and true—as did the men and women throughout our history whom we now honor."[78]

Louise visited her husband again in mid-August and found him shaken by the sudden death of Vito Marcantonio and the passing of Mary Church Terrell. Particularly reflective, he soon lamented in a letter to his wife that he would miss enjoying with her their anniversary and her birthday: "I am extremely sorry. I send thanks to you that the first can be celebrated and thanks to your parents that the second is possible. Have some friends in for the occasion and dance with Mary Lou."[79]

The authorities released Patterson on September 28, but he faced a return to prison if he remained noncompliant. For Louise, this naturally meant another round of strategizing. With Angie Dickerson, Dorothy Hunton, and Eslanda Robeson, she took the lead in forming the Committee of One Hundred Women, which promptly staged the Mass Rally for the Defense of William Patterson at the Renaissance Casino on November 8.[80] Though ailing, Bass, her trusted ally, wrote from the West Coast to request a list of all of

Louise's contacts in Los Angeles and Pasadena so that she might solicit assistance. She added optimistically, "And with the New Year may we win a great victory over the evil forces that darken our good land. The liberation of Mr. Patterson will be a great and long stride forward toward that goal."[81]

Fortunately, this struggle did not become protracted. Although Pat was taken back into custody in late November, remaining housed at the Metropolitan Detention Center on West Street, he was freed when the Court of Appeals for the Second Circuit reversed his conviction early in 1955. But the bone of contention, the Civil Rights Congress, would not be similarly saved, nor would the CAA and a host of other leftist organizations, which were forced to cease functioning.

By the spring of 1956, the Pattersons were leading a relatively quiet life in Brooklyn, having relocated to 1268 President Street in the Crown Heights section. Pat still functioned as a party leader, although with a much lower profile. Louise backed him and never broke with the reconstituted CPUSA, even when legions fled after the Soviet invasion of Hungary and Nikita Khrushchev's revelations at the Twentieth Communist Party Congress about Stalin's purges.[82] She spent many weekends, often accompanied by Mary Lou, doing clerical work at Twenty-Sixth Street, as insiders referred to the antiquated townhouse that served as the party headquarters.[83] And, in her late fifties, Louise still mustered up the energy for an occasional parade.[84]

Several prominent comrades resided nearby, including Esther Cooper Jackson and James Jackson, Doxey Wilkerson, and the writer John Oliver Killens, who triumphed with his debut novel of black affirmation, *Youngblood*, the same week the Supreme Court handed down the *Brown v. Board of Education* ruling. Louise always cared about the cultural front and helped to involve Killens and other artists in the efforts of the Afro-American Committee for Gifts of Art and Literature to Ghana. Following the lead of Langston Hughes, who had approached Ghanaian officials about having African Americans donate art as a show of admiration and support, the working committee formed early in 1959 under the leadership of Doris Du Bissette. Its members included Charles Alston, Ida Cullen Cooper, and Jean Blackwell Hutson. Louise, whose interest in Africa had first been spurred by Du Bois and Alphaeus Hunton, assumed a familiar role as its secretary. Hughes and Aaron Douglas served as honorary chairmen, though they did most of the heavy lifting in terms of securing commitments. The writers responded robustly, donating dozens of books and original manuscripts. The painters, though, expressed concerns about economics and plans for exhibits and felt they had played second fiddle to the writers throughout the process.[85] The project was completed but without the envisioned response from visual artists. They would not match Margaret Burroughs and the Chicago group, which had delivered twenty-five paintings to Ghana when the nation achieved independence.[86]

Perhaps Mary Lou experienced the greatest tension in the Patterson household during those days. On the one hand, she was proud of her parents and never ashamed of being a red-diaper baby. She marveled at the headquarters' library and enjoyed the recreational classes at the Jefferson School of Social Science. She relished her time at Higley Hill, a left-wing summer camp in Vermont run by Max Granich, the younger brother of Mike Gold (Itzok Isaac Granich) and Grace Granich. Furthermore, she fit in with the other teenagers in a Brooklyn community of left-wing activists. Her peers included the Burnham daughters (Claudia, Linda, and Margaret), Harriet Jackson, Bettina Aptheker, Phyllis Strong, and Angela Davis, who visited the Burnhams for several summers while her mother, Sallye Davis, who knew the Burnhams, Jacksons, and Strongs through the Southern Negro Youth Conference in Birmingham, worked on a graduate degree in education at New York University. Angela Davis eventually relocated to Brooklyn and lived with the progressive Reverend W. Howard Melish and his family while attending Elisabeth Irwin High School in Manhattan.

On the other hand, Mary Lou lived a life of fear. In school she was afraid of being found out with respect to her party connections, although she apparently leaked enough of her politics to be dubbed "Little Stalin" by a teacher and "Little Lenin" by a classmate.[87] She usually felt compelled to confine her political remarks in school to the narrow range of mainstream integrationist politics. Participating in a youth march for integrated schools when she was fifteen seemed pretty safe; she organized three busloads of students from Wingate High for the ride to Washington, DC. Ironically, she was found out by the FBI, which noted her appearance.[88] Mary Lou must also have been fearful, at least subconsciously, about the vulnerability of her parents. She often noticed the unmarked cars outside of their home.

Predictably, Mary Lou's inner turmoil, as well as her sharp mind and strong will, which her parents cultivated, did not always result in actions they would approve of or even foresee. Even the teenagers of leftist parents can sometimes desire to be free of them, at least temporarily. One day, in her adolescent wisdom, she phoned her mother at her job to inform her that she was running away from home. Using money earned as a babysitter, Mary Lou headed for Penn Station to purchase a ticket to Chicago, where she planned to stay with Uncle Claude, as she referred to close family friend and comrade Claude Lightfoot. An elaborate planner, she pretended to smoke a cigarette, hoping to appear older. She apparently picked up company in Buffalo, or at least that is how she interpreted the presence of two neatly dressed men who boarded the train and sat near her for the remainder of the trip. Lightfoot promptly escorted her back to New York City to face the music. Louise, who always struggled with the demands of motherhood, either had not been flustered by her daughter's intentions or simply had chosen a deadpan approach. Before the elaborate trip had gotten under way, she had told her daughter over the phone to make sure to put on dinner.[89]

CHAPTER 11

A Fairer Public Hearing, 1960–1969

On March 13, 1960, Pat flew abroad to discuss trade initiatives with his contacts in England, Czechoslovakia, Hungary, and the Soviet Union. He also aimed to raise funds for "Negro work" in the United States and to champion the cause of Henry Winston, who was still in prison after being convicted under the Smith Act and had gone virtually blind owing to medical neglect. Unlike in recent years, Louise did not remain in the United States while Pat was gone. Taking leave from her latest job, at the Foundation for Cooperative Housing, Louise, together with new high school graduate Mary Lou, boarded a TWA flight to France shortly after midnight on July 1. After a week in Paris, where they lodged at the Hotel Vaneu, the two headed for the Soviet Union with the intent to link up with Pat. By the time they arrived, however, he had accepted an opportunity to visit the People's Republic of China. Such a trip violated U.S. passport regulations, which prohibited travel to Red China, Cuba, North Korea, and North Vietnam. However, Chinese ambassadors frequently extended invitations to their American acquaintances, and U.S. authorities could not always track the resultant excursions.[1] Indeed, Louise and Mary Lou followed the same path as Pat and spent six weeks in China. They arrived in Beijing on July 9, although FBI records suggest that Louise did not leave the Soviet Union until she traveled to Czechoslovakia on October 18.[2]

Louise had been particularly curious about China since Eslanda Robeson's visit to the emerging republic a decade earlier; Robeson had reported on her trip on a speaking tour Louise organized on behalf of the CAA.[3] During her own trip, Louise got a glimpse of the controversial Great Leap Forward, the government-driven process of collectivization and industrialization that Mao Tse-tung considered the best approach to the development of the Chinese socialist state. No evidence exists that she took copious notes as she had in the Soviet Union—perhaps because her husband recorded many of their observations.[4] They saw production teams in action and visited industrial exhibits. They traveled from Beijing to Dalian, the gateway port to the Pacific about three hundred miles to the southeast, to visit a research center and Dalian Medical College. They saw the so-called people's communes in action in several suburbs. Although China was experiencing a great famine—historians debate the correlation between widespread hunger and official economic policy—Louise saw enough signs of progress among the masses to be optimistic about China's future. Yet she was keenly aware by then that "none of these countries is a paradise. Building socialism is a long tough struggle."[5]

Mary Lou had a more urgent concern; she was ready to enroll in college. Her first choice had been Oberlin, which admitted her but did not offer a scholarship.[6] Continuing to look for the best, which also meant the most affordable, opportunity to study medicine, a lifelong interest of hers, she considered going to school in Beijing.[7] But her father considered the possibility "too complicated" because of worsening Sino-Soviet relations resulting from the clash of Marxist-Leninist and Maoist ideologies.[8] In fact, in the same month that Louise arrived in China, Nikita Khrushchev pulled Soviet advisers and technical experts out of the country. Pat, with his international support system rooted firmly in Soviet and Soviet-supported political alliances, did not feel comfortable leaving his daughter at a Chinese university.[9] Louise had not made the same political analysis; her concern was practical: regular communication with Mary Lou would be difficult.[10]

Back in Russia, Pat brokered a better solution, striking a deal that allowed his daughter to enroll in the newly established People's Friendship University in southern Moscow, an institution designed to help so-called developing nations in Africa, Asia, and Latin America by providing technical, professional, and research training to their students, although, given the institution's potential for excellence, young scholars from other nations would attend as well.[11] The initiative sprang from the efforts of the Central Council of Trade Unions, the Committee of Youth Organizations of the USSR, the Union of Soviet Societies of Friendship and Cultural Relations with Foreign Countries, and the Soviet Afro-Asian Solidarity Committee. Khrushchev had announced the creation of the university during a speech in Indonesia in February 1960. Since then more than thirty-five thousand applications had poured in for the five hundred available slots. Headed by Professor Sergei Rumyantsev, the school offered free tuition, accommodations, and medical care along with free books, access to laboratories, and fare to Moscow and back. The school occupied an entire block that had once been the site of a military academy. Five years of rigorous study lay ahead for students; the first year focused on the learning of Russian.[12]

Perhaps Mary Lou's matriculation at the university was pushed most strongly by her father, but Louise had no objection. Given the markedly improved infrastructure over the decades and the opportunities for women and students of all nationalities, she remained quite enthusiastic about the Soviet Union, the land in which she had seen so much promise in 1932, albeit through a restricted lens. If the dream had worked for her, maybe the reality could work for her daughter. Mary Lou enrolled in September. Asked about the daring involved in attending a Russian school at such a young age, she responded, "It makes sense when you understand how I was raised."[13] Interestingly, she had relatives in Russia. During a stopover in Leningrad, Pat found his other two daughters, Lola and Anna, whom he had previously tried to locate and whom he erroneously believed had perished along with two million others during the two-and-a-half-year Siege of Leningrad by the German army during World War II. Both daughters were married with children.

After several more stops in Eastern Europe, including a three-week stay in Prague, Louise traveled to London. There she got in touch with colleague and comrade Claudia Jones, who had been living in England since December 1955. In December 1950, authorities had ordered Jones deported from the United States under the McCarran Act, a judgment she had contested for five years, during which time she also served a prison sentence after her Smith Act conviction. With seemingly boundless energy despite a history of heart disease, Jones remained active in progressive political circles, including the Communist Party of Great Britain and the Caribbean Labour Congress. Remaining true to her journalistic roots, she had founded the *West Indian Gazette* in 1958.[14] The two decided to visit Paul Robeson, whom Jones frequently crossed paths with in London. He had recently returned from a historic and lucrative eight-week concert tour of Australia and New Zealand and was in a buoyant mood.[15] Louise and Jones dropped by for a noontime visit, but Robeson kept them there until midnight.[16]

Louise arrived back in New York on the evening of December 19. Almost as soon as she returned, she began trying to convert her renewed avidity for socialist experiments into action. Within weeks, she sought out the stellar sociologist Oliver Cromwell Cox, on the faculty of Lincoln University in

Missouri. Probably the most accomplished Marxist teaching at a historically black college or university (HBCU), Cox had published the classic *Caste, Class, and Race* in 1948; he was currently writing *Capitalism and American Leadership* for release in 1962. Louise wondered whether Cox thought feasible a plan to get HBCU presidents and bishops to tour socialist countries at their own expense.[17] Apparently, she imagined that these prominent mainstream figures would be impressed enough by the economic and social advances to speak favorably of those countries and become more compelling representatives of socialism in the eyes of the American public than increasingly marginalized political figures such as herself. Cox offered moral support but little hope. "The socialist countries, I am sure, represent the promise of the future," he declared, noting that he had recently visited Africa, the West Indies, and Europe. Nevertheless, he wrote off black college presidents and bishops as a conservative bunch.[18] With Louise's best lead at an HBCU lukewarm at best, this sketch remained on the drawing board.

Louise's activities were limited for several months after she slipped on a plastic bag in wet conditions outside a store on Nostrand Avenue in her neighborhood and fractured her ankle. The only consolation was that Nebby Crawford, her dearest friend for more than forty years, was in New York for an extended stay to visit Nebby Lou, who was pursuing graduate work at Columbia University. Nebby was, in fact, with Louise at the time of the accident.[19] She helped keep Louise's spirits up during part of her recovery. The two enjoyed each other enormously, as always. But for all their merriment and conversation, their reminiscences and conjectures, they had no idea that a major family event was on the horizon. That Mary Lou, now matriculated at Patrice Lumumba University, as the school had been renamed in February, would thrive in her studies was easy enough to foretell. The big news was harder to forecast: just as full of surprises as her mother had been, Mary Lou, only eighteen years old, married fellow student and Cuban national Roberto Camacho on October 12, 1961.[20] "Cheer up," advised Nebby from California. "When you settle back after the surprise of the wedding and the snafu about the announcements, you will be stronger than ever and good for another 50 years."[21] Nebby was referring to the fact that three hundred wedding announcements had been stolen from a post office box, thus delaying notification to many friends of the Pattersons.

Congratulations trickled in for months, most of them with a political spin. Rockwell Kent mentioned the pictures of Mary Lou taken at abolitionist John Brown's grave in upstate New York that hung on a wall in his home.

Then he conveyed his wishes for her well-being, concluding, "I realize that in this world of ours today I might be suspected of irony. But Mary Lou is not in America, and my wish to her is backed with confidence that in a free Cuba she will have her hopes for happiness fulfilled."[22] Shirley Graham Du Bois, who had recently relocated to Ghana with her husband (now ninety-three years old), confessed that the wedding "did knock us out." She sent their best wishes. Catching Louise up on news in Ghana, she described a libation ceremony that had been held for writer Julian Mayfield's newborn son and expressed her reactions to recent press clippings about W. E. B., as she referred to her spouse. Summarizing her impressions of Ghana, she reasoned, "Living among these very straight-forward, upstanding, straight-speaking black folks, I am more and more convinced that there are a lot of crazy people in this world! Just keep a cool head, girl. If you could see what I am seeing these days you would have no doubt about what will come out on top."[23] Fred Ptashne, who had been a faculty member at the Abraham Lincoln School, capped the political theme surrounding the union: "A marriage between Mary Louise, girl of the future, to a rising star from Cuba, in the surroundings of the land of the future. . . . It all fits perfectly."[24]

Louise needed no familial connection to support the regime of Fidel Castro, the most popular international cause for U.S. leftists since the Spanish Civil War. Ironically, she had already written a review, in summer 1961, of novelist Warren Miller's journalistic book about the new Cuba, *90 Miles from Home*. The venue was *Freedomways*, a quarterly journal that had been launched in April 1961. A brainchild of the late Louis Burnham and Edward Strong, the venture was a follow-up to Paul Robeson's defunct *Freedom* newspaper, which Burnham had edited during the 1950s. This new enterprise helped to revitalize the old Robeson–Du Bois axis and connect it to an emerging generation of readers, writers, and thinkers concerned with worldwide black liberation. It seemed quite logical for Louise to contribute articles.[25]

Louise called Miller's book a "balanced and composite picture of a people in revolutionary ferment, dedicated to forging a new life, solidly supporting a beloved Fidel Castro, despite a pathetic appendage of dissenters of an era gone never to return." With no political axe to grind, Miller had interviewed Cubans from all walks of life and published their words. Contrary to most U.S. media coverage, he favored description over prescription. Louise appreciated the way several interviewees explained the actions of dissidents and defectors; they were, in brief, seen as the beneficiaries of the Batista regime's corruption. Noting that 40 percent of Cuba's 6.5 million residents were Negroes, she focused on the remarks of a young Afro-Cuban teacher who maintained, "It is unthinkable that there could be a Cuban Negro who is not for the revolution. Our whole lives have been transformed by it. In two years, discrimination has been wiped out. How many years is it since your Emancipation Proclamation?" Although the claim that Cuba was discrimination-free was overstated, it was undeniable that when Louise's article appeared, it had been ninety-eight years since Abraham Lincoln's fiat, and America still lacked a civil rights act and a voting rights act. A young Afro-Cuban mother, proud of her new cottage with its modern utilities, expressed to Miller, "You don't understand, if any counterrevolutionaries showed themselves around here, we would eat them."[26]

A few months after her review was published, Louise and Pat hosted a fund-raising party for the Fair Play for Cuba Committee, an organization founded in 1960 that made a flashy debut with a full-page advertisement in the *New York Times* titled "What Is (Really) Happening in Cuba."[27] The committee was led by Robert Taber and Edmonde Haddad, and its founding members included writers James Baldwin, John Oliver Killens, and Norman Mailer; historian John Henrik Clarke; and prototypical black power advocate Robert Williams. At the Patterson gathering, reminiscent of Louise's salon work in the 1930s, three documentaries were shown. One focused on housing improvements and social equality in post-Batista Cuba: rents had been slashed, land redistributed, and segregation abolished. A second film covered the Bay of Pigs invasion on April 17, 1961, a failed attack sponsored by the Central Intelligence Agency. The final movie highlighted the First Declaration of Havana, a document drafted by Castro on September 2, 1960, and approved by the National General Assembly.[28] Spelling out the aims of the revolution, the manifesto condemned American imperialism in Latin America, provided the rationale for the seizure of American corporate assets in Cuba, affirmed self-determination for Cuba, and welcomed military assistance. A passage that struck at America's racial Achilles heel and would play well with those of Louise's ilk expressed that "democracy is incompatible with the financial oligarchy, racial discrimination, and the outrages of the Ku Klux Klan, the persecutions that prevented the world from hearing for many years the wonderful voice of Paul Robeson, imprisoned in his own country."[29]

That summer, Louise headed for her oldest source of practical political inspiration, accepting an invitation to be a delegate at the Moscow Conference, held on July 9–14. She set sail on June 22, 1962, almost thirty years to the day from her first trip across the ocean. After disembarking from the *New Amsterdam* in London, she transferred to the ss *Kallinen*, bound for Leningrad. In Moscow she sat among twenty-one hundred delegates, including many from Africa, listening to Khrushchev (she would read the remarks in translation) speak of complete disarmament as a guarantee for peace and security in the world. She also attended the plenary address of Oginga Odinga, leader of the Kenyan delegation. A key figure in the Kenyan African National Union, Odinga would become the Republic of Kenya's first vice president, serving under Jomo Kenyatta. In her typical manner, Louise took copious notes on the sites she visited, such as the recently opened New Palace of Pioneers with its units devoted to science, film, photography, ballet, music, theater, graphic arts, and architecture. Of course, she noted the facilities at Patrice Lumumba University and spent time with Mary Lou and Roberto. The three spent the month of August in Sochi, the summer resort on the Black Sea that Louise had visited in 1932.

Turning back to domestic developments, Louise returned to *Freedomways* and the review format to comment on the South, the region that was becoming, in her words, "the yardstick used by world opinion to evaluate our nation's democratic institutions, practices and pretensions."[30] Although not on the front lines of the modern phase of the civil rights movement, she supported the struggle while simultaneously seeking to contextualize it. Assessing Daisy Bates's memoir, *The Long Shadow of Little Rock*, she wrote that the shadow was "so deep it touches every facet of American life: the venal politicians who make racism their stock in trade; the muted white community afraid to oppose the outrages of a virulent organized racist minority; the failure of Federal government to act because of the 'exclusive jurisdiction of state and local authorities'; and the Negro community like a rock, absorbing the shocks and fighting on, setting heroic standards for courage and moral fortitude unmatched in American history."[31] After referencing the Battle of Little Rock, as she called the attempt to desegregate Central High School in 1957, she relayed some of the particulars of Bates's life, noting that she and her husband, L. C. Bates, were continuing their civil rights and community work. For Louise, the example of Bates served as a microcosm of the entire spectrum of contemporary anti–Jim Crow, civil rights activists. She pointed out that James Meredith, the first African American student to attend the University of Mississippi, still studied there although he labored under tremendous duress. She also reminded readers that the legions involved in the

Albany Movement, with which Martin Luther King Jr. had been involved (though with limited immediate success), were pressing onward despite jailing and persecution. Of Meredith, the Albany protesters, and others, she declared, "*The Long Shadow of Little Rock* is primarily their story, the story of an aroused and courageous people who have made up their minds that come what may they will make their sufferings 'count for something.'" "Their victory," Louise continued, "can be the nation's salvation."[32]

In a subsequent issue of *Freedomways*, Louise took as provocation a second book on life south of the Mason-Dixon line, Ralph McGill's *The South and the Southerner*, which appeared in 1963. A Pulitzer Prize winner and the publisher of the *Atlanta Constitution*, McGill had opposed for decades the racial hierarchy in Dixie. In his "Letter from Birmingham Jail," King asserted that McGill was one of the "few enlightened white persons."[33] Indeed, Louise found fascinating McGill's graphic descriptions of how post-Reconstruction propaganda campaigns and terrorism disinformed poor whites and played a large part in consigning them and blacks to the bottom of the economic order. She thought that his profiles of racist demagogues Thomas Roderick Dew, Ben Tillman, James Vardaman, and Tom Watson helped readers to understand the rise and role of Orval Faubus, George Wallace, and Ross Barnett. In addition, she admired the author's analysis of the revival of the Ku Klux Klan, his optimism concerning possibilities in the South after the *Brown v. Board of Education* decision, and his argument about the debilitating effects of Jim Crow on the nation in economic, educational, and moral terms. At the same time, Louise felt that the liberal McGill failed to draw conclusions that would enable white southerners to comprehend more deeply their own position and the need to join forces with black militants. In her estimation, "enlightened self-interest must accompany moral indignation and to awaken this, basic causes cannot be glossed over by treating effects."[34] To her, this liberal trap had ensnared McGill even though his volume was commendable overall.

McGill, unwittingly in Louise's view, lent credence to post-Reconstruction repression by writing naively that the masses of newly freed slaves were unready for citizenship. She wondered whether McGill was aware of Du Bois's monumental *Black Reconstruction* or the valiant Reconstruction-era legislative efforts made by former slaves and landless white allies. Expressing a Marxist line that had been articulated by many others, including Harry Haywood in *Negro Liberation*, she suggested that the Dews, Tillmans, Vardamans, and Watsons, though despicable, were but the emissaries of the real destroyers of Reconstruction, part of the formula of "rising northern capital in collusion with the southern bourbons."[35] The hearty embrace of Booker T. Washington by both entities after his "Atlanta Compromise" address in 1895 signaled to Louise the complete merger of those interests, a relationship McGill probed only lightly. Moreover, because McGill indulged in stereotypes about kindly paternalism and carefree slaves, Louise surmised that for all his liberalism, or perhaps because of it, he reflected a measure of caste bias. She questioned whether he really understood the militancy of those leading the freedom rides and sit-ins.[36]

Louise considered undertaking graduate work in English, perhaps to strengthen her chops as a reviewer or critic. Or perhaps she saw possibilities for employment. In any event, she reached out to Oakley C. Johnson, someone she knew in Communist Party circles. A historian and writer who would also write reviews for *Freedomways*, Johnson was a founding member of the party and had taught at several colleges and universities. He began his teaching career in the 1920s as an instructor of rhetoric at the University of Michigan, where he received his doctorate. For a radical, Johnson's advice seemed exceedingly traditional and not particularly inspiring, though he could be commended for taking Louise's ambition seriously, as his lengthy, single-spaced letter showed. He was not condescending, merely staid. After apprising her of two strands of potential study, literature and composition, and warning her that she might have to enroll in some prerequisite classes for no credit, he described several survey courses and special seminars she could take and recommended books she should buy. Additionally, Johnson stressed that Louise should read the *New York Times Book Review* (she already did) to keep abreast of developments in the literary world. He advised her to be clear on the meanings of technical terms such as *semantics, linguistics, philology, phonetics, syntax,* and *accidence*; to avoid confusing *infer* and *imply*; and to steer clear of clichés.[37]

If the somewhat-deadening response failed to dim Louise's fire for graduate school, it certainly did nothing to make it rage. In any event, by the time she heard from Johnson, who had taken quite a while to reply, she had moved in another direction that was obviously more pressing to her. After being fired from her job as a clerk for the New York City chapter of the National Lawyers Guild at their office on Park Row in Lower Manhattan—the group sought to distance itself from all things related to Pat—she joined Herbert Aptheker, a historian, Marxist theoretician, and member of the Communist Party's National Committee, to establish the American Institute of Marxist Studies (AIMS) in a fifth-floor suite at 20 East Thirtieth Street. The FBI quickly noted that she was working there.[38] Louise, in her own words, helped to "lay the foundation, structure the physical setup, and chart its course."[39] The threefold purpose of AIMS, as articulated by the director Aptheker, was to foster Marxist scholarship, serve the cause of academic freedom and scientific inquiry, and assist in the production of a dialogue between Marxist and non-Marxist scholars. In short, he imagined "a fairer public hearing for Marxism."[40] Because Louise was always a pedagogue at heart, though not fated for an English classroom (except for that summer on the Delta), her participation in AIMS and her embrace of the notion of "a fairer hearing" were a logical sequel to teaching at Pine Bluff and Hampton, running cultural salons in Harlem, working for the CES, undergirding the Abraham Lincoln School, promoting proletarian fraternalism for the IWO, and serving as a public instructor on a host of civil rights issues—not to mention her travels to the Soviet Union, Eastern Europe, and China, as well as her interest in Cuba and her daughter's journey. Further articulating the need for AIMS, Aptheker explained, "The late C. Wright Mills stated that all social science for the past century was a dialogue with Marx, but in the United States since World War II it has been closer to a monologue and diatribe."[41] Specific initiatives would include publishing a newsletter and monographs, undertaking study and analysis of hegemonic public school curricula, and staging symposia, the first of which, "Marxism and Democracy," attracted four hundred presenters and attendees to the Sheraton-Atlantic Hotel on April 23, 1964.[42]

Although Marxism certainly remained relevant to African American struggles, theoreticians would have to come to grips with the question of black power as the key legislative tussles of the civil rights movement neared resolution and urban riots loomed, such as the third major outburst in Harlem.[43] On July 16, 1964, during a dispute between Patrick Lynch, a building superintendent, and several students attending summer school at nearby Robert Wagner Junior High School, Lynch trained a water hose on the adolescents. During the ensuing commotion, police officer Thomas Gilligan shot and killed fifteen-year-old James Powell, who he claimed had tried to attack him with a knife. No knife was recovered during the investigation. At the height of the riot following Powell's funeral on Saturday, July 18, some Harlem residents hurled rocks and bottles at the police. When Bayard Rustin, the chief architect of the March on Washington for Jobs and Freedom, implored the crowd to stop, they derided him as an Uncle Tom and chanted that they wanted Malcolm X.[44]

This militant mood erupted into urban rebellions throughout the rest of the decade, including in the Watts section of Los Angeles, Cleveland, Newark, and, most massively, Detroit. Louise did not oppose the fierce outpouring of frustration, and she read the literature of the black power movement diligently.[45] However, ever the organizing strategist, she believed that the young generation of activists could benefit from deeper consideration of previous black liberation efforts. Malcolm thought as much himself. The month before he was assassinated, he expressed a wish to meet Paul Robeson, about as good a resource as Louise could have recommended.[46] She would also promote the insights of another iconic figure from the labor struggles of the 1930s, Angelo Herndon, now moving through his fifties in relative obscurity. Urging him to become a public figure again, she wrote, "So many, too many of the young militants don't know anything of the history of the liberation struggle, nor of the people like you and Ben and Pat and many, many others who paved the way."[47] But Herndon would not resurface to any significant degree.

Louise's husband needed no coaxing to maintain a high profile during heightened black resistance. Despite mounting health woes, Pat became an early supporter of and fund-raiser for the Black Panther Party, whose leadership had embraced *We Charge Genocide*. The now-elderly Patterson even served as an attorney for the party's cofounder and minister of information, Huey P. Newton. However, their comradeship would dissolve after Pat, as Louise thought reasonable, proffered a lengthy, largely laudatory, and constructive critique of the Panthers titled "The Black Panther Party: A Force against U.S. Imperialism" that was published, in fact, in the *Black Panther*, the organization's newspaper.[48] Contrasting the Panthers to his old nemesis, the leadership of the NAACP, Pat asserted that the Panthers had admirably stepped into a political vacuum partly caused by the NAACP's lack of willingness or ability to "wage a militant class struggle for the rights of Blacks or for labor's unity with Blacks."[49] But Pat's bottom lines were that the science of Marxism-Leninism remained pertinent, that the Panthers had made reckless assertions about violence, and that Communists should play a leading role in a broad black liberation front.[50] A perturbed Newton, increasingly prone to prefacing comments with "Chairman Mao tells us" (symbolizing the Sino-Soviet tension that had worried Pat several years earlier), responded that his new foil was a bourgeois ideologue and revisionist opponent of armed struggle. He added that the Communist Party political line belonged in a museum.[51] Although he did not refer to Louise directly, Newton had little regard, at least rhetorically, for comments about Communist "others who paved the way." He observed, "We find the road so rocky until we are sure that no one has cleared the way."[52]

Louise knew better. No upbraiding by Newton could erase her record and that of her comrades. Nor could Maoist formations diminish her or her husband's interest in Soviet political, economic, and social approaches. As a matter of fact, on the afternoon of July 10, 1969, they were aboard Aeroflot Flight SUOC4 en route to Moscow. Louise continued on to a conference in Uzbekistan, the largest and most economically advanced republic in Central Asia and one of the places that had long fascinated her and Langston Hughes. She returned to Tashkent, the capital city, comprising more than 1.2 million residents and seemingly countless nationalities.[53] Although the city was still recovering from the earthquake in April 1966, which had left seventy-five thousand Tashkent families temporarily homeless, Louise could judge that the pace of technological and social progress was remarkable. The power stations of Uzbekistan generated seven times more electricity than the whole of prerevolutionary Russia. The literacy rate in Tashkent stood at 100 percent, ten times higher than in pre-Bolshevik times.[54] More than twelve hundred Uzbek woman were doctoral candidates or doctors of science, and more than a third of the people serving in the republic's Supreme Soviet were workers and collective farmers. These developments aligned with a presentation, "The Daughters of Turkmenia," by Dr. Amangul Annageldyyeva of the Turkmen Medical Institute, which reinforced and updated the narrative that Louise had heard during her first visit in 1932.[55] Dr. Annageldyyeva recounted the tale of downtrodden and humiliated prerevolutionary women with their faces covered with yashmaks and their voices stilled while they were sold into unwanted marriages, their circumstances justified by religious and civic law. In 1969 numerous Turkmen women were teachers, engineers, scientists, doctors, and legislators.

Louise could take pride in the fact that Mary Lou fit the revolutionary mold as well, having become the first African American to complete medical studies at a university in the Soviet Union. After resuming residence in the United States in 1968, she worked as a pediatrician. She was the mother of two lovely daughters, five-year-old Sandra and three-year-old Evelyn. However, she and Roberto had divorced, ending their dream marriage for the Left.

Then, also mixed with triumphs, were the major sorrows of recent years, such as the death of the elderly Du Bois, the man who, in Jean Toomer's terms, set Louise flowing.[56] There were also the tragic, seemingly premature demises of a string of close associates all younger than Louise—comrades Louis Burnham, Edward Strong, and Ben Davis; fellow Sojourners Claudia Jones and Lorraine Hansberry; and bosom buddy Langston Hughes. She was living only about a mile from Hughes after she and Pat relocated to 147th Street in February 1967. Although Louise energetically honored all of her fallen comrades, especially Davis when his book *Communist Councilman from Harlem* was published posthumously in 1969, she penned the most about Hughes, effectively eulogizing him over the course of several years. Speaking to his basic humanity, she recounted scenarios from their most extended adventure, the trip to the USSR in 1932: "Whether driving through the hot, dusty Turkoman desert in an old jalopy, sharing a tea bowl with Uzbeks in a chaikhanna, wandering the streets of Samarkand and Old Bukhara (cities whose civilizations date back to B.C.), or visiting new factories and collective farms in Tashkent, Langston got to know the people of the land."[57]

Later she addressed his literary significance. She recalled that on the eve of the appearance of *Shakespeare in Harlem*, Hughes wrote to her in Chicago to inform her of the book's import: "folk, blues, lyric verse in the lighter manner—*but not too light*." He drew her attention to lines from "Mississippi Levee": "Levee, levee, how high does you have to be / To keep them cold muddy waters from / washing over me?" Becoming a critic of his own work and explicating his indirectness, he wrote, "You can take that for a text and say: Our levee has to be so high the exploiters can't get over it, neither can they get under it, neither can they get through it. It has to stretch so far they can't get by it, and they can't do nothing about it. It has to be built with the sandbags of the working class. Can't nobody else build a levee that won't break down."[58]

Reflecting on Hughes's letter and the scope of his poetry, Louise saw her article as a corrective to bland interpretations. She later confided to Nicolás Guillén regarding the immediate attempts to construct Hughes's legacy, "His funeral was for me a great tragedy—not because of his death but in the manner in which it was treated. Arna Bontemps—his literary executor—gave the main obituary. He characterized Langston as a 'Poet of Death.' Nothing was said of his hatred of oppression and his militant revolutionary works."[59] In her writing she cast Hughes the way she wanted him remembered most, as a "revolutionary poet who saw the future of a world free from racism, human exploitation and war through the unity of the workers of his land in common struggle with the exploited peoples the world over."[60]

CHAPTER 12

Confirming Commitments, 1970–1984

W hile Louise was involved politically in the 1960s, her most significant street action did not occur until 1970 when Angela
Davis faced the gas chamber in California after seventeen-year-
old Jonathan Jackson, the younger brother of celebrated prison
activist and writer George Jackson, led a revolt at the Marin County courthouse on August 7. During the ensuing shootout in the parking lot, Jonathan
Jackson was killed along with inmates William Christmas, James McClain,
and the presiding judge at McClain's assault trial, Harold Haley, who had been
taken hostage. Because authorities recovered at the scene a .380 handgun
registered to Davis, she was subject under California law to charges of murder, conspiracy to commit murder, and kidnapping. However, no evidence
indicated that Davis had given the gun to Jackson or been involved in planning the revolt. Pessimistic about her prospects for fair treatment in the legal
system, Davis, who had observed police repression during her work with the
Communist-affiliated Che-Lumumba Club and the Black Panther Party, decided to go underground.[1] Federal agents captured her in New York City on
October 13 and confined her in the Women's House of Detention in New York
City's Greenwich Village.

Louise could hardly have avoided, even at the age of sixty-nine, deep involvement in that cause célèbre. In addition to her political sympathies and
personal history with Davis, the high-stakes proceeding possessed the grav-
ity and weight, even the international appeal, of the Scottsboro and Ingram
cases, without disputes about grassroots tactics and Communist participation in the defense. After all, Davis, a well-known member of the CPUSA
since 1968, counted as one of their own. Moreover, she not only favored mass
political agitation on her behalf but instigated, even from behind bars, as

much of it as she could.[2] Davis became so popular largely because she was a professional black woman. She had been fired that spring from her teaching position at the University of California, Los Angeles, despite overwhelming support from faculty and students. Even the reluctant NAACP leadership could not forsake her.[3]

As many would have expected, Louise became the executive secretary of the New York Committee to Free Angela Davis, while Jose Stevens, a young Harlem organizer, served as the chair. Operating out of several downtown offices, they orchestrated events around the city, including a forum at Columbia University and a large rally on Greenwich Avenue outside of the jail shortly before Davis was extradited to California in December. Several weeks later, Louise, following the classic ILD playbook, took the fight overseas. Loaded with material about the Davis case, she arrived in London at the end of February.

On the evening of February 28, as the guest of George Matthews, editor of the daily *Morning Star*, and John Gollan, the general secretary of the Communist Party, she attended a rally at Royal Festival Hall to celebrate the forty-first anniversary of the Communist-supported paper. The next day, she addressed a large demonstration, telling the audience, "Angela never sees the sunlight in so-called sunny California." She added, punctuating her remarks with black power salutes, "The only guarantee that she will be free is that the people of our country and the people of the world demand her freedom."[4] Then Louise, although much grayer and plumper than in her heyday, led protesters on a march to the U.S. embassy, where she presented a letter criticizing the treatment of Davis and demanding her release.

After meeting in smaller sessions with labor activists and students on March 1, she caught a train to Manchester on the morning of March 2. Along the way she reflected on the fact that Manchester was where Frederick Douglass received the document legally granting him freedom from enslavement and Karl Marx issued a major appeal for the British to support the North during the U.S. Civil War.[5] After she arrived at Piccadilly Station, her hosts rushed her to a press conference covered by the independent franchise Granada TV. Next on the itinerary came an afternoon at Manchester University, where she addressed an enthusiastic crowd of several hundred, and an appearance that evening at the West Indian Centre on Carmoor Road.

Continuing with her arduous schedule, although now battling a cold, Louise left Manchester the next morning by train, headed for Leeds and a rendezvous with a group of academics called the Left Luncheon Club. She attended an event that night at the Guildford Hotel before pushing on to England's second-largest city, Birmingham. She found it interesting that many residents knew of the city in Alabama with the same name, an appellation they felt had been "discredited" in America. They could not adopt too superior an attitude, though. While not the "Bombingham" of the American South, England's Birmingham had its share of racial issues, as students conveyed to Louise during her visit to Birmingham University.[6]

Louise labored through a speech the next evening at the Coventry College of Education, twenty-five miles from Birmingham. But not much rest ensued, as she had to be at the airport early the following morning for a flight to Glasgow; from there, she would be driven to Edinburgh for an afternoon demonstration organized by the Young Communist League. By nine o'clock that night she was on a flight to London. Up early again the next morning, she left the Paddington train station for Cardiff, where she received a rousing ovation from a crowd of three hundred supporters. After a late-night return to London, she managed to get a few hours' sleep before arising to participate in several activities on International Women's Day.

Before returning to the United States, Louise made a brief but intense stop in Paris, where three weeks earlier the French Communist Party, the French Association of Democratic Lawyers, the General Confederation of Labor, and the Human Rights League had sponsored a rally and a mass march to the U.S. embassy. She squeezed in an interview with the newspaper *L'Humanité* and a meeting with several Communist officials, including the vibrant Marie-Claude Vaillant-Couturier, a fifty-eight-year-old representative in parliament. Vaillant-Couturier's activist credentials were extensive, dating back to her days as a leftist journalist and member of the French Resistance. She had been imprisoned in several concentration camps, including Auschwitz, and served as a witness at the Nuremberg Trials. Vaillant-Couturier told Louise about a group of prominent French women who were demanding a fair trial for Davis. Some of them had cabled New York governor Nelson Rockefeller in an attempt to block Davis's extradition to California. Vaillant-Couturier pledged to remain involved in the cause.[7]

Although weary and still feeling under the weather when she returned to Harlem, where much of the chatter was not about Davis but about the colossal clash between Muhammad Ali and Joe Frazier a day or so earlier, Louise recovered quickly. Carl Bloice noted the energy in her voice and eyes when he visited her 147th Street apartment in Esplanade Gardens, a six-building Mitchell Lama complex. Bloice, an outstanding journalist from the West

Coast (he would become the founding moderator of the web forum Portside), had joined the Communist Party in 1959 at the age of twenty. He interviewed Louise for a story in *People's World*.[8] He knew Davis personally and, in fact, would testify at her trial that she was working on articles with him at the newspaper's office at the time of the courthouse incident.

Displaying her usual confidence, Louise declared to Bloice that her trip had been a tremendous success, claiming that evidence of this already existed.[9] She perhaps referenced the follow-up letter to that effect from George Matthews, as well as the extensive media coverage in Europe.[10] As in the Scottsboro case, her efforts were not in vain. The first payoff occurred in February 1972, when, after sixteen months behind bars, Davis was released on bail. This represented an emotional peak for Louise, one that was desperately needed because she had just suffered a major setback the previous month when Nebby, her virtual sibling, succumbed to cancer at the age of seventy-two. Louise, accompanied by Pat, had spent a week with Nebby and her husband, Matt, in California shortly before her best friend died. She did not return for the funeral. "It must have been horrible for her," surmised Mary Lou. "It must have brought back memories of Mother Thompson. Must have been difficult."[11] Characteristically a private person regarding personal matters, Louise revealed little. But Nebby Lou discerned that "Louise's only consolation was in knowing that her 'sister' was finally released from the pain of her long illness." Speaking to Louise's political tenacity, she remarked, "Even in grief she soldiered on, determined to actively fight for the acquittal of Angela Davis."[12]

After April, Davis no longer faced the prospect of capital punishment because the California Supreme Court, in the case of *The People of the State of California v. Robert Page Anderson*, struck down the death penalty on the grounds that it violated the state constitution. On June 4, with seemingly the whole world watching, after it had become increasingly clear that the prosecution had a very weak case, the jury acquitted Davis.

Although case 52613 had been safely tucked away in the win column, Louise, who kept copies of both issues of *Jet* that featured Davis on the cover, still felt a need to defend her.[13] When *Angela Davis: An Autobiography* appeared in 1974, Louise grew distressed by the reviews of some "bourgeois critics" and addressed the preliminary critical reception, sketching what she termed a "review of reviews."[14] She noted the popularity of Davis's book, which she correctly predicted would become a "classic in revolutionary literature."[15] Sales were brisk for Random House. The journal *Black Scholar*, for which Davis was a board member, purchased three thousand copies for a subscription drive. The Bantam paperback edition would arrive soon, and foreign-language versions were slated for release. *Angela Davis* also became a Book of the Month Club alternative selection and had been excerpted in *Book Digest*. The *New York Times* reviewed the book, which Louise claimed was unusual because the paper generally shunned books by avowed Communists, instead, as she put it, "pretending they have not been published." She reasoned that the present exception resulted from the periodical's worry that "their virulent anti-communism [would] show up the hypocrisy of their 'concern' for the Solzhenitsyns and freedom of the arts."[16] Not that Christopher Lehmann-Haupt, the paper's senior daily book reviewer, did Davis any favors, according to Louise. He reflected the quest for the "private and real" Angela that, along with anti-Communism, racism, male chauvinism, and contradictions, were the main threads Louise detected in the numerous reviews she had collected from around the nation.[17] Lehmann-Haupt wrote, "She appears so unusually intelligent, articulate, and well grounded in her beliefs that one almost instinctively looks to her for explanations one wouldn't expect from others of the same militancy and political persuasion."[18] Louise rejected Lehmann-Haupt's words partly because, in defending Davis, she was defending herself. She had once been an intelligent, articulate, college-educated woman in her early thirties who rationally chose the Left. Good political reasons were enough, she figured, and those should not be discounted because observers sought emotional explanations such as a flawed parent-child relationship or other psychological duress.

By the same logic, Louise dismissed Karen Durbin's assessment in *Ms.* magazine because Durbin argued that Davis's choice of radical discomfort over almost-guaranteed mainstream comfort represented an extraordinary decision and that there were actually three Angela Davises: the black woman, the middle-class intellectual, and the revolutionary activist.[19] Many could forgive Durbin for being awestruck as well as for her popular and generally unobjectionable though imprecise phrasing. But, to Louise, neither she nor Davis was special or fractured, and both were sanely on the side of most of humanity. Similarly, she took exception to Ivan Webster's piece in the *New Republic*, Robert Kirsch's in the *Los Angeles Times*, and Marc Larson's in the *Minneapolis Tribune*.[20] She also lambasted the *New Yorker* for terming the book "grim and hostile" and received coolly Francis Carney's remarks in the *New York Review of Books* that the autobiography was "agitprop" and had been written "under discipline"—Carney being familiar with some of the political jargon of the 1930s.[21]

In contrast, Louise respected Maya Angelou's opinion. Writing in the *Chicago Daily News*, Angelou, a literary star after *I Know Why the Caged Bird Sings*, contended, "Davis explains her belief and membership in the Communist Party so rationally that this reader is impelled to see it as logically following her experience. There is no hysteria or ranting in this book—rather, the telling of events."[22] And, to be fair to the *New York Times*, Louise noted that in the *Sunday Book Review*, Elinor Langer, four days after Lehmann-Haupt's review, lauded Davis's rendering for its "precision and individuality." Furthermore, Langer wrote of Davis's effort, "Her account of her involvement with the Party is so plausible and fresh it turns back the burden of explanation to those who feel that the Communist Party is so irrelevant, drenched with the blood of history or populated by Government agents, that anyone who would willingly join it is stupid, unserious and against him/her self or fond of losing."[23]

Faith Berry, who had a year earlier edited Langston Hughes's *Good Morning Revolution* and would publish a biography of him in 1983, penned the best review of those that appeared in the "capitalist newspapers," in Louise's opinion.[24] Berry acknowledged that the book lacked intimate details and that readers came to know Davis only through her narration of political ideas and events. But this was not a negative for Berry. In fact, she saw this as the reason that "some of the most forceful, cogent passages of the book are about her experiences in jail; she is able to project the pain of her incarceration by fully exposing all the inhuman conditions of our penal institutions." Berry concluded, "What the book unveils most of all is a series of events in the making of a revolutionary, told with a clarity that highlights all the circumstances which made her one."[25]

It sounded like a project Louise could eventually undertake, though it is not known whether Davis's book directly inspired her to write her own memoir, a task she began several years later. She settled at that point for defusing bad reviews and praising an autobiography she considered "a breath of fresh air midst the plethora of books flooding the market by Watergate conspirators and others seeking to make millions of dollars titillating the reader with salacious gossip about people in the news and 'dirty tricks' exposures."[26] Louise hoped that *Angela Davis* would help oppressed people, including the underemployed and overincarcerated African American population, identify the real enemy, which she uncompromisingly saw as "world imperialism with the monopoly capitalism of the United States as the spearhead."[27]

Continuing her quest to view socialist experiments up close, Louise visited Cuba with Pat for a month in 1974. Traveling first through Mexico, where they arrived on February 20, they stayed briefly in Mexico City with Elizabeth Catlett, who had renounced her American citizenship in 1962, and her husband, Pancho Mora. After securing visas from the Cuban embassy and airline tickets, the Pattersons were met at the airport in Havana on February 23 by Julián Torres Rizo from the Cuban Communist Party's Department of Foreign Relations. Accompanying Rizo were the two comrades who would serve as their guides.

Their hosts mapped out an auto trip, with frequent stops, from Havana to Santiago de Cuba. But before they got deep into the trip, Louise and Pat underwent extensive physical exams at a Cuban hospital and were found to be in relatively good health. After that, they drove to Cienfuegos and then Ciego de Ávila before arriving in Camagüey in the central part of the island, the heart of the country's cattle industry. Camagüey was also the home of Louise's granddaughters, who both had birthdays that week. After a celebration and sightseeing, the Pattersons traveled to Bayamo and then to Santiago de Cuba. They visited the Moncada Barracks, where the Cuban Revolution had begun on July 26, 1953.[28] Reflecting on her trip through the land where, in her estimation, "revolution is a watchword and socialism a reality," Louise recalled seeing some of the positive changes in nourishment and health care, and women's increasing role in the labor sector. She saw the impressive improvements in education facilities, which enabled a soaring literacy rate.[29]

After a flight back to Havana, Louise met with Nicolás Guillén at the Union of Writers and Artists of Cuba, the organization he had founded in 1961. She gave Guillén, the great Afro-Cuban poet who had been a friend and admirer of Hughes, as well as an influence on him, a copy of *Good Morning Revolution*. In response, Guillén informed her that he and his comrades wished to publish a special issue of *La Gaceta de Cuba* on Hughes. As she left the office, she thought of how similar Guillén and Hughes were as *revolutionary* writers, and she imagined that Cuba represented the realization of Hughes's vision as expressed in "A Letter to the Academy": "Speak about the Revolution—where the flesh triumphs (as well as the spirit) and the hungry belly eats, and there are no best people, and the poor are mighty and no longer poor, and the young by the hundreds of thousands are free from hunger to grow and study and love and propagate, bodies and souls unchained."[30]

Louise charged that the U.S. government was trying to prevent Americans from obtaining full information about the Cuban Revolution, seeking instead to undermine it with boycotts and offensives such as the Bay of Pigs invasion. Moreover, in her view, the United States welcomed counterrevolutionaries with open arms. Nonetheless, she applauded that "a new form of society—socialism—is arising in Cuba, the first in the Western Hemisphere and it is already a beacon of light for all the poverty-stricken, underdeveloped countries under foreign domination whose resources do not benefit their own people."[31]

While in Havana, Louise was fascinated by the outpouring of emotion upon the death of Cuba's greatest trade union leader, Lázaro Peña, on March 11. He had risen through the union ranks to become the general secretary of the Confederation of Cuban Workers and a member of the Central Committee of the Communist Party. He was also a founder of both the Confederation of Labor of Latin America and the World Federation of Trade Unions. His bier lay at the base of the José Martí monument in the great Plaza of the Revolution for more than twenty-four hours, precipitating what Louise called a "human wave of grief-stricken people." She joined the procession to Colon Cemetery, led by Fidel Castro and President Osvaldo Dorticós Torrado. She later reflected that it was her "first opportunity to see a great black freedom fighter receive such honor."[32]

Back on the turf of a white-supremacist, capitalist patriarchy, Louise followed and supported the activities of the National Association against Racist and Political Repression (NAARPR), a broad coalition she helped found in the aftermath of the Angela Davis case. The coalition united under a bold motto: Unity + Struggle + Organization = Victories.[33] This remains the organization's mantra and, of course, represents what Louise was all about. During this period, NAARPR agitators contributed to several legal triumphs, perhaps most notably in the cases of the Wilmington Ten, Joan Little, Delbert Tibbs, Carlos Feliciano, Paul "Skyhorse" Durant, and Richard "Mohawk" Billings.

Louise celebrated these triumphs, but the circumstances had to seem like the endless looping of a bad tape from the past. The Wilmington Ten, for example, were convicted on specious evidence of arson and conspiracy after the firebombing of a grocery store in North Carolina on February 6, 1971. No casualties occurred, but that proved to be beside the point. The judge sentenced one of the defendants, Ann Shepard, to fifteen years. The nine men, none older than the twenty-four-year-old Reverend Benjamin Chavis Jr., who would later become the executive director of the NAACP, were slapped with prison terms ranging from twenty-eight to thirty-four years. After a nine-year legal battle, a federal appeals court set aside the convictions, ruling that the trial judge had violated the defendants' constitutional rights. Also in North Carolina, Joan Little, barely past adolescence, faced a charge of first-degree murder—and an automatic death sentence—in the killing of jail guard Clarence Alligood in August 1974; Little stated that Alligood had entered her cell for the purposes of sexual assault. The semen on his half-naked body seemed to support her allegation and her contention that she had used an ice pick in self-defense. Amid numerous protests and the tension that only capital cases generate, an integrated jury acquitted Little on August 15, 1975.

Delbert Tibbs faced a similar fate in Florida. A former seminary student, the twenty-five-year-old was falsely accused of having committed murder and rape while hitchhiking in 1974. He received the death penalty but was freed in 1977 after the state supreme court vacated the conviction. In 1975 NAARPR also claimed success with the freeing of Carlos Feliciano of the Movimiento Independentista Revolucionario Armado, who had been held in jail in New York for five years after being accused of planting bombs around the city. Also in 1975, the organization rallied behind "Skyhorse" and "Mohawk," as they were commonly known, two members of the Los Angeles branch of the American Indian Movement, a prime target of the FBI's Counter Intelligence Program. Falsely accused of killing a cab driver, they were acquitted three years later.[34] The post-1960s establishment response to radicalism remained aggressive, and NAARPR continued its vigilance and activism. Indeed, the mission to destabilize radical protest, which included the Machiavellian twist of unchecked drug flow, contributed to current high rates of incarceration.

As America began commemorating its bicentennial in 1976, Herbert Aptheker wrote to request that Louise facilitate the featured session at a proposed conference "Marxism and the Bicentennial," to be held at Columbia University in April. Referencing her long association with AIMS, he stated, "I know no one who so ably handles the difficult and crucial task of chairing this kind of effort."[35] If nothing else, a few months short of seventy-five years old, she had experience. She no longer was central to the collective that held the institute together; Zarya Schwartz had assumed a leading role. But Louise remained part of the AIMS family, and she wouldn't refuse the man she deemed "the hardest working, typing, hitting, prolific outputter I ever met!"[36] The panel, titled "The Working Class and the Bicentennial," would include presentations by Gus Hall, the CPUSA's general secretary and presidential candidate; Philip Foner, a labor historian and faculty member at Lincoln University in Pennsylvania; Dennis Serette, the president of the Coalition of Black Trade Unionists; and Ernest DeMaio, a representative of the World Federation of Trade Unions. Indeed, most of the people who participated in the symposium were open or congressionally identified members of the CPUSA, documented supporters, or Marxists from other groups. These included Aptheker himself, Dorothy Burnham, and Johnetta Cole, an anthropologist and the future president of Spelman College who was then a member of the pro-Castro Venceremos Brigade and had authored articles supporting the Cuban regime.[37]

Speaking in McMillan Theater on April 23, Louise framed the occasion for the audience, asserting that "this symposium stands out as an example of how such a bicentennial should be observed if it is to have meaning and substance, and be a guideline for the American people through the critical period in which we live."[38] She surely had in mind the economic crises both nationally and locally. The country was trying to overcome a recession, the sixth since the end of World War II. The downturn lasted from the end of 1973 through the first quarter of 1975, with high unemployment continuing into 1976. Furthermore, just six months before the symposium, New York City had verged on bankruptcy. President Gerald Ford had taken a stern stance toward the city, not quite uttering the "drop dead" that has been popularly attributed to him but coming close to it before reversing course.[39] Ford, to Louise's alarm, still was a strong threat to carry the state of New York against Jimmy Carter in the upcoming presidential election. Stressing the need for radical thought, she pointed proudly to some of the achievements of AIMS—a newsletter with a circulation of thirty-six hundred, thirteen volumes published through Humanities Press, eighteen occasional papers, eleven bibliographies—on the way to her main point: "I think we can say AIMS has won a distinct role in the life and struggle of the people of our land to make a better world, helping to provide that knowledge that will lead to socialism as the solution of man's exploitation, an end to war, and to true equality."[40]

That same year, Louise cofounded yet another entity to facilitate such a vision, teaming with entertainer Ossie Davis to establish the William L. Patterson Foundation. Davis was a longtime admirer of Pat, whom he referred to as his "communist guru."[41] Before he developed the confidence to go public with the script for his hit play *Purlie Victorious* (1961), he invited the Pattersons to his home for a special reading at which they provided feedback.[42] Pat, now halfway through his ninth decade and suffering from various illnesses—the lengthening list included a heart attack and a fractured hip—sensed the end was not far off. So did Louise. Thinking of his legacy, an especially poignant reflection after Paul Robeson's death in January and the shocking demise of sixty-seven-year-old comrade Hy Lumer in July, she wanted not so much to celebrate her husband as to ensure that his specific brand of advocacy continued beyond his physical presence.[43] The foundation was conceived as "an independent institution, responsible to and funded by people who seek an end to racism, exploitation, and war."[44] While Louise assumed her familiar role of executive secretary, Carlton Goodlett became the foundation's president. A medical doctor and influential newspaperman who published the *San Francisco Sun-Reporter*, which had a circulation of more than a hundred thousand, Goodlett considered himself a protégé of Pat and had affiliated with a number of progressive groups, including the CPUSA.[45] The group staged several events, including awards luncheons with Pat in attendance. Those feted for making outstanding contributions toward the realization of the foundation's objectives included Benjamin Chavis Jr., George W. Crockett Jr., and Esther Cooper Jackson.[46]

As Louise considered Pat's legacy, she received several reminders of her own when writers and scholars sought her input for their projects. She belonged to a dwindling group of people who had participated directly in the Harlem Renaissance. Robert Hemenway of the University of Kentucky, then working on the manuscript that evolved into *Zora Neale Hurston: A Literary Biography*, contacted Louise in the fall of 1975. He had been given her address by Nathan Irvin Huggins, a history professor at Columbia University, who had published *Harlem Renaissance* a few years earlier. Hemenway expressed admiration for Louise's career; however, for his book he wanted her take on Hurston and Hughes, particularly the developments surrounding *Mule Bone*. He conjectured, not unreasonably, that Hurston had been in love with Hughes and jealous of Louise. According to him, Hurston had admitted as much to Arna Bontemps, whom Hemenway had interviewed. But Hemenway remained properly cautious about any story spun by such a master of mischief and intrigue as Hurston.[47] At any rate, Louise did not swallow the bait, at least not right away. She conveyed, somewhat cagily, that while she was present for much of the composing, she lacked firsthand knowledge of the dispute about authorship. She sent Hemenway her phone number, which was unlisted, and invited him to call her whenever he visited New York. She felt that any detailed conversation, at least to begin with, should take place in person.[48]

Hemenway traveled to New York in January to interview Hurston's brother Everette and consult with Alice Walker, who had recently published her essay "Looking for Zora" in *Ms.* magazine, where she served on the staff. Walker would be credited more than anyone else for the revival of interest in Hurston. Hemenway missed connecting with Louise on that trip, however, because he had not received her return note in time.[49] Indeed, given her worries over and struggles with Pat's declining health, she was not as rapid a correspondent as she had typically been.

Writing from Lexington in February, Hemenway offered to send Louise a portion of his draft chapter on *Mule Bone* for fact checking. He also inquired about Charlotte Osgood Mason and disclosed that Arthur Fauset, for a brief time a recipient of Mason's largesse, had actually despised his patron. Like Hurston, a combination of literary figure, folklorist, and anthropologist, Fauset, the brother of the better-known writer Jessie Fauset, had found Mason "imperious."[50] Louise desired to push the point further. She responded to Hemenway that Mason may have been overbearing but most certainly had been a racist. Louise opined that Mason thought Negroes should act like primitives and derisively charged them with acting like "white folks" if they failed to conform to her expectations. Louise had been insulted in that manner, as had, perhaps only behind his back, Alain Locke. Concerning the offer to read the section on *Mule Bone*, Louise accepted but wasn't sure what she could contribute. Moreover, she wanted clarification regarding Hemenway's overall thesis. She considered books about the Harlem Renaissance to be important but felt that none had yet dealt with the phenomenon comprehensively. She wrote, "I feel very keenly that we must discuss and write about Black creative activities not in a vacuum, but within the framework of the entire society in which these artists lived. Certainly today we could not write about Africa, which is in the midst of fierce struggles for liberation, as was done." Declining an offer to talk at length over the phone, Louise again asserted that she would be pleased to meet Hemenway in person.[51] That finally happened in June.

Other researchers who consulted Louise during the 1970s included Walker, who wanted to know more about both Hurston and Hughes, and Mark Naison, a young assistant professor in the Department of Afro-American Studies at Fordham University.[52] Naison aspired to tell a "true story of the left."[53] He had already conversed with Pat, and before interviewing Louise he spoke with her by phone and sent her a copy of his article, "The Communist Party in Harlem in the Early Depression Years," which had appeared in *Radical History Review*. His interests eventually sprouted into the book *Communists in Harlem during the Depression*, which appeared in 1983. Phyllis Klotman of Indiana University contacted Louise near the end of the summer in 1979 seeking information about another topic from long ago: Wallace Thurman. Although increasingly worried about Pat—he had to be hospitalized that fall—Louise fielded Klotman's query and met with her when she traveled to New York.[54]

Early in January 1980, Pat again entered Union Hospital in the Bronx, suffering from assorted ailments, including kidney failure. A fretful Louise spent most of each day sitting with him, providing as much comfort as she could. Several friends, touched by the plight of the man they venerated as "Mr. Civil Rights," sent contributions to offset the treatment cost of ninety dollars per day.[55] In mid-February Mary Lou sent out an appeal for funds that yielded results as well.[56] However, the campaign was short-lived because Pat succumbed to his illness on March 5, 1980.

Louise and Mary Lou had Pat's remains cremated promptly, but the official homegoing ceremonies and the outpouring of affection for Pat stretched over two months. The first memorial service took place on the afternoon of March 15 at Harlem's Convent Avenue Baptist Church. Recorded music by Paul Robeson greeted the two thousand attendees. A large portrait of Pat framed by a simple floral arrangement was placed on the dais, directly opposite Louise's front-row seat.[57] Ossie Davis presided. Beah Richards, a favorite of Pat, could not make the event but sent a poem, which was read by fellow actress Ruby Dee. Dee also recited a poem of her own, "Thinking about Pat and Louise," which read in part, "Pat and Louise / Bedrocks of involvement / Of Compassion / On-across which / To build the better days / For all our sakes."[58] Henry Winston served as the main speaker, and Howard Mann Sr. ended the ceremony with a rendition of Ludwig van Beethoven's "Ode to Joy." The family asked that financial contributions be sent to the William L. Patterson Foundation, a scholarship fund that Louise and Davis had cofounded four years earlier.[59]

On March 29 Louise left for several weeks on the West Coast. The California trustees of the William L. Patterson Foundation, including Matt Crawford and Frances Williams, held a tribute at St. Augustine's Episcopal Church in Oakland on April 19. Speakers included Angela Davis and Maya Angelou. Ron Dellums, the U.S. congressman from California's eighth district, issued a statement. On April 25 Louise arrived in Chicago as the guest of Ishmael Flory, who was concerned about her health. She had been suffering from bronchitis and needed rest, not additional travel. The next morning, more than a hundred people, including Richard Durham, Claude Lightfoot, and Gus Hall, showed up at the Waldheim Cemetery Chapel in Forest Park, which was the burial site of Eugene Dennis, Elizabeth Gurley Flynn, William Z. Foster, Emma Goldman, Lucy Parsons, and the Haymarket martyrs. Two weeks later, Louise was in Los Angeles for the service held at Holman United Methodist Church, then pastored by iconic civil rights activist James Lawson, who had moved to Los Angeles in 1974. Frances Williams, Kendra Alexander, and Beah Richards were among the speakers, with Richards reading "Poem to William Patterson." Actor William Marshall, best known for his *Blacula* performances, also recited verse.

From New York, Louise wrote to thank Angelou for her participation in the Oakland tribute and for their outing with Jessica Mitford, a leftist writer and former member of the Civil Rights Congress, to the landmark T.J.'s Gingerbread House, located in Louise's old West Oakland stomping grounds. She also updated Angelou, a trustee of the William L. Patterson Foundation, on the thinking of the directors. Three compelling ideas had surfaced: a booklet collecting the accolades uttered at the four formal tributes along with testimony sent from around the world, an edited selection of Pat's own writings, and a collection of essays by other writers dealing with Pat's ideology and work. She thought Angelou might be enticed to contribute to the third effort.[60] She made the same overture a few days later to Julian Mayfield, a novelist, playwright, essayist, and activist whom she had known since the Peekskill days, when he was a bodyguard for Robeson.[61] Mayfield had worked with Robert Williams in North Carolina and had been a neighbor to the Du Boises in Ghana. He had been so in awe of Pat that when he once picked him up during his days driving a cab in New York City, he could not answer when his passenger, having arrived at his destination, asked about the fare.[62]

Louise's ability to actualize these publishing dreams was compromised after she accepted a full-time job with the Harlem Restoration Project. Headquartered on West 125th Street off of Amsterdam Avenue and thus a convenient bus ride from her home, the nonprofit tenants' rights corporation was started in 1977 by Marie Runyon, a flamboyant and aggressive former assemblywoman from the seventieth district. A native North Carolinian who abhorred Jim Crow, Runyon had been a respected activist in Harlem for decades. Her efforts over the years included organizing rent strikes and raising money for the legal defense of the Black Panthers. She reasoned, "All they wanted was what we need today—freedom, justice and an end to racism."[63]

Employing several former inmates, the Harlem Restoration Project enjoyed such spectacular early success advocating for tenants and rehabilitating some of the community's most dilapidated properties that the city began awarding it contracts to subsidize its work. However, although an effective firebrand, Runyon was not an astute businesswoman or fiscal manager, traits that would lead to the project's downfall in the 1990s. In the 1980s, however, Louise kept financial matters in order. According to Dorothy Keller, the project's former assistant director and general counsel, Louise, still putting that Berkeley education to use, was instrumental in straightening out the books. She handled the bank accounts, payroll obligations, and necessary fiscal reports to authorities impeccably.[64] Also, because the Harlem Restoration Project's employees worked more elastically than their titles and job descriptions indicated, Louise also served as a counselor and agitator against landlords, as did Keller.

Keller's activist credentials were impressive. Raised in Rochester, New York, she had graduated from Western Reserve University in 1951. Long attracted to issues of civil liberty and prisoner rights, she collaborated with attorney Haywood Burns on the trials that grew out of the Attica riots of September 1971. As she neared fifty, she sought to make a bigger impact and entered Hofstra University Law School.[65] As a practicing attorney, she often visited Rikers Island, where she would encounter inmates who yelled, "Why aren't you at 10 Delaware?" They were referring to the Erie County jail on Delaware Avenue in Buffalo, where they had seen her.[66]

Louise and Keller, almost thirty years Louise's junior, embarked on a great friendship. We "clicked and became very close," the latter recalled, adding, "Between Louise and my mother, that's what I wanted to be like as an older woman." Keller especially appreciated Louise's wit and humor: "She could see something funny in anything." The two stayed fairly low-key in the office because they weren't sure of Runyon's reaction to their bond. Outside of work, they often met at Louise's apartment or Keller's home in the West Village. They had mutual friends, such as Burns, who had defended Angela Davis as well as the Attica defendants, and Keller attended several of the parties that Louise threw in Esplanade Gardens.[67]

At some of those gatherings, people such as Burns suggested that Louise write a memoir, an idea she had been considering for some time. But she always felt blocked after having been around writers such as Hughes, Bontemps, Hurston, and Alice Childress.[68] However, early in 1983, she approached writer Linda Trice to request assistance. Trice responded that she could not help with drafting the manuscript; she suggested that Burns would know someone. But Trice did offer to work on the final rewrite and to accompany Louise to meet with publishers.[69]

Although Louise remained intellectually sharp and possessed a continued lust for community work, she was increasingly affected by physical ailments. A severe case of pneumonia left her homebound for several months. She still smoked, which did not help matters. By the spring of 1984, she had decided to retire permanently. Moreover, she would vacate her apartment and move to Oakland, a pivotal scene of her youth and the current home of Mary Lou. On June 19 she sent notice to the board of directors at her apartment complex that she would be moving in September. Therefore, her party at Savoy Manor Ballroom in the Bronx on Sunday, September 16, exactly one week after she turned eighty-three, served a fourfold purpose: it celebrated her birthday, commemorated her career, served as a farewell bash, and functioned as a benefit for the NAARPR, which continued to educate and organize around democratic rights and antiracism.[70] The group was then under the directorship of Frank Chapman, with Angela Davis, Reverend David Garcia, and attorney Lennox Hinds as cochairs. The organization was working on cases like that of Johnny Imani Harris, on death row in Alabama for merely participating as an inmate in a protest during which a prison guard was killed, and Leonard Peltier, the American Indian Movement member serving consecutive life sentences after being convicted on less-than-compelling evidence in 1977 of killing FBI agents Jack Coler and Ronald Williams.

Veteran activist Charlene Mitchell, a familiar figure in Communist Party circles who lived one floor above Louise, chaired the celebration committee; Ossie Davis presided. Celebrated author John Oliver Killens delivered a written tribute, "In the Great Tradition of Black Womanhood," in which he noted Louise's struggles with the racism she encountered in her youth.[71] He also praised some of her subsequent achievements: graduating from Berkeley, teaching in Arkansas and Virginia, and working with the Urban League, the IWO, the CAA, and AIMS. More than 150 people sent greetings; several dozen additional people were listed in the "welcome home to California" section of the program, including Beah Richards, the artist whom Pat valued above all others; the tireless Angela Davis; the now-transplanted Apthekers (Herbert and Faye); Sue Bailey Thurman, her pal from Hampton; and Nebby Lou. Friends old and new offered toasts, including lawyer John Abt, Dorothy Burnham, and Faith Berry.[72] The most sentimental gift was perhaps provided by Bruce Nugent, who gave her a replica copy of *Fire!!* Decades beyond the personality conflicts of the Harlem Renaissance, Nugent had generously inscribed, "For Louise, whom I have known *and* loved forever."[73]

On September 28, after two stints in New York that amounted to forty-seven tumultuous yet productive years touching every progressive political cause from Russian friendship to ex-cons rehabilitating tenements, and with yet another major project in mind, Louise Patterson (the name she mostly went by then) departed from the New York scene.

CHAPTER 13

Still Reaching, 1984–1999

Mayor Eugene "Gus" Newport declared October 7, 1984, to be Louise Toles Thompson Patterson Day in Berkeley. As part of the celebration, Beah Richards and others hosted a gala in the Tilden Room of the student union building on the university campus. No one in attendance could have known that the guest of honor's second residency in California would be longer and perhaps as memorable as her first or that, after she had supposedly retired, she would take part in significant activities at the University of California, Berkeley. For example, Louise joined with African American students to found the Black Awards Ceremony, an annual affair designed to commend black faculty, staff, and students for "accomplishments and excellence in the face of constant struggle."[1] In addition, she delivered several speeches on campus and became a familiar presence at a variety of events, including the Berkeley Black Graduation ceremony, conducted each spring since 1977 by the Department of Afro-American Studies.

As she settled in with her daughter at 558 Fifty-Sixth Street, she drew a steady stream of visitors from the surrounding community and beyond. She remained in good spirits, continued to be an adept card player, and was nearly unbeatable at Scrabble. But she could be too competitive at table tennis. During one spirited game with her daughter, she wound up slamming the ball so aggressively that she lost her balance and, instinctively using her hand to break her fall, broke her wrist. Charlene Mitchell quipped in a letter, "I thought ping pong was a mild game."[2]

Louise also pursued her lifelong habit of reading voraciously and amassing information about politics, education, and culture. With the aid of friends who sent her newspaper and magazine items they thought would be of interest, she built extensive files on Jesse Jackson's presidential aspirations, the death of Huey P. Newton, the trials and tribulations of Nelson Mandela and Winnie Mandela, and the Clarence Thomas–Anita Hill proceedings. She kept the entire issue of the *New York Times Magazine* that contained the cover story "Henry Louis Gates Jr.: Black Studies' New Star," and she clipped from her cherished *Jet* magazine the news that Derrick Bell was taking a leave of absence from his professorship at Harvard Law School to protest the school's lack of a black female professor.[3]

Through Jessica Mitford, Louise kept abreast of one of the raging cultural controversies of the mid-1980s, the dispute over the film version of Alice Walker's *The Color Purple*. Shortly after the movie's release, Mitford saw it during a trip to Atlanta. Back in California, she discussed it with Maya Angelou, who argued that criticism of Walker and the film, which Angelou had not seen, was motivated by envy. That was certainly part of the truth but could not totally mitigate the charge, with which Mitford concurred, that the negative depictions of black men saturating the movie conveyed a problematic message.[4] More than a casual or lightweight observer, Mitford had penned a positive profile on Walker and Angelou for the *London Sunday Times*.[5] After their conversation, she wrote Angelou a letter the same night, asserting, "Alice said to you that 'the work is a gift,' true. But that doesn't hold it exempt from criticism of its message." She quoted Voltaire, "qui plume a, guerra a," meaning, roughly, "to hold a pen is to be at war."[6]

In a subsequent letter, following a mild and playful response from Angelou, Mitford disclosed that she had talked at length with Louise about *The Color Purple* and that "she agrees with me about the whole impact of the film." She anticipated that Angelou might consider the two senior women to be "hidebound Old Lefties stuck in the United Front days" but pushed her point nonetheless. Referencing feminist writer Andrea Dworkin's argument that men saw abusing women as a fundamental right, she asked Angelou, "Could [Alice Walker] actually be taking MORE of a lead from the A. Dworkin militant-feminist line than from her own community?"[7]

Louise had limited patience with white feminists because they had not contributed much to the protests against the imprisonment of Angela Davis. At any rate, she requested to see the written exchange between her writer friends, which Mitford provided along with a slew of reviews. Aware that Angelou was slated to appear soon at the National Black Writers Conference in Brooklyn, hosted by veteran social realist John Oliver Killens, with whose family she had once lived, Mitford knew that Angelou as a headliner could hardly defend the movie strongly at that showcase. "She does seem to be in a bit of a quandary," Mitford wrote Louise.[8] Conversing years later with Nebby Lou regarding Walker's work, Louise stated succinctly, "I don't go along with it. I think that's as much a criticism of us as it is of the black men who mistreated the women."[9]

The question of positive portrayal also concerned Louise with respect to Arnold Rampersad's emerging two-volume biography of Langston Hughes. The Rutgers University professor knew she disagreed with his approach even as she supported his work and remained a valuable interviewee. She felt, not surprisingly, that the scholar was failing to cast Hughes majestically enough. Rampersad, with obvious admiration and affection for Louise, sincerely hoped that she would see the value of the finished product.[10] Apparently, she saw much worth promoting. Upon the publication of the second installment, she teamed with Mary Perry Smith, the president of the Black Filmmakers Hall of Fame, to mark the occasion at the Oakland Museum on February 12, 1989. In addition to a book signing as well as a dialogue between her and Rampersad, the event, billed overall as a tribute to Hughes, included a screening of St. Clair Bourne's *The Dreamkeeper* in the museum's James Moore Theater.

It seems that all of Louise's associates made it to the West Coast sooner or later. Sally Goldmark (née Inge), who had worked with Louise at the CES more than fifty years earlier, wrote from Seattle.[11] She had tracked down her former office mate through her neighbor Mary Bassett, a great-niece of Ted Bassett, who had been active with Louise in the Harlem section of the Communist Party. Like Louise, Goldmark, a Brooklyn native now seventy-eight years old, had moved leftward after leaving the CES. After marrying John Goldmark in 1942, she moved with him to the state of Washington and entered a life of ranching and electoral politics. Her husband, who passed away in 1979, became a very liberal, often red-baited state senator. Very ill by 1985, Goldmark was unable to travel to Oakland as Louise desired. She died less than three months after contacting her old friend.[12] In fact, she never got to tell Louise about the most tragic aspect of her story. Because of her family's liberal and radical history, a disgruntled right-winger, David Rice, targeted her son Charles Goldmark, an attorney. Rice had broken into Goldmark's home the previous Christmas Eve; chloroformed him, his wife, and his kids; and then stabbed and beat them all fatally. Goldmark wanted Louise to come see her in Seattle, but, practically speaking, not enough time remained to make that happen.[13]

Dorothy Keller, for whom Louise was a mother figure, came to Oakland to check on her.[14] Actress Vinie Burrows spent two months in the area to play the lead in a production of *Medea* at the University of Santa Clara. New Yorker Sarah Wright, author of the classic novel *This Child's Gonna Live*, presented Louise with a copy of her new book on A. Philip Randolph. Roger Keeran, affiliated with the Harry Van Arsdale Jr. School of Labor Studies at Empire State College and the author of *The Communist Party and the Auto Workers Unions*, needed Louise's input for a book he was writing on the CIO. He conducted several hours of interviews with her about her work for the IWO. John Henrik Clarke, associate editor of *Freedomways* and once co-chair with Louise of a memorial for Alphaeus Hunton, included an Oakland stop as he delivered a lecture titled "African Background in the Teachings of Dr. Martin Luther King, Jr."[15]

Margaret Walker, whom Louise had not seen in many years, toured California to push her *New and Collected Poems*. During the Bay Area phase of her trip, which included appearances at Berkeley and Solano Community College, Walker stayed with Louise and Mary Lou. They treasured the opportunity to reminisce—at least in the case of the elder women—and to share current news.[16] It's not hard to imagine that as they touched on literary matters they discussed not only Walker's poetry but her book on Richard Wright, *Daemonic Genius*. Certainly, members of Sojourner: A Black Women's Book Club, to which Louise and her daughter belonged, expressed interest in placing *Daemonic Genius* on their agenda.[17]

Even while maintaining a robust social calendar, Louise tried to work on her memoir, having seriously answered the call to place a sensible frame around her entire life from the vantage point of her ninth decade. With a historian's sense, she also became obsessed with gathering secondary materials about African American life in the western United States during the period of her youth. She wrote to numerous libraries and historical societies and collected such texts as Jack D. Forbes's *Afro-Americans in the Far West: A Handbook for Educators*; *The Negro in the State of Washington, 1788–1967: A Bibliography*, compiled by the Washington State Library; Elizabeth McLagan's *A Peculiar Paradise: A History of Blacks in Oregon, 1788–1940*; and *Oakland's Black Community: An Historical Bibliography*, compiled by the Oakland Public Library.

Now serving as a walking library to new waves of students, cultural workers, and scholars, Louise would, in turn, rely on those people, as well as some longtime or rediscovered friends, to sharpen her perspective on her own journey. Daphne Muse, a former student at Fisk University and Mills College who had been a researcher for the legal defense team of Angela Davis, developed a proposal to help Louise grasp the budgetary dimensions of the memoir project, the funding required for phone calls, postage, travel, recording, reproduction, supplies, clerical support, and legal fees.[18] Margaret Wilkerson, a theater scholar, a faculty member at the University of California, Berkeley, and the director of the university's Center for the Study, Education, and Advancement of Women, took a special interest in the endeavor and secured some of the needed resources.[19] A product of black Los Angeles of the 1940s and 1950s, Wilkerson also became the first of several interviewers to help generate lengthy recordings, leading Louise, over the first few months of 1986, to recount on audiotape the story of her formative decades, including her time teaching in Arkansas. As Louise used these interviews to draft chapters—sometimes typing, sometimes working in longhand on yellow legal pads—she revealed definite writing ability, a narrative style that was uncluttered and engaging yet nonetheless weighty. She had a feel for what made a good anecdote and seemed capable of producing a book at least the equal of those that were probably her primary models, Hughes's *The Big Sea* and *I Wonder as I Wander* and Pat's *The Man Who Cried Genocide*.

This activity paid dividends when Louise accepted an invitation to address students at her alma mater on May 6, 1989. Relying on her memoir writing, she shared with the audience in Pauley Ballroom several of her postcollege experiences, emphasizing her role as an educator in the South. She wanted the Berkeley students, young enough to be her great-grandchildren, to understand that they were only the most recent enrollees, but surely welcome, in a long battle for equity and inclusion in higher education.[20] In her view, they were indispensable reinforcements, and she wished for them what she had claimed for herself: academic excellence and fulfilling work with the mission of creating the "kinds of universities, society and, indeed, world that treasure the contributions of all, regardless of color, gender and other differences."[21] She saluted the activists among them and surmised how difficult it had to be for them to establish unity among those with clashing viewpoints.[22] "Organizing is a fine art," she intoned. "I have worked at it all of my adult life."[23] Drawing on that vast experience, she advised the students "to study and to learn how to bring the disparate parts of our own group together and to continue your efforts to strengthen alliances and coalitions with those who are not black."[24] She cautioned them, "In your organizing, keep strong contact with your community. Never separate yourself from your larger community base or you will find yourself isolated and fair game for any predator."[25] Louise wondered why a black person had to be a superstar to be hired by the University of California as opposed to being simply a "good, solid academician," as were most of the seven thousand faculty in the system.[26] She stressed that the university was a land-grant institution and therefore had a responsibility to "remove obstacles to black academic achievement by hiring more black faculty, improving student support services, and ending racism in all its forms in its classrooms and in every corner of its campuses."[27] Given the enthusiastic applause at the conclusion of her speech, Louise might have been as inspiring a speaker as the one she witnessed in Wheeler Hall as an undergraduate.

Work on the memoir proceeded in fits and starts. Linda Burnham, a daughter of Dorothy Burnham and at that time a whirlwind activist and journalist in the Bay Area and soon-to-be founder and director of the Women of Color Resource Center, pushed Louise forward with a round of interviews. They preliminarily covered Louise's arrival in New York City, the Harlem Renaissance, the *Black and White* fiasco, her IWO involvement, her visit to Spain during the Spanish Civil War, and the Harlem Suitcase Theater. However, acutely aware of the limitations of memory, Louise continued to think more expansively about her writing and kept deepening the context beyond her recollections or her conversations with much younger interlocutors. This obsession led her to take a road trip to Nevada during the summer of 1987, escorted by a new and valued associate, Chuck Fields.

On Sunday, July 12, the travelers pulled into Reno around six o'clock in the evening. The following morning, Louise, dressed in an airy blouse, pedal pushers, and open-toe shoes, braved the heat to visit the Nevada Historical Society to consult with archivists there. In the course of conversation, she learned of Elmer Rusco, a scholar who had written extensively about blacks in Nevada, including the book *"Good Time Coming?": Black Nevadans in the Nineteenth Century*, published in 1975. Louise inquired about meeting Rusco but found no immediate lead she could follow to make it happen. She also pored over coverage of the fight between Joe Gans and Oscar Mathaeus Nielsen in the pages of the *Goldfield Daily Sun* and of the fight between Jack Johnson and Jim Jeffries in several newspapers, including the *St. Louis Republic*, *Denver Post*, and *New Orleans Daily Picayune*. Before leaving town, Louise and Fields stopped by the plaque, located at Fourth and Toano, that commemorated the Fight of the Century. Louise, clearly enjoying herself, read the words aloud while Fields videotaped her.

While driving south, Fields pointed out some of the cuts in the mountains where silver had been extracted. Louise revealed an environmentalist side and likened the mining industry to the lumber companies destroying the forests of the state of Washington. "In search of profits they don't give a dang about what they do to the country or the people," she sighed.[28] They stopped in Virginia City, taking in sights such as the historic Piper's Opera House, where Mark Twain once performed. After pushing through the desert for nearly four more hours, with copper-colored mountains a constant backdrop, they decided to spend the night in Tonopah, still about twenty-five miles short of Goldfield. They stayed at Old Corral, hit Jerry's Diner for dinner, and went to bed exhausted at one o'clock in the morning.

On July 14 Louise completed the journey to the site of some of her earliest memories. She stood in front of the camera, announcing, as she would in her memoir, that Goldfield was the town where she first became conscious of racism.[29] But no traces of that story could be discerned in a location with not a single black resident. After riding somewhat somberly around the ruined shacks and buildings of a virtual ghost town, noting that there were still no sidewalks and thinking of how she and her mother had walked the dark roads eighty years earlier, Louise remarked in disappointment, "It has been an interesting experience."[30] The liveliest activity involved the buzzing chainsaws of those at work on the Goldfield Hotel restoration project. A visit to the Goldfield Historical Society, where Louise smoked a cigarette while conversing with a curator, failed to yield much useful information.

After returning to Tonopah for a visit to the Central Nevada Museum, Louise and Fields then headed back north toward Carson City and, beyond that, Lake Tahoe. There was obviously something in Louise that connected emotionally with rural Nevada, perhaps just a line of memory to her mother. Nonetheless, she reminded herself that she never wanted small-town life. Fields agreed, recalling the summers he spent in Plum, Texas. "They don't have a decent newspaper," Louise observed of Tonopah residents. "I imagine they watch a lot of TV," she added. "Maybe they have softball teams."[31] But they certainly had nothing that could ever have held her.

By the end of the year, seeking to capture in print the Oregon phase of her life, Louise had reached out to connect with eighty-one-year-old Kathryn Bogle in Portland, long active in civil rights struggles in the state, as well as

Verdell Burdine Rutherford, a younger sister of the Dolores Burdine whom Louise used to babysit in Coos Bay. Bogle had also lived in Coos Bay for a year during her childhood but did not remember Louise, five years her senior. Rutherford possessed no direct memories of Louise either; she had been only two years old when Louise moved to California. However, her mother often spoke of her former neighbors over the years, making Louise Thompson "a name stored in my memory bank since a child."[32] She thus considered Louise a long-lost family member. Rutherford and her husband, Otto, a Portland native, made a hobby of collecting memorabilia and were eager to help with research. She thought it sad, though, that Louise missed reuniting with Dolores and their mother. The two had died in March 1986, Margaret Burdine Cash at the age of one hundred and, two days prior, Dolores Burdine Goodman, a former chair of the NAACP in Yakima, Washington, at seventy-seven. But Louise did have a chance to see her other former fan, Nattie Boles Gordon, who was still living in Coos Bay.

Accompanied by Wilkerson and Beverly John, Louise made the trip to Oregon at the end of May 1988, an experience she found "exhilarating" despite the inclement weather, which included a snowstorm during their excursion to Crater Lake National Park.[33] The three visitors, with the audiotape running, interviewed Gordon in Coos Bay on May 31. A couple of days later, they were at the Rutherford home in Portland. Louise met with Bogle on June 3 and visited with her the Oregon Historical Society on Park Avenue. The information she collected on the trip through conversation and perusal of secondary sources, as well as the materials—articles, letters, and pictures—that Verdell Rutherford and Gordon began to send through the mail, gave Louise more confidence in her ability to compose what she had envisioned.[34]

The impulse to provide a more panoramic view of her times also slowed her progress, however. On a visit to Beah Richards in Los Angeles, her fellow Sojourner advised her to scale back the archival work. When Louise conveyed that she was having trouble framing certain events and was looking for old issues of the *California Eagle*, specifically for details about Paul Robeson's visits to the city, Richards countered, "Louise, you're the detail. When you open your mouth, you don't need anything else."[35] On another subject, they agreed that they disliked Martin Duberman's biography of Robeson. Louise had declined to be interviewed for the book and later refused a request from Knopf to publish excerpts of letters from her and Pat to the Robesons.[36] Aside from questions about Duberman's qualifications and perspective with regard to Robeson's life—and those questions were considerable—Louise and a significant segment of the black Left held a grudge against Duberman for not only defending William Styron and his novel, *The Confessions of Nat Turner* (1967), but vehemently criticizing editor John Henrik Clarke and the writers who had contributed to *William Styron's Nat Turner: Ten Black Writers Respond.* Lloyd Brown, a close colleague of Robeson, opined, "In some 50-odd years of reading the *New York Times Book Review*, I cannot recall a more blatantly anti-black essay than Martin Duberman's attack on a group of black writers and scholars who had expressed opposition to a book that gravely slandered their people."[37] Based on this, Brown, whom Robeson himself had chosen as his authorized biographer, expressed misgivings to Clarke about Duberman's capabilities.[38]

Despite Richards's urging to trust her memory, Louise remained hesitant during interviews. Nebby Lou handled much of the taping for a year beginning in the spring of 1989, retracing Louise's account of the early years from a different angle than Wilkerson had. During these sessions Louise exhibited a very sharp memory although she sometimes shifted the focus to secondary material or remarked that they could later corroborate some point or another.

Even if she had had an optimal approach, Louise would still have been up against an unforgiving clock as ailments, trips to the doctor, and hospital stays were going to continue. She always affirmed that she was working hard on the project and did generate several hundred pages, but she produced multiple drafts of the period through the 1930s rather than writing about the later times, which for whatever reason, she had trouble framing, as she acknowledged to Richards. Friends, typically with a political message, tried to push or pull her to victory. Chicago colleagues Claude Lightfoot and Ishmael Flory solicited funds on her behalf.[39] Flory told her, "Muhammad Ali made one mistake. He's not the greatest—Louise Patterson is the greatest."[40] The playwright Loften Mitchell wrote, "I am rooting for you. And I am rooting against warmongers and perpetrators of poverty and racism."[41] Maya Angelou assisted with fund-raising, performing a benefit to a packed audience at Glide Memorial Church in San Francisco.[42]

Not long after the fund-raiser, Louise made her first trip back east in nearly five years. Battling the high humidity and missing the Pacific breezes, she attended her granddaughter Joanna's graduation on June 27, 1989, from the High School of Performing Arts in New York City.[43] While there, she heard a great deal of clamor accompanying the release of another hot-topic movie of the 1980s, director Spike Lee's *Do the Right Thing.* She visited radio station WOR with Ossie Davis and Ruby Dee, who had played the roles of Da

Mayor and Mother Sister and were fulfilling their promotional obligations. Davis, knowing that Louise had not cared at all for Lee's previous movie, *School Daze*, informed her that while the film had weaknesses, the "man is growing."[44]

After returning to Oakland, she went to view the movie on Friday afternoon, July 7, with Mary Lou, Fields, and Jim Massey, after which they retreated to Louise's home for a long and spirited discussion of their initial reactions. Mary Lou thought the rising filmmaker "had upped the ante for Hollywood," showing that a film could deal with serious social issues and yet be commercially successful. More circumspect, Louise admitted that she had been "very moved." Shifting quickly to an analytical frame of mind, she wondered, "What happens to those people who do not have a social position on racism? What do they get out of the film?" She immediately continued, "I'd be very interested in talking to people who have not been a part of any race relations organizations, any political organizations that had discussed racism. First of all, how would they define it?" She stated furthermore, "It was a Brooklyn I was not familiar with." Mary Lou tried to break through the distancing and the generational denial, explaining that the Bedford-Stuyvesant setting symbolized urban black life. She knew that her eighty-seven-year-old mother, who had wandered slowly and observantly through the first major riot in Harlem, could certainly understand black communities suffering from high unemployment, police brutality, and a dearth of black proprietorship. The connection was made. Louise turned to Massey to make sure he was recording Mary Lou, declaring, "What she's saying is good."[45]

Although Louise still refrained from issuing a summative judgment, she was clear that the movie was not degrading: "It's not Uncle Tomming." She had enjoyed the general display of "ethnic validity" and the vernacular speech, even offering an exquisitely rhythmic "that motherfucker" of her own. Regarding Lee's directing talent, she warmed to the task of criticism by pointing out that the "genius of his filmmaking" resided in some of his subtle, nuanced moves as well as in his photography, for example, the distorted facial shots of Radio Raheem during the movie's climactic scene in Sal's Famous Pizzeria. Lee's surrealism, as she labeled it, reminded her of Jean-Paul Sartre. In contrast, she remained puzzled by Ruby Dee's role: "She's typical of a woman sitting in the window. I've seen it in Harlem. But I'm not clear what she's talking about." For Louise, on the whole, "the women's characters were not as strong. . . . There wasn't one woman that I could think of as strong—and black women are strong."[46]

The following month Louise would be before professional cameras herself when she went to Los Angeles to film footage for KCET, the public television station serving southern and central California. The project, a docudrama written by Dee, was *Zora Is My Name!*[47] It aired nationally on February 14, 1990, as part of the series *American Playhouse.* In private settings Louise could be pointed and sometimes harsh in her comments concerning Hurston, charging her with supporting "some of the greatest enemies of blacks" and with denouncing Communists and "anybody who was progressive."[48] However, she generally tempered her remarks for the public, focusing on the writer's abundant talent and vibrant, mostly generous personality. After Verdell Rutherford saw the film and accompanying commentary, she wrote with compliments: "You were so beautiful and spoke with so much authority."[49]

Interest in Hurston continued to surge from the late 1980s into the 1990s, as evident by the announcement of the First Annual Zora Neale Hurston Festival of the Arts, to take place in Hurston's hometown of Eatonville, Florida, in late January 1990. As soon as she learned of the celebration, Louise was inclined to attend but was slow to accept the invitation of N. Y. Nathiri, the president of the Association to Preserve the Eatonville Community, because of health issues, which involved several weeks in the hospital and a battery of tests.[50] On the coronary care unit at Merritt Hospital, Louise barely survived one of her own experiments. Although she was being administered oxygen, as were other patients on the floor, she extracted a pack of cigarettes from her pocketbook and proceeded to light up until the frantic shouting of a nurse halted her. Of course, her cigarettes and matches were seized. Otherwise, she was the darling of the unit, holding court among patients and employees alike.[51]

Eventually released and cleared for travel, and funded by Nathiri and Wilkerson, Louise arrived in Eatonville on January 25 to participate in the oral history session. Always diligent in preparation, she read from a text she had written for the occasion. She recounted the story of her own relationship with Charlotte Osgood Mason, a tale not favorable to Mason, and characterized her experience with Hurston as "brief and happy." She explained that Hurston was "creative in so many ways" and that she had "never met anyone like her." But Louise never claimed to understand the writer and concluded her presentation with a mix of praise, sympathy, and vague criticism:

> To understand her you have to understand what the fight for survival has meant for Blacks here in the US and the effect that racism has had on all of

us here. For me to understand Zora I needed much more experience than I had at that time. She was a very complex person who had to go through a lot to get where she was. In honoring Zora, recognizing her talent, we also have to see and understand things that crippled her and many of us. And to know these things is to know much better how to combat certain things that are still here. And because she was such an individualist, she tried to do it alone.[52]

Back home, Louise, when feeling well enough, resumed her normal run of activities, which included interviewing for her memoir, responding to scholars' requests for information, and fulfilling speaking engagements. The Association of Black Graduate Students in Education at Stanford University identified her as a "pioneer black educator" and invited her to take part in a symposium featuring her, Robert Bragg, Laurence Crouchette, Wilhelmina Henry, and Lois Powell. Norma Francisco, representing the organization, arranged round-trip car transport from Oakland to Palo Alto, a trip that originated from Valdez Plaza on Twenty-Eighth Street, where Louise was living after Mary Lou had relocated to Riverside to join her husband, Lance Gilmer. Apparently, the session at Stanford didn't last long enough. Louise wrote to inform Francisco that, health permitting, she would like to meet with a group of education students, a meeting Francisco said she would be glad to facilitate.[53]

Education always remained a vital political issue for Louise, who had spoken in public about the fact that schools in Oakland were inferior to those in the suburbs. This was related in her mind to the doubling of poverty rates in the city since the mid-1960s; more than a third of Oakland's children were living in poverty in the 1990s, and three-fourths of these were black, as she was quick to point out.[54] On occasion she reflected, "I think the black question is the thing that most disturbs in the United States."[55] She feared that matters would become worse if George H. W. Bush were reelected president. "He is the establishment," she explained. "Reagan was a puppet. But Bush knows what he is doing every step of the way."[56] If she needed confirmation that the insights of her generation remained relevant, she received it when an update arrived from the indomitable Vicki Garvin: "I've managed to keep fairly active at forums on Malcolm X, as a member of Sisters Against South African Apartheid, of the Committee to Eliminate Media Offensive to African People, and at demos against the Persian Gulf War. . . . I feel confident that the ongoing struggles will produce positive results for progress and justice during this decade. The majority peoples of the world will finally defeat the minority who have exploited and oppressed us over the centuries!"[57]

Regarding international issues, Louise did not wear her political ideology on her sleeve much during those days. But she naturally had to grapple intellectually and emotionally with the fall of Communism in Eastern Europe, the so-called Revolution of 1989 that originated in Poland and spread through the Eastern bloc, much of which she had visited in 1962 when, in her estimation, she "got a good look at the socialist world."[58] The sweeping changes, mostly nonviolent except in Romania, eventually led to the dissolution of the Soviet Union and the resignation of Mikhail Gorbachev. The Soviet Union was not as old as Louise and would not last as long. Yet she remained far from contrite even as she acknowledged, thinking about her memoir, "That's going to be a difficult period for me to deal with now with what's happened, though I don't take it as some people do, you know, that everything's gone and they're heartbroken and they're disillusioned and so forth and so on. I don't know exactly where I am. I'm thinking about it a lot." Remaining pensive, she mused, "When you think that socialism, the forms that it took in Eastern Europe, had only about seventy years, the time of trial till this present business. . . . I talk to people who are Christians. How many years have you had this Christianity? 2,000? And where is the church today? And what is done in the name of the church?"[59]

Ruminating about state control, Louise pondered its strengths and drawbacks. She saw value in compelling people to live ethically while she understood the danger in allowing bureaucracies to determine ethical value. "People have to learn to live as civilized people together," she calmly explained to an interviewer, "and thinking that way is difficult."[60] Bracketing socialism and any other economic issues, she announced, "To me, the two questions most difficult to handle are sex and race. The man still feels he's superior to the woman. And the race question, ethnic groups . . ." Louise deplored the ethnic one-upmanship she observed in the United States and felt that competition does not lead to respect. Mentioning an episode of *Donahue* that featured the Ku Klux Klan, she confided, "It was really frightening. These young ignorant-looking white folks with their children running all over the place talking about the niggers. It was enough to turn your stomach."[61]

So Russia, for Louise, despite accounts of Russian racism such as those by Homer Smith and Robert Robinson, still ranked ahead of the United States with respect to ethnic relations.[62] This was symbolized by the reactions of young *Moscow News* reporter Yelena Khanga, the granddaughter of Oliver

Golden, whom Louise met during her tour of Central Asia in 1932. While visiting the United States in 1988, Khanga expressed bewilderment over all the fuss about the "first black headquarters" (she meant quarterback), a reference to Doug Williams, the signal caller for the Washington Redskins in Super Bowl XXII, who was the first African American quarterback to start a National Football League championship game. Also, Khanga was shocked that network television would cover the theories of Jimmy "The Greek" Snyder about the superiority of black athletes owing to their breeding and physiology.[63]

May 12, 1991, Mother's Day, found a relaxed Louise in the Riverside home of her daughter and Gilmer. With wind chimes playing in a gentle breeze and Mary Lou at the video camera, she met in the backyard with a friend of theirs, the historian Sterling Stuckey, who had left Northwestern University to join the faculty at Riverside in 1989. Stuckey was keen to ask about her recollections of Paul Robeson, a heroic figure to him. His family had hosted Robeson in their Chicago home in the early 1950s. Louise graciously shared her perceptions of Robeson's generosity and exuberance as well as his solemn commitment to struggle. She waxed eloquent about Peekskill, the subsequent concert tour on behalf of the CAA, and her visits to Robeson's London home in the 1960s.[64]

Interested in Louise's background and opinions as well, Stuckey informed her that President Bush had delivered the commencement address at Hampton University the day before and had been met with student protests. "I would say that's positive," replied the Hampton instructor of generations ago. She asked about the substance of the speech by the man she called the "most dangerous president we have had." She discounted Bush's obligatory remarks about fighting discrimination, knowing that seven months earlier he had vetoed the Civil Rights Act of 1990. Also, neither she nor Stuckey cared for Bush's Republican pleading for cuts in the capital gains tax.[65]

Louise had been unaware of Stuckey's scholarship, so, ever intellectually curious, she inquired about it. When he told her about his book, *Slave Culture: Nationalist Theory and the Foundations of Black America*, she expressed a desire to read it. At one point, she asked Stuckey his opinion of a journal she had been reading, *Callaloo*, giving her opinion that it was "too pretentious. It will not reach the masses." Stuckey agreed, "They don't have independence of spirit to pioneer anything of their own. It has to be modeled after . . . even when they're talking about black writers, they can't utter ten words in succession without mentioning the word *canon* or *discourse*." Aware of his exaggeration and admitting that he was not the most devoted reader of the literary publication, Stuckey added, though not softening much, "Maybe you can run across a piece that runs a page or two without *canon* being used or the word *discourse* being used."[66]

While Louise was in Riverside, Mary Lou also taped a two-hour conversation between her mother, her husband, and a friend named Mildred that touched on a wide array of issues, beginning with health care. Louise, mindful of her success with the IWO, imagined that the average American would rally behind the idea of adequate health insurance for all. She dismissed in her own mind the rape allegation against William Kennedy Smith—anticipating the jury's later decision—because she thought it was a maneuver, Chappaquiddick notwithstanding, to keep Ted Kennedy out of the presidential race of 1992. She criticized Operation Desert Storm, embraced affirmative action, endorsed the continued use of sanctions against apartheid South Africa, sided with Mayor Tom Bradley of Los Angeles after he called for the resignation of Police Chief Daryl Gates in the wake of the beating of Rodney King, tweaked white feminists for not being attentive enough to black issues, and ridiculed the decision of the Federal Deposit Insurance Corporation to close Freedom National Bank when the federal government had bailed out banks such as Silverado Savings and Loan. Becoming quite animated, she exclaimed, "I wish I had more time to learn and participate actively." Throughout the session, she stressed the need for people to develop their critical faculties: "You have to know how to read a newspaper. You have to know how to see the media. . . . It's the whys we've got to turn to. . . . It's the why of the thing."[67]

At several junctures, Gilmer, a former sports writer for the *San Francisco Examiner*, turned the conversation to the exploitation of athletes. Louise remained respectfully attentive; she understood exploitation but didn't worry too much about sports. During her weekly reading of *Jet*, she stopped when she got to that section of the magazine, mainly because she didn't want to read another account of opulence. However, her interest spiked when her son-in-law told her that the Los Angeles Lakers had been a powerhouse with a starting lineup of five African American players. Then, seemingly out of the blue, Louise asked about the progress of Bo Jackson, the multisport star who had been seriously injured in January while playing running back for the Raiders, her once and future hometown team, which was then headquartered in Los Angeles.[68]

Louise returned to the Bay Area in time to attend the Seventeenth Annual Black Graduation ceremony at Berkeley, an event at which she would receive the Fannie Lou Hamer Award, a fitting tribute given her own social justice work over the decades and her admiration for the civil rights warrior. Adorned in a black cap and gown with a scarf of kente cloth draped around her neck, she proudly climbed to the stage as part of the graduation procession and tapped her cane on the floor to the beat of the lively music played by a pianist and percussionist as she stood waiting for the signal to be seated. About an hour into the ceremony, following remarks by her friend and collaborator Wilkerson, Barbara Christian, and others about developments involving the Department of Afro-American Studies—and before a stirring keynote address by June Jordan—Wilkerson guided Louise to the podium and introduced her formally, impressing the audience and thrilling the Deltas on hand when she announced the honoree's membership in that sorority.

Faltering slightly at the outset, Louise gained confidence throughout her six-minute address. She briefly recounted the story of her graduation, registered her solidarity with the Hampton University students who had protested against President Bush, and spoke of advances that needed to be made with respect to issues of peace, unemployment, and poverty. "Oh, you young graduates," she exclaimed, "I'm so happy to be here. This is a great moment of my life. And though I'll be ninety in several months, I have decided that I'm going to stick around for a little longer. There's much work to do for all of us. I'm gonna be here with you a little while and see how you stir things up a bit."[69]

Louise received a boost when Nikky Finney, a future recipient of the National Book Award, began to assist her with her writing style. She reported excitedly to Ossie Davis, who raised the funds for the work, "She is helping me pull on my creative juices!!! She is a younger version of me and I am an older version of her. It works!"[70] Margaret Burroughs, in a letter from Chicago, jokingly called the proposed book "our autobiography" and hoped it would be available soon.[71] Burroughs probably did not realize the telling nature of her word choice. Louise and an actual collaborator, Wilkerson, who had resumed interviewing, had signed no formal contract specifying the nature of their collaboration with respect to ownership, entitlement rights, exclusivity, distribution, royalties, and spinoffs.[72] Indeed, the title was in question, with Wilkerson imagining the book as an authorized biography.[73]

Although not a controversy that rose to the level of the *Mule Bone* affair, the matter needed to be resolved, at least from the perspective of Wilkerson and Mary Lou. The latter consulted attorney Cy Epstein, a family friend who had been impressed by what he had seen of the manuscript, quickly discerning that the "writing therein showed professional quality and may approach a level of stylistic skill that would be appreciated by critical audiences." He argued that contract issues were secondary to the goal of finishing the work, reasoning, "I would rather have a legal dispute over such issues with respect to a finished product than resolve a legal dispute at the expense of finishing the project." Epstein considered the completion of a first draft the higher priority because "it will constitute an appropriate emblem of the life and times of Louise, a tribute to the memory of Mr. Patterson, and, finally, quite possibly a source of moral sustenance to a generation or generations of young people." But the most important point, as Louise had confided to Epstein, was that delays, both past and future, were and would be largely a function of her increasingly fragile health.[74] In a subsequent letter to Mary Lou, Wilkerson explained that she hoped that a draft would be ready by the end of the year.[75] However, Louise focused primarily on the material already accumulated, and even though she tried to minimize distractions by, for example, increasingly turning down requests for interviews, she failed to make appreciable progress. Eventually, her daughter became her primary interlocutor, though period coverage was not extended much as a result. Mary Lou pushed instead for more psychological depth.[76]

In 1994 Louise made her last trip abroad, a junket to Italy inspired by a friend of Mary Lou. Matt Crawford made the journey along with Sterling Stuckey and his wife. Mostly confined to a wheelchair, Louise nonetheless saw a number of sights, and she participated fully at restaurants as she enjoyed her food and wine.[77] For her ninety-third birthday a few weeks later, Faith Berry, by then a friend of twenty-two years (Berry considered herself Louise's foster daughter), came up from Santa Barbara to take her to dinner and a small celebration at a favorite haunt, T.J.'s Gingerbread House.[78] The following night, *Oakland Tribune* columnist Brenda Payton and her husband, Steve, hosted a party at their home overlooking the dotted lighting of the surrounding hills. In this picturesque setting, surrounded by friends, Louise, with a head full of completely white hair, felt "overcome with joy." Mary Lou, radiantly commanding the living room from the center of the floor, announced, to knowing laughter, "There is no program as such. And anybody who knows Louise knows there *would* have been a program had *we* organized it." As Louise sat with Nebby Lou at her side, she listened as Mary Lou read touching tributes from Charlene Mitchell, Jim Johnson, Vinie Burrows, and the couple Jessica Mitford and Bob Treuhaft. Salutes were offered in person by the Paytons, Linda Burnham, Fania Davis, Faith Berry, Norville Smith from the Black Alumni Club at Berkeley, a bespectacled and distinguished-looking Matt Crawford, and Sterling Stuckey.[79]

Stuckey probably had not fully weighed his words when he remarked, "I don't think there's any living figure in this country who's been involved in more important social struggles over the years."[80] Whether true or not, such a declaration, despite the mirthful occasion, betokened the fact that Louise had few years left. Or perhaps Stuckey had struck the precise tragicomic chord for the entire group: hope against hope for many more productive years for the guest of honor.

She tried valiantly, her reach far exceeding her grasp, which is precisely what her particular heaven was for. She did more interviews, this time with Linda Burnham, who outlined all of the prospective chapters.[81] As late as the spring of 1995, Berry provided the solicited feedback—but on the portion of the manuscript dealing once again with Louise's first trip to Russia.[82]

Louise spent her last two years in the Amsterdam Nursing Home in New York. She was an author. Her articles and memoir stamped her as such. Therefore, in addition to all of her other accomplishments, she was the last surviving writer of the cultural formation known as the Harlem Renaissance. With a literary flourish, she died on August 27, 1999. Mary Lou had once noted the irony that the birth of William L. Patterson and the death of W. E. B. Du Bois occurred on the same day of the year. Moreover, she knew of a movement to have August 27 set aside as a special day to recognize Pat and Du Bois.[83] Louise would never miss the opportunity to also be featured at such a celebration.

Perhaps her final text for the public was the commentary she gave about her life to Philadelphia filmmaker Louis Massiah: "I may not leave you any earthly possessions. But you don't need them. That you can get for yourself. What I would like to leave you is a feeling that whatever small contribution I have made has not been a sacrifice—it has been a pleasure; it has been the thing that has given me the greatest pleasure—and that you will build and you will do more and that no one is free until all people are free."[84]

Introduction

1. Lee, a sixty-year-old black man, had been convicted of murder in Maryland. After the U.S. Supreme Court refused to overturn his conviction, Maryland executed him on October 28, 1933. Mooney, a white labor leader, had been convicted of the Preparedness Day Bombing, which occurred in San Francisco on July 22, 1916. He was pardoned in 1939 after twenty-two years in prison. Herndon, who turned twenty years old two days before the march, had been arrested in Atlanta the previous year for possessing Communist literature and organizing industrial workers, both black and white. After several convictions and appeals—and two years in prison—Herndon was cleared for good in 1937.

2. See T. R. Poston, "145,000 Protest to Roosevelt," *New York Amsterdam News*, May 10, 1933.

3. Figure given by Louise Thompson in "And So We Marched," *Working Woman*, June 1933, 6.

4. Farrakhan was the leading figure in the Million Man March on October 16, 1995. Estimates of the actual crowd size vary, but some do claim that there were a million participants.

5. L. Patterson, interview by Evelyn Louise Crawford, June 17, 1989, transcript, 24, box 28, folder 7, Louise Thompson Patterson Papers, Stuart A. Rose Manuscript, Archives, and Rare Book Library, Emory University, Atlanta, GA.

6. FBI Report, September 24, 1941, Louise Thompson Patterson FBI/FOIA Chicago File 100-4092.

7. Louise Thompson to Nebby Crawford, January 16, 1931, quoted in Crawford and Patterson, *Letters from Langston*, 38.

8. L. Patterson with Verdell Burdine and Otto Rutherford, interview by Margaret Wilkerson and Beverly John, June 2, 1988, transcript, 24, box 27, folder 16, Louise Thompson Patterson Papers.

9. L. Patterson, "What Makes One an American Negro," box 20, folder 22, Louise Thompson Patterson Papers.

10. L. Patterson, interview by Evelyn Louise Crawford, March 18, 1990, transcript, 28, box 28, folder 13, Louise Thompson Patterson Papers.

11. Erik S. McDuffie attributes the term *black left feminism*, a concept that frames his book *Sojourning for Freedom*, to Mary Helen Washington. See McDuffie, *Sojourning for Freedom*, 3; Washington, "Alice Childress," 185. For discussion of the radical black female subject, see Davies, *Left of Karl Marx*, xv, 1–27.

Chapter 1: Louise Alone, 1901–1916

1. Louise, in an unpublished memoir segment titled "Chapter 1," claims that her mother was nineteen years old at the time. "Chapter 1," unpublished memoir, 3, box 19, folder 15, Louise Thompson Patterson Papers. However, both U.S. census records and Lulu's Illinois marriage license indicate that she had reached the age of twenty-four by September 9, 1901.

2. L. Patterson, "Chapter 1," unpublished memoir, 6.

3. Spear, *Black Chicago*, 1.

4. Spear, *Black Chicago*, 12.

5. Spear, *Black Chicago*, 7, 29.

6. The council was the successor to the Afro-American League, which operated from 1890 to 1893. Inspired by the journalist T. Thomas Fortune, who also founded the league, the council, mainly headed by Alexander Walters, lasted until 1907.

7. Attempting to attract people who were disenchanted with some of the established congregations, the Institutional Church and Social Settlement eventually featured a nursery and a kindergarten; a mother's club; an employment bureau; a print shop; a gymnasium; classes in sewing, cooking, and music; lectures by prominent figures; concerts; and space for meetings. See Spear, *Black Chicago*, 95–96.

8. See Addams, *Twenty Years at Hull-House*.

9. State of Illinois Marriage License 307578.

10. L. Patterson, "Chapter 1," unpublished memoir, 7.

11. Although she began calling herself Louise at this time, I have used Lulu, rather than Louise, throughout to avoid confusion.

12. L. Patterson, "Chapter 1," unpublished memoir, 6–7. I cannot confirm the diagnosis or speak to the combination of health problems she might have encountered, but the symptoms reported are more associated with polio than measles.

13. L. Patterson, "Chapter 1," unpublished memoir, 6–7.

14. See Hobbs, *Cayton Legacy*, 15–16.

15. Hobbs, *Cayton Legacy*, 16–18.

16. See H. Cayton Jr., *Long Old Road*, 21.

17. The Klondike Gold Rush is also known as the Yukon Gold Rush, the Alaska Gold Rush, and the Last Great Gold Rush.

18. See Berton, *Klondike*, 396.

19. Population statistic cited from Hobbs, *Cayton Legacy*, 24.

20. H. Cayton Jr., *Long Old Road*, 3.

21. L. Patterson, "Chapter 1," unpublished memoir, 8–9.

22. L. Patterson, "Chapter 1," unpublished memoir, 7–8.

23. Population figure from Aycock and Scott, *Joe Gans*, 153.

24. Population figure from "Goldfield's Building Boom." http://www.goldfield historicalsociety.com/buildingboom.html. Accessed February 22, 2017.

25. L. Patterson, "Chapter 1," unpublished memoir, 9.

26. See Porter, "Foreword," xii; Rusco, *"Good Time Coming?,"* 203–6.

27. See Porter, "Foreword," xii; Rusco, *"Good Time Coming?,"* 206–7.

28. Rusco, *"Good Time Coming?,"* 207.

29. Newlands, quoted in Rusco, *"Good Time Coming?,"* 212.

30. Rusco, *"Good Time Coming?,"* 207.

31. Rusco, *"Good Time Coming?,"* 208.

32. Ellison, *Invisible Man*, 17–29.

33. Early, "Introduction," 24–31.

34. Quoted in Aycock and Scott, *Joe Gans*, 6–7.

35. See Ashe, *Hard Road to Glory*, 29. Reviewing the incidents attributed to the bouts, Ashe noted that three white customers fractured the skull of William Conway, a black patron, in Flushing, New York, and that in Manhattan a black doorman fought off a pair of white attackers at the St. Urban apartments on Central Park West.

36. Quoted in Aycock and Scott, *Joe Gans*, 162.

37. L. Patterson, "Chapter 2," unpublished memoir, 2, box 19, folder 15, Louise Thompson Patterson Papers.

38. "Oral History—Louise Patterson," 1, box 28, folder 16, Louise Thompson Patterson Papers.

39. L. Patterson, "Chapter 1," unpublished memoir, 15.

40. See Du Bois, *Souls of Black Folk*, 4.

41. L. Patterson, "Chapter 1," unpublished memoir, 12.

42. L. Patterson, "Chapter 1," unpublished memoir, 12–13.

43. L. Patterson, "Chapter 1," unpublished memoir, 13.

44. L. Patterson, "Chapter 1," unpublished memoir, 13.

45. L. Patterson, "Chapter 1," unpublished memoir, 15.

46. I follow a different sequence than Louise does in her memoir. She suggests a series of moves from Goldfield to Oakland and back to Goldfield. She also indicates that her time in Walla Walla came after stints in Utah and Idaho and immediately before living in Oregon. However, she relates specific memories of seeing Booker T. Washington in Walla Walla in the fall of 1909; dreading the appearance of Halley's comet while living in Oakland, which had to be during the spring of 1910; and meeting Jack Johnson en route to Goldfield in June 1910. Because I find the specificity of those memories convincing, I believe that part of the sequence had to be from Goldfield to Walla Walla to Oakland to Goldfield. In any case, portraying a collage of Louise's childhood experiences in the West is more important than establishing a perfectly accurate timeline.

47. L. Patterson, "Chapter 1," unpublished memoir, 21.

48. L. Patterson, "Chapter 1," unpublished memoir, 20.

49. L. Patterson, "Chapter 1," unpublished memoir, 21.

50. L. Patterson, untitled segment of unpublished memoir, 9, box 19, folder 15, Louise Thompson Patterson Papers.

51. L. Patterson, "Chapter 1," unpublished memoir, 27.

52. L. Patterson, interview by Margaret Wilkerson, February 21, 1986, transcript, 19–20, box 27, folder 5, Louise Thompson Patterson Papers.

53. L. Patterson, interview by Margaret Wilkerson, February 21, 1986, transcript, 17.

54. Louise speaks of claiming 160 acres. "Chapter 1," unpublished memoir, 33. That would have been the case under the original Homestead Act of 1862. In 1909 applicants became eligible for up to 320 acres under the Enlarged Homestead Act. Because Louise is speaking of interactions within her family that transpired after 1909, I have opted for the larger number.

55. L. Patterson, "Chapter 1," unpublished memoir, 32.

56. L. Patterson, "Chapter 1," unpublished memoir, 32.

57. L. Patterson, "Chapter 1," unpublished memoir, 33.

58. After Johnson won the title from Tommy Burns, a Canadian, in 1908, some whites sought to reclaim a key symbol of racial superiority by identifying promising challengers, popularly dubbed "white hopes," who might capture the crown. Jeffries, a former heavyweight champion who had retired undefeated, became the most celebrated of the bunch. On the aftermath of Johnson's win, see Geoffrey C. Ward's *Unforgivable Blackness*, 216–19. Ward wrote, "No event since emancipation forty-five years earlier seemed to mean so much to Negro America as Johnson's victory. And no event yielded such widespread racial violence until the assassination of Dr. Martin Luther King, Jr., fifty-eight years later" (217).

59. L. Patterson and Beah Richards, April 2, 1989, audio, box AV, Louise Thompson Patterson Papers.

60. Norman Taurog, dir., *Mrs. Wiggs of the Cabbage Patch*, 1934.

61. L. Patterson, "Chapter 1," unpublished memoir, 25. Mrs. Wiggs's actual phrase is, "All I got to do is to put a little more water in the soup." See Hegan, *Mrs. Wiggs*, 9.

62. L. Patterson, "Chapter 1," unpublished memoir, 19.

63. L. Patterson, "Chapter 1," unpublished memoir, 19.

64. L. Patterson, "Chapter 1," unpublished memoir, 23.

65. L. Patterson, "Chapter 1," unpublished memoir, 22.

66. L. Patterson, "Chapter 1," unpublished memoir, 22.

67. L. Patterson, "Chapter 1," unpublished memoir, 22–23.

68. L. Patterson, "Chapter 1," unpublished memoir, 23.

69. L. Patterson, "Chapter 1," unpublished memoir, 29.

70. Massachusetts native J. C. Tolman founded Marshfield in 1853, naming it after his hometown, which was also located along a bay and was named for the surrounding salt marshes. In 1944 the citizens of Marshfield, Oregon, unwilling to continue being associated with the Massachusetts city, voted to change the name to Coos Bay.

71. L. Patterson, "Chapter 1," unpublished memoir, 30.

72. L. Patterson, "Harlem in the 1920s," unpublished memoir, 1, box 19, folder 20, Louise Thompson Patterson Papers.

73. L. Patterson, interview by Chuck Fields, April 2, 1989, audio, box AV, Louise Thompson Patterson Papers.

74. L. Patterson, "Chapter 1," unpublished memoir, 25.

75. L. Patterson, "Chapter 1," unpublished memoir, 34.

76. L. Patterson, "Chapter 1," unpublished memoir, 28.

77. L. Patterson, "Chapter 1," unpublished memoir, 28.

78. L. Patterson, "Chapter 1," unpublished memoir, 28.

79. L. Patterson, "Chapter 2," unpublished memoir, 1.

Chapter 2: California Community, 1917–1925

1. Located at 4322 Fourth Avenue, Dunlap's Dining Room operated from 1930 to 1968. The building is listed on the National Register of Historic Places.

2. L. Patterson, "Chapter 1," unpublished memoir, 33, box 19, folder 15, Louise Thompson Patterson Papers.

3. Lulu Thompson to Margaret Burdine, June 27, 1917, box 23, folder 3, Louise Thompson Patterson Papers.

4. For discussion of the family downfall, see H. Cayton Jr., *Long Old Road*, 22–25; and Hobbs, *Cayton Legacy*, 47–52.

5. Louise Thompson to Delores Burdine, March 18, 1917, box 4, folder 1, Louise Thompson Patterson Papers.

6. Louise Thompson to Delores Burdine, March 18, 1917.

7. L. Patterson, interview by Linda Burnham, December 10, 1994, audio, box AV3, Louise Thompson Patterson Papers.

8. For population data, see Bagwell, *Oakland*, 84–85.

9. "The Great Pandemic: The United States in 1918–1919: California," U.S. Department of Health and Human Services website. Posted on September 4, 2008, to the University of North Texas Web Archive. https://webarchive.library.unt.edu/eot2008 /20090116052333/http://1918.pandemicflu.gov/.

10. L. Patterson, interview by Evelyn Louise Crawford, May 13, 1989, transcript, 7, box 28, folder 3, Louise Thompson Patterson Papers.

11. L. Patterson, interview by Evelyn Louise Crawford, May 13, 1989, transcript, 36.

12. L. Patterson, interview by Evelyn Louise Crawford, May 13, 1989, transcript, 38.

13. L. Patterson, interview by Evelyn Louise Crawford, May 13, 1989, transcript, 39.

14. L. Patterson, interview by Evelyn Louise Crawford, May 13, 1989, transcript, 39.

15. L. Patterson, interview by Evelyn Louise Crawford, May 13, 1989, transcript, 37.

16. L. Patterson, interview by Evelyn Louise Crawford, May 13, 1989, transcript, 13.

17. L. Patterson, interview by Evelyn Louise Crawford, May 13, 1989, transcript, 13.

18. For background on real estate practices in Berkeley, see Wollenberg, *Berkeley*, 82–83.

19. First envisioned by Wilhelm von Humboldt during the early nineteenth century, the German model broke from the traditional university focus on student mastery of canonical knowledge to incorporate discovery as a primary educational value. An extensive network of seminars and laboratories was central to the conception.

20. Wollenberg, *Berkeley*, 58–63.

21. See Ida Louise Jackson, "Ida Louise Jackson," 253–54.

22. *California Pelican*, September 1919.

23. *California Pelican*, January 1921, 17.

24. *California Pelican*, November 1919, 14.k

25. *California Pelican*, December 1919, 15.

26. *California Pelican*, December 1920, 21.

27. *California Pelican*, February 1921, 19.

28. *California Pelican*, December 1922, 29.

29. *California Pelican*, September 1920, 35.

30. See Anderson, *This Was Harlem*, 117–20.

31. L. Patterson, interview by Evelyn Louise Crawford, May 13, 1989, transcript, 31.

32. L. Patterson, interview by Evelyn Louise Crawford, May 13, 1989, transcript, 49.

33. L. Patterson, interview by Evelyn Louise Crawford, May 13, 1989, transcript, 29.

34. L. Patterson, interview by Evelyn Louise Crawford, May 13, 1989, transcript, 23–24.

35. L. Patterson, interview by Evelyn Louise Crawford, May 13, 1989, transcript, 25.

36. L. Patterson, interview by Evelyn Louise Crawford, May 13, 1989, transcript, 23–26.

37. L. Patterson, interview by Evelyn Louise Crawford, May 13, 1989, transcript, 23, 27.

38. Tarea Hall Pittman, interview by Joyce Henderson, June 10, 1971, transcript, the Earl Warren Oral History Project, subseries Northern California Negro Political Leaders, the Bancroft Library, University of California at Berkeley.

39. Pittman, interview by Joyce Henderson, June 10, 1971.

40. According to Ida Louise Jackson, seventeen African Americans, eight female and nine male, attended Cal in 1920. See "Ida Louise Jackson," 254. In the introduction to *Head of the Class*, Gabrielle Morris indicates that eight thousand to nine thousand undergraduates attended the University of California each year during the 1920s (xvii).

41. In Morris's *Head of the Class*, Tarea Hall Pittman related that the Deltas encountered resistance from an intrafraternal council, which did not want them represented in the council. Council members argued that the Deltas did not belong because they had no sorority house. Dean Stebbins interceded and ruled that as long as the Deltas maintained the proper grade point averages they would be allowed on the council (33–34).

42. Ida Louise Jackson, president of the campus chapter of Alpha Kappa Alpha, recalled, "Rho chapter decided to take a page in the *Blue and Gold*, at forty-five dollars per page. We paid the required fee, went on the date assigned to us to the photographer and posed as directed for our picture. The eagerly awaited date when the B&G was off the press arrived; we could hardly wait to see a copy. *But our picture was not included!* Our disappointment knew no bounds. We were never able to see the editor or anyone else in charge. We went to the dean of women's office. She tried to explain in words that would comfort us, but she was unable to offer any acceptable answer. This was a bruise that did not quickly heal." In "Ida Louise Jackson," 255. Certainly, Deltas fared or would have fared no better gaining inclusion in *Blue and Gold*.

43. See Roberta J. Park, "Ida Louise Jackson, Class of '22," *Chronicle of the University of California*, fall 1998, 95–97. Also, in "Ida Louise Jackson," Jackson related that both sororities grew from the Braithwaite Club, formed in 1920, an attempt by African

American female students to construct a viable social life on campus. Louise was likely a member of that club (254).

44. See "U.C. Talk on Negro Economic Condition," *Berkeley Daily Gazette*, March 10, 1923; "Today in Brief," *Daily Californian*, March 12, 1923.

45. See Du Bois, "Economic Future" and "Economics of Negro Emancipation."

46. Massiah, *Louise Thompson Patterson*.

47. See "Upperclasswomen to Hold Dixieland Party," *Daily Californian*, March 6, 1923; "Upper Class and Graduate Women Entertained with Southern Party," *Daily Californian*, March 8, 1923.

48. "Upperclasswomen to Hold Dixieland Party," *Daily Californian*, March 6, 1923; "Upper Class and Graduate Women Entertained with Southern Party," *Daily Californian*, March 8, 1923.

49. Quoted in "Stanford Cancels Boxing Matches with California," *Daily Californian*, March 9, 1923.

50. Quoted in "Stanford Cancels Boxing Matches with California," *Daily Californian*, March 9, 1923.

51. Louise recounted many times her determination to get to New York City. See, for example, L. Patterson, "Chapter 2: Pine Bluff/Hampton," 5, box 19, folder 18, Louise Thompson Patterson Papers. Three years after his speech at Berkeley, Louise asked Du Bois for a job. See Louise Thompson to W. E. B. Du Bois, July 13, 1926, box 6, folder 4, Louise Thompson Patterson Papers.

52. Broussard, *Black San Francisco*, 76.

53. On Du Bois's importance as an education theorist, see Aldridge, *Educational Thought*.

54. See *University of California Bulletin*, 3rd ser., 16, no. 1, p. 88.

55. See University of California, The Sixtieth Commencement, May 1923, pp. 15–19, 81.

56. See *Directory of Graduates of the University of California, 1864–1916*, p. 89 and p. 134.

57. L. Patterson "Chapter 1," unpublished memoir, 28.

58. L. Patterson "Chapter 1," unpublished memoir, 28.

59. Population figure given in L. Patterson, "Pine Bluff/Hampton," unpublished memoir, 1.

60. L. Patterson, "Pine Bluff/Hampton," unpublished memoir, 2.

61. L. Patterson, "Pine Bluff/Hampton," unpublished memoir, 3.

62. L. Patterson, "Pine Bluff/Hampton," unpublished memoir, 3.

63. L. Patterson, "Pine Bluff/Hampton," unpublished memoir, 3–4.

64. L. Patterson, "Pine Bluff/Hampton," unpublished memoir, 3.

65. Originally referring to Esau's sale of his birthright for food, or pottage, in Genesis 25:29–34, *mess of pottage* connotes the bad or shortsighted end of an exchange. The narrator of James Weldon Johnson's *The Autobiography of an Ex-Coloured Man* reflects on the material gains he achieved by passing for white. He concludes ruefully, "My love for my children makes me glad that I am what I am and keeps me from desiring to be otherwise; and yet, when I sometimes open a little box in which I still keep my fast yellowing manuscripts, the only tangible remnants of a vanished dream, a dead

ambition, a sacrificed talent, I cannot repress the thought that, after all, I have chosen the lesser part, that I have sold my birthright for a mess of pottage" (142).

66. L. Patterson, "Harlem in the 1920s," unpublished memoir, 1, box 19, folder 20, Louise Thompson Patterson Papers.

Chapter 3: Shades of Control, 1925–1928

1. Population figures from C. Reed, *Chicago NAACP*, 9.

2. For use of the term *black metropolis*, see Spear, *Black Chicago*, 91. *Black metropolis* is used throughout Christopher Robert Reed's *The Chicago NAACP and the Rise of Black Professional Leadership*.

3. On the riot and bombings in Chicago, see Spear, *Black Chicago*, vii, 219–21.

4. See C. Reed, *Chicago's Black Metropolis*, 2, 24, 76.

5. Quoted in C. Reed, *Chicago NAACP*, 19.

6. L. Patterson, interview by Louis Massiah, June 13, 1992, transcript, 7, box 6, folder 6, Louise Thompson Patterson Papers.

7. L. Patterson, "Pine Bluff/Hampton," unpublished memoir, 6, box 19, folder 18, Louise Thompson Patterson Papers.

8. Louise Thompson to W. E. B. Du Bois, July 13, 1926, box 6, folder 4, Louise Thompson Patterson Papers.

9. Louise Thompson to W. E. B. Du Bois, September 22, 1926, box 6, folder 4, Louise Thompson Patterson Papers.

10. See "University of Arkansas at Pine Bluff," en.wikipedia.org. Accessed February 23, 2017.

11. Enrollment figures taken from Faison, "University of Arkansas at Pine Bluff (UAPB)."

12. L. Patterson, "Pine Bluff/Hampton," unpublished memoir, 12.

13. Massiah, *Louise Thompson Patterson*; L. Patterson, "Pine Bluff/Hampton," unpublished memoir, 19.

14. L. Patterson, "Pine Bluff/Hampton," unpublished memoir, 15.

15. L. Patterson, "Pine Bluff/Hampton," unpublished memoir, 16.

16. L. Patterson, "Pine Bluff/Hampton," unpublished memoir, 17.

17. L. Patterson, "Pine Bluff/Hampton," unpublished memoir, 17.

18. L. Patterson, "Pine Bluff/Hampton," unpublished memoir, 16.

19. L. Patterson, "Pine Bluff/Hampton," unpublished memoir, 19.

20. See Leinwand, *1927*, 159

21. Leinwand, *1927*, 160.

22. L. Patterson, "Pine Bluff/Hampton," unpublished memoir, 21.

23. L. Patterson, "Pine Bluff/Hampton," unpublished memoir, 21.

24. L. Patterson, "Pine Bluff/Hampton," unpublished memoir, 22.

25. L. Patterson, "Pine Bluff/Hampton," unpublished memoir, 22.

26. L. Patterson, "Pine Bluff/Hampton," unpublished memoir, 23.

27. See Brian Greer, "Little Rock's Last Lynching Was in 1927, but the Terrible Memories Linger," *Arkansas Times*, August 4, 2000.

28. Greer, "Little Rock's Last Lynching Was in 1927," *Arkansas Times*, August 4, 2000.

29. L. Patterson, "Pine Bluff/Hampton," unpublished memoir, 21.

30. Greer, "Little Rock's Last Lynching Was in 1927," *Arkansas Times*, August 4, 2000.

31. Greer, "Little Rock's Last Lynching Was in 1927," *Arkansas Times*, August 4, 2000.

32. L. Patterson, "Pine Bluff/Hampton," unpublished memoir, 19–20.

33. L. Patterson, "Pine Bluff/Hampton," unpublished memoir, 24.

34. L. Patterson, "Pine Bluff/Hampton," unpublished memoir, 25.

35. L. Patterson, "Harlem in the 1920s," unpublished memoir, 2, box 19, folder 20, Louise Thompson Patterson Papers.

36. See "20th Century Limited," en.wikipedia.org. Accessed February 23, 2017.

37. Phrase used in Anderson, *This Was Harlem*, 190.

38. For overview of black migration to Harlem, see Anderson, *This Was Harlem*, 3–12, 42–50.

39. Sacco and Vanzetti were anarchists who had been convicted on July 14, 1921, of murdering two men during an armed robbery on April 15, 1920. The trial was widely considered to be unfair. Massachusetts governor Michael Dukakis issued a proclamation to that effect in 1977.

40. Sinclair, *Boston*, 683–84.

41. W. Patterson, *Man Who Cried Genocide*, 93–94.

42. See Van Vechten, *Splendid Drunken Twenties*, 85, 90.

43. L. Patterson, "Pine Bluff/Hampton," unpublished memoir, 32.

44. See E. Graham, "Hampton Institute Strike," 672.

45. L. Patterson, "Pine Bluff/Hampton," unpublished memoir, 35.

46. Walter Scott Copeland, "Integrity of the Anglo-Saxon Race," *Newport News Daily Press*, March 15, 1925, 4.

47. See J. Smith, *Managing White Supremacy*, 117.

48. J. Smith, *Managing White Supremacy*, 117, 123.

49. Founded in Chicago in 1919, the National Association of Negro Musicians, Inc., is the oldest organization in the United States dedicated to the preservation, encouragement, and advocacy of all genres of African American music.

50. Guggisberg established the school in 1924 in what is now Accra, Ghana. In her memoir ("Pine Bluff/Hampton," unpublished memoir, 38), Louise recalled incorrectly that the visitor was South African statesman Jan Smuts, but Smuts was not in the United States in 1927. Louise attended a talk Smuts gave in New York City in 1930, which perhaps accounts for her confusion. At any rate, Guggisberg coauthored a book, *The Future of the Negro*, in which he reflected on his 1927 tour.

51. In his memoir, *Rough Steps on My Stairway*, Cecil Lloyd Spellman suggests that the event could be considered as much a lockout as a strike (100, 105).

52. Quoted in Spellman, *Rough Steps*, 100.

53. L. Patterson, "Pine Bluff/Hampton," unpublished memoir, 40.

54. Accounts vary with respect to the actual size of the elected committee. The *Crisis* printed a photo of a twenty-two-member committee on page 15 of its issue dated January 1928. The men depicted were Claud J. Amis, John Casey, Theester Coleman, Robert A. Coles Jr., G. James Fleming, J. T. Henderson, J. Llewelyn Houck, C. Orin Jeffries, Denton Johnson, Roger Laws, E. A. Mebane, Stephen Mims, Alfred V. Moore,

Saul Perdue, Rudolph B. Renfrow, Howard Rollins, Cecil Lloyd Spellman, Cyril W. Stephens, Lee A. Valentine, Fleming R. Waller, William A. Willie, and Evan T. Wood.

55. L. Patterson, "Pine Bluff/Hampton," unpublished memoir, 42.

56. L. Patterson, "Pine Bluff/Hampton," unpublished memoir, 45. The *Crisis* misprinted some of her wording when it published her remarks. The journal printed "too great for good to come out of it" (345). See "The Hampton Strike," December 1927, 345–46.

57. See Du Bois, "Hampton Idea." Du Bois was eventually invited back in 1936.

58. L. Patterson, "Pine Bluff/Hampton," unpublished memoir, 46.

59. L. Patterson, "Pine Bluff/Hampton," unpublished memoir, 41.

60. See Leinwand, *1927*, 234–39.

61. E. Graham, "Hampton Institute Strike," 677.

62. Spellman, *Rough Steps*, 104.

63. Spellman, *Rough Steps*, 105–6.

64. Quoted in Spellman, *Rough Steps*, 110.

65. L. Patterson, "Pine Bluff/Hampton," unpublished memoir, 49.

66. L. Patterson, interview by Evelyn Louise Crawford, June 11, 1989, transcript, 18, box 28, folder 6, Louise Thompson Patterson Papers.

67. For an account of Louise's initial engagement with *Das Kapital*, see Nelson, "Louise Thompson Patterson," 216–19. Nelson is too speculative about Louise's immediate and specific responses to the book, but her general argument about how and why the volume influenced Louise while she taught at Hampton is sound. Moreover, Nelson's primary premise—that Louise had been radicalized in the South and therefore brought a radical perspective concerning ethics to Harlem intellectual circles in 1928—is accurate.

68. See "The Hampton Strike," *Crisis*, December 1927, 345–46.

69. L. Patterson, interview by Evelyn Louise Crawford, June 17, 1989, transcript, 22–25, box 28, folder 7, Louise Thompson Patterson Papers.

70. Quoted in Spivey, *Schooling*, 26.

71. L. Patterson, interview by Evelyn Louise Crawford, June 17, 1989, transcript, 22–25.

72. L. Patterson, "Pine Bluff/Hampton," unpublished memoir, 51.

73. L. Patterson, "Pine Bluff/Hampton," unpublished memoir, 51.

74. See Armfield, *Eugene Kinckle Jones*, 23–35.

75. The New York School of Philanthropy, established in 1904, became the New York School of Social Work in 1917. The New York School of Social Work operated until 1963 and later was incorporated into Columbia University as the Columbia University School of Social Work.

76. L. Patterson, interview by Evelyn Louise Crawford, June 17, 1989, transcript, 24.

77. L. Patterson, interview by Evelyn Louise Crawford, June 17, 1989, transcript, 24.

Chapter 4: Harlem Kaleidoscope, 1928–1932

1. The owner of the tenement, Iolanthe Sydney, provided rent-free rooms to artists, including, on occasion, Wallace Thurman, Bruce Nugent, and Langston Hughes. The coinage *Niggerati Manor* is usually attributed to Zora Neale Hurston.

2. "Call for Talent Issued by Experimental Theatre," *Amsterdam News*, January 30, 1929.

3. In his essay Hughes addressed the problem of the "desire to pour racial individuality into the mold of American standardization, and to be as little Negro and as much American as possible." "Negro Artist," 55. Exhorting artists not to be afraid of racial and vernacular content, he closed,

> Let the blare of Negro jazz bands and the bellowing voice of Bessie Smith singing Blues penetrate the closed ears of the colored near-intellectuals until they listen and perhaps understand. Let Paul Robeson singing "Water Boy," and Rudolph Fisher writing about the streets of Harlem, and Jean Toomer holding the heart of Georgia in his hands, and Aaron Douglas drawing strange black fantasies cause the smug Negro middle class to turn from their white, respectable, ordinary books and papers to catch a glimmer of their own beauty. We younger Negro artists who create now intend to express our individual dark-skinned selves without fear or shame. We know we are beautiful. And ugly too. The tom-tom cries and the tom-tom laughs. If colored people are pleased we are glad. If they are not, their displeasure doesn't matter either. We build our temple for tomorrow, strong as we know how, and we stand on top of the mountain, free within ourselves. (59)

4. L. Patterson, interview by Linda Burnham, May 7, 1987, transcript, 1, box 27, folder 6, Louise Thompson Patterson Papers.

5. See "Society," *Amsterdam News*, April 10, 1929; "Charles S. Johnsons on Way to Nashville," *Amsterdam News*, September 11, 1929; "Other Celebrities Are Listed among Guests of the Afternoon," *Amsterdam News*, April 2, 1930; "Society," *Amsterdam News*, April 9, 1930.

6. West, "Elephant's Dance," 167.

7. L. Patterson, interview by Evelyn Louise Crawford, July 8, 1989, transcript, 6, box 28, folder 8, Louise Thompson Patterson Papers.

8. L. Patterson, interview by Evelyn Louise Crawford, May 13, 1989, transcript, 5, box 28, folder 3, Louise Thompson Patterson Papers.

9. L. Patterson, interview by Evelyn Louise Crawford, July 8, 1989, transcript, 9.

10. Hughes, *Big Sea*, 238.

11. Thurman to Langston Hughes, November 1928, quoted in van Notten, *Wallace Thurman's Harlem Renaissance*, 206.

12. Thurman to Claude McKay, October 4, 1928, quoted in van Notten, *Wallace Thurman's Harlem Renaissance*, 204.

13. L. Patterson, interview by Evelyn Crawford, July 8, 1989, transcript, 10.

14. See van Notten, *Wallace Thurman's Harlem Renaissance*, 207–8.

15. Thurman to William Jourdan Rapp, ca. April 1929, in *Collected Writings*, 133–34.

16. Thurman to William Jourdan Rapp, May 7, 1929, in *Collected Writings*, 139.

17. Thurman to William Jourdan Rapp, ca. May 1929, in *Collected Writings*, 141.

18. Thurman to William Jourdan Rapp, ca. June 1929, in *Collected Writings*, 143.

19. L. Patterson, "Harlem in the 1920s," unpublished memoir, 14, box 19, folder 20, Louise Thompson Patterson Papers.

20. Thurman to William Jourdan Rapp, ca. July 1929, in *Collected Writings*, 149–50.

21. Thurman, *Infants of the Spring*, 71.

22. Thurman, *Infants of the Spring*, 131.

23. Thurman, *Infants of the Spring*, 274–75.

24. Thurman to William Jourdan Rapp, ca. August 1929, in *Collected Writings*, 159–60.

25. Thurman to William Jourdan Rapp, ca. August 1929, in *Collected Writings*, 159–60.

26. L. Patterson, interview by Evelyn Louise Crawford, July 8, 1989, transcript, 17.

27. L. Patterson, interview by Evelyn Louise Crawford, July 8, 1989, transcript, 14.

28. L. Patterson, interview by Evelyn Louise Crawford, July 29, 1989, transcript, 14, box 28, folder 10, Louise Thompson Patterson Papers.

29. Hughes's biographer, Arnold Rampersad, who interviewed Louise, makes it clear, as did Louise, that no romantic relationship took place between her and Hughes. *Life of Langston Hughes*, 1:196. He also remarks on Hughes's general aversion to intimacy (268–69).

30. Alvin J. Moses, "18,000 See Lincoln Lions Win over Hampton," *Inter-State Tattler*, November 8, 1929.

31. L. Patterson, interview by Evelyn Louise Crawford, July 15, 1989, transcript, 26, box 28, folder 9, Louise Thompson Patterson Papers.

32. See Rampersad, *Life of Langston Hughes*, 1:174.

33. L. Patterson, interview by Evelyn Louise Crawford, July 15, 1989, transcript, 26–28.

34. L. Patterson, interview by Evelyn Louise Crawford, July 29, 1989, transcript, 16–17.

35. L. Patterson, interview by Linda Burnham, May 7, 1987, transcript, 11.

36. See Hubert C. Herring, "Union Seminary Routs Its Reds," *Christian Seminary*, June 13, 1934, 799–801.

37. L. Patterson, interview by Linda Burnham, May 7, 1987, transcript, 10.

38. L. Patterson, interview by Linda Burnham, May 7, 1987, transcript, 11.

39. See "To Air Labor Problems of Negro at Brookwood," *Amsterdam News*, December 24, 1930; and "Labor College Host to Interracial Meeting," *Amsterdam News*, December 31, 1930.

40. Quoted in Rampersad, *Life of Langston Hughes*, 1:196.

41. For commentary on the origin and growth of the Communist Party in Harlem, see Naison, *Communists in Harlem*, 3–56.

42. L. Patterson, interview by Evelyn Louise Crawford, July 29, 1989, transcript, 26.

43. See W. Patterson, *Man Who Cried Genocide*, 109.

44. W. Patterson, *Man Who Cried Genocide*, 139.

45. See "Radicals Promote First Annual Dance," *Amsterdam News*, December 23, 1931.

46. See "Plans Laid for Harlem's Friends of Soviet Union," *Amsterdam News*, December 23, 1931.

47. See "Films on Soviet Union Viewed by Harlemites," *Amsterdam News*, February 17, 1932.

48. Quoted in E. Brown, *Mayakovsky*, 275.

49. It has commonly been reported that Mayakovsky shot himself. But his daughter, Yelena Vladimirovna Mayakovskaya, known more popularly by her adoptive name, Patricia Thompson, has disputed that claim.

50. L. Patterson, interview by Margaret Wilkerson, January 21, 1986, transcript, 41, box 27, folder 4, Louise Thompson Patterson Papers.

51. See "Speaker Urges Negro Join Militant Unions," *Amsterdam News*, March 30, 1932.

52. Louise Thompson to Langston Hughes, April 24, 1932, box 12, folder 7, Louise Thompson Patterson Papers.

53. Louise Thompson to Langston Hughes, May 16, 1932, box 12, folder 7, Louise Thompson Patterson Papers.

54. Louise Thompson to Langston Hughes, May 16, 1932.

55. Louise Thompson to Langston Hughes, May 16, 1932.

56. Louise Thompson to Langston Hughes, May 16, 1932.

57. L. Patterson, interview by Evelyn Louise Crawford, July 15, 1989, transcript, 13.

58. Langston Hughes to Louise Thompson, June 6, 1932, quoted in Rampersad, *Life of Langston Hughes*, 1:241.

59. Alain Locke to Charlotte Osgood Mason, June 1, 1932; June 5, 1932; and June 9, 1932, all in box 9, folder 10, Louise Thompson Patterson Papers.

60. Alain Locke to Charlotte Osgood Mason, June 5, 1932.

61. W. A. Domingo to friends, May 31, 1932, box 12, folder 3, Louise Thompson Patterson Papers.

Chapter 5: Madam Moscow, 1932

1. L. Patterson, "Trip to Russia," unpublished memoir, 10, box 20, folder 2, Louise Thompson Patterson Papers.

2. L. Patterson, "Trip to Russia," unpublished memoir, 11.

3. L. Patterson, "Trip to Russia," unpublished memoir, 13.

4. L. Patterson, "Trip to Russia," unpublished memoir, 12.

5. L. Patterson, "Trip to Russia," unpublished memoir, 12.

6. See Berry, *Langston Hughes*, 155–58.

7. Quoted in Harris and Molesworth, *Alain L. Locke*, 269.

8. See Berry, *Langston Hughes*, 155.

9. Louise Thompson to Mother Thompson [June 1932], box 1, folder 24, Louise Thompson Patterson Papers.

10. L. Patterson, "Trip to Russia," unpublished memoir, 15.

11. Louise Thompson to Mother Thompson [June 1932].

12. H. Smith, *Black Man*, 25.

13. H. Smith, *Black Man*, 25.

14. L. Patterson, "Trip to Russia," unpublished memoir, 20.

15. Carew, *Blacks, Reds*, 125.

16. Quoted in Hassan, *Loren Miller*, 63.

17. H. Smith, *Black Man*, 28.

18. H. Smith, *Black Man*, 28.

19. Hughes, *I Wonder*, 89.

20. Hughes, *I Wonder*, 88. Also see Gilmore, *Defying Dixie*, 143. Gilmore notes that the Russian woman involved, who served as a translator for the *Black and White* group, was banished to Siberia.

21. Louise Thompson to Mother Thompson, August 24, 1932, box 1, folder 24, Louise Thompson Patterson Papers.

22. See Hauke, *Ted Poston*, 51.

23. Louise Thompson to Mother Thompson, August 24, 1932.

24. L. Patterson, "Trip to Russia," unpublished memoir, 21.

25. L. Patterson, "Trip to Russia," unpublished memoir, 20.

26. Hughes, *I Wonder*, 77.

27. See Berry, *Langston Hughes*, 167–70; and Gilmore, *Defying Dixie*, 146–47.

28. L. Patterson, "Trip to Russia," unpublished memoir, 22.

29. L. Patterson, "Trip to Russia," unpublished memoir, 22.

30. L. Patterson, "Trip to Russia," unpublished memoir, 23.

31. Quoted in Hughes, *I Wonder*, 95.

32. Louise Thompson to Mother Thompson, August 24, 1932.

33. L. Patterson, "Trip to Russia," unpublished memoir, 28.

34. L. Patterson, "Trip to Russia," unpublished memoir, 29.

35. L. Patterson, "Trip to Russia," unpublished memoir, 29.

36. *New York Amsterdam News*, October 26, 1932.

37. "Langston Hughes Spikes Lies on Negro Film," *Daily Worker*, September 8, 1932.

38. Henry Lee Moon and T. R. Poston, "*Amsterdam News* Reporters Tell Why Soviet Russia Dropped Film: American Prejudice Triumphs over Communism," *Amsterdam News*, October 5, 1932.

39. *New York Times*, October 5, 1932.

40. "Make New Plans for Soviet Film," *Amsterdam News*, October 19, 1932.

41. "Returns Scoring Soviet Attitude," *Amsterdam News*, October 5, 1932.

42. W. A. Domingo to Louise Thompson, October 6, 1932, box 1, folder 22, Louise Thompson Patterson Papers.

43. "Players Denounce Attack on Soviet," *Amsterdam News*, October 26, 1932.

44. See Louise Thompson, "The Soviet Film," *Crisis*, February 1933, 37.

45. Louise Thompson to Mother Thompson, September 4, 1932, box 1, folder 24, Louise Thompson Patterson Papers.

46. For Louise, such discussion would have been framed by party member Harry Haywood's Black Belt thesis, a position that had been adopted by the Comintern. In the mid-1920s, Haywood had studied in Moscow, where he tried to theorize the best way to entwine Marxism-Leninism with African American liberation efforts. He was guided, in part, by V. I. Lenin's "Preliminary Draft Theses on the National and Colonial Questions" and Joseph Stalin's "Marxism and the National Question." In 1927 a colleague known as Nasonov suggested to Haywood that African Americans constituted an oppressed nation whose struggle would become autonomous and result in an agrarian and democratic revolution in the South. Haywood sought to rescue progressive black nationalism from being diverted into Garvey-like separatism. See Haywood, *Black Bolshevik*, 218–44.

47. L. Patterson, interview by MaryLouise Patterson, October 1993, audio, box AV3, Louise Thompson Patterson Papers.

48. L. Patterson, interview by MaryLouise Patterson, October 1993.

49. Hassan, *Loren Miller,* 57, 73.

50. L. Patterson, "Trip to Russia," unpublished memoir, 40.

51. L. Patterson, "Trip to Russia," unpublished memoir, 38.

52. L. Patterson, "Trip to Russia," unpublished memoir, 38.

53. L. Patterson, "Trip to Russia," unpublished memoir, 40.

54. L. Patterson, "Trip to Russia," unpublished memoir, 41.

55. L. Patterson, "Trip to Russia," unpublished memoir, 41.

56. L. Patterson, "Trip to Russia," unpublished memoir, 41.

57. "To the Workers and Peasants of Uzbekistan Soviet Socialist Republic," October 5, 1932, box 1, folder 22, Louise Thompson Patterson Papers.

58. Louise Thompson to Mother Thompson, October 7, 1932, box 1, folder 24, Louise Thompson Patterson Papers.

59. I am, of course, referring to Reed's journalistic account, in *Ten Days That Shook the World,* of the Bolshevik victory over the Kerensky government.

60. L. Patterson, "Trip to Russia," unpublished memoir, 43.

61. L. Patterson, "Trip to Russia," unpublished memoir, 44.

62. Louise Thompson to Mother Thompson, October 18, 1932, box 1, folder 24, Louise Thompson Patterson Papers.

63. For Poston's designation, see Hauke, *Ted Poston,* 141–85. For Patterson's comment about Poston being her enemy, see L. Patterson, "Trip to Russia," unpublished memoir, 47.

64. L. Patterson, "Trip to Russia," unpublished memoir, 47.

Chapter 6: The Struggle Has Nine Lives, 1932–1934

1. Louise Thompson to Langston Hughes, February 26, 1933, in Crawford and Patterson, *Letters from Langston,* 107.

2. "Prefers Russia Now to Living in America," *Amsterdam News,* November 23, 1932.

3. The *Amsterdam News* announced that she would appear at Savage's on December 11. "Many Hear Lecture at Augusta Savage's," December 7, 1932. And it announced her lecture to the Harlem Interracial Forum on January 21. See "The Harlem Sketch Book," *Amsterdam News,* January 11, 1933.

4. L. Patterson, interview by Carol Yates, May 19, 1998, audio, box AV3, Louise Thompson Patterson Papers.

5. In *The New York Intellectuals,* Alan Wald explained that the National Committee for the Defense of Political Prisoners was one of the "two most important organizations of revolutionary intellectuals that existed during the early 1930s" (54). The other was the League of Professionals. For more extended commentary, see pp. 54–60.

6. "Obtains New Scottsboro Evidence," *Amsterdam News,* February 8, 1933.

7. "Letter Exonerates Scottsboro Boys," *Amsterdam News,* February 15, 1933; "Police Are Blamed by White Girl," *Amsterdam News,* February 15, 1933.

8. For summaries of the initial incident, see Carter, *Scottsboro,* 4–8; Reynolds, *Courtroom,* 254–56.

9. L. Patterson, "Return to America and Scottsboro," unpublished memoir, 17, box 20, folder 4, Louise Thompson Patterson Papers.

10. L. Patterson, "Return to America and Scottsboro," unpublished memoir, 17.

11. "From the Testimony of Ruby Bates in the Trial of Haywood Patterson, April 7, 1933," http://library.thinkquest.org/12111/scottsboro/rubybate.htm. Accessed August 13, 2013.

12. "From the Testimony of Ruby Bates in the Trial of Haywood Patterson, April 7, 1933," http://library.thinkquest.org/12111/scottsboro/rubybate.htm.

13. For this claim, see Solomon, *Cry*, 240.

14. On Leibowitz's mindset, see Solomon, *Cry*, 240–41; and Carter, *Scottsboro*, 181–83. For mention of the Capone defense, see Reynolds, *Courtroom*, 315.

15. See L. Patterson, "Return to America and Scottsboro," unpublished memoir, 13–14; Wald, *New York Intellectuals*, 60.

16. Wald, *New York Intellectuals*, 60.

17. Reynolds, *Courtroom*, 277.

18. Quoted in Reynolds, *Courtroom*, 275.

19. Quoted in Naison, *Communists in Harlem*, 83–85.

20. Carter, *Scottsboro*, 243–49.

21. Louise Thompson, "And So We Marched," *Working Woman*, June 1933, 6.

22. L. Patterson, "Return to America and Scottsboro," unpublished memoir, 7–8.

23. L. Patterson, interview by Evelyn Crawford, August 31, 1989, transcript, 6, box 28, folder 12, Louise Thompson Patterson Papers.

24. "Ruby Bates Tells Scottsboro Story," *Washington Post*, May 7, 1933.

25. Louise Thompson, "And So We Marched," *Working Woman*, June 1933, 6.

26. For discussion of Judge Horton's decision, see Reynolds, *Courtroom*, 277–80.

27. L. Patterson, "Return to America and Scottsboro," unpublished memoir, 9–10.

28. L. Patterson, "Return to America and Scottsboro," unpublished memoir, 9.

29. L. Patterson, "Return to America and Scottsboro," unpublished memoir, 10.

30. L. Patterson, "Return to America and Scottsboro," unpublished memoir, 11.

31. L. Patterson, interview by Ruth Schultz and Bud Schultz, August 12, 1984, transcript, 10, box 27, folder 3, Louise Thompson Patterson Papers.

32. L. Patterson, "The Harlem Riot of 1935," unpublished memoir, 8, box 20, folder 5, Louise Thompson Patterson Papers.

33. L. Patterson, interview by unidentified source, April 20, 1989, transcript, 33, box 28, folder 2, Louise Thompson Patterson Papers.

34. L. Patterson, "The Harlem Riot of 1935," unpublished memoir, 10.

35. L. Patterson, "The Harlem Riot of 1935," unpublished memoir, 9.

36. Du Bois, "Marxism and the Negro Problem," *Crisis*, May 1933, 103–04, 118.

37. L. Patterson, "The Harlem Riot of 1935," unpublished memoir, 9.

38. L. Patterson, "The Harlem Riot of 1935," unpublished memoir, 12. Also, see McGlamery, "Race Based Underwriting," 533–34, for an explanation of debt routes: "An agent of the insurance company would travel door-to-door along a weekly or monthly route, sometimes called a 'debt,' to collect premiums from the policyholders. The logic behind the product was that the working poor that needed inexpensive insurance would not budget effectively enough to pay on a quarterly basis, or afford the

minimum level of benefits that ordinary life insurance demands. Personal collection was used because mailing was not cost effective and, theoretically, the policyholder did not have the time or motivation to deliver their payments themselves."

39. For discussion of the links between industrial insurance and racial discrimination, see McGlamery, "Race Based Underwriting," 531–70.

40. Louise Thompson, "The Role of Proletarian Fraternalism in the Liberation Struggle of the Negro People," *Negro Liberator*, July 28, 1934.

41. She made this assessment in L. Patterson, "Return to America and Scottsboro," unpublished memoir, 18.

42. Robin Kelley indicated that there were about fifteen hundred Communist and Communist-affiliated activists in the Birmingham area during 1934. *Hammer and Hoe*, 33.

43. Kelley, *Hammer and Hoe*, 70.

44. Kelley, *Hammer and Hoe*, 67.

45. L. Patterson, "Return to America and Scottsboro," unpublished memoir, 20.

46. Louise Thompson, "Southern Terror," *Crisis*, November 1934, 327.

47. ILD press release, May 19, 1934, box 1, folder 19, Louise Thompson Patterson Papers.

48. Louise Thompson, "Southern Terror," *Crisis*, November 1934, 327.

49. L. Patterson, "Return to America and Scottsboro," unpublished memoir, 21.

50. L. Patterson, "Return to America and Scottsboro," unpublished memoir, 22.

51. Louise Thompson, "Southern Terror," *Crisis*, November 1934, 327.

52. Louise Thompson, "Southern Terror," *Crisis*, November 1934, 327.

53. "Upbraids Judge," *Amsterdam News*, May 19, 1934.

54. Louise Thompson, "Southern Terror," *Crisis*, November 1934, 328.

55. Patterson, "Return to America and Scottsboro," unpublished memoir, 22.

56. Louise Thompson to C. B. Powell, May 21, 1934, box 8, folder 8, Louise Thompson Patterson Papers.

57. "Birmingham Police Arrest Louise Thompson," *Negro Liberator*, May 18, 1934; Thompson to Sadie Doroshkin, May 21, 1934, box 8, folder 8, Louise Thompson Patterson Papers.

58. Louise Thompson to Sadie Doroshkin, May 21, 1934.

59. Louise Thompson to Joseph Brodsky, May 21, 1934, box 8, folder 8, Louise Thompson Patterson Papers.

60. Louise Thompson to Joseph Brodsky, May 21, 1934.

61. Louise Thompson to Joseph Brodsky, May 21, 1934.

62. C. B. Powell to Louise Thompson, May 28, 1934, box 8, folder 8, Louise Thompson Patterson Papers.

63. Jeannette Triplett Jones to Louise Thompson, June 1, 1934, box 6, folder 2, Louise Thompson Patterson Papers.

64. L. Patterson, "Southern Terror," *Crisis*, November 1934, 327. Also see Maxwell, *New Negro, Old Left*, 144–51, on "Southern Terror" as a remarkable piece of journalism. Maxwell sees the article as a needed response to masculinist, homosocial Communist

Party rhetoric. Such rhetoric, according to Maxwell, cast interracial proletarian unity as white men's work and elided black female presence.

65. L. Patterson, "Southern Terror," *Crisis*, November 1934, 328.

66. Carter, *Scottsboro*, 182.

67. Solomon, *Cry*, 245.

68. For background on the bribery case and on Leibowitz's political maneuvering, see Solomon, *Cry*, 244–48. Leibowitz's statement threatening to withdraw is included in Reynolds, *Courtroom*, 286–87.

69. Patterson, "Return to America and Scottsboro," unpublished memoir, 15.

70. "I.L.D. Negligence May Doom Patterson, Lawyers Charge," *Amsterdam News*, October 27, 1934.

71. "Coins Fall Slowly at I.L.D. Meeting Here," *Amsterdam News*, November 3, 1934.

72. "Coins Fall Slowly at I.L.D. Meeting Here," *Amsterdam News*, November 3, 1934.

73. "Death Claims Noted Writer," *Amsterdam News*, December 29, 1934.

74. L. Patterson, interview by Evelyn Louise Crawford, July 8, 1989, transcript, 17, box 28, folder 8, Louise Thompson Patterson Papers.

75. See Thurman, *Collected Writings*, 130.

76. L. Patterson, interview by Evelyn Louise Crawford, July 29, 1989, transcript 30, 36, box 28, folder 10, Louise Thompson Patterson Papers.

77. L. Patterson, interview by Evelyn Louise Crawford, July 29, 1989, transcript, 36.

78. L. Patterson, interview by MaryLouise Patterson, October 1993, audio, box AV3, Louise Thompson Patterson Papers.

79. L. Patterson, interview by MaryLouise Patterson, October 1993.

Chapter 7: Popular Fronts, 1935–1937

1. Fogelson and Rubenstein, *Mass Violence in America*, 7.

2. Fogelson and Rubenstein, *Mass Violence in America*, 8.

3. L. Patterson, "The Harlem Riot of 1935," unpublished memoir, 5–6, box 20, folder 5, Louise Thompson Patterson Papers. She recalled, "But nobody believed that I just accidentally happened to be there at the right moment and had nothing to do even with agitating them."

4. Fogelson and Rubenstein, *Mass Violence in America*, 2, 8.

5. L. Patterson, "The Harlem Riot of 1935," unpublished memoir, 2–3.

6. L. Patterson, "The Harlem Riot of 1935," unpublished memoir, 3.

7. L. Patterson, "The Harlem Riot of 1935," unpublished memoir, 6.

8. L. Patterson, "The Harlem Riot of 1935," unpublished memoir, 2–3.

9. *New York American*, March 20, 1935; March 21, 1935; and March 22, 1935.

10. Ford had graduated from Fisk University, Burroughs from Hunter College, and Davis from Amherst College and Harvard University. Louise, of course, had attended the University of California, Berkeley.

11. See Naison, *Communists in Harlem*, 144.

12. L. Patterson, "The Harlem Riot of 1935," unpublished memoir, 5.

13. Quoted in L. Patterson, "The Harlem Riot of 1935," unpublished memoir, 5.

14. L. Patterson, "The Harlem Riot of 1935," unpublished memoir, 5.

15. Fogelson and Rubenstein, *Mass Violence in America*, 14.

16. Fogelson and Rubenstein, *Mass Violence in America*, 10.

17. Quoted in Fogelson and Rubenstein, *Mass Violence in America*, 12.

18. Quoted in Fogelson and Rubenstein, *Mass Violence in America*, 11.

19. Quoted in Fogelson and Rubenstein, *Mass Violence in America*, 18.

20. Naison, *Communists in Harlem*, 178.

21. *Official Proceedings of the National Negro Congress 1936*, 41. The National Negro Congress claimed that 585 organizations participated: 81 churches and religious organizations, 71 fraternal societies, 83 trade unions, 2 farm organizations, 26 youth organizations, 226 civic groups and societies, 46 political groups and parties, 23 women's organizations, 14 educational organizations, 6 professional groups, 2 business organizations, and 5 newspaper groups.

22. Haywood, *Black Bolshevik*, 461–62.

23. Quoted in *Official Proceedings of the National Negro Congress 1936*, 3.

24. *Official Proceedings of the National Negro Congress 1936*, 22.

25. *Official Proceedings of the National Negro Congress 1936*, 22–23.

26. Louise Thompson, "Toward a Brighter Dawn," *Woman Today*, April 1936, 30.

27. Louise Thompson, "Toward a Brighter Dawn," 14.

28. Louise Thompson, "Toward a Brighter Dawn," 14.

29. Ella Baker and Marvel Cooke, "The Bronx Slave Market," *The Crisis*, November 1935, 330–31, 340.

30. Louise Thompson, "Toward a Brighter Dawn," 14, 30.

31. "Louise Thompson Is Made IWO Executive," *Amsterdam News*, February 29, 1936.

32. "Leaders to Discuss Minimum Wage Law," *Amsterdam News*, April 25, 1936; "Stage, Screen, Nite Spots," *Amsterdam News*, April 18, 1936.

33. Arnold Rampersad and Lawrence Jackson discuss the influence of Hughes and Louise on Ellison. See Rampersad, *Ralph Ellison*, 90–93; and Jackson, *Ralph Ellison*, 163–75.

34. For commentary on the climax and resolution of the Scottsboro case, see Reynolds, *Courtroom*, 301–14; and Carter, *Scottsboro*, 369–98.

35. Haywood, *Black Bolshevik*, 467.

36. Quoted in Donlon, "Introduction," 2–3.

37. "Many Join in Parade vs. War and Fascism," *Amsterdam News*, August 29, 1936.

38. Beevor, *Battle for Spain*, 232. Germany and Italy bombed Guernica on April 26, 1937.

39. Berry, *Langston Hughes*, 255.

40. Rampersad, *Ralph Ellison*, 94.

41. H. Graham, *Spanish Civil War*, 87–91; G. Jackson, *Spanish Civil War*, 58–63.

42. Rolfe, *Lincoln Battalion*, 5–9; Haywood, *Black Bolshevik*, 473.

43. L. Patterson, untitled memoir segment, 6, box 20, folder 5, Louise Thompson Patterson Papers.

44. L. Patterson, untitled memoir segment, 6.

45. L. Patterson, untitled memoir segment, 8.

46. L. Patterson, "The Paris Conference and the Harlem Suitcase Theatre," unpublished memoir, 2, box 20, folder 6, Louise Thompson Patterson Papers.

47. Carr, *Spanish Civil War*, 83

48. Carr, *Spanish Civil War*, 95. The poster reads in English, "All the peoples of the world are in the International Brigades on the side of the Spanish people."

49. See Branch, *At Canaan's Edge*, 768.

50. For commentary on the Battle of Jarama, see H. Graham, *Spanish Civil War*, 161.

51. Haywood, *Black Bolshevik*, 479–93.

52. The *Afro-American* published a picture of Louise together with those three, captioned "Time Out behind Spanish Lines." The accompanying article is by Hughes: "Organ Grinder's Swing Heard above Gunfire in Spain," *Afro-American*, November 6, 1937. See also G. Jackson, *Spanish Civil War*, 132.

53. L. Patterson, "The Paris Conference and the Harlem Suitcase Theatre," unpublished memoir, 3.

54. "Walter Garland, Radio Broadcast, Station E.A.R.—Madrid [1937]," box 10, folder 11, Louise Thompson Patterson Papers.

55. H. Graham, *Spanish Civil War*, 45.

56. "Harry Haywood, Radio Speech, Station E.A.R.—Madrid [1937]," box 10, folder 11, Louise Thompson Patterson Papers.

57. "Louise Thompson, Radio Speech, Station E.A.R.—Madrid [1937]," box 13, folder 9, Louise Thompson Patterson Papers.

58. L. Patterson, "The Paris Conference and the Harlem Suitcase Theatre," unpublished memoir, 3. See Beevor, *Battle for Spain*, 171.

59. L. Patterson, "The Paris Conference and the Harlem Suitcase Theatre," unpublished memoir, 3.

60. Carr, *Spanish Civil War*, 134–35.

61. L. Patterson, "The Paris Conference and the Harlem Suitcase Theatre," unpublished memoir, 2–3.

62. Quoted in Richard Wright, "American Negroes in Key Posts of Spain's Loyalist Forces," *Daily Worker*, September 20, 1937.

63. Quoted in L. Patterson, untitled memoir segment, 10, box 20, folder 6, Louise Thompson Patterson Papers.

64. L. Patterson, interview by Linda Burnham, March 2, 1988, transcript, 36, box 27, folder 11, Louise Thompson Patterson Papers.

65. H. Graham, *Spanish Civil War*, 120.

66. See Paul Hofmann, "Dolores Ibarruri, 'La Pasionaria' of Spanish Civil War, Dies at 93; An Indomitable Leftist," *New York Times*, November 13, 1989.

67. Haywood, *Black Bolshevik*, 469.

68. L. Patterson, "The Paris Conference and the Harlem Suitcase Theatre," unpublished memoir, 4.

69. L. Patterson, "The Paris Conference and the Harlem Suitcase Theatre," unpublished memoir, 7.

70. "Manifesto of the Second World Congress against Racism and Anti-Semitism [1937]," box 10, folder 10, Louise Thompson Patterson Papers.

71. "Report of the Committee for Action and for Propaganda" and "Legislation Committee [ca. 1937]," both in box 10, folder 10, Louise Thompson Patterson Papers.

72. L. Patterson, untitled memoir segment, 1–3, box 10, folder 5, Louise Thompson Patterson Papers.

73. Gregg Andrews, *Thyra J. Edwards*, 100.

Chapter 8: Ba Ba Ba Bop, 1937–1940

1. "Speech at Hotel Commodore, October 6, 1937," box 20, folder 17, Louise Thompson Patterson Papers.

2. "150 Nurses Attend Banquet Honoring Salaria Kee Here," *Amsterdam News*, May 28, 1938.

3. The *Amsterdam News* announced that Edwards was staying with Louise until November 14. See "Details Explain Herndon Death," *Amsterdam News*, November 13, 1937.

4. Gregg Andrews, *Thyra J. Edwards*, 105–8.

5. Gregg Andrews, *Thyra J. Edwards*, 105–8.

6. Louise Thompson to Hughes, November 13, 1937, in Crawford and Patterson, *Letters from Langston*, 136. *Bombas* and *obuses* are the Spanish words for "bombs" and "cannon shells."

7. Quoted in Donlon, "Langston Hughes and Louise Thompson," 30.

8. Hughes, *New Song*, 24–25.

9. Hughes, *New Song*, 3.

10. Quoted in Donlon, "Langston Hughes and Louise Thompson," 36.

11. Fifty-four nations signed the pact after Germany, France, and the United States signed in August 1928. The Nine-Power Treaty of 1922 was signed by China, Japan, the United States, Great Britain, Italy, France, Belgium, Portugal, and the Netherlands.

12. Although he did not name the countries, Roosevelt strongly implied that Germany, Italy, and Japan had violated the Kellogg-Briand Pact and the Nine-Power Treaty, as well as the Covenant of the League of Nations. He suggested that those countries had to be "quarantined" as some patients are during outbreaks of disease to protect the broader community.

13. Randolph, "Crisis of the Negro," n.p.

14. S. Brown, "Negro Writer," n.p.

15. Locke, "Resume of Talk and Discussion," n.p.

16. C. Brown, "What Negro Youth," n.p.

17. According to Louise in "Toward a Brighter Dawn," a third of the delegates at the convention in 1936 were women. Thompson, "Toward a Brighter Dawn," *Woman Today*, April 1936, 14. Of the 1,149 delegates in 1937, 444, or 39 percent, were women.

18. "Ask Goldwater to Give Job to Alma Vessells," *Amsterdam News*, September 24, 1938.

19. "Louise Thompson Patterson" interview [ca. 1955], transcript, 19, box 27, folder 1, Louise Thompson Patterson Papers.

20. "Louise Thompson Patterson," interview, transcript, 25.

21. See Mishler, *Raising Reds*, 4–12, 64.

22. "Louise Thompson Patterson," interview, transcript, 34.

23. L. Patterson, "The Harlem Riot of 1935," unpublished memoir, 23, box 20, folder 5, Louise Thompson Patterson Papers.

24. L. Patterson, "The Harlem Riot of 1935," unpublished memoir, 24.

25. L. Patterson, "The Harlem Riot of 1935," unpublished memoir, 23.

26. "Louise Thompson Patterson," interview, transcript, 38–39.

27. "Louise Thompson Patterson," interview, transcript, 38.

28. L. Patterson, interview by Ruth Schultz and Bud Schultz, August 12, 1984, transcript, 13, box 27, folder 3, Louise Thompson Patterson Papers.

29. L. Patterson, "The Harlem Riot of 1935," unpublished memoir, 21.

30. The "Little Steel" companies were Republic Steel, Bethlehem Steel, National Steel, Inland Steel, American Rolling Mills, and Youngstown Sheet and Tube.

31. "Louise Thompson Patterson," interview, transcript, 34.

32. L. Patterson, "The Harlem Riot of 1935," unpublished memoir, 27.

33. "Richard Wright Given Literary Post for Work," *Amsterdam News*, June 25, 1938.

34. L. Patterson, "The Harlem Riot of 1935," unpublished memoir, 17.

35. "Celebrate the Blues," *Amsterdam News*, November 26, 1938.

36. Arnold Rampersad noted Hughes's intent to collaborate in 1931 with Whittaker Chambers, Paul Peters, and John Burck to establish a suitcase theater inside the John Reed Club. The plan did come to fruition. Rampersad, *Life of Langston Hughes*, 1:356. Both Rampersad and Faith Berry cite the letter that Hughes wrote while traveling from Europe to Noel Sullivan on January 15, 1938, expressing the desire to start a theater. Rampersad, *Life of Langston Hughes*, 1:356; Berry, *Langston Hughes*, 274.

37. L. Patterson, "The Paris Conference and the Harlem Suitcase Theatre," unpublished memoir, 8, box 20, folder 6, Louise Thompson Patterson Papers.

38. The full title of the published work is *Don't You Want to Be Free? A Poetry Play: From Slavery through the Blues to Now—and Then Some!—with Singing, Music, and Dancing.*

39. McLaren, *Langston Hughes*, 121.

40. L. Patterson, "On the Harlem Suitcase Theatre," unpublished fragment, 6A, box 20, folder 7, Louise Thompson Patterson Papers.

41. "Rules and Regulations" [ca. 1938], 2, box 7, folder 4, Louise Thompson Patterson Papers.

42. McLaren, *Langston Hughes*, 118.

43. L. Patterson, "The Paris Conference and the Harlem Suitcase Theatre," unpublished memoir, 14. Executive committee members were Louise, Hughes, Mary Savage, Dorothy Peterson, Robert Earl Jones, Grace Johnson, Hilary Phillips, Ernest Goldstein, and Muriel Unis.

44. L. Patterson, "The Paris Conference and the Harlem Suitcase Theatre," unpublished memoir, 9.

45. For Hughes's explanation, see Marvel Cooke, "Suitcase Theatre Group Is Brilliant in Premiere," *Amsterdam News*, April 30, 1938.

46. L. Patterson, "The Paris Conference and the Harlem Suitcase Theatre," unpublished memoir, 13.

47. L. Patterson, "The Paris Conference and the Harlem Suitcase Theatre," unpublished memoir, 13.

48. Robert Earl Jones played in the production of *Mule Bone* that opened at the Ethel Barrymore Theatre on February 14, 1991.

49. "Rules and Regulations," 2.

50. Cooke, "Suitcase Theatre Group Is Brilliant in Premiere," *Amsterdam News*, April 30, 1938.

51. McLaren, *Langston Hughes*, 128.

52. L. Patterson, "On the Harlem Suitcase Theatre," unpublished memoir, 6A.

53. L. Patterson, "The Paris Conference and the Harlem Suitcase Theatre," unpublished memoir, 16.

54. L. Patterson, "On the Harlem Suitcase Theatre," unpublished memoir, 9A.

55. McLaren, *Langston Hughes*, 119.

56. See Rampersad, *Life of Langston Hughes*, 1:360.

57. Scholars typically state that *Don't You Want to Be Free?* ran for 135 or so performances. See, for example, McLaren, *Langston Hughes*, 120. I opt for the larger number because the play was staged a handful of times at additional sites.

58. Mark Naison describes how black Communists reinvented themselves as radical democrats. *Communists in Harlem*, 178–79.

59. For discussion of the impact of the Nazi-Soviet Pact in African American communities, see Gilmore, *Defying Dixie*, 300–307; and Naison, *Communists in Harlem*, 287–320. Naison lists Louise, James Ford, Ben Davis, Abner Berry, Audley Moore, Bonita Williams, Rose Gaulden, Theodore Bassett, Claudia Jones, Howard Johnson, James Burnham, Emmett May, and Richard Moore as the core of the Communist Party in Harlem (288).

60. See Naison, *Communists in Harlem*, 290.

61. Naison, *Communists in Harlem*, 287.

62. For background on the convention, see Gilmore, *Defying Dixie*, 307–11.

63. Gilmore, *Defying Dixie*, 307–11.

64. Randolph, "Crisis of the Negro," n.p.

65. Bedacht, *Labor Fraternalism*.

66. See *Wikipedia*, s.v. "International Workers Order," en.wikipedia.org. Last updated December 15, 2015; and "International Workers Order (1922–1946)," http://www.marxisthistory.org/subject/eam/iwo.html. Accessed March 2, 2017.

67. See "Swarthmore Peace Collection," https://www.swarthmore.edu/library/peace/CDGA.A-L/ampeoplesmob.htm. Last updated August 21, 2015.

68. W. Patterson, *Man Who Cried Genocide*, 139.

69. W. Patterson, *Man Who Cried Genocide*, 140.

70. L. Patterson, interview by MaryLouise Patterson, October 1993, audio, box AV3, Louise Thompson Patterson Papers. The talk about article writing is most likely a reference to several pieces by Louise that appeared in *Fraternal Outlook* in 1940.

71. See W. Patterson, *Man Who Cried Genocide*, 140.

72. "Wed 3 Weeks Ago in Chicago," *Amsterdam News*, September 28, 1940.

73. McDuffie, *Sojourning for Freedom*, 123.

74. "Dinner Party," *Amsterdam News*, October 12, 1940.

1. For population figures, see Hirsch, *Making the Second Ghetto*, 17.

2. Wright, "Introduction," xvii.

3. Enrollment numbers taken from Mullen, *Popular Fronts*, 7.

4. Drake and Cayton, *Black Metropolis*, 736. For their broader discussion of the Communists' relationship to the black community, see 734–37.

5. In *Communist Front?* Gerald Horne quotes Pat: "My own wife goes by her name and is addressed as Louise Thompson as often as Louise Patterson. Frankly I think she should be addressed as Louise Thompson. That is her name" (37).

6. Max Bedacht, "Report of the General Secretary to the General Executive Board, February 22–23, 1941, New York City," 2, box 2, folder 5, International Workers Order Records, Kheel Center for Labor-Management Documentation and Archives, Martin P. Catherwood Library, Cornell University, Ithaca, NY.

7. Bedacht, "Report of the General Secretary to the General Executive Board, February 22–23, 1941, New York City," 3.

8. Bedacht, "Report of the General Secretary to the General Executive Board, February 22–23, 1941, New York City," 3–4.

9. Mullen, *Popular Fronts*, 81.

10. "Minutes of the Annual Plenary Session of the General Executive Board, September 6–7, 1941, New York City," 1, box 1, folder 8, International Workers Order Records.

11. *The Negro People Will Defend America*, 3.

12. Louise Thompson and S. Patterson, *IWO*, 4.

13. Louise Thompson and S. Patterson, *IWO*, 4.

14. "Minutes of the General Executive Board, June 27, 1942, New York City," 3, box 1, folder 9, International Workers Order Records.

15. "Minutes of the General Executive Board, June 27, 1942, New York City," 2.

16. "Minutes of the General Executive Board Plenary Sessions, February 7–8, 1942, New York City," 1–6, box 1, folder 9, International Workers Order Records.

17. The elder Evelyn Crawford was born on August 17, 1899, in San Francisco.

18. L. Patterson to Langston Hughes, November 5, 1942, box 17, folder 49, Louise Thompson Patterson Papers.

19. Edward Strong, Thelma Dale, and Hermina Dumont to L. Patterson, March 25, 1943, box 23, folder 8, Louise Thompson Patterson Papers.

20. Langston Hughes to Mary Louise Patterson, March 23, 1943, box 17, folder 41, Louise Thompson Patterson Papers.

21. Max Bedacht, Peter Shipka, John Middleton, and Sylvia Schatzkammer to L. Patterson [1943], box 23, folder 9, Louise Thompson Patterson Papers.

22. Rubin Saltzman to L. Patterson [1943], box 23, folder 9, Louise Thompson Patterson Papers.

23. Sidney Jones and Roma Jones to Mary Louise Patterson [March 1943], box 23, folder 8, Louise Thompson Patterson Papers.

24. Geraldyne Lightfoot and Claude Lightfoot to L. Patterson [March 1943], box 23, folder 8, Louise Thompson Patterson Papers.

25. James Ford to Mr. and Mrs. William Patterson, May 3, 1943, box 23, folder 9, Louise Thompson Patterson Papers.

26. Thyra Edwards to L. Patterson [1943], box 23, folder 8, Louise Thompson Patterson Papers

27. Evelyn "Nebby" Crawford to L. Patterson, March 21, 1943, box 23, folder 8, Louise Thompson Patterson Papers.

28. See Mrs. Allen to L. Patterson, April 21, 1943, box 23, folder 9, Louise Thompson Patterson Papers.

29. For discussion of othermothers, see Collins, *Black Feminist Thought*, 119; and Patton, *Grasp*, 1–2.

30. Susie Revels Cayton to L. Patterson, April 10, 1943, box 23, folder 8, Louise Thompson Patterson Papers.

31. Mrs. Allen to L. Patterson, April 21, 1943, box 23, folder 9, Louise Thompson Patterson Papers.

32. L. Patterson and Sterling Stuckey [ca. 1991], video, box AV5, Louise Thompson Patterson Papers.

33. Browder, *Victory and After*, 78. Also see comments on 80, 84, and 87.

34. Pat ultimately denounced Browder; on Pat's perspective, see Horne, *Black Revolutionary*, 93–96.

35. *Proceedings of the 6th National Convention*, 18, box 3, folders 1–6, International Workers Order Records.

36. *Proceedings of the 6th National Convention*, 218–19.

37. *Proceedings of the 6th National Convention*, 28.

38. *Proceedings of the 6th National Convention*, 112–13.

39. Louise Thompson to Sam Milgrom, June 23, 1944, box 6, folder 5, International Workers Orders Records.

40. Louise Thompson to Sam Milgrom, September 5, 1944, box 6, folder 6, International Workers Orders Records.

41. Louise Thompson to Sam Milgrom, May 23, 1945, box 6, folder 7, International Workers Orders Records.

42. Louise Thompson to Sam Milgrom, May 23, 1945.

43. Halpern, *Killing Floor*, 218.

44. Quoted in Halpern, *Killing Floor*, 214.

45. Halpern, *Killing Floor*, 202–5.

46. Halpern and Horowitz, *Meatpackers*, 42–45.

47. Quoted in Halpern and Horowitz, *Meatpackers*, 48.

48. Quoted in Halpern and Horowitz, *Meatpackers*, 54.

49. Quoted in Halpern and Horowitz, *Meatpackers*, 54–55.

50. "Back Living Wage Demand," *Chicago Defender*, January 19, 1946.

51. Halpern, *Killing Floor*, 221.

52. Halpern, *Killing Floor*, 221.

53. "Clerics Demand Purge of Mayor's Commission," *Chicago Defender*, April 6, 1946.

54. Quoted in "Clerics Demand Purge of Mayor's Commission," *Chicago Defender*, April 6, 1946.

55. W. Patterson, *Man Who Cried Genocide*, 149–50.

56. W. Patterson, *Man Who Cried Genocide*, 150.

57. W. Patterson, *Man Who Cried Genocide*, 151.

58. On the course Davis taught, see his memoir, *Livin' the Blues*, 283–85.

59. W. Patterson, *Man Who Cried Genocide*, 154.

60. See Rob Roy, "Horne, Vaughn, Carpenter in Week's Spotlight: The Trio Are Held Over in Exclusive Cabarets," *Chicago Defender*, April 26, 1947, 18.

61. See Earl Calloway, "Lena and the Best of Everything," *Chicago Defender*, August 16, 1975.

62. See Denning, *Cultural Front*, 77.

63. Officially termed the European Recovery Program, the Marshall Plan, dubbed such in honor of Secretary of State George Marshall, refers to the U.S. government's $13 billion relief effort to rebuild Europe after World War II. Both *Iron Curtain* and *Cold War* denote the political tension between the Eastern and Western blocs from the late 1940s until the early 1990s, including the construction of physical barriers such as the Berlin Wall. The Czech coup took place on February 21–25, 1948.

64. W. Patterson, *Man Who Cried Genocide*, 155.

65. Halpern, *Killing Floor*, 229–30.

66. See Culver and Hyde, *American Dreamer*, 495.

67. "Louise Thompson Patterson," interview [ca. 1955], transcript, 43, box 27, folder 1, Louise Thompson Patterson Papers.

68. Hunton, *Alphaeus Hunton*, 61.

69. See Duberman, *Paul Robeson*, 330–33.

70. In September 1948 Du Bois, working as a special researcher for the association, refused to cooperate with White because he felt the latter was too beholden to Truman and had not been properly responsive to Du Bois's suggestions about foreign policy, especially concerning the Third World. See Lewis, *W. E. B. Du Bois*, 534.

Chapter 10: Sojourns and Sojourners, 1949–1959

1. The eleven defendants were Eugene Dennis, Ben Davis, Robert Thompson, John Gates, Gus Hall, Jack Stachel, Gilbert Green, Henry Winston, Carl Winter, Irving Potash, and John Williamson. The case of national chairman William Z. Foster was separated from those of the others because of his illness. He took part in the trials through depositions.

2. Hollis Lynch reported that membership stood at fifty-seven on September 17, 1948, the date of the meeting at which Yergan was expelled. Shortly thereafter, the council ceased publishing its membership list to protect members from political reprisals. Lynch, *Black American Radicals*, 39.

3. L. Patterson in conversation with Sterling Stuckey [ca. 1991], video, box AV5, Louise Thompson Patterson Papers.

4. L. Patterson in conversation with Sterling Stuckey [ca. 1991].

5. Quoted in Duberman, *Paul Robeson*, 342.

6. Quoted in Duberman, *Paul Robeson*, 342.

7. Vincent Boyle, letter to the editor, *Peekskill Evening Star*, August 18, 1949.

8. *Peekskill Evening Star,* August 22, 1949.

9. L. Patterson in conversation with Beah Richards, audio, April 2, 1989, box AV1, Louise Thompson Patterson Papers.

10. Duberman, *Paul Robeson,* 363–80.

11. L. Patterson in conversation with Sterling Stuckey [ca. 1991], DVD, box AV5, Louise Thompson Patterson Papers.

12. L. Patterson in conversation with Sterling Stuckey [ca. 1991].

13. On different phases of media coverage of Robeson, see Hoyt, *Paul Robeson,* 197.

14. L. Patterson in conversation with Sterling Stuckey [ca. 1991].

15. "Paul Robeson in Detroit" [ca. 1986], 3, box 11, folder 12, Louise Thompson Patterson Papers.

16. "Paul Robeson in Detroit," 3.

17. George Schermer to members of the Interracial Committee, September 16, 1949, box 11, folder 12, Louise Thompson Patterson Papers.

18. Olive R. Beasley to co-worker, September 29, 1949, box 11, folder 12, Louise Thompson Patterson Papers.

19. "Paul Robeson in Detroit," 3.

20. Robeson, "I Am the Same Man," 234.

21. Paul Robeson Jr., *Undiscovered Paul Robeson,* 181.

22. L. Patterson in conversation with Beah Richards, April 2, 1989.

23. L. Patterson in conversation with Beah Richards, April 2, 1989.

24. L. Patterson in conversation with Beah Richards, April 2, 1989.

25. Quoted in "17,000 Hear Robeson in Concert Here," *California Eagle,* October 6, 1949.

26. Louise Thompson in conversation with Sterling Stuckey [ca. 1991].

27. The dollar figure is taken from Horne, *Black Revolutionary,* 138.

28. Duberman, *Paul Robeson,* 388.

29. Duberman, *Paul Robeson,* 701.

30. Horne, *Black Revolutionary,* 122–23.

31. The National Negro Congress submitted a petition to the secretary general of the United Nations on June 6, 1946; Du Bois, representing the NAACP, presented one on October 23, 1947.

32. Article 2 of the Genocide Convention deemed genocide to be "any of the following acts committed with intent to destroy, in whole or in part, a national, ethnical, racial or religious group, as such: (a) killing members of the group; (b) causing serious bodily or mental harm to members of the group; (c) deliberately inflicting on the group conditions of life calculated to bring about its physical destruction in whole or in part; (d) imposing measures intended to prevent births within the group; (e) forcibly transferring children of the group to another group." See "Convention on the Prevention and Punishment of the Crime of Genocide. Adopted by the U.N. General Assembly on December 9, 1948," historyplace.com. Accessed March 2, 2017.

33. W. Patterson, *We Charge Genocide,* 56–125.

34. W. Patterson, *We Charge Genocide,* 57.

35. W. Patterson, *We Charge Genocide,* 125–26.

36. Louise Thompson in conversation with Sterling Stuckey [ca. 1991].

37. Louise Thompson in conversation with Sterling Stuckey [ca. 1991].

38. For figures concerning IWO membership, see Sabin, *Red Scare in Court*, xiv.

39. Jones, who was born in Trinidad, was arrested in 1948 under the Immigration Act of 1918, in 1950 under the McCarran Act, and in 1951 under the Smith Act. She was convicted under the Smith Act and eventually ordered to leave the country in 1955. See C. Davies, *Left of Karl Marx*, xxiv–xv.

40. Sabin, *Red Scare in Court*, 37.

41. Sabin, *Red Scare in Court*, 261.

42. Sabin, *Red Scare in Court*, 263.

43. Sabin, *Red Scare in Court*, 299.

44. Hamilton, *Beah*.

45. See Richards, *A Black Women Speaks*.

46. "A Call to Negro Women" [1951], box 13, folder 3, Louise Thompson Patterson Papers.

47. President Harry S. Truman, "Address at the Constitution Day Ceremonies at the Library of Congress," September 17, 1951. See Gerhard Peters and John T. Woolley, American Presidency Project, http://www.presidency.ucsb.edu/ws/?pid=13916. Accessed March 2, 2017.

48. B. Richardson to the White House, September 25, 1951, box 12, folder 17, Louise Thompson Patterson Papers.

49. B. Richardson to Alexander Pace, September 25, 1951, box 12, folder 17, Louise Thompson Patterson Papers. The collaborators used the wrong name on the letter. The intended recipient was not Alexander Pace but Frank Pace Jr., the secretary of the army. Louise and Richardson also referred to him as the secretary of war, but that post no longer existed. Derrick, twenty-four years old and unarmed, was killed by policemen in Harlem twelve hours after his discharge from the military. He was wearing his uniform when he died, and his discharge pay was not recovered. The implication is that the police might have robbed him. See Biondi, *To Stand and Fight*, 192–93. According to the *Afro-American*, Gilbert, serving in the Twenty-Fourth Infantry in Korea, was court-martialed for "misconduct in the face of the enemy." "Lt. Gilbert Rejoined by Family, Plans 'New Start' in California," *Afro-American*, April 23, 1955. More specifically, he was accused of refusing an order to advance his men to a forward position during heavy artillery fire during the summer of 1950 in Yongdong. Upon conviction, he was sentenced to death, a sentence that was reduced to twenty years at hard labor by President Truman in November 1950 and eventually to twelve years by army officials. Gilbert was paroled on December 1, 1954. See also "Group Seeks Funds to Reunite Gilberts," *Afro-American*, April 2, 1955; and Michael Ollove, "A Soldier's Disgrace," *Baltimore Sun*, April 28, 1996.

50. B. Richardson to Dean Acheson, September 25, 1951, box 12, folder 17, Louise Thompson Patterson Papers.

51. B. Richardson to J. Howard McGrath, September 25, 1951, box 12, folder 17, Louise Thompson Patterson Papers.

52. B. Richardson to the Democratic National Committee [September 1951], box 13, folder 5, Louise Thompson Patterson Papers.

53. B. Richardson to William L. Dawson, September 25, 1951, box 13, folder 5, Louise Thompson Patterson Papers.

54. "Digest of Proceedings" [October 1951], 1, box 12, folder 17, Louise Thompson Patterson Papers.

55. Claudia Jones to Beulah Richardson, September 30, 1951, box 13, folder 5, Louise Thompson Patterson Papers.

56. "Digest of Proceedings," 1.

57. "Digest of Proceedings," 1–2.

58. "A Call to Negro Women" [1951], box 13, folder 3, Louise Thompson Patterson Papers.

59. "Digest of Proceedings," 2–3.

60. "Digest of Proceedings," 3.

61. "Digest of Proceedings," 4.

62. "Digest of Proceedings," 4.

63. "Our Cup Runneth Over: Statement Issued by the Sojourners for Truth and Justice, Relative to the Murder by Bombing of Mr. and Mrs. Harry T. Moore of Mims, Florida" [1951], box 13, folder 2, Louise Thompson Patterson Papers.

64. "Summary Proceedings" [1952], 1–2, box 12, folder 18, Louise Thompson Patterson Papers.

65. "Summary Proceedings," 2.

66. Evelyn Burrell to L. Patterson, April 5, 1952, box 12, folder 19, Louise Thompson Patterson Papers.

67. According to Erik McDuffie, the Sojourners for Truth and Justice had stopped functioning by the end of 1952. McDuffie, *Sojourning for Freedom*, 182.

68. On April 5, 1952, Bass wrote to White requesting a formal aligning of the NAACP with the Sojourners for Truth and Justice. She described how the organization had formed in September 1951, and she referred to the denial of a pardon to Rosa Lee Ingram and her two sons before adding, "While many in our organization are members of the NAACP, with the understanding of the strength there is in unity we want to organizationally join hands with the National Association in working toward the freedom of Mrs. Ingram." Bass to White, April 5, 1952, box 8, folder 5, Louise Thompson Patterson Papers.

69. On the politics of the Cold War and the relationship of the U.S. government to African American moderates and African American radicals, see Horne, *Black Revolutionary*, 109–56. McDuffie suggests that the Communist Party did not solidly back the Sojourners. McDuffie, *Sojourning for Freedom*, 183.

70. The *Yates* decision distinguished between espousing belief in a doctrine and fomenting particular acts of violence. Belief in Communist doctrine in and of itself could not be the basis of criminal guilt.

71. Future U.S. poet laureate Lowell served a sentence as a conscientious objector during World War II. Lardner was one of the Hollywood Ten, members of the film

industry who refused to answer questions in 1947 before the House Un-American Activities Committee.

72. Horne, *Black Revolutionary*, 147.

73. W. Patterson to L. Patterson, July 16, 1954, and W. Patterson to L. Patterson, July 20, 1954, both in box 208-5, folder 3, William L. Patterson Papers, Moorland-Spingarn Research Center, Founders Library, Howard University, Washington, DC.

74. W. Patterson to L. Patterson, July 12, 1954, box 208-5, folder 3, William L. Patterson Papers.

75. W. Patterson to L. Patterson, July 2, 1954, box 208-5, folder 3, William L. Patterson Papers.

76. W. Patterson to Mary Louise Patterson, July 11, 1954, box 208-5, folder 3, William L. Patterson Papers. Mary Lou is the name her parents called her. Therefore, I use it in the latter portions of the book.

77. W. E. B. Du Bois to L. Patterson, July 23, 1954, box 208-5, folder 7, William L. Patterson Papers.

78. L. Patterson to friends, July 29, 1954, box 208-5, folder 7, William L. Patterson Papers.

79. W. Patterson to L. Patterson, August 25, 1954, box 208-5, folder 3, William L. Patterson Papers.

80. Committee of One Hundred Women to friends, November 3, 1954, box 208-5, folder 8, William L. Patterson Papers.

81. Charlotta Bass to L. Patterson, December 14, 1954, box 208-5, folder 2, William Patterson Papers.

82. According to Sabin, the Communist Party lost 75 percent of its membership in 1956–1957. Sabin, *Red Scare in Court*, 5.

83. M. Patterson, "Black and Red," 111–12.

84. M. Patterson, "Black and Red," 113.

85. "Memo to Members of the Committee on Gifts to Ghana," March 2, 1960, box 1, folder 3, Louise Thompson Patterson Papers.

86. "Minutes of Meeting of Afro-American Committee for Gifts of Art and Literature to Ghana," July 29, 1959, box 1, folder 3, Louise Thompson Patterson Papers.

87. M. Patterson, "Black and Red," 111, 113.

88. Horne, *Black Revolutionary*, 161.

89. Author interview with MaryLouise Patterson, August 11, 2015.

Chapter 11: A Fairer Public Hearing, 1960–1969

1. See Horne, *Black Revolutionary*, 173–79.

2. L. Patterson, interview by Carol Yates, May 19, 1998, audio, box AV3, Louise Thompson Patterson Papers. In this interview Louise indicated that the stay in China lasted six weeks. MaryLouise Patterson confirms that she and her mother visited China—for two months, as she recalls. Author interview with MaryLouise Patterson, August 11, 2015. Also see MaryLouise Patterson, "Black and Red," 114. An FBI informant relayed the official line that Louise had remained in the Soviet Union until October. See FBI Report, February 3, 1961, Louise Thompson Patterson FBI/FOIA

Bureau File 100-407934. However, the agency, based on information from another informant, had reason to believe that Louise had gone to China, in violation of passport regulations. See FBI Report, October 20, 1960, Louise Thompson Patterson FBI/FOIA Bureau File 100-407934. The FBI did not pursue the matter because it determined that it was not worth compromising the identity of the informant.

3. Eslanda Robeson entered China in December 1949 and returned to the United States in January 1950. The purpose of the tour was, as her biographer Barbara Ransby phrased it, "to describe China's progress and promise." Ransby, *Eslanda*, 201, 332.

4. William Patterson's notes on China are included in box 208-1, folders 9–13, William L. Patterson Papers.

5. L. Patterson, interview by Carol Yates, May 19, 1998.

6. Author, interview with MaryLouise Patterson, August 11, 2015.

7. Author, interview with MaryLouise Patterson, August 11, 2015.

8. MaryLouise Patterson, "Black and Red," 114.

9. MaryLouise Patterson, "Black and Red," 114.

10. MaryLouise Patterson, "Black and Red," 114.

11. The USSR government founded the People's Friendship University on February 5, 1960. On February 22, 1961, the school was renamed Patrice Lumumba University after the slain Congolese independence leader.

12. Alexander Usvatov, "The First Bell at the Friendship University," *Moscow News*, October 1, 1960.

13. Author interview with MaryLouise Patterson, August 11, 2015.

14. See Davies, *Left of Karl Marx*, xxv–xxvi, 177, 186.

15. Paul Robeson Jr. reported that his father generated close to $150,000 in concert fees and television appearances on that particular tour. *Undiscovered Paul Robeson*, 307.

16. L. Patterson and Sterling Stuckey [ca. 1991], video, box AV5, Louise Thompson Patterson Papers.

17. L. Patterson to Oliver Cromwell Cox, January 26, 1961, box 15, folder 19, Louise Thompson Patterson Papers.

18. Oliver Cromwell Cox to L. Patterson, January 30, 1961, box 15, folder 19, Louise Thompson Patterson Papers.

19. Author phone interview with MaryLouise Patterson, October 19, 2015.

20. Horne, *Black Revolutionary*, 185, 272.

21. Nebby Crawford to L. Patterson, December 1, 1961, box 23, folder 14, Louise Thompson Patterson Papers.

22. Rockwell Kent to L. Patterson, December 1, 1961, box 23, folder 14, Louise Thompson Patterson Papers.

23. Shirley Graham Du Bois to L. Patterson, December 18, 1961, box 23, folder 13, Louise Thompson Patterson Papers.

24. Fred Ptashne to L. Patterson, January 2, 1962, box 23, folder 14, Louise Thompson Patterson Papers.

25. *Freedomways* was published from 1961 to 1985, *Freedom* from 1950 to 1955. Along with the Robesons and the Du Boises, key members of the *Freedom* circle included Lloyd Brown, John Henrik Clarke, Alice Childress, and Lorraine Hansberry.

26. Louise Thompson, "David and Goliath," *Freedomways*, summer 1961, 215–16.

27. The party took place on March 31, 1962. The Fair Play for Cuba Committee placed the advertisement in the *New York Times* on April 6, 1960.

28. FBI Report, April 2, 1962, Louise Thompson Patterson FBI/FOIA New York File 100-24624.

29. As printed in the The First and Second Declarations of Havana, point 6 of the preamble reads in full: "The National General Assembly of the People reaffirms—and is certain of doing so as an expression of a view common to all the people of Latin America—that democracy is incompatible with the financial oligarchy, racial discrimination, and the outrages of the Ku Klux Klan, the persecutions that prevented the world from hearing for many years the wonderful voice of Paul Robeson, imprisoned in his own country, and that killed the Rosenbergs, in the face of the protests and the horror of the world and despite the appeal of the rulers of many countries, and of Pope Pius XII, himself" (29).

30. Louise Thompson, "Southern Editor's Analysis," *Freedomways*, first quarter, 1964, 168.

31. Louise Thompson, "A Shadow That Covers a Whole Nation," *Freedomways*, winter 1963, 115.

32. Louise Thompson, "A Shadow That Covers a Whole Nation," *Freedomways*, winter 1963, 116–17.

33. In the portion of the letter in which he discussed his disappointment with white moderates and conjectured that "perhaps the South, the nation, and the world are in dire need of creative extremists" (198), King concluded with the following statement:

> I had hoped the white moderate would see this need. Perhaps I was too optimistic; perhaps I expected too much. I suppose I should have realized that few members of the oppressor race can understand the deep groans and passionate yearnings of the oppressed race, and still fewer have the vision to see that injustice must be rooted out by strong, persistent, and determined action. I am thankful, however, that some of our white brothers in the South have grasped the meaning of this social revolution and committed themselves to it. They are still too few in quantity, but they are big in quality. Some—such as Ralph McGill, Lillian Smith, Harry Golden, James McBride Dabbs, Ann Braden, and Sarah Patton Boyle—have written about our struggle in eloquent and prophetic terms. Others have marched with us down nameless streets of the South. They have languished in filthy, roach-infested jails suffering the abuse and brutality of policemen who view them as "dirty nigger lovers." Unlike so many of our moderate brothers and sisters, they have recognized the urgency of the moment and sensed the need for powerful "action" antidotes to combat the disease of segregation. (198–99)

34. Louise Thompson, "Southern Editor's Analysis," *Freedomways*, first quarter, 1964, 168–70.

35. Louise Thompson, "Southern Editor's Analysis," *Freedomways*, first quarter, 1964, 170. Also see Haywood, *Negro Liberation*, 49–65.

36. Louise Thompson, "Southern Editor's Analysis," *Freedomways*, first quarter, 1964, 170.

37. Oakley C. Johnson to Mrs. William L. Patterson, April 4, 1964, box 15, folder 2, Louise Thompson Patterson Papers. For literary study, Johnson suggested anthologies in world literature, English literature, and American literature. He offered no specific titles for the first two subjects but for the last expressed a preference for *A College Book of American Literature* (edited by Milton Ellis, Louise Pound, and George Spohn). Turning to composition, Oakley listed five books that he claimed to rely on both to write and to teach: *Webster's New Collegiate Dictionary, The King's English* (by Henry Watson Fowler and George Fowler), *The Gift of Language* (by Margaret Schlauch), *Words and Their Ways in English Speech* (by James Bradstreet Greenough and George Lyman Kittredge), and *Learning to Write in College* (by Reed Smith, revised by William Hastings).

38. FBI Report, March 4, 1965, Louise Thompson Patterson FBI/FOIA Bureau File 100-407934.

39. L. Patterson, "Address to Members of the Forum and Friends of AIMS," April 23, 1976, 1, box 1, folder 11, Louise Thompson Patterson Papers.

40. Aptheker, "The American Institute of Marxist Studies" [ca. 1963], box 9, folder 7, Herbert Aptheker Papers, Manuscripts Division of the Department of Special Collections, Stanford University Libraries, Palo Alto, CA.

41. Aptheker, "The American Institute of Marxist Studies" [ca. 1963].

42. *AIMS Newsletter*, June 1964, 1, box 140, folder 1, Herbert Aptheker Papers.

43. See chapter 7 of this volume for commentary on the Harlem riot of 1935. The outbreak in 1943 occurred on August 1–2 after a white police officer shot a black man. This riot is alluded to in books such as Ralph Ellison's *Invisible Man* and Sidney Poitier's *The Measure of a Man*.

44. Gilyard, *John Oliver Killens*, 196; D'Emilio, *Lost Prophet*, 382–83.

45. For example, she saved among her papers a copy of Eldridge Cleaver's *On the Ideology of the Black Panther Party, Part I*.

46. Duberman, *Paul Robeson*, 527–28; Paul Robeson Jr., *Undiscovered Paul Robeson*, 344–45.

47. L. Patterson to Angelo Herndon, May 26, 1969, box 16, folder 3, Louise Thompson Patterson Papers.

48. Excerpts included in Newton, *To Die*, 164–74.

49. Newton, *To Die*, 168.

50. Newton, *To Die*, 168–74.

51. Newton, *To Die*, 174–79.

52. Newton, *To Die*, 179.

53. From *Uzbekistan* [1969], 7, 46–47, box 14, folder 8, Louise Thompson Patterson Papers.

54. "Tashkent" [1969], fact sheet, box 14, folder 6, Louise Thompson Patterson Papers.

55. Annageldyyeva, "Daughters of Turkmenia," August 1, 1969, box 14, folder 6, Louise Thompson Patterson Papers.

56. In the "Seventh Street" section of *Cane*, Jean Toomer wrote, "Black reddish blood. Pouring for crude-boned soft-skinned life, who set you flowing? Blood suckers of the War would spin in a frenzy of dizziness if they drank your blood. Prohibition would put a stop to it. Who set you flowing? White and whitewash disappear in blood. Who set you flowing? Flowing down the smooth asphalt of Seventh Street, in shanties, brick office buildings, theaters, drug stores, restaurants, and cabarets? Eddying on the corners? Swirling like a blood-red smoke up where the buzzards fly in heaven? God would not dare to suck black red blood. A Nigger God! He would duck his head in shame and call for the Judgment Day. Who set you flowing?" (39).

57. L. Patterson, "With Langston Hughes in the USSR," 157.

58. Quoted in L. Patterson, "A Levee That Won't Break Down," *Freedomways*, second quarter, 1974, 150. In the version of Hughes's poem that appears in *The Collected Poems of Langston Hughes*, the lines read, "Levee, levee / How high have you got to be / To keep them cold muddy waters / From washin' over me?" (249).

59. Untitled draft of interview questions, box 5, folder 4, Louise Thompson Patterson Papers.

60. L. Patterson, "A Levee That Won't Break Down," *Freedomways*, second quarter 1974, 150.

Chapter 12: Confirming Commitments, 1970–1984

1. Davis, *Angela Davis*, 3–12.

2. Davis, *Angela Davis*, 64–65, 382–83.

3. Horne, *Black Revolutionary*, 205–6.

4. Carl Bloice, "Triumphant Tour of Britain for Angela's Freedom," *People's World*, March 27, 1971.

5. Bloice, "Triumphant Tour of Britain for Angela's Freedom," *People's World*, March 27, 1971.

6. Bloice, "Triumphant Tour of Britain for Angela's Freedom," *People's World*, March 27, 1971.

7. FBI Report, March 24, 1971, Louise Thompson Patterson FBI/FOIA Bureau File 100-407934.

8. Bloice, "Triumphant Tour of Britain for Angela's Freedom," *People's World*, March 27, 1971.

9. Bloice, "Triumphant Tour of Britain for Angela's Freedom," *People's World*, March 27, 1971.

10. George Matthews to L. Thompson, March 11, 1971, box 5, folder 13, Louise Thompson Patterson Papers.

11. Author phone interview with MaryLouise Patterson, October 19, 2015.

12. Evelyn Louise (Nebby Lou) Crawford email to author, October 21, 2015.

13. These were the *Jet* issues of May 6, 1971, and May 16, 1974.

14. L. Patterson, untitled book review [1975], 3, 11, box 19, folder 1, Louise Thompson Patterson Papers.

15. L. Patterson, untitled manuscript, 2.

16. L. Patterson, untitled manuscript, 3–4. An outspoken critic of the gulag, the Russian writer Aleksandr Solzhenitsyn, winner of the Nobel Prize in Literature in 1970, was expelled from the Soviet Union in 1974. He eventually returned in 1994.

17. L. Patterson, untitled book review, 4.

18. Christopher Lehmann-Haupt, "Not Quite Speaking Out," *New York Times*, October 23, 1974.

19. Karen Durbin, "First Person Impersonal," *Ms.*, February 1975, 38.

20. Ivan Webster, "Political Fury," *New Republic*, November 16, 1974, 30. Robert Kirsch, "Angela Davis and the Path Taken," *Los Angeles Times*, November 6, 1974; Marc Larson, "Behind Angela's Propaganda," *Minneapolis Tribune*, November 17, 1974.

21. See *New Yorker*, November 11, 1974, 214; and Francis Carney, "George Jackson and His Legend," *New York Review of Books*, November 28, 1974.

22. Maya Angelou, "Angela Davis' Odyssey in Her Own Words," *Chicago Daily News*, November 23, 1974.

23. Elinor Langer, "Angela Davis," *Sunday Book Review*, October 27, 1974.

24. L. Patterson, untitled manuscript, 8.

25. Berry, review of *Angela Davis: An Autobiography*, *Washington Star-Times*, October 20, 1974.

26. L. Patterson, untitled manuscript, 9.

27. L. Patterson, untitled manuscript, 10.

28. W. Patterson, "The Cuban Trip," unpublished notes [ca. 1974], box 208-1, folder 15. William L. Patterson Papers.

29. L. Patterson, "A Levee That Won't Break Down," *Freedomways*, second quarter, 1974, 152.

30. Quoted in L. Patterson, "A Levee That Won't Break Down," *Freedomways*, second quarter, 1974, 153.

31. L. Patterson, untitled essay [ca. 1974], box 5, folder 4, Louise Thompson Patterson Papers.

32. L. Patterson, untitled essay, box 5, folder 4.

33. See brochure, "Louise Patterson Celebration" [1984], box 24, folder 6, Louise Thompson Patterson Papers.

34. See brochure, "Louise Patterson Celebration."

35. Herbert Aptheker to L. Patterson, January 9, 1976, box 1, folder 11, Louise Thompson Patterson Papers.

36. L. Patterson, "Address to Members of the Forum and Friends of AIMS," April 23, 1976, 3, box 1, folder 11, Louise Thompson Patterson Papers.

37. See Cole, "Afro-American Solidarity with Cuba."

38. L. Patterson, "Address to Members of the Forum and Friends of AIMS," April 23, 1976, 1.

39. After a hard-line speech by Ford on October 29, 1975, the *New York Daily News* headline on October 30 read "Ford to City: Drop Dead." The president had not used that phrase. In fact, a couple of months later, the president signed off on federal loans to New York. He lost the election of 1976 to Carter by a margin of 297 electoral votes to

240. Doing poorly in New York City—Carter took two-thirds of the vote—cost Ford New York State's forty-one electoral votes. Had he garnered those, he would have won the presidency. What also probably worked against Ford rhetorically was that the Democratic National Convention took place in New York City in 1976.

40. L. Patterson, "Address to Members of the Forum and Friends of AIMS," April 23, 1976, 4–5.

41. O. Davis and Dee, *With Ossie and Ruby*, 292.

42. O. Davis and Dee, *With Ossie and Ruby*, 292.

43. Robeson died on January 23, 1976, in Philadelphia. Hy Lumer, the husband of Burnham, passed away on July 22, 1976, in New York City. During his activist career, Lumer was imprisoned under the Taft-Hartley Act, was editor of *Political Affairs* and *Jewish Affairs*, and served as the educational director of district 7 of the International Brotherhood of Electrical Workers. Louise assisted with the ceremonies for Lumer. See Henry Winston to L. Patterson, July 28, 1976, and Charlene Mitchell to L. Patterson, July 30, 1976, both in box 9, folder 17, Louise Thompson Patterson Papers.

44. Program for the William L. Patterson Foundation First Annual Awards Luncheon [ca. 1977], box 10, folder 12, Louise Thompson Patterson Papers.

45. Horne, *Black Revolutionary*, 207–9.

46. Program for the William L. Patterson Foundation First Annual Awards Luncheon.

47. Robert Hemenway to L. Patterson, November 18, 1975, box 16, folder 5, Louise Thompson Patterson Papers.

48. L. Patterson to Hemenway, January 12, 1976, box 16, folder 5, Louise Thompson Patterson Papers.

49. Robert Hemenway to L. Patterson, February 16, 1976, box 16, folder 5, Louise Thompson Patterson Papers.

50. Robert Hemenway to L. Patterson, February 16, 1976.

51. L. Patterson to Robert Hemenway, March 19, 1976, box 16, folder 5, Louise Thompson Patterson Papers.

52. Alice Walker to L. Patterson, January 21, 1976, box 16, folder 36; Alice Walker to L. Patterson, April 26, 1976, box 16, folder 36; Mark Naison to L. Patterson, November 13, 1976, box 15, folder 2. All three letters in the Louise Thompson Patterson Papers.

53. Mark Naison to L. Patterson, November 13, 1976.

54. Phyllis Klotman to L. Patterson, September 5, 1979; January 23, 1980; February 19, 1980; and July 22, 1980, all in box 16, folder 13, Louise Thompson Patterson Papers.

55. For examples of references to Pat as "Mr. Civil Rights," see Theresa Watanabe, "Longtime Black Communist Dead," *Los Angeles Times*, March 10, 1980; and Antar Mberi, "Mister Civil Rights," *World Magazine*, April 17, 1980, 16.

56. MaryLouise Patterson-Gilmer to friends of Pat, February 14, 1980, box 24, folder 1, Louise Thompson Patterson Papers.

57. See J. J. Johnson, "2,000 Pay Tribute to Wm. L. Patterson," *Daily World*, March 18, 1980.

58. Ruby Dee, "Thinking about Pat and Louise" [1980], box 15, folder 28, Louise Thompson Patterson Papers.

59. See "Memorial Service," *New York Amsterdam News*, March 15, 1980.

60. L. Patterson to Maya Angelou, June 13, 1980, box 24, folder 5, Louise Thompson Patterson Papers.

61. L. Patterson to Julian Mayfield, June 18, 1980, box 23, folder 3, Louise Thompson Patterson Papers.

62. Julian Mayfield to L. Patterson, April 27, 1980, box 23, folder 3, Louise Thompson Patterson Papers.

63. Quoted in Tamar Kaplan-Marans, "Fifty Years In, Runyon Continues Struggle," *Columbia Daily Spectator*, February 2, 2001.

64. Author phone interview with Dorothy Keller, June 10, 2015.

65. Since 2011, the institution has been known officially as the Maurice A. Deane School of Law.

66. Author, phone interview with Dorothy Keller, June 10, 2015.

67. Author, phone interview with Dorothy Keller, June 10, 2015.

68. L. Patterson, interview by Pele deLappe [ca. 1989], transcript, 1, box 27, folder 2, Louise Thompson Patterson Papers.

69. Linda Trice to L. Patterson, February 2, 1983, box 15, folder 3, Louise Thompson Patterson Papers.

70. Savoy Manor Ballroom is not to be confused with the Savoy Ballroom, which operated on Lenox Avenue in Harlem from 1926 to 1958.

71. John Oliver Killens, "In the Great Tradition of Black Womanhood," 1984.

72. See brochure, "Louise Patterson Celebration," box 24, folder 6, Louise Thompson Patterson Papers.

73. Contained in box 6, folder 11, Louise Thompson Patterson Papers.

Chapter 13: Still Reaching, 1984–1999

1. See "Recognizing Our Own: The 1st Annual Black Award Ceremony" [1988], box 24, folder 7, Louise Thompson Patterson Papers.

2. Charlene Mitchell to L. Patterson, August 31, 1987, box 15, folder 4, Louise Thompson Patterson Papers.

3. See Adam Begley, "Henry Louis Gates, Jr.: Black Studies' New Star," *New York Times Magazine*, April 1, 1990; see *Jet*, May 14, 1990.

4. Jessica Mitford to Maya Angelou, February 1, 1986, box 4, folder 9, Louise Thompson Patterson Papers.

5. Jessica Mitford, "Black Eloquence," *London Sunday Times*, October 20, 1985.

6. Jessica Mitford to Maya Angelou, February 1, 1986.

7. Maya Angelou to Jessica Mitford, February 3, 1986, box 4, folder 9, Louise Thompson Patterson Papers; Jessica Mitford to Maya Angelou, February 8, 1986, box 4, folder 9, Louise Thompson Patterson Papers.

8. Jessica Mitford to L. Patterson, February 9, 1986, box 4, folder 9, Louise Thompson Patterson Papers.

9. L. Patterson, interview by Evelyn Louise Crawford, March 18, 1990, transcript, 38, box 28, folder 13, Louise Thompson Patterson Papers.

10. Arnold Rampersad to L. Patterson, July 17, 1985, box 16, folder 23, Louise Thompson Patterson Papers.

11. Sally Goldmark to L. Patterson, March 5, 1985, box 6, folder 15, Louise Thompson Patterson Papers.

12. Mary Bassett to L. Patterson, June 6, 1985, box 6, folder 15, Louise Thompson Patterson Papers.

13. Mary Bassett to L. Patterson, June 6, 1985.

14. Author, phone interview with Dorothy Keller, June 10, 2015.

15. Clarke spoke at the Family Resource House of Unity on January 15, 1989.

16. L. Patterson to Margaret Walker, May 1, 1989, box 14, folder 11, Louise Thompson Patterson Papers.

17. L. Patterson and Margot Dashiell to Sojourners, October 14, 1989, box 12, folder 15, Louise Thompson Patterson Papers.

18. "Work in Progress on the Life of Louise Alone Toles Patterson," May 14, 1985, box 20, folder 24, Louise Thompson Patterson Papers.

19. The center has since been renamed as the Gender Equity Resource Center.

20. L. Patterson, "Chapter 2: Pine Bluff/Hampton," 52–54, box 19, folder 18, Louise Thompson Patterson Papers.

21. L. Patterson, "Chapter 2: Pine Bluff/Hampton," 56.

22. L. Patterson, "Chapter 2: Pine Bluff/Hampton," 54.

23. L. Patterson, "Chapter 2: Pine Bluff/Hampton," 54–55.

24. L. Patterson, "Chapter 2: Pine Bluff/Hampton," 54.

25. L. Patterson, "Chapter 2: Pine Bluff/Hampton," 55.

26. L. Patterson, "Chapter 2: Pine Bluff/Hampton," 56.

27. L. Patterson, "Chapter 2: Pine Bluff/Hampton," 56.

28. "Nevada Trip" [1987], video, box AV5, Louise Thompson Patterson Papers.

29. "Nevada Trip" [1987].

30. "Nevada Trip" [1987].

31. "Nevada Trip" [1987].

32. Verdell Burdine Rutherford to L. Patterson, January 26, 1988, box 4, folder 1, Louise Thompson Patterson Papers.

33. L. Patterson to Verdell Rutherford [1988], box 4, folder 1, Louise Thompson Patterson Papers.

34. Verdell Burdine Rutherford to L. Patterson, March 24, 1990, and March 25, 1990, box 4, folder 1, Louise Thompson Patterson Papers.

35. L. Patterson with Beah Richards, audio, April 2, 1989, box AV1, Louise Thompson Patterson Papers.

36. See Barbara Bristol to L. Patterson, July 18, 1988, and L. Patterson to Barbara Bristol, September 2, 1988, box 11, folder 9, Louise Thompson Patterson Papers.

37. Lloyd L. Brown, "Memorandum on Paul Robeson Biography," March 16, 1982, box 11, folder 9, Louise Thompson Patterson Papers.

38. Lloyd L. Brown to John Henrik Clarke, March 16, 1982, box 11, folder 9, Louise Thompson Patterson Papers. Brown's agreement with Robeson expired seven months after Robeson's death. Paul Robeson Jr. subsequently granted Duberman exclusive

use of the Robeson archives. Brown is referring to "Historical Fictions," Duberman's review in the *New York Times* (August 11, 1968).

39. Claude Lightfoot and Ishmael Flory to friends, April 14, 1989, box 15, folder 30, Louise Thompson Patterson Papers.

40. Ishmael Flory to L. Patterson, June 14, 1989, box 15, folder 30, Louise Thompson Patterson Papers.

41. Loften Mitchell to L. Patterson, June 25, 1991, box 9, folder 22, Louise Thompson Patterson Papers.

42. See Mildred Penn Lee, "Bay Area Activist Life to Be Subject of Book," *East Bay Monitor*, April 1989, 3.

43. L. Patterson to Tom Wirth, July 6, 1989, box 9, folder 12, Louise Thompson Patterson Papers.

44. L. Patterson with MaryLouise Patterson and others, July 7, 1989, audio, box AV2, Louise Thompson Patterson Papers.

45. L. Patterson with MaryLouise Patterson and others, July 7, 1989.

46. L. Patterson with MaryLouise Patterson and others, July 7, 1989.

47. Directed by Neema Barnette, the film featured Dee along with Louis Gossett Jr., Flip Wilson, Oscar Brown Jr., Paula Kelly, Roger Mosley, Beah Richards, Count Stovall, and Lynn Whitfield.

48. L. Thompson, interview, June 2 and June 6, 1989, transcript, 39, box 28, folder 4, Louise Thompson Patterson Papers.

49. Verdell Burdine Rutherford to L. Patterson, February 15, 1990, box 4, folder 1, Louise Thompson Patterson Papers.

50. L. Patterson to N. Y. Nathiri, November 11, 1989, box 7, folder 12, Louise Thompson Patterson Papers.

51. Author phone interview with MaryLouise Patterson, October 19, 2015.

52. L. Patterson, "Notes for Zora Neale Hurston Presentation" [1990], unpublished manuscript, box 7, folder 14, Louise Thompson Patterson Papers.

53. L. Patterson to Norma Francisco [ca. April 1990], and Norma Francisco to L. Patterson, May 1, 1990, box 13, folder 12, Louise Thompson Patterson Papers.

54. See "Black Elders Day Celebration," February 10, 1988, box 19, folder 4, Louise Thompson Patterson Papers.

55. L. Patterson, edited interview transcript, June 24, 1991, 21, box 28, folder 14, Louise Thompson Patterson Papers.

56. L. Patterson, edited interview transcript, June 24, 1991, 21.

57. Vicki Garvin to L. Patterson, April 1, 1991, box 15, folder 5, Louise Thompson Patterson Papers.

58. L. Patterson, interview by unidentified person regarding memoir project [ca. 1990], video, box AV5, Louise Thompson Patterson Papers.

59. L. Patterson, interview by unidentified person, June 24, 1991, transcript.

60. L. Patterson, interview by unidentified person, June 24, 1991, transcript.

61. L. Patterson, interview by unidentified person, June 24, 1991, transcript.

62. H. Smith, *Black Man*; on Robinson, see Simeon Booker, "Black Man Returns Home after 47 Years in Russia," *Ebony*, June 1987.

63. Itabari Njeri, "Black Russian," *Los Angeles Times*, February 8, 1988.

64. L. Patterson and Sterling Stuckey [ca. 1991], video, box AV5, Louise Thompson Patterson Papers.

65. L. Patterson and Sterling Stuckey [ca. 1991].

66. L. Patterson and Sterling Stuckey [ca. 1991].

67. L. Patterson and others regarding current events and politics [ca. 1991], video, box AV5, Louise Thompson Patterson Papers.

68. L. Patterson and others regarding current events and politics [ca. 1991]. The Raiders were based in Los Angeles from 1982 to 1994 before moving back to Oakland.

69. University of California Black Graduation [1991], video, box AV5, Louise Thompson Patterson Papers.

70. L. Patterson to Ossie Davis, April 28, 1992, box 15, folder 28, Louise Thompson Patterson Papers.

71. Margaret Burroughs to L. Patterson, March 12, 1992, box 15, folder 16, Louise Thompson Patterson Papers.

72. Cy Epstein to Mary Louise Patterson, August 25, 1992, box 24, folder 8, Louise Thompson Patterson Papers.

73. Proposal for "The Life and Times of Louise Thompson" by Margaret B. Wilkerson [ca. 1991], box 24, folder 8, Louise Thompson Patterson Papers.

74. Epstein to Mary Louise Patterson, August 25, 1992.

75. Margaret Wilkerson to Mary Louise Patterson, October 20, 1992, box 24, folder 8, Louise Thompson Patterson Papers.

76. L. Patterson, interview by MaryLouise Patterson, October 1993, audio, box AV3, Louise Thompson Patterson Papers.

77. "Trip to Italy" [ca. 1994], video, box AV5, Louise Thompson Patterson Papers.

78. Author, phone interview with Faith Berry, October 8, 2015.

79. "Louise Thompson Patterson's Birthday (93rd) Party," September 10, 1994, video, box AV5, Louise Thompson Patterson Papers.

80. "Louise Thompson Patterson's Birthday (93rd) Party," September 10, 1994.

81. "Louise Thompson Patterson Project Chapter Outline, October 30, 1994," box 4, folder 3, Louise Thompson Patterson Papers.

82. Faith Berry to L. Patterson, May 8, 1995, box 15, folder 11, Louise Thompson Patterson Papers.

83. MaryLouise Patterson-Gilmer, "Commentary," *California Voice*, August 21, 1982.

84. Massiah, *Louise Thompson Patterson*.

Addams, Jane. *Twenty Years at Hull-House*. 1910. New York: Signet, 1999.

Aldridge, Derrick P. *The Educational Thought of W. E. B. Du Bois: An Intellectual History*. New York: Teachers College Press, 2008.

Aleksandrov, Grigori, and Sergei Eisenstein, dirs. *October*. Sovkino, 1928.

Anderson, Jervis. *This Was Harlem: A Cultural Portrait, 1900–1950*. New York: Farrar, Straus and Giroux, 1981.

Andrews, Gordon. *Undoing Plessy: Charles Hamilton Houston, Race, Labor, and the Law, 1895–1950*. Newcastle upon Tyne, UK: Cambridge Scholars, 2014.

Andrews, Gregg. *Thyra J. Edwards: Black Activist in the Global Freedom Struggle*. Columbia: University of Missouri Press, 2011.

Angelou, Maya. *I Know Why the Caged Bird Sings*. New York: Random House, 1969.

Anthony, David Henry. *Max Yergan: Race Man, Internationalist, Cold Warrior*. New York: New York University Press, 2006.

Aptheker, Herbert. Papers. Manuscripts Division of the Department of Special Collections, Stanford University Libraries, Stanford, CA.

Armfield, Felix L. *Eugene Kinckle Jones: The National Urban League and Black Social Work, 1910–1940*. Urbana: University of Illinois Press, 2012.

Ashe, Arthur R., Jr. *A Hard Road to Glory: A History of the African-American Athlete, 1619–1918*. New York: Amistad, 1988.

Aycock, Colleen, and Mark Scott. *Joe Gans: A Biography of the First African American World Boxing Champion*. Jefferson, NC: McFarland, 2008.

Bagwell, Beth. *Oakland: The Story of a City*. Oakland, CA: Oakland Heritage Alliance, 1982.

Baldwin, Kate A. *Beyond the Color Line and the Iron Curtain: Reading Encounters between Black and Red, 1922–1963*. Durham, NC: Duke University Press, 2002.

Bates, Daisy. *The Long Shadow of Little Rock: A Memoir*. New York: David McKay, 1962.

Bedacht, Max. *Labor Fraternalism*. New York: National Education Department, International Workers Order, 1941.

Beevor, Antoy. *The Battle for Spain: The Spanish Civil War, 1936–1939*. New York: Penguin, 2001.

Berry, Faith. *Langston Hughes: Before and beyond Harlem*. New York: Wings Books, 1983.

Berton, Pierre. *Klondike: The Last Great Gold Rush, 1896–1899*. Toronto: Pierre Berton, 1972.

Biondi, Martha. *To Stand and Fight: The Struggle for Civil Rights in Postwar New York City*. Cambridge, MA: Harvard University Press, 2006.

Boyd, Valerie. *Wrapped in Rainbows: The Life of Zora Neale Hurston*. New York: Scribner, 2003.

Branch, Taylor. *At Canaan's Edge: America in the King Years, 1965–68*. New York: Simon and Schuster, 2006.

Brock, Lisa. "The 1950s: Africa Solidarity Rising." In *No Easy Victories: African Liberation and American Activists over a Half Century, 1950–2000*, edited by William Minter, Gail Hovey, and Charles Cobb Jr., 59–81. Trenton, NJ: Africa World Press, 2008.

Broussard, Albert S. *Black San Francisco: The Struggle for Racial Equality in the West, 1900–1954*. Lawrence: University Press of Kansas, 1993.

Browder, Earl. *Victory and After*. New York: International Publishers, 1942.

Brown, Charlotte Hawkins. "What Negro Youth Have a Right to Expect from the Constitution of These United States." In *Official Proceedings, Second National Negro Congress, Metropolitan Opera House, Philadelphia, Pennsylvania, October 15, 16, 17, 1937*. Washington, DC: National Negro Congress, 1937.

Brown, Edward J. *Mayakovsky: A Poet in the Revolution*. Princeton, NJ: Princeton University Press, 1973.

Brown, Sterling A. "Negro Characters as Seen by White Authors." *Journal of Negro Education* 2, no. 2 (April 1933): 179–203.

———. "The Problems of the Negro Writer." In *Official Proceedings, Second National Negro Congress, Metropolitan Opera House, Philadelphia, Pennsylvania, October 15, 16, 17, 1937*. Washington, DC: National Negro Congress, 1937.

Brundenius, Claes. "Growth with Equity: The Cuban Experience (1959–1980)." *World Development* 9, nos. 11/12 (1981): 1083–96.

Carew, Joy Gleason. *Blacks, Reds, and Russians: Sojourners in Search of the Soviet Promise*. New Brunswick, NJ: Rutgers University Press, 2008.

Carr, Raymond. *The Spanish Civil War*. New York: Norton, 1986.

Carter, Dan T. *Scottsboro: A Tragedy of the American South*. Rev. ed. Baton Rouge: Louisiana State University Press, 2007.

Cayton, Horace R., Jr. *Long Old Road: An Autobiography*. Seattle: University of Washington Press, 1963.

Cayton, Susie Revels. *Stories by Cayton*. Seattle, WA: Association of African American Historical Research and Preservation, 2002.

Chaney, Michael A. "International Contexts of the Negro Renaissance." In *The Cambridge Companion to the Harlem Renaissance*, edited by George Hutchinson, 41–54. New York: Cambridge University Press, 2007.

Clarke, John Henrik, ed. *William Styron's Nat Turner: Ten Black Writers Respond*. Boston: Beacon, 1968.

Cleaver, Eldridge. *On the Ideology of the Black Panther Party, Part I.* San Francisco: Black Panther Party, [ca. 1968].

Cole, Johnetta. "Afro-American Solidarity with Cuba." *Black Scholar* 8, nos. 8–10 (1977): 73–80.

Collins, Patricia Hill. *Black Feminist Thought: Knowledge, Consciousness, and the Politics of Empowerment.* New York: Routledge, 1991.

Collum, Danny Duncan, ed. *African Americans in the Spanish Civil War: "This Ain't Ethiopia, but It'll Do."* New York: G. K. Hall, 1992.

Cox, Oliver Cromwell. *Capitalism and American Leadership.* New York: Philosophical Library, 1962.

———. *Caste, Class, and Race: A Study in Social Dynamics.* New York: Monthly Review Press, 1948.

Crain, William, dir. *Blacula.* American International Pictures and Power Productions, 1972.

Crawford, Evelyn Louise, and MaryLouise Patterson, eds. *Letters from Langston: From the Harlem Renaissance to the Red Scare and Beyond.* Oakland: University of California Press, 2016.

Culver, John C., and John Hyde. *American Dreamer: The Life and Times of Henry A. Wallace.* New York: W. W. Norton, 2000.

Curtis, Nancy C. *Black Heritage Sites: The South.* New York: New Press, 1996.

Davies, Carole Boyce. *Left of Karl Marx: The Political Life of Black Communist Claudia Jones.* Durham, NC: Duke University Press, 2008.

Davis, Angela. *Angela Davis: An Autobiography.* New York: International Publishers, 1974.

Davis, Benjamin J. *Communist Councilman from Harlem: Autobiographical Notes Written in a Federal Penitentiary.* New York: International Publishers, 1969.

Davis, Frank Marshall. *Livin' the Blues: Memoirs of a Black Journalist and Poet.* Madison: University of Wisconsin Press, 1992.

Davis, Ossie, and Ruby Dee. *With Ossie and Ruby: In This Life Together.* New York: William Morrow, 1998.

D'Emilio, John. *Lost Prophet: The Life and Times of Bayard Rustin.* Chicago: University of Chicago Press, 2003.

Demme, Jonathan, dir. *Beloved.* Harpo Films, Clinica Estetico, and Touchstone Pictures, 1998.

Denning, Michael. *The Cultural Front: The Laboring of American Culture in the Twentieth Century.* London: Verso, 1997.

Dickerson, Dennis C. *African American Preachers and Politics: The Careys of Chicago.* Jackson: University Press of Mississippi, 2010.

Directory of Graduates of the University of California, 1864–1916. Berkeley: California Alumni Association, 1916.

Donlon, Anne. "Introduction." In *Poetry, Politics, and Friendship in the Spanish Civil War: Langston Hughes, Nancy Cunard, and Louise Thompson,* edited by Anne Donlon, 1–9. New York: Lost and Found, the CUNY Poetics Document Initiative, 2012.

———. "Langston Hughes and Louise Thompson." In *Poetry, Politics, and Friendship in the Spanish Civil War: Langston Hughes, Nancy Cunard, and Louise Thompson,* edited by Anne Donlon, 28–40. New York: Lost and Found, the CUNY Poetics Document Initiative, 2012.

Drake, St. Clair, and Horace R. Cayton. *Black Metropolis: A Study of Negro Life in a Northern City*. New York: Harcourt, Brace, 1945.

Duberman, Martin. *Paul Robeson: A Biography*. New York: New Press, 1989.

Du Bois, W. E. B. *Black Reconstruction*. 1935. New York: Atheneum, 1992.

———. "Criteria of Negro Art." *Crisis*, October 1926, 290–97.

———. "The Economic Future of the Negro." *Publications of the American Economic Association*, 3rd ser., 7, no. 1 (February 1906): 219–42.

———. "The Economics of Negro Emancipation in the United States." *Sociological Review* A4, no. 4, October 1911, 303–13.

———. "The Hampton Idea." In *The Education of Black People: Ten Critiques, 1906–1960*, edited by Herbert Aptheker, 5–15. New York: Monthly Review Press, 1973.

———. *The Souls of Black Folk*. 1903. New York: Penguin, 1989.

Dunnigan, Alice A. *The Fascinating Story of Black Kentuckians: Their Heritage and Traditions*. Washington, DC: Associated Publishers, 1982.

Dwyer, William L. *The Goldmark Case: An American Libel Trial*. Seattle: University of Washington Press, 1984.

Early, Gerald. "Introduction." In *My Soul's High Song: The Collected Writings of Countee Cullen, Voice of the Harlem Renaissance*, edited by Gerald Early, 1–73. New York: Anchor, 1991.

Eisenstein, Sergei, dir. *Battleship Potemkin*. Goskino, Mosfilm, 1925.

Ellis, Milton, Louise Pound, and George Spohn, eds. *A College Book of American Literature*. 2nd ed. New York: American Book Company, 1949.

Ellison, Ralph. *Invisible Man*. 1952. New York: Vintage, 1995.

Faison, Othello. "University of Arkansas at Pine Bluff (UAPB)." In *The Encyclopedia of Arkansas History and Culture* (encyclopediaofarkansas.net), edited by Guy Lancaster. Little Rock: Butler Center for Arkansas Studies at the Central Arkansas Library System (CALS). Entry last updated June 29, 2015.

Fast, Howard. *Peekskill USA: Inside the Infamous 1949 Riots*. Mineola, NY: Dover, 1951.

Fogelson, Robert M., and Richard E. Rubenstein, eds. *Mass Violence in America: The Complete Report of Mayor LaGuardia's Commission on the Harlem Riot of March 19, 1935*. New York: Arno, 1969.

Forbes, Jack D. *Afro-Americans in the Far West: A Handbook for Educators*. Berkeley, CA: Far West Laboratory for Educational Research and Development, 1968.

Fowler, Henry Watson, and George Fowler. *The King's English*. 3rd ed. Oxford: Clarendon, 1931.

Frazier, Robeson Taj. *The East Is Black: Cold War China in the Black Radical Imagination*. Durham, NC: Duke University Press, 2015.

Giddings, Paula J. *Ida, a Sword among Lions: Ida B. Wells and the Campaign against Lynching*. New York: Amistad, 2008.

Gilmore, Glenda Elizabeth. *Defying Dixie: The Radical Roots of Civil Rights, 1919–1950*. New York: W. W. Norton, 2008.

Gilyard, Keith. *John Oliver Killens: A Life of Black Literary Activism*. Athens: University of Georgia Press, 2011.

Gold, Mike. "Introduction." In *A New Song* by Langston Hughes. New York: International Workers Order, 1938.

Gore, Dayo. *Radicalism at the Crossroads: African American Women Activists in the Cold War*. New York: New York University Press, 2011.

Goudsouzian, Aram. *Sidney Poitier: Man, Actor, Icon*. Chapel Hill: University of North Carolina Press, 2004.

Graham, Edward K. "The Hampton Institute Strike of 1927: A Case Study in Student Protest." *American Scholar* 38, no. 4 (Autumn 1969): 668–683.

Graham, Helen. *The Spanish Civil War: A Very Short Introduction*. New York: Oxford University Press, 2005.

Greenough, James Bradstreet, and George Lyman Kittredge. *Words and Their Ways in English Speech*. London: Macmillan, 1931.

Griffith, D. W., dir. *The Birth of a Nation*. David W. Griffith Corporation and Epoch Producing Corporation, 1915.

Guggisberg, Sir Gordon, and A. G. Fraser. *The Future of the Negro*. New York: Negro Universities Press, 1929.

Halpern, Rick. *Down on the Killing Floor: Black and White Workers in Chicago's Packinghouses, 1904–54*. Urbana: University of Illinois Press, 1997.

Halpern, Rick, and Roger Horowitz, eds. *Meatpackers: An Oral History of Black Packinghouse Workers and Their Struggle for Racial and Economic Equality*. New York: Monthly Review Press, 1999.

Hamilton, LisaGay, dir. *Beah: A Black Woman Speaks*. New York: Clinica Estetico/LisaGay, Inc., 2003. DVD.

Handy, Robert T. *A History of Union Theological Seminary in New York*. New York: Columbia University Press, 1987.

Harley, Sharon. "Race Women: Cultural Productions and Radical Labor Politics." In *Women's Labor in the Global Economy: Speaking in Multiple Voices*, edited by Sharon Harley, 9–27. New Brunswick, NJ: Rutgers University Press, 2007.

Harris, Leonard, and Charles Molesworth. *Alain L. Locke: The Biography of a Philosopher*. Chicago: University of Chicago Press, 2008.

Hassan, Amina. *Loren Miller: Civil Rights Attorney and Journalist*. Norman: University of Oklahoma Press, 2015.

Hauke, Kathleen A. *Ted Poston: Pioneer American Journalist*. Athens: University of Georgia Press, 1998.

Haywood, Harry. *Black Bolshevik: Autobiography of an Afro-American Communist*. Chicago: Liberator, 1978.

———. *Negro Liberation*. 1948. Chicago: Liberator, 1976.

Hegan, Alice Caldwell. *Mrs. Wiggs of the Cabbage Patch*. New York: Century, 1901.

Hemenway, Robert E. *Zora Neale Hurston: A Literary Biography*. Urbana: University of Illinois Press, 1980.

Hill, George Roy, dir. *The Sting*. Zanuck/Brown Productions and Universal Pictures, 1973.

Hirsch, Arnold R. *Making the Second Ghetto: Race and Housing in Chicago, 1940–1960*. Cambridge: Cambridge University Press, 1983.

Hobbs, Richard S. *The Cayton Legacy: An African American Family*. Pullman: Washington State University Press, 2002.

Horne, Gerald. *Black Revolutionary: William Patterson and the Globalization of the African American Freedom Struggle*. Urbana: University of Illinois Press, 2013.

———. *Communist Front? The Civil Rights Congress, 1946–1956*. Rutherford, NJ: Fairleigh Dickinson University Press, 1988.

———. *Race Woman: The Lives of Shirley Graham Du Bois*. New York: New York University Press, 2000.

Horowitz, Roger. *"Negro and White, Unite and Fight!": A Social History of Industrial Unionism in Meatpacking, 1930–90*. Urbana: University of Illinois Press, 1997.

Hoyt, Edwin P. *Paul Robeson: The American Othello*. Cleveland, OH: World Publishing, 1967.

Huggins, Nathan Irvin. *Harlem Renaissance*. 1971. New York: Oxford University Press, 2007.

Hughes, Langston. *The Big Sea*. 1940. New York: Hill and Wang, 1993.

———. *The Collected Poems of Langston Hughes*. Edited by Arnold Rampersad and David Roessel. New York: Vintage, 1995.

———. *Good Morning Revolution: Uncollected Writings of Social Protest*. Edited by Faith Berry. New York: Lawrence Hill, 1973.

———. *I Wonder as I Wander*. 1956. New York: Hill and Wang, 1993.

———. "The Negro Artist and the Racial Mountain." 1926. In *Within the Circle: An Anthology of African American Literary Criticism from the Harlem Renaissance to the Present*, edited by Angelyn Mitchell, 55–59. Durham, NC: Duke University Press, 1994.

———. *A New Song*. New York: International Workers Order, 1938.

———. *Shakespeare in Harlem*. New York: Knopf, 1942.

Hunton, Dorothy K. *Alphaeus Hunton: The Unsung Valiant*. Richmond Hill, NY: D. K. Hunton, 1986.

Ibarruri, Dolores. *They Shall Not Pass: The Autobiography of La Pasionaria*. New York: International Publishers, 1966.

International Workers Order. "Foreword." In *A New Song* by Langston Hughes. New York: International Workers Order, 1938.

International Workers Order Records. Kheel Center for Labor-Management Documentation and Archives, Martin P. Catherwood Library, Cornell University, Ithaca, NY.

Jackson, Gabriel. *A Concise History of the Spanish Civil War*. New York: John Day, 1974.

Jackson, Ida Louise. "Ida Louise Jackson." In *There Was Light: Autobiography of a University, Berkeley: 1868–1968*, edited by Irving Stone, 249–66. New York: Doubleday, 1970.

Jackson, Lawrence P. *Ralph Ellison: Emergence of Genius*. New York: John Wiley and Sons, 2002.

Jenkins, Robin Dearmon. "Linking Up the Golden State: Garveyism in the San Francisco Bay Area, 1919–1925." *Journal of Black Studies* 39, no. 2 (2008): 266–80.

Johnson, James Weldon. *The Autobiography of an Ex-Coloured Man.* 1912. New York: Pelican Mentor, 1948.

Joseph, Peniel E. *Waiting 'til the Midnight Hour: A Narrative History of Black Power in America.* New York: Henry Holt, 2006.

Keeran, Roger. *The Communist Party and the Auto Workers Unions.* New York: International Publishers, 1986.

Kelley, Robin D. G. *Freedom Dreams: The Black Radical Imagination.* Boston: Beacon, 2002.

——. *Hammer and Hoe: Alabama Communists during the Great Depression.* Chapel Hill: University of North Carolina Press, 1990.

Killens, John Oliver. Papers. Stuart A. Rose Manuscript, Archives, and Rare Book Library, Emory University, Atlanta, GA.

——. *Youngblood.* New York: Dial, 1954.

Kelljan, Bob, dir. *Blacula II (Scream Blacula Scream).* American International Pictures and Power Productions, 1973.

King, Martin Luther, Jr. "Letter from Birmingham Jail." In *The Autobiography of Martin Luther King, Jr.,* edited by Clayborne Carson, 187–204. New York: Warner Books, 1998.

Kirschke, Amy Helene. *Aaron Douglas: Art, Race, and the Harlem Renaissance.* Jackson: University of Mississippi Press, 1995.

Knupfer, Anne Meis. *The Chicago Black Renaissance and Woman's Activism.* Urbana: University of Illinois Press, 2006.

Lee, Spike, dir. *Do the Right Thing.* 40 Acres and a Mule Filmworks, 1989.

Leinwand, Gerald. *1927: High Tide of the 1920s.* New York: Four Walls Eight Windows, 2001.

Lenin, V. I. "Preliminary Draft Theses on the National and Colonial Questions." In *Collected Works,* 31:144–51. Moscow: Progress, 1966.

Lewis, David Levering. *W. E. B. Du Bois: The Fight for Equality and the American Century, 1919–1963.* New York: Holt, 2003.

Locke, Alain. "Resume of Talk and Discussion: Alain Locke." In *Official Proceedings, Second National Negro Congress, Metropolitan Opera House, Philadelphia, Pennsylvania, October 15, 16, 17, 1937.* Washington, DC: National Negro Congress, 1937.

Lynch, Hollis. *Black American Radicals and the Liberation of Africa: The Council on African Affairs, 1937–1955.* Ithaca, NY: Cornell University Africana Studies and Research Center, 1978.

Makalani, Minkah. *In the Cause of Freedom: Radical Black Internationalism from Harlem to London, 1917–1939.* Chapel Hill: University of North Carolina Press, 2011.

Marx, Karl. *Das Kapital.* 1867.

Massiah, Louis, dir. *Louise Thompson Patterson: In Her Own Words.* Philadelphia: Scribe Video Center, 2005. DVD.

Maxwell, William J. *New Negro, Old Left: African-American Writing and Communism between the Wars.* New York: Columbia University Press, 1999.

McDuffie, Erik S. *Sojourning for Freedom: Black Women, American Communism, and the Making of a Black Left Feminism.* Durham, NC: Duke University Press, 2011.

McGill, Ralph. *The South and the Southerner*. Boston: Little, Brown, 1963.

McGlamery, J. Gabriel. "Race Based Underwriting and the Death of Burial Insurance." *Connecticut Insurance Law Journal* 15, no. 2 (Spring 2009): 531–70.

McLagan, Elizabeth. *A Peculiar Paradise: A History of Blacks in Oregon, 1788–1940*. Portland, OR: Georgian, 1980.

McLaren, Joseph. *Langston Hughes: Folk Dramatist in the Protest Tradition, 1921–1943*. Westport, CT: Greenwood, 1997.

Miller, James A. *Remembering Scottsboro: The Legacy of an Infamous Trial*. Princeton, NJ: Princeton University Press, 2009.

Miller, Warren. *90 Miles from Home*. Boston: Little, Brown, 1961.

Miller, Wayne F. *Chicago's South Side, 1946–1948*. Berkeley: University of California Press, 2000.

Minnelli, Vincente, dir. *Cabin in the Sky*. Metro-Goldwyn-Mayer, 1943.

Mishler, Paul C. *Raising Reds: The Young Pioneers, Radical Summer Camps, and Communist Political Culture in the United States*. New York: Columbia University Press, 1999.

Mitchell, Verner D., and Cynthia Davis. *Literary Sisters: Dorothy West and Her Circle, a Biography of the Harlem Renaissance*. New Brunswick, NJ: Rutgers University Press, 2012.

Morris, Gabrielle. "Introduction." In *Head of the Class: An Oral History of African-American Achievement in Higher Education and Beyond*, edited by Gabrielle Morris, xvi–xxvii. New York: Twayne, 1995.

———, ed. *Head of the Class: An Oral History of African-American Achievement in Higher Education and Beyond*. New York: Twayne, 1995.

Mullen, Bill V. *Popular Fronts: Chicago and African-American Cultural Politics, 1935–46*. Urbana: University of Illinois Press, 1999.

Naison, Mark. "The Communist Party in Harlem in the Early Depression Years: A Case Study in the Reinterpretation of American Communism." *Radical History Review* 3, no. 4 (1976): 68–95.

———. *Communists in Harlem during the Depression*. Urbana: University of Illinois Press, 1983.

The Negro People Will Defend America. Washington, DC: National Negro Congress, 1941.

Nelson, Claire Nee. "Louise Thompson Patterson and the Southern Roots of the Popular Front." In *Women Shaping the South: Creating and Confronting Change*, edited by Angela Boswell and Judith N. McArthur, 204–28. Columbia: University of Missouri Press, 2006.

Newton, Huey P. *To Die for the People*. 1972. San Francisco: City Lights Books, 2009.

Oakland Public Library, comp. *Oakland's First Black Community: An Historical Bibliography Compiled by the Oakland Public Library, Oakland History Room*. N.d.

Patterson, Louise Thompson. "With Langston Hughes in the USSR." *Freedomways* 8, no. 2 (Spring 1968): 152–58.

———. "A Levee That Won't Break Down." *Freedomways* 14, no. 2 (Spring 1974): 149–53.

———. Papers. Stuart A. Rose Manuscript, Archives, and Rare Book Library, Emory University, Atlanta, GA.

Patterson, MaryLouise. "Black and Red All Over." In *Red Diapers: Growing Up in the Communist Left*, edited by Judy Kaplan and Linn Shapiro, 110–15. Urbana: University of Illinois Press, 1998.

Patterson, William L. *The Man Who Cried Genocide*. New York: International Publishers, 1971.

———. Papers. Moorland-Spingarn Research Center, Founders Library, Howard University, Washington, DC.

———, ed. *We Charge Genocide: The Crime of Government against the Negro People*. 1951. New York: International Publishers, 1970.

Patton, Venetria. *The Grasp That Reaches beyond the Grave: The Ancestral Call in Black Women's Texts*. Albany: State University of New York Press, 2013.

Poitier, Sidney. *The Measure of a Man: A Spiritual Autobiography*. New York: Harper-Collins, 2000.

Porter, Kenneth Wiggins. "Foreword." In *"Good Time Coming?": Black Nevadans in the Nineteenth Century*, by Elmer R. Rusco, ix–xiv. Westport, CT: Greenwood, 1975.

Praetzellis, Mary, and Adrian Praetzellis, eds. *Putting the "There" There: Historical Archaeologies of West Oakland*. Rohnert Park, CA: Anthropological Studies Center, Sonoma State University, 2004.

Rampersad, Arnold. *The Life of Langston Hughes*. 2 vols. New York: Oxford University Press, 1986–1988.

———. *Ralph Ellison: A Biography*. New York: Knopf, 2007.

Randolph, A. Philip. "The Crisis of the Negro and the Constitution." In *Official Proceedings, Second National Negro Congress, Metropolitan Opera House, Philadelphia, Pennsylvania, October 15, 16, 17, 1937*. Washington, DC: National Negro Congress, 1937.

Ransby, Barbara. *Eslanda: The Large and Unconventional Life of Mrs. Paul Robeson*. New Haven, CT: Yale University Press, 2013.

Reed, Christopher Robert. *The Chicago NAACP and the Rise of Black Professional Leadership, 1910–1966*. Bloomington: Indiana University Press, 1997.

———. *The Rise of Chicago's Black Metropolis, 1920–1929*. Urbana: University of Illinois Press, 2011.

Reed, John. *Ten Days That Shook the World*. New York: Boni and Liveright, 1919.

Reynolds, Quentin. *Courtroom: The Story of Samuel S. Leibowitz*. New York: Farrar, Straus and Giroux, 1950.

Richards, Beah. *A Black Woman Speaks: And Other Poems*. Los Angeles: Inner City, 1974.

Ritt, Martin, dir. *The Great White Hope*. Lawrence Turman Films, Inc., 1970.

Robeson, Paul. "I Am the Same Man." In *Paul Robeson Speaks: Writings, Speeches, Interviews, 1918–1974*, edited by Philip S. Foner, 233–34. New York: Brunner/Mazel, 1978.

Robeson, Paul, Jr. *The Undiscovered Paul Robeson: Quest for Freedom, 1939–1976*. Hoboken, NJ: John Wiley and Sons, 2010.

Rolfe, Edwin. *The Lincoln Battalion: The Story of the Americans Who Fought in Spain in the International Brigades*. New York: Random House, 1939.

Rusco, Elmer R. *"Good Time Coming?": Black Nevadans in the Nineteenth Century*. Westport, CT: Greenwood, 1975.

Ryan, James G. *Earl Browder: The Failure of American Communism*. 2nd ed. Tuscaloosa: University of Alabama Press, 1997.

Sabin, Arthur J. *Red Scare in Court: New York versus the International Workers Order*. Philadelphia: University of Pennsylvania Press, 1993.

Schlauch, Margaret. *The Gift of Language*. New York: Dover, 1955.

Schultz, Bud, and Ruth Schultz, eds. *We Will Be Heard: Voices in the Struggle for Constitutional Rights Past and Present*. London: Merrell, 2008.

Seiter, William A., dir. *Dimples*. Twentieth Century Fox, 1936.

Sherrard-Johnson, Cherene. *Dorothy West's Paradise: A Biography of Class and Color*. New Brunswick, NJ: Rutgers University Press, 2012.

Sinclair, Upton. *Boston*. Vol. 2. New York: Albert and Charles Boni, 1928.

Smith, Homer. *Black Man in Red Russia*. Chicago: Johnson, 1964.

Smith, J. Douglas. *Managing White Supremacy: Race, Politics, and Citizenship in Jim Crow Virginia*. Chapel Hill: University of North Carolina Press, 2002.

Smith, Reed. *Learning to Write in College*. Revised by William Hastings. Lexington, MA: D. C. Heath, 1949.

Solomon, Mark. *The Cry Was Unity: Communists and African Americans, 1917–1936*. Jackson: University Press of Mississippi, 1998.

Spear, Allan H. *Black Chicago: The Making of a Negro Ghetto, 1890–1920*. Chicago: University of Chicago Press, 1969.

Spellman, Cecil Lloyd. *Rough Steps on My Stairway: The Life History of a Negro Educator*. New York: Exposition Press, 1953.

Spivey, Donald. *Schooling for the New Slavery: Black Industrial Education, 1868–1915*. Westport, CT: Greenwood, 1978.

Stahl, John M., dir. *Imitation of Life*. Universal Pictures, 1934.

Stalin, Joseph. "Marxism and the National Question." In *Works*, 2:300–381. Moscow: Foreign Languages Publishing, 1954.

Starobin, Joseph R. *American Communism in Crisis, 1943–1957*. Cambridge, MA: Harvard University Press, 1972.

Stone, Andrew. *Stormy Weather*. Twentieth Century Fox, 1943.

Stone, Irving, ed. *There Was Light: Autobiography of a University, Berkeley, 1868–1968*. Garden City, NY: Doubleday, 1970.

Stowe, Harriet Beecher. *Uncle Tom's Cabin; or, Life among the Lowly*. 1852.

Stuckey, Sterling. *Slave Culture: Nationalist Theory and the Foundations of Black America*. New York: Oxford University Press, 1987.

Styron, William. *The Confessions of Nat Turner*. New York: Random House, 1967.

Swindall, Lindsey, R. *Paul Robeson: A Life of Activism and Art*. Lanham, MD: Rowman and Littlefield, 2013.

Taurog, Norman, dir. *Mrs. Wiggs of the Cabbage Patch*. Paramount Pictures, 1934.

Thompson, Louise. "David and Goliath. *Freedomways* 1, no. 2 (Summer 1961): 214–17.

———. "The Negro in America." *Fraternal Outlook*, September 1940, 10–11.

———. "Negro Women in Our Party." *Party Organizer*, August 1937, 25–27.

———. "Now Is the Time to Build the Order." *Fraternal Outlook*, January 1940, 31, 34.

———. "The Role of Proletarian Fraternalism in the Liberation Struggle of the Negro People." *Negro Liberator*, July 28, 1934.

———. "A Shadow That Covers a Whole Nation." *Freedomways* 3, no. 1 (Winter 1963): 115–17.

———. "Southern Editor's Analysis." *Freedomways* 4, no. 1 (Winter 1964): 168–71.

———. "Southern Terror." *Crisis*, November 1934, 327–28.

———. "The Soviet Film." *Crisis*, February 1933, 37, 46.

———. "What Happened in Harlem: An Eye-Witness Account." *New Masses*, April 2, 1935, 15–16.

———. "Wipe Out Lynch Law!" *Fraternal Outlook*, March 1940, 12–13, 27.

Thompson, Louise, and Samuel C. Patterson. *The IWO and the Negro People: A Message and an Appeal.* New York: International Workers Order, 1942.

Thurman, Wallace. *The Blacker the Berry.* 1929. New York: Collier, 1970.

———. *The Collected Writings of Wallace Thurman.* Edited by Amritjit Singh and Daniel M. Scott III. New Brunswick, NJ: Rutgers University Press, 2003.

———, ed. *Fire!!* 1, no. 1, November 1926.

———, ed. *Harlem: A Forum of Negro Life* 1, no. 1 (Fall 1928).

———. *Infants of the Spring.* 1932. Boston: Northeastern University Press, 1992.

Toomer, Jean. *Cane.* 1923. New York: Liveright, 1993.

Tramble, Thomas, and Wilma Tramble. *Images of America: The Pullman Porters and West Oakland.* Charlestown, SC: Arcadia, 2007.

Travis, Dempsey. *An Autobiography of Black Chicago.* Chicago: Urban Research Institute, 1981.

van Notten, Eleonore. *Wallace Thurman's Harlem Renaissance.* Amsterdam: Rodopi, 1994.

Van Vechten, Carl. *The Splendid Drunken Twenties: Selections from the Daybooks, 1922–1930.* Edited by Bruce Kellner. Urbana: University of Illinois Press, 2003.

von Eschen, Penny M. *Race against Empire: Black Americans and Anticolonialism, 1937–1957.* Ithaca, NY: Cornell University Press, 1997.

Wald, Alan M. *The New York Intellectuals: The Rise and Decline of the Anti-Stalinist Left from the 1930s to the 1950s.* Chapel Hill: University of North Carolina Press, 1987.

Walker, Alice. *The Color Purple.* New York: Harcourt Brace Jovanovich, 1982.

Walker, Margaret. *Richard Wright, Daemonic Genius: A Portrait of the Man, a Critical Look at His Work.* New York: Dodd, Mead, 1988.

———. *This Is My Century: New and Collected Poems.* Athens: University of Georgia Press, 1989.

Walker, Thomas J. E. *Pluralistic Fraternity: The History of the International Worker's Order.* New York: Garland, 1991.

Ward, Geoffrey C. *Unforgivable Blackness: The Rise and Fall of Jack Johnson.* New York: Knopf, 2004.

Washington, Mary Helen. "Alice Childress, Lorraine Hansberry, and Claudia Jones: Black Women Write the Popular Front." In *Left of the Color Line: Race, Radicalism, and Twentieth Century Literature of the United States*, edited by Bill V. Mullen and James Smethurst, 183–204. Chapel Hill: University of North Carolina Press, 2003.

————. *The Other Black List: The African American Literary and Cultural Left of the 1950s*. New York: Columbia University Press, 2014.

Washington State Library, comp. *The Negro in the State of Washington, 1788–1967: A Bibliography*. 1968.

Waters, Mary-Alice, ed. *The First and Second Declarations of Havana: Manifestos of Revolutionary Struggle in the Americas Adopted by the Cuban People*. New York: Pathfinder, 2007.

Watson, Steven. *The Harlem Renaissance: Hub of African-American Culture, 1920–1930*. New York: Pantheon Books, 1995.

Webster's New Collegiate Dictionary. Springfield, MA: G and C Merriam, 1951.

West, Dorothy. "Elephant's Dance: A Memoir of Wallace Thurman." 1970. In *Where the Wild Grape Grows: Selected Writings, 1930–1950*, edited by Verner D. Mitchell and Cynthia Davis, 167–75. Amherst: University of Massachusetts Press, 2005.

Williams, Rhonda Y. *Concrete Demands: The Search for Black Power in the 20th Century*. New York: Routledge, 2015.

Wollenberg, Charles. *Berkeley: A City in History*. Berkeley: University of California Press, 2008.

Wolters, Raymond. *The New Negro on Campus: Black College Rebellions of the 1920s*. Princeton, NJ: Princeton University Press, 1975.

Wright, Richard. 1940. "Bright and Morning Star." In *Uncle Tom's Children*, 221–63. New York: HarperPerennial, 2008.

————. "Fire and Cloud." 1938. In *Uncle Tom's Children*, 157–220. New York: HarperPerennial, 2008.

————. "Introduction." In *Black Metropolis: A Study of Negro Life in a Northern City*, by St. Clair Drake and Horace R. Cayton, xvii–xxxiv. New York: Harcourt, Brace, 1945.

Wright, Sarah. *A. Philip Randolph: Integration in the Workplace*. New York: Silver Burdett, 1990.

————. *This Child's Gonna Live*. New York: Delacorte, 1969.

Zaki, Hoda M. *Civil Rights and Politics at Hampton Institute: The Legacy of Alonzo G. Moron*. Urbana: University of Illinois Press, 2007.

Zeigler, James. *Red Scare Racism and Cold War Black Radicalism*. Jackson: University Press of Mississippi, 2015.

Grand Hotel, 85, 89
Granich, Grace, 180
Granich, Max, 180
Graves, Evelyn Phyllis "Nebby," 33–36, 40–41,
    50, 63, 69, 79, 150–51, 185, 198
Graves, Milton, 34
Graves, Wilbur, 34, 40
Gray, Harriette, 154
Grayson, Francis DeSales, 168, 173
Grayson, Josephine, 173
Great Depression, the, 71, 85, 98, 135, 206
Great Leap Forward, the, 182–83
Great Migration, the, 51
Great White Hope, The (film), 19
Grebner, Georgi, 83
Green, Abner, 166
Green, Theodore, 154
Green and Gold Studio, 79
Greenberg, Henry Clay, 170
Greene, Dave, 147
Green River, Wyoming, 69
Gregg, James Edgar, 53–58, 60
Griffith, D. W., 39
Grimke, Francis J., 14
Grimley, John, 116
Guernica, 121
Guggisberg, Gordon, 55, 239n50
Guillén, Nicolás, 194, 201
Gunther, John, 177

Haddad, Edmonde, 187
hair, 27–29, 34
Hairston, Frank, Jr., 168
Hairston, Howard Lee, 168
Hairston, James Luther, 168
Haley, Harold, 195
Hall, Gus, 203, 207
Hall, Tarea, 36, 40. *See also* Pittman, Tarea Hall
Hall, Wheeler, 217
Hammett, Dashiell, 166
Hammond, John Henry, Jr., 77
Hampton, Joe, 168
Hampton Institute, 2–3, 50, 53–60, 67, 73–74,
    191
Hampton-Lincoln football game, 71
Hampton University, 225, 227
Handy, W. C., 135
Hansberry, Lorraine, 173, 194, 261n25
Harlem, 51; activism in, 76, 101, 196; commu-
    nism in, 74–75, 90, 96, 111–19, 135, 140–41,
    206; culture in, 42, 51; politics in, 75, 78,

80, 120–21, 140, 163; Renaissance, 2, 14, 41,
    61–65, 112, 132, 139, 205–6, 217, 229; restora-
    tion of, 208; riots in, 114–19; violence in, 113,
    172, 221, 258n49
Harlem: A Forum of Negro Life, 65
Harlem: A Melodrama of Negro Life in Harlem
    (Thurman and Rapp), 65
Harlem Committee to Aid Spanish Democ-
    racy, 129
Harlem Experimental Theatre, 61
Harlem Hellfighters, 33
Harlem Hospital, 126, 132
Harlem Interracial Forum, 98
Harlem Renaissance, 2, 14, 61–64, 112, 132, 139,
    205–6, 217, 229
Harlem Renaissance (Huggins), 205
Harlem Restoration Project, 208–9
Harlem Suitcase Theater, 136–39, 217, 252n36
Harper, Toy, 135, 137–38
Harris, Abram, 74
Harris, Johnny Imani, 210
Harry Van Arsdale Jr. School of Labor Studies,
    215
Hart, Pearl, 158
Hartford Avenue Baptist Church, 154, 165
Harvard Law School, 213
Hayes, Charles, 156
Haymarket martyrs, 207
Hays, Arthur Garfield, 116
Haywood, Harry, 62, 76, 112, 121–27, 145, 189,
    244n46
Hazell, Nellie, 119
HBCU (Historically Black Colleges or Univer-
    sities). *See* Historically Black Colleges or
    Universities (HBCU)
Head of the Class (Morris), 236nn40–41
Hearst, Phoebe Apperson, 31
Hearst, Randolph, 115
Hedrick, La Ursa, 155
Hegan, Alice Caldwell, 20
Heineray, John, 115
Hemenway, Robert, 205–6
Hemingway, Ernest, 124
Henry, James B., 170
Henry, Wilhelmina, 223
Herndon, Angelo, 1, 99, 118, 121, 192, 231n1
Herrick, E. M., 120
Herring, Hubert C., 72–73, 76, 78
Hill, Anita, 213
Hill, Charles A., 154
Hill, Leonard, 78, 82, 88

Hill City, 10
Hinds, Lennox, 210
Historically Black Colleges or Universities (HBCU), 73, 185. *See also specific colleges and universities*
Hitler, Adolf, 122, 128, 140, 148, 150
Hobbs, Lloyd, 115
Hofstra University Law School, 209
Hollums, E. I., 105
Hollywood Ten, 259n71
Holman United Methodist Church, 208
Holt, Nora, 53
Homestead Act, 18, 234n54
Hopkins, Irma, 34
Horace, James, 157
Horne, Frank, 144
Horne, Gerald, 4
Horne, Lena, 158
Horton (Judge), 102
House Lobbying Committee, 166
House Un-American Activities Committee, 150, 259n71
housing, 8, 30, 157, 209
Houston, Charles, 118
Howard University, 37, 55, 59, 73–74, 82, 98, 118, 160
Howe, McHenry, 1–2
Hubbard, Maceo, 174
Huggins, Nathan Irvin, 205
Hughes, Langston: biography of, 214, 216; in Central Asia, 92, 94; Harlem Suitcase Theater and, 138–39, 252n36; Mezhrabpom-film project and, 78, 88–90, 136; *Mule Bone* controversy and, 71–74, 205; personal life of, 2, 61–62, 64, 78, 120, 194, 209, 240n1; social activism of, 60, 74, 121, 135, 179; Soviet Union and, 77, 81, 84–85, 91, 96; in Spain, 123–24; writings by, 70–71, 130, 137, 148, 150–51, 200, 241n3; World War II and, 142. *See also specific works*
Hugo, Victor, 177
Huiswood, Otto, 62, 92
Hull House, 8
Humanities Press, 204
Human Rights League, 197
Humboldt, Wilhelm von, 235n19
Humphrey, Lyman, 10
Hungary, 168, 182
Hunter, Oscar, 121
Hunton, Alphaeus, 160–61, 166, 173–75, 179, 215
Hunton, Dorothy, 171, 173, 175, 178

Hurley, Charles, 113
Hurricane Katrina, 47
Hurst, Fanny, 138
Hurston, Zora Neale, 2, 62, 71–74, 79, 137, 205–6, 209, 222, 240n1
Hutson, Jean Blackwell, 179
Hyde Park, Chicago, 42

Ibarruri, Dolores, 127
Idaho, 21, 26, 233n46
I Know Why the Caged Bird Sings (Angelou), 200
ILD (International Labor Defense). *See* International Labor Defense (ILD)
Imes, William Lloyd, 129
immigrants, 103, 133–34, 146, 157, 161, 166
imperialism, 88, 94, 140, 147, 160, 187, 192
Independence Day battle, 19
Indiana, 146
Indiana University, 206
Indians, 13
Industrial Areas Foundation, 158
industrialization, 28, 42, 105, 145, 182–83
Infants of the Spring (Thurman), 68
influenza pandemic of 1918, 28
Ingram, Rosa Lee, 159, 174, 177, 195, 259n68
Ingram, Zell, 135
Inside U.S.A. (Gunther), 177
Institutional Church and Social Settlement, 8, 232n7
insurance, 104–5, 132, 226
integration, 42, 134, 153; jury, 169
Internal Revenue Service (IRS), 177
International Brigades, 121–22, 127
International Brotherhood of Electrical Workers, 266n43
International Committee on African Affairs, 141
International Federation of Leagues against Racism and Anti-Semitism, 122
International Labor Defense (ILD), 76, 99, 101–3, 109–11, 159, 196
International League against Anti-Semitism, 127
International Union of Mine, Mill and Smelter Workers, 105
International Women's Day, 197
International Workers Order (IWO), 103–7, 114, 120–36, 142–59, 169–70, 191, 210, 217, 226
interracial solidarity, 2, 102, 136, 156–57, 164, 216–17

Moore, Harriet, 175
Moore, Harry, 175
Moore, Richard B., 52, 59, 62, 74, 118
Moore Shipbuilding Company, 28
Mora, Pancho, 201
Morehouse College, 73
Morgan, Emma Lou, 63
Morley, S. Griswold, 39
Morning Star, 196
Morris, Gabrielle, 236nn40–41
Moscow, Russia, 52, 86–88, 92
Moscow Conference, 187
Moscow News, 224
Moser, J. T., 105–6
Mother Thompson. *See* Thompson, Louise
Moton, Robert, 174
Mount Carmel Baptist Church, 102
Movimiento Independentistia Revolucionario Armado, 203
Moyer, Charles, 48
Mrs. (magazine), 199, 205
Mrs. Wiggs of the Cabbage Patch (Hegan), 20
Mule Bone (Hughes and Hurston), 71–74, 137, 205–6, 227
murder, 48–49, 119, 174–75
Muse, Daphne, 216
Muslims, 126, 145, 178
Mussolini, Benito, 117, 119, 122, 124–25
Muste, A. J., 74

NAARPR (National Association against Racist and Political Repression), 202–3, 210
Naison, Mark, 206
Nathiri, N. Y., 222
National Afro-American Council, 8
National Association against Racist and Political Repression (NAARPR), 202–3, 210
National Association for the Advancement of Colored People (NAACP), 36–51, 76–77, 109, 116, 160, 165, 175, 192, 196, 202, 219, 259n68
National Association of Negro Musicians, 54, 239n49
National Black Writers Conference, 213
National Committee for the Defense of Political Prisoners, 78, 99, 101–2, 117, 152, 245n5
National Committee of the Communist Party, 118
National Committee to Defend the Rights of William L. Patterson, 178

National Council of Churches, 72
National Federation for Constitutional Liberties, 159
National Football League, 225
National General Assembly, 187
National Guard, 49, 170
nationalism, 117, 133, 145, 163, 244n46
National Labor Relations Board, 120
National Lawyers Guild, 190
National Negro Congress, 117–24, 130–51, 159–60, 167
National Sponsoring Committee, 118
National Urban League, 59, 63
Nazism, 122, 128, 148, 150
Nazi-Soviet nonaggression pact, 140–42
Nebby. *See* Graves, Evelyn Phyllis "Nebby"
Negro Agricultural and Technical College of North Carolina, 57
Negro Democratic League of Philadelphia, 119
Negro Experimental Theatre, 61
Negro in the State of Washington, The (Washington State Library), 215
Negro Liberation (Haywood), 189
Negro Liberator (newspaper), 104–5, 107–8
Negro People Will Defend America, The (pamphlet), 149
Nelken, Margarita, 127
Nevada, 12–13, 16, 26, 66, 217–18
New and Collected Poems (Walker), 215
New Deal, 121, 140, 153
New Harlem Casino, 76
Newlands, Francis G., 13
New Masses, 135, 142
New Negro, 14, 41, 55
New Negro Theater, 139
New Orleans Daily Picayune, 217
New Orleans jazz, 34
New Palace of Pioneers, 188
Newport, Eugene "Gus," 212
Newport News Daily Press, 54
New Republic, 199
New Song, A (Hughes), 130, 136
Newton, Huey P., 192–93, 213
New York American, 115
New York City, 41–43, 51–53, 60–74, 83, 99, 120, 135, 143–47, 159–63, 169, 174–76, 203–11. *See also* Harlem
New York Committee to Free Angela Davis, 196
New York Daily News, 265n39